A Will to Serve

Stories of Patience, Persistence,
and Friends Made Along the Way

by Jim Ellis

With contributions by Jennifer Ott

Foreword by Sally Jewell

Afterword by Gary Locke

HistoryLink and Documentary Media

Seattle, WA

A WILL TO SERVE: Stories of Patience, Persistence, and Friends Made Along the Way
by JIM ELLIS

First Edition
Printed in South Korea

HistoryLink
admin@historylink.org
www.historylink.org
(206) 447-8140

Documentary Media LLC
books@docbooks.com
www.documentarymedia.com
(206) 935-9292

Author: Jim Ellis
Additional contributions: Jennifer Ott
Foreword: Sally Jewell
Afterword: Gary Locke

Fact checking: Jim Kershner and Kit Oldham
Editing and book production: Tori Smith
Photo research and productions: Elisa Law
Book Design: Marilyn Esguerra
Editorial Director: Petyr Beck

Available through the University of Washington Press
uwapress.uw.edu

ISBN: 978-1-933245-70-6
Library of Congress Cataloging-in-Publication Data:

Names: Ellis, James R. (James Reed), 1921-2019, author. | Ott, Jennifer, 1971-
Title: A will to serve : stories of patience, persistence, and friends made along the way / by Jim Ellis ; with contributions by Jennifer Ott.
Other titles: Stories of patience, persistence, and friends made along the way
Description: First edition. | Seattle, WA : HistoryLink and Documentary Media, [2024] | Includes bibliographical references and index. |
Identifiers: LCCN 2023041730 | ISBN 9781933245706 (hardcover)
Subjects: LCSH: Ellis, James R. (James Reed), 1921-2019. | Civic leaders–Washington (State)–Seattle–Biography. | Lawyers–Washington (State)–Seattle–Biography. | Seattle (Wash.)–Biography. | Seattle (Wash.)–History–20th century.
Classification: LCC F899.S453 E66 2024 | DDC 979.7/772092 [B]–dc23/eng/20231211
LC record available at https://lccn.loc.gov/2023041730

Front Cover photo: Zee Wendell

FOR THE LOVE OF MARY LOU

Mary Lou once said,
"If I ever write a book of my life, it will be called, For the Love of Jim."

—*Jim Ellis*

JIM'S BOYS

"When Mary Lou died, Walter took it upon himself to see that I would get back among the living and not remain isolated at home. The group of guys Walt called were my old, good friends who were there when I needed them the most. They liked to call themselves "Jim's Boys," and those dinners at Vito's Restaurant on First Hill became my lifeline to healing."

—*Jim Ellis*

Mary Lou Earling Ellis
April 7, 1921 – November 17, 1983

James Reed Ellis
August 5, 1921 – October 22, 2019

Contents

✦

Foreword *by Sally Jewell*

WITHIN THE PAGES OF THIS BOOK, Jim Ellis tells the stories of his many efforts to bring people and perspectives together in service to our shared community. He provides timeless examples of civic leadership from which current and future generations can learn. His spirit and insight are cornerstones for many of our region's major accomplishments from his time volunteering as a young Seattle lawyer in the 1950s through his years as an elder statesman into the 2010s.

Jim was 69 and I was 35 when we first met in 1991. Thanks to the recommendation of a bank executive for whom I worked, Jim asked me to join the board of a new organization he had agreed to lead, the Mountains to Sound Greenway Trust, an effort to thoughtfully manage and protect the rapidly urbanizing lands along Interstate 90. Ours was the beginning of a relationship that would shape my life over three-plus decades. The experience provided a roadmap for respectful listening and collaboration that I practiced time and again in addressing controversial and complex challenges in service to our country as US Secretary of the Interior, as well as in my professional and personal life.

Jim worked hard on this book for decades, interweaving his personal and professional journeys to share real-world experiences of love and loss, mistakes and triumphs, brilliance and naivete. A *Will to Serve* is Jim's story, but his wife, Mary Lou, is with him every step of the way. I wish I had had the opportunity to meet Mary Lou, a thoughtful advisor and confidant who passed before I met Jim. In the many stories he shared with me as we worked together on the Greenway, a common thread was Mary Lou's influence, helping him channel the grief and anger he felt after losing his brother Bob in World War II into making Jim's own life count for Bob's. This inspired a philosophy of living a life in thirds—a third for work, a third for home, and a third for community. For me, and for countless other people Jim influenced over his long and productive life, his example was an inspiration to find balance, not only creating space for family, friends, and professional growth, but leaving our communities better than we found them.

Perhaps best known for his personal commitment to cleaning up our beloved Lake Washington—so polluted in the 1940s and '50s by raw sewage and industrial discharges that it was rendered unsafe for swimming—Jim had a positive impact on our region and our world in many ways. In his own words, "Participants at any level in our system of self-government will find that success is carried on a tide of patience and persistence." Jim's visionary, but failed effort in the 1960s to secure voter support for a largely federally funded regional light rail and rapid transit system required patience and persistence to shape what the region now has in Sound Transit's Link Light Rail, Metro, and regional bus networks that are so important to reducing traffic and congestion. This was demonstrated as Jim and Mary Lou advocated to preserve farmland, raising awareness of how unchecked development was overtaking farms and how new tools, like conservation easements, could enable farmers to economically continue their work, while creating breathing space for the character and history that define many rural and suburban communities today. Patience and persistence were vital to Jim's leadership in supporting development of the Washington State Convention Center and Freeway Park, and in resolving concerns of those opposed. This created new valuable public space by building over the Interstate 5 Freeway, welcoming visitors from around the world and driving economic activity, while reducing freeway traffic noise.

One of my favorite phrases is "Progress moves at the speed of trust," an idea Jim understood to his core, and a sentiment that is equally true for projects of any scale. I witnessed it in action as US Secretary of the Interior, pulling states, energy companies, cattle ranchers, environmentalists, hunters, developers, and scientists together to find common ground and protect over 144 million acres of the "Sagebrush Sea" in the American West. I saw it work in the Mojave Desert to support thoughtful development of renewable energy by listening to diverse perspectives to protect Native American sacred sites, viewsheds, critical habitat, wildlife connectivity, recreation, and local community interests across 10 million acres of federal lands. I also saw it work in the Greenway time and again.

When he first spoke to me about joining the board of the Greenway, I said, "Jim, this sounds like at least a 25-year project!" to which he responded, "Yes, it will be." I could hardly picture myself being age 60 by the time we finished, which seemed so far into the future. I'm now well past that mark and, like so many involved in that effort, continue to find inspiration in how critical the Greenway has become with increasing population, climate change, and the vital role nature plays in our region's health, productivity, and wellbeing.

Building on an idea conceived by activists from the Issaquah Alps Trail Club, Jim recruited a large board for the Greenway representing diverse interests. He insisted on providing dinner at every meeting, which were held along the Greenway corridor at the Preston Community Hall, 22 miles east of Seattle and close to the Raging River where he and his brother Bob built a log cabin as teenagers. Those dinners continue today, with business executives still sharing tables with local community activists, environmentalists with timber company representatives, tribal leaders with recreation organization leaders, and many more. Board members and guests build trusting, respectful relationships across ideologies and differences to find common ground. The results continue to be extraordinary, which visitors can feel as they immerse themselves in the beauty and serenity of the connected landscapes and abundant wildlife traversing this east-west corridor that shaped the lives and cultures of Indigenous people of our region before settlers arrived and continue to nurture all of us today.

As you read Jim's words, stories, and tributes to many people along his life's journey, I hope you will be inspired in your activities to listen to each other, find common ground, and advocate for lasting solutions that will shape our region and world for the generations to come.

Editor's Note

Jim Ellis intended his book to be a telling of his full life. A prolific writer and public speaker, his manuscript for this book was a draft with material enough for several books, but it remained unfinished. Jim's completed passages are the heart of *A Will to Serve* and his detailed outline provided a guide for completing the story.

Some elements of his original vision have been slightly reshaped to bridge the interrupted narrative. In editing this work, Jim's interweaving of storylines from the personal and public sides of his life has been honored. The conversational approach of using "casual quotes" that he favored is maintained as a literary device, particularly in his rapport with his wife, Mary Lou, his family, and occasionally others in memorable moments when the context is clear. Additionally, there are a few notations along the way to provide context when needed.

Historian Jennifer Ott worked with Jim's original collection of material and with historical records to complete select topics. She also added a few sections to bring some of his life's work up to date, particularly in his later years.

Jim's intention to highlight the contributions of the many friends, colleagues, and mentors who walked the civic journey with him was clearly indicated in the original material. To provide readers with a reasonable volume of content in a book format, much of this material has been made available on HistoryLink.org and in the Seattle Public Library's Seattle Room collections. This content and Jim's many public speeches and written papers are well worth diving into for a more detailed look at individual campaigns and projects.

Those close to Jim may notice some incomplete elements or missing individuals, particularly from his later career years and circle of close friends. While Jim did not have time to complete his manuscript, his intentions, his warmth, and his respect for so many people permeated his drafts and outlines.

We readers are lucky to hear Jim's easy storytelling voice and compelling style in *A Will to Serve*. Sit down with a plate of sliced oranges (one of Mary Lou's specialties) and enjoy your time with him.

Introduction

The city that is alive is never completed and always needs work. Just as natural systems cannot be taken for granted nor distant suffering long ignored, so the institutions of free people cannot exist unwatched and untended. The safety of liberty rests upon the everyday duties of life, the willingness of citizens to pursue the common good, to teach their children well, to defend justice, to be stewards of the planet and to respect each other.

—*Jim Ellis, "Garden of Remembrance Dedication" speech, July 4, 1998*

ON A SNOWY NIGHT at Mountain Home Air Base in the winter of 1945, my wife of four months, Mary Lou, inspired a life commitment to public service in honor of my brother Bob. He had been killed in action during the Battle of the Bulge in World War II. Mary Lou pulled me out of shock, denial, and revenge with a challenge to "make your life count for his by doing something you and Bob believe in—like conservation." We began to focus our life goals to our family and community.

This is an auto-biographical sketch book. Much as you might carry a flashlight to guide an evening walk, this account shines on events from a long life and the wonderful people who shared them. They are examples of the love and leadership we witnessed.

Our civic struggles often read like old-time movies. Good causes meet unexpected hazards. Ideals run up against real world hungers and ironies. Through crosscurrents of political tides and project campaigns, Mary Lou tried to "keep our eyes on things that will make life better for people."

Fairness requires that events of history and actions of people be measured against the values and conditions of their time. This was particularly true during the rapid changes of the last half of the twentieth century. I have tried to respect this truth. Excerpts from speeches and election results are included to mark places and times on the path we took.

Fortunately for readers of these stories, our friends were fascinating people and some of our causes were cliffhangers. These sketches tell how good luck, hard work, and reasoned risk-taking can help citizens improve urban living and conserve natural places.

This book is also about family. From the beginning, my life was molded by my parents Floyd and Hazel Reed Ellis, my Reed grandparents, my brother Bob, and the teachers in Seattle's John Muir Elementary School. The parenting of Floyd and Hazel was a lucky strike for their three sons and illuminated everything that followed. In adult years, Mary Lou's parents, Roy and Mary Earling, our children Bob, Judi, Lynn, and Steve, my brother John, and life-time friends in law practice and public service became major sources of ideas and strength.

Mary Lou tried "to keep our eyes on things that will make life better for people."

Mary Lou was the inspiration for this book as she was of my life. Hers were the adventures of a joyous, curious, creative, and courageous woman who charted her own course beginning with graduation from pilot training in 1944.

I hope these sketches of people and events along our path will give the reader a small part of the pleasure it has given me to recall them.

Like some men of my generation I seldom said, "I love you" to those I loved or "Thank you" to friends for the gift of their friendship. With this book I do so now.

BOOK ONE

Foundations

✦

CHAPTER 1

My Family Roots and Beginnings

I WAS BORN AUGUST 5, 1921, in Oakland, California, where my father, Floyd Earl Ellis, was working as a co-founder and partner in a new importing and exporting firm, The Wilbur-Ellis Company. A few months later, our family moved from Oakland to Los Angeles.

My father was born October 22, 1894, in Dayton, Washington, and grew up in Dayton and Spokane, one of two sons of Leonidas Lee Ellis and Amy Andrus Ellis. Floyd supported himself through law school at the University of Washington Law School in Seattle. After graduating in 1919, he was employed by Rogers Brown & Company, a Seattle firm which traded commodities and general merchandise across the Pacific. The company immediately sent him to Dairen, Manchuria, where he earned the respect of the Chinese trading community and was soon joined by his younger brother Harold. They developed a system for cleaning empty Standard Oil tankers using local Chinese labor so these ships could return to America with a paying cargo of vegetable oils. Working together, Floyd and Harold earned enough money in a little over a year to come back to the states and marry their college sweethearts.

Floyd Ellis with Jim and infant Bob, 1924.

My mother, Hazel Reed, grew up in Spokane, Washington, one of two daughters of Dr. James S. Reed and Wilhelmina Mannel Reed. Hazel graduated from North Central High School in Spokane and the University of Washington in Seattle where she majored in home economics and was active in the Pi Beta Phi sorority. She returned home in 1920 to work briefly as a reporter for the *Spokane Chronicle*.

Hazel and Floyd had known each other in high school and at the university. On September 15, 1920, they were married in the church across the street from the Reed family home in Spokane. Their honeymoon at Banff and Lake Louise in Canada was interrupted when Floyd received a wire that his employer, Rogers Brown and Company, was bankrupt.

Floyd had planned to continue working for Rogers Brown and to be sent to Japan. Instead, because of the unexpected company failure, he started a new firm in partnership with his fraternity brothers Brayton Wilbur and Tom

Frank. The Wilbur-Ellis Company established headquarters in California and engaged in the import and export of vegetable and fish oils and meals.

From 1922 to 1926—until I was five years old—our family lived in Los Angeles, California, a beautiful city of about 600,000. Our first home was a rented house on Rimpaugh Street in Hollywood. We later moved to a stucco house on Bronson Avenue near Wilshire. When I was two years old, my brother Bob was born and we were sometimes left in the watchful care of Ola, a kind woman with a large lap and a big heart. She called Bob "a little angel" and me "a little devil." On weekends, I remember picnic lunches on nearby Pacific Ocean beaches.

In 1926, the Wilbur-Ellis Company decided to open a Seattle office, with Floyd as partner in charge. I viewed the coming move as a disaster and alerted next door neighbor, Joan Worthington. We built a street barricade of brush in an unsuccessful attempt to prevent the Bekins Moving Co. vans from taking the Ellises away from Los Angeles.

Floyd drove the family north to Seattle in a Packard touring sedan with glass flower vases mounted inside each door jam.

In the 1920s and 1930s, Seattle was a deep-water trading port of 300,000 connected to the rest of the country by four transcontinental railroads. The young city had boomed during the Alaska Gold Rush period and was sustained by regional timber and fishery resources. A system of electric streetcars, cable cars, and "interurbans" furnished public transportation. There were few automobiles on the streets, and the doors of most homes were not locked. Floyd's office was in the Central Building on Third Avenue and later in the Hoge Building on Second Avenue.

Our family lived in a brick house on Shoreland Drive in the Mount Baker neighborhood where my youngest brother, John, was born in September 1928. I walked to and from John Muir Elementary School. The school was run by a staff of teachers dedicated to high ideals and the conservation principles of the school's namesake. At the end of each day, all students marched out, room by room, past Principal Jessie Lockwood and the American flag to the sound of a drum and bugle.

Some of my fondest memories of childhood were the trips to Spokane by car in summer and by train at Christmas to visit grandparents. Spokane's

Friends join Jim and Bob in barricading the street
to halt the family move from Los Angeles to Seattle.

major attraction for Bob and me was our much-loved grandfather, Dr. James S. Reed. As little kids, Bob and I would sneak into "Gramps" Reed's bed for a "big toe" war. During grade school summer vacations, Gramps drove his old Rickenbacker over bumpy roads on fishing and camping trips to Priest Lake or Pend Oreille Lake. This car was well remembered for the smell of cigars and the stains of tobacco juice on the driver's window.

The Wilbur-Ellis Company prospered during the boom of the late 1920s and our family moved about a mile south of the Mount Baker neighborhood and into a large house on a point overlooking Lake Washington Boulevard and the lake. The property contained a clay tennis court and madrona woods where the three Ellis boys built tree houses in partnership with the five Ring brothers who lived across the street. During construction of the first tree house, a neighbor saw us "borrowing" some scrap lumber from a new home being built about a block away. I remember my father's chagrin and disappointment when he found out what we had done. Rich Ring and I (as the oldest brothers) were required to work for a week to pay the builder for the lumber we had taken.

*Bob, baby John, Hazel, and Jim at the family home on
Shoreline Drive in Seattle's Mt. Baker neighborhood.*

The Floyd and Hazel Ellis family home at 4016 50th Street in Seattle.

When I was nine years old, my father returned to the Far East to develop new business and to purchase a Far East trading firm, the Connell Company. I was taken out of the fourth grade to accompany my parents on the five-month trip to Japan, China, and the region. Our Reed grandparents moved to Seattle for the five months of this trip to stay with my brothers.

The long ocean voyages, the poverty and disease, the international enclaves for business, and the presence of British and American gunboats in the harbors reflected the last years of a colonial era. As one of the only Caucasian children for part of the trip I keenly felt the alienation of culture and language. The sight of deliberately deformed beggars and starving children left a lasting impact, and I was shocked to see dead bodies in the streets in one Chinese city.

When we left Shanghai for the trip home on the *Canadian Pacific Empress* of Japan, my father's Chinese business friends arranged an elaborate farewell display of fireworks which were set off from small junks following our vessel down the Wang Po River.

Every few years at John Muir Grade School, a pageant on the theme of conservation or chivalry was performed involving most of the students. For the Galahad Pageant each boy made his own shield and sword in shop class. In the sixth grade I performed as "youth" in a large nature pageant where my brother Bob was one of many "bears" and my brother John was among younger children walking under sewn-together sheets as a moving "glacier." My epilogue speech called for saving "the wonder and glory of the big trees."

"The spirit of John Muir shall not die. Rise, all youth, to my call! We shall climb the mountains and get their good tidings. The spirit of John Muir lives forever!"

A complete student government was organized for seventh and eighth graders. In the first semester of eighth grade, I was appointed student body president and in the second semester conservation commissioner. When the school dedicated a grove of trees near Naches Pass, I made the dedication speech.

In 1932, young Bob was stricken critically ill with rheumatic fever which confined him in bed for almost two years. My parents were frantic, and the entire household learned to tip-toe around this life-threatening illness. Under the intensive care of Dr. Frank Douglass, Bob finally began to improve, and he and Hazel spent a winter in Arizona to assist with his recovery. A few years later, Bob became a football player and inspirational award winner at Franklin High School.

Bob and I were only two years apart, followed by John, five years after Bob. Bob and I usually went to the same school and engaged in similar activities. One of our street pastimes in summer was following the ice truck around and picking up chips of ice which broke off when the big blocks were cut into smaller sizes for home ice boxes. This was before the days of refrigerators.

During the deep depression of the 1930s, some of the people living in the neighborhood of 50th and Genesee Streets were out of work and on relief. The good fortune of the Wilbur-Ellis Company, and our big house at 4016 50th Avenue South, created a self-consciousness in Bob and me that we were "rich" and therefore "not as good" as other kids. We acquired a strong desire to conform to norms in the neighborhood and at school.

Bob and I saw that some kids did not have any lunch during these Depression years and when we told my mother, she included an extra sandwich in our school lunches. I explained that "Mother always makes too much" and gave the "extra" sandwich to a friend who needed it.

Ours was a family of boys. Under our code, wrestling and fighting were considered OK, but loving touches, hugging, or crying was frowned on as "sissy stuff." Our parents allowed no profanity or foul language at home, and we always stood up when a woman entered the room. Hazel made active efforts to develop our cultural awareness, including piano lessons—which were largely wasted on me—and attendance at dancing classes which were regarded in early years as a serious form of torture.

My father was a devoted family man. Indeed, his hobby was his family. In summers there were family fishing trips, often with friends like candymaker W. A. Nagel. Backyard games of softball and touch football were frequent and hotly contested. I remember Dad calling time out from a softball game in 1926 so we could listen to the radio broadcast of Lindbergh landing in Paris after the first solo flight across the Atlantic. Floyd was finally compelled to stop playing touch football with his boys when he slipped during a game on the tennis court and broke his arm. Both parents gave strong support for school activities, whether athletic or political. At least one parent always attended significant school events.

Hazel, called "Tilly" by her boys, was a participant in all of our early activities. She drove us to the mountains for fishing trips and during earlier grade-school years she wielded a saw and hammer to help build tree houses or clubhouses, even when these projects were not aesthetically pleasing. She was a voracious reader of Book-of-the-Month-Club selections, and the boys followed her lead. Piano lessons became very important to John, and my reluctant attendance at dancing classes made it possible for me later to meet the love of my life, Mary Lou.

Entertainment at home consisted of family bridge and poker games and listening to the big radio in the living room. On Friday evenings we often had dinner in downtown Seattle at the American Oyster House, the Betsy Jarvis Tearoom, Rippe's, or Manca's, followed by a movie at the 5th Avenue, Orpheum, Paramount, Blue Mouse, or Music Box Theaters.

Floyd was determined that his sons would be self-reliant and make their own way. He frequently told stories of his boyhood in Dayton when he worked for every nickel that he spent. It was his view that an able-bodied man was not a man if he lived off the charity of others or was supported by his family after school years. To instill this concept, he set up a system of jobs for me which involved the summertime care of our large lawn from age ten to fourteen.

In the spring of 1937, our parents decided that Bob and I should have an outdoor living experience and learn to get along on our own. I was fifteen years old, and Bob was thirteen, when Dad challenged us one night at dinner:

"You boys are growing up with silver spoons in your mouths. How would you like to spend this summer at the place where we went fishing last month and build a log cabin there? I will grubstake you two the land, tools, and materials. You would do the work and own the property in equal shares."

We jumped up cheering loudly and quickly accepted Hazel's terms for approval which were: A wood floor under our tent, a nap each afternoon for Bob, fresh milk for him every day, and inspection by parents at least every other Sunday. Floyd then bought seven acres of second-growth forest land on Raging River near the end of the Upper Preston Road in the Cascade foothills. At that time, this was a two-hour drive from home in Seattle through Renton and Issaquah. The purchase price was $700.00, and title was taken in the names of Bob and me. Seeing this deed made us feel very responsible.

In early June, we were dropped off at the end of the upper Preston Road with lumber for a tent floor, sleeping bags, canned goods, and our two dogs. It took both of us all day to take everything down to the river, clear a camp site, and build a tent floor. By the time a mountain of canned goods had been stored in the tent there was barely room for two sleeping bags and two dogs. Rain had just started and continued for the next four days while we huddled in the tent with two wet sheepdogs. We quickly used up all our paper trying to make fires with wet wood and ate very little hot food.

On the fourth day, while sitting in the tent trying to keep dry, we noticed a short, stocky man covered with a poncho fishing up the river toward us. We saw that whether a fish was of legal size or not it disappeared into the poncho, and we figured that the fisherman was some sort of bad guy. Bob hoped he wouldn't see our tent, but no such luck. He climbed up the bank, put his head in the tent, and pulled back his poncho hood to reveal that "he" was a woman.

"What are you boys doing here?" she said.

Bob replied, "We own this property."

She looked at this forlorn 13-year-old and spoke magic words. "When was the last time you had any hot food?"

Bob poured out that we hadn't had any hot food for three days and said, "My brother is a terrible cook."

She saw the wet dogs and wet clothes and commanded, "Follow me!" We meekly followed her up to the road and down to a tiny farmhouse where she lived with her 5'2" husband Johnny Brown. "Take off those wet clothes and hang 'em by the stove."

Our temporary camp tent and cooking fire pit in the early summer of 1937.

Signpost marking Jim's and Bob's camp at the Raging River cabin.

We complied and soon something that smelled awfully good was cooking on the wood range. It tasted great, we had seconds, and our morale rose quickly. "The stew was delicious, Mrs. Brown, what is it?" I asked.

"It's head cheese from the pig we killed last week," she answered. I almost barfed but recovered enough to eat a piece of blackberry pie.

Mr. and Mrs. Brown had no children, and by a stroke of providence Mrs. B. decided to "keep an eye on these polite boys." I asked her where I could find fresh milk for my brother.

She responded, "Carl, across the road, is milking a cow. I'll ask him to put a bottle of milk for you in the spring behind his kitchen. You can pay him what he asks. Carl is always fair."

Our spirits quickly perked up and the next day the sun came out. We learned how to find dry wood in a wet forest, how to keep fires going overnight, how to catch fish with periwinkles or salmonberries, how to cook, and we began to cut trees for a 24-foot-by-14-foot log cabin with a 24-foot-by-10-foot front porch.

These were exciting times for two young boys. The experience developed physical strength and confidence. In addition to a regular toolbox, we used a small Forest Service booklet on cabin building, two shovels, a pick, two light-weight single-bitted axes, and a two-person crosscut saw to begin a huge project. In this logged-off country, homes were few and far between. Our only close neighbors were John Brown, Carl Lilljmark, and Frank Noland, a disabled World War I veteran who had built his own log cabin. The second-growth forest around the cabin site was just the right age for cabin-size logs. Frank Noland gave us key tips on safely cutting straight trees in a dense forest. He showed us how to use iron wedges to guide the fall and a length of manila rope tied far enough up a tree to allow us to shake it loose if it got stuck against other trees on the way down.

A small cluster of subsistence farmers and mill workers lived in "Upper Preston" about a mile down river. Every morning we took turns walking to get a bottle of raw milk which was cooling in Carl's spring. Mrs. Brown influenced the close-knit, mostly Swedish community, to accept us and occasionally she contributed home-cooked food to our otherwise monotonous diet of canned beans, spaghetti, or meatballs.

A major surprise for us was the weight of newly cut logs. When we had cut enough trees for the cabin, help was needed to move these heavy logs to the building site. Mrs. Brown suggested that I walk a mile down the road to a yellow house owned by a man with a small, gas-powered winch. I timidly knocked on the door and the 6-foot-2-inch owner opened the door, towering over me. When I asked if we could hire him to pull our logs into the cabin clearing, he quickly dismissed the request with, "Aye don't vork for children!" and slammed the door. When I reported this rejection to Mrs. Brown she frowned, "Why that old bastard! Don't worry. Carl will pull your logs in." While getting milk one morning, I discovered that Carl had trouble seeing and said, "But, Mrs. Brown, Carl is half blind and so is his horse." "Doesn't matter," she replied. "They do fine in the woods."

Early next morning when it was still dark, I woke to the sound of crashing through the trees and got up to see Carl approaching the clearing with his big horse. I quickly put on pants and shoes and ran out to meet him. He said, "I'm here to pull your logs. Do you know how to set choker?" I shook my head, and he painstakingly showed me how to wrap a chain and iron hook around a log so it would not slip off, warning me, "If this slips, it could cut your leg off."

The next six hours I worked feverishly with no breakfast while Bob watched. The horse was powerful, whipping the logs around as they turned corners. Both Carl and his horse frequently bumped into trees but shortly after noon they had dragged the last log down and onto the peeling rack. I was completely worn out, while Carl did not even seem winded. "How much do we owe you, Carl?" I asked.

He thought a minute and said, "Five dollars."

Knowing how hard they had worked I said, "That's not enough for you and the horse." He said with firmness, "Aye don't vant to rob you." I thanked him, paid him the five dollars, and staggered back to our tent. Bob had watched the whole morning and had made me a sandwich. I gulped the sandwich down and fell into a sleep of exhaustion.

After cutting foundation blocks from a downed old cedar tree for the four corners, we selected from our log rack the largest four logs and put them in place. When these bottom logs were spiked together, Frank showed us how to lift the upper logs into place. We tied a set of rope pulleys to each end of

Bob cutting rafter ends as he and Jim rush to get a roof in place in late August before halting work for the start of school.

the bottom log of the front wall and ran the ropes over the back wall to an inclined plane of peeled poles leading from the wall to the ground. We would roll a new cabin log from the log rack to the slanting poles and "grease" these poles with a bucket of water. Then Bob and I each worked one set of pulleys. The freshly cut trees were heavy with sap. For each log we notched and put in place, spikes were set to permit later cut outs for windows and doors. Progress was very slow, but during July the cabin walls began to rise. In August, my father hired a Scotch mason to camp with us for two weeks to build a stone chimney and fireplace. Bob and I hauled all the rocks from the river to the chimney site.

One August morning, we cut some small trees for roof rafters. After lopping off the branches, we dragged each log from the woods to the clearing. Our system was to hitch ourselves to a crossbar with a rope running back to the log. We strained together against the crossbar like a team of horses, grunting, sweating, and goading each other. We would slip and fall, sometimes we got angry, but often we found ourselves laughing. After several hours we quit to eat a lunch of sandwiches and milk and Bob went to sleep for his daily nap. As had been agreed, my brother faithfully took his afternoon naps. Our family doctor believed these would prevent any severe fatigue which might cause a recurrence of Bob's rheumatic fever.

The shell of a one-room log cabin was in place by the end of the first summer.

During our second summer of cabin building in 1938, Bob and I purchased about 250 feet of used two-inch iron pipe for $20.00 from Aldarra Farm near Fall City. We used the pipe to run water from a spring on the hillside down to the back porch of the cabin. We built a 2-foot-by-4-foot enclosure under the eve of the roof and a cedar septic tank a few feet away. We installed a real toilet to replace the original outhouse. There was a sink outside the back door draining into the septic tank. There would be no hot water heater until 1946.

We still had no electricity and often worked after dark using kerosene lamps. There was the endless job of removing the blackened surface of the log walls using hand paint scrapers. We worked hard, but also took days off to go fishing up the river or hiking in the surrounding hills.

The cabin was livable by the end of the second summer.

After three summers Bob and I were inseparable.

Three blocks north of John Muir Grade School was the white terra cotta of Franklin High School which seemed like a new adult world. With the help of grade school friends, I was elected freshman class president. I would much rather have made the freshman football team, but at 125 pounds I found tackling 200-pound Dewey Soriano to be harder than it looked and was cut from the squad.

In sophomore year, my circle of friends widened. I was encouraged to enter the school oratorical contest and won first place with a clenched-fist version of "Ireland Worth Dying For." This led to joining the debate team and, a year later, to a high point of my high school years—leading a student assembly in an effort to rally the school after we had lost the championship basketball game.

Ellis family, circa 1943.

I wanted to earn my way through college just as my father had done. In senior year, I applied for a scholarship to Yale based on a good high school grade average. When our family finances exceeded the scholarship limits and the offer was withdrawn, my father made a deal to pay for school if I worked summers.

In September 1939, I left my family for the first time. Everyone came down to the King Street Station to see the Great Northern Empire Builder pull out of Seattle for the trip east. My grandparents, aunt and uncle, and close family friends were standing on the platform to wish me well when the train reached Spokane that night. A few minutes later, I watched the lights of Spokane disappear and wiped away a few tears. A much-loved home and family, and a happy childhood, seemed to be slipping away forever behind the clicking of Pullman car wheels.

✦

CHAPTER 2

Mary Lou's Roots and Beginnings

Her voice always had a smile.

—Mardie Demming

MARY LOU'S MOTHER, Mary Gazzam graduated from Smith College in Northampton, Massachusetts in 1918 and returned to Seattle where she met Roy Brown Earling at a Rainier Club dance on New Year's Eve.

On September 2, 1919, Roy and Mary were married at Crystal Springs. They spent their honeymoon on a trip to Honolulu aboard the steamship *Lurline* and stayed at the new Moana Hotel on Waikiki. They made their first home in Metcalf, Arizona, where Roy was serving as superintendent of the Metcalf Division of the United States Smelting, Refining & Mining Company (USSR & M Co.). A year later they were transferred to Massachusetts.

Mary Louise "Mary Lou" Earling was born on April 7, 1921, at her parents' home in Egypt, Massachusetts. Roy Earling was then working in nearby Boston as an assistant construction engineer in the headquarters of the USSR & M Co.

After Mary Lou was born, the Earling family moved to Cohasset, a few miles from Egypt in the same township of Scituate. The family enjoyed living on the New England coast and occupied comfortable colonial homes in Egypt and Cohasset where Mary Lou's younger sister, Nancy, was born in 1923. These were conservative communities. Mary was once asked to leave the

Roy and Mary Gazzam Earling, circa 1919.

public beach because she was not wearing "stockings" in addition to her more than ample bathing suit.

Roy was a proud father who delighted in playing with his daughters. He built a large, elaborately engineered toy elephant for Mary Lou. They called this burlap masterpiece "the only Heffalump in Cohasset" and stationed it in the front yard of their home.

While leading a quiet life in this ordered setting, Roy was working with the officers of the USSR & M Co. to hatch a major gold mining venture. This venture would shape the future of the Earling family and take them thousands of miles away from Boston to a cold, remote frontier. In 1925, when Mary Lou was four and her sister Nancy two, the USSR & M Co. transferred the Earling family to Nome, Alaska, where Roy began a lifetime career developing placer gold mining properties. The family booked passage with the Alaska Steamship Company on the round-bottomed passenger-supply ship *Victoria*. Roy sailed in June and Mary and the girls followed in October.

At the time of their arrival in 1925, Nome was a small town of about 500 people located on the edge of the Bering Sea. The town boasted a few wood-

*Mary Lou and Nancy in the front yard with "the
only Heffalump in Cohasset" built by Roy Earling.*

The Earling family in Alaska, circa 1926.

frame commercial buildings and board sidewalks. All building materials were brought in by ship because there were no trees on the tundra to make lumber. Driftwood logs were dragged from the beach and piled in tepee-like stacks to dry for fuel.

The family lived there for two years while Roy supervised a thawing and dredging operation on the nearby gravels of the Hammond Consolidated Gold Fields. During winter months the children took dogsled rides and in summer they played on two swings and a slide in the yard of the Coast Guard station on Front Street. Although there were no tourists, each summer the population swelled with Native families from the nearby islands. The Earling girls delighted in watching Iñupiat dancing and blanket tossing, a game in which a group of people hold an outstretched walrus- or seal-skin blanket and toss one person into the air. There were lots of Malamute and Husky dogs in town and the girls never tired of playing with them.

Family members still recall how Mary Lou climbed onto the roof of the four-story company apartment building at the age of four and managed to get down safely by herself after causing much community consternation.

In 1928, the Earling family moved to Fairbanks in the central interior of Alaska. Fairbanks was then a town of about 1,700 people with some log and frame buildings left behind from the turn-of-the-century gold rush. They lived in Fairbanks until Roy retired from the company in 1952.

The local subsidiary of the USSR & M Co. was called the Fairbanks Exploration Company, or F.E. Company for short, and was the principal employer in the town. Roy developed an improved method for the cold-water thawing of permanently frozen ground and a new method for hydraulic stripping of the overburden of muck. The exposed and thawed gold-bearing gravels were then washed through large gold dredges. Roy was known to company employees as "R. B." Company associates considered him an effective leader and employees thought of him as a strong-minded, but reasonable, boss. He was a familiar figure in the F.E. Company mining camps. The operations were profitable. As Roy rose in the company ranks, the family occupied an increasingly important position in town.

When Roy became manager of the Fairbanks mining operations in 1934, the Earling family moved into a larger home on Cowles Street. Finally, from

1940 to 1952, they lived in a new colonial-style house built by the company a few blocks from the office and smelter. Roy was especially proud of the huge pansies that bordered the path to their house, the sixteen-foot sunflower plants, and thirty-pound cabbages that grew fast in the long Arctic summer days.

Just about everyone knew everyone else in interior Alaska in the 1920s, 1930s, and early 1940s. Doors were never locked in Fairbanks and cars used for winter shopping trips were left on the street with the engines running. Twice-monthly family-style Scandinavian dances were organized by the Sourdough Dance Club. The girls especially liked these warm, lively parties. There were picnics and baseball games during July's daylight evenings and cross-country skiing and ice skating during the snow-covered winter.

Winter in Fairbanks arrived early and departed late. The temperature sometimes reached fifty degrees below zero. This season was Mary Lou's favorite. The days were dark, but lacy birch trees, telephone wires, and the air itself glistened with frost crystals. The fast-moving curtains of the Northern Lights were a special treat. Even the quiet was conspicuous, broken only by the crunch of boots on the snow and the droning of wood saws.

When spring approached, the girls began taking off layers of clothes and the whole town began to focus on the precise second of the natural ice breakup in the Chena and Tanana Rivers. Their banks would overflow, and the girls would find poles and push themselves around the submerged streets on the parts of wood sidewalks that were floating loose. During school days they used a canoe to cross the flooded area between their house on Cowles Street and the Crawford's house where family friend Alta Crawford then drove the children to school.

The streets and paths all turned to mud until gradually the warmer and longer days of sunshine began to dry the mud into the dust of summer. There were hardly any paved roads, so dust was everywhere. During the long, dry days, the Earling girls took turns every hour watering the dirt roadway of Cowles Street.

The birches and aspens put on a spectacular show in September, but once Mary Lou left Fairbanks to attend ninth grade at Bush School in Seattle in 1935, fall always seemed sad to her sister Barbara. Mary Lou's departure was a sign that their childhood together was ending and that separate paths were leading to different futures. The whole neighborhood joined the family at the

The Earling home in Fairbanks, Alaska, 1927.

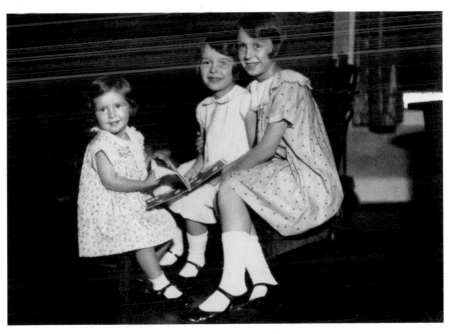

The Earling girls, circa 1929.

train station and later at the airfield to wave goodbye to Mary Lou each year when she left, sometimes tying eight or ten handkerchiefs together so they could be seen a few minutes longer and waving until the little Electra flew beyond the hills.

The girls adored their father and Roy was a gentle and affectionate parent. For summer fun, he made bows and arrows and a pair of stilts for Mary Lou, Nancy, and Barbara, who had become the third Earling child in 1927. In the winter, Roy flooded the back lawn to make an ice-skating rink and hollowed out playhouse igloos from the big snowdrifts by their backdoor.

Mary Lou's love for her father showed in her scrawled childhood notes and that love never diminished. When the family was together, Roy devoted considerable time to his daughters and when they were away, he would sometimes include elaborate cartoons in his letters.

Mary Earling also served as a caring supervisor of the girls' activities and was a faithful and loving letter writer when they were away at school. She was a leader in the small Christian Science community and raised her girls in this faith. No liquor was served in the Earling home and, like most parents in this small mining camp community, Mary and Roy taught their daughters never to be seen in a Fairbanks tavern.

Her younger sisters admired "Em," as Mary Lou was affectionately called, because she was a natural leader and never let them down. Of her sister, Nancy later wrote:

I'll try to paint a simple word portrait of Mary Lou as a girl: patient, kind-hearted and generous, interesting to be with, straightforward, totally alert, romantic but without a shred of vanity, absolutely loyal, and creative in everything she did.

I feel fortunate to have been close enough to her age to be a participant in her growing-up years. I think the best indication of the strong influence she was in my life and how much I looked up to her is the fact that for several years after Sam and I were married I kept calling him 'Mary Lou.'

In the early 1930s, Roy purchased a piece of property with a small cabin on Harding Lake, located about fifty miles southeast of Fairbanks. For Mary Lou, Nancy, and Barbara, this little cabin without running water became their

The Earling Family, 1943.

favorite place on earth. After gathering around a cozy kerosene lamp each evening for dinner, the girls climbed into their sleeping porch bunks.

Mary Lou loved the natural beauty of Alaska and its warm and friendly people. She shared her father's passion for photography and her scrapbook of photos was entitled *Alaska, My Alaska*. Mary Lou and her father captured some of the people and scenes of frontier Alaska in their photographs—the traders, trappers, miners, bush pilots, teachers, salesmen, and settlers who pioneered that vast North Country. Mary Lou talked with Will Rogers and Wiley Post when they stopped at Harding Lake on their ill-fated attempt to fly around the world. Bush pilots like Sam White were among her heroes.

Bush School for Girls was then operated by its founder, Helen Bush, with "day" students and boarding students. Two years later Mary Lou was joined by Nancy, and a year after by Barbara in 1938.

Mary Lou was homesick for her family for the first few months at Bush School, but soon made life-long friends, among them were Mary Lou "Louie" Minor from Seattle, her roommate Mary "Mardie" Deming from Bellingham, Washington, and Ruth Pullen ("Pulley") from South Dakota. Mary Lou was known by her classmates as a girl who never made unkind remarks about people and wouldn't tolerate those who did. Whenever she heard unkind words, Mary Lou would respond with an instant defense or some positive comment. She was the first to welcome Pulley warmly and made her feel at home when she felt like "a hick from the sticks." Whenever the tears came in Barbara's first homesick year at Bush, Mary Lou held her in her arms. When Mardie's mother died, Mary Lou appointed herself as someone to watch over her roommate with special care.

Mardie recalled:

". . . her naturalness and her natural affection for people were the keys to her attractiveness. . . Mary Lou was always the first to defend a friend, assist an underdog, or support a cause she believed in—and often at great inconvenience to herself. Mary Lou lived with joy. . . Her voice always had a smile."

During her four years at Bush, Mary Lou developed into a pretty young woman, winning the school contest for "most beautiful eyes" in her senior year as well as student body president. She was a popular partner in the dancing classes and parties sponsored by the Women's University Club, the Sunset Club, and the Daughters of the American Revolution.

In February of 1938, Roy and Mary took Mary Lou and her sisters out of school for a three-month trip to Europe and the Middle East. It was an exciting cruise in grand style aboard the *S. S. Roma*, with stops around the Mediterranean—from Casablanca to Egypt, Palestine, Greece, Rhodes, and Italy—before taking the train through Europe. They were in Holland when Hitler occupied Austria.

Mary Lou was a good student at Bush, getting high grades all four years. She planned on going to Smith College in Massachusetts like her mother had and was disappointed when she wasn't admitted. Instead, she and her friend Louie entered Pine Manor College in Wellesley, Massachusetts.

⁂

CHAPTER 3

High School and College: Riding Different Trains

I FIRST MET MARY LOU in November of 1937, when we were sixteen years old. Mary Deming brought her as a date for my friend, Dolph Hoyt, to a dancing class party given by my mother. We first really noticed each other a few weeks later when the four of us attended a party in the Mount Baker neighborhood, followed by a farm dance at Bush School. Mary Lou wore a red gingham peasant dress and with that one dance she enchanted me for a month.

However, Mary Lou and I traveled separate paths for most of our high school years, only occasionally seeing one another. She spent her summers in Alaska with her family, while I spent my summers at Raging River building the cabin with my brother.

Under heavy urging by my parents, I attended the Women's University Club dancing parties. These dances drew a mix of public and private school students, mostly from well-to-do families in Seattle. At one of those parties in September 1938, I noticed that Mary Lou looked especially pretty and I asked for a place on her dance program. Her signal of encouragement was to squeeze the hand of a boy she liked. That night after our program dance and a couple warm hand squeezes, I invited Mary Lou onto my turf for a high school dance.

After the dance, when we parked in front of the Bush Annex, Mary Lou misread my nervous fumbling with the door handle and quickly opened her car door. I remember thinking, "Opening her door means she doesn't want a goodnight kiss." She later told me, "I was hoping you would reach for me instead of the door." Mary Lou and I each came away from that date thinking that the other was reserved but we exchanged dances more successfully at later events.

During our high school years Mary Lou and I struck occasional sparks together, but my shyness, the patterns of our lives, and the presence of other more experienced partners, kept us on different tracks most of the time. We later laughed over these near misses. In September of 1939, we didn't even know that we each left Seattle for the East on the same day, on different trains.

"Last station! Grand Central!" The conductor called through the cars and an 18-year-old from Seattle began to feel the excitement of New York City—the great station, the towering skyscrapers, subway trains shaking the streets above. I spent two awestruck days in New York City feeling its pulse and visited the 1939 World's Fair.

The final leg of the trip on the New Haven Railroad traveled through the backyards of industrial cities, a far cry from my mental picture of postcard New England. In New Haven, the cab driver helped me unload my suitcases where the Yale campus fronts on the City Green and said, "Good luck, young man." I carried the bags through the old campus gate to begin four years of college.

My room assignment was in Wright Hall. Wright was a central gathering spot because the university post office was located in the basement. My roommate was an Andover graduate, John Makepeace, known to his friends as "J. G.," a good tennis player with a self-conscious grin.

Both Yale and New England seemed like a long way from Seattle and family. I was homesick for weeks. I learned that nobody cared if I slept late or didn't do homework. The absence of girls was a vacuum and the change from open Western friendliness to Eastern reserve bothered me. But the historic buildings of the campus pulled me in and the statue of Nathan Hale in front of Connecticut Hall was inspiring.

I occasionally visited my mother's cousin, Harold E. Mitchell, and his wife, Beth, in nearby West Hartford. Hal was a practicing attorney, Speaker of the House of Representatives for the state of Connecticut, and a national leader in the Republican Party. He introduced me to his political friends and invited me to listen to a few strategy sessions in his smoke-filled study. Some lively discussions occurred over the dining room table and their hospitality provided a welcome home away from home.

Summer vacation highlights back at home included a backpacking trip in the high Cascades with Bob, Dolph Hoyt, and Walt Ring, and weekend family fishing trips with my father, grandfather, and brother Bob. The outdoors, especially the mountain country, held a visceral attraction for Bob and me.

In 1940, J. G. and I were assigned to Saybrook College. Yale was organized into residential dormitories which were called "colleges." All upper classmen lived and took their meals in these residential colleges in a system modeled after Oxford and Cambridge. We made our closest Yale friendships in Saybrook. We both liked playing bridge and intramural basketball, but there was a big difference in our study habits. J. G. excelled in disciplined effort and grades, while I continued to daydream, miss classes, and get average grades. There were a few all-night "beer and bridge" parties and lots of singing in the courtyard.

I became active in the Political Union, a student forum for the discussion of public issues, and made the Yale debate team. From 1938 to 1941, my political views were colored by pacifist leanings, a long admiration for childhood hero Charles Lindberg, and by a strong desire not to be entangled in a European War, which some of my teachers believed was caused by profiteering munitions makers.

In February 1941, I wrote to Mary Lou to invite her to the Yale Junior Prom, a major winter event involving a three-day weekend. Her girlfriend Louie later recalled that Mary Lou was very excited when she received my letter. She carefully planned her wardrobe and arranged to stay at the home of Christian Science friends in nearby Hamden.

I was delighted when she said "Yes," and borrowed my Uncle Hal Mitchell's new car to meet the Boston train in Hartford. When Mary Lou walked off the train, she looked like she had just stepped out of a bandbox. We hadn't seen each other for almost two years, and she was prettier than I remembered. I took her suitcase and noticed that she still wore no lipstick!

We stopped at the Mitchell house in West Hartford so Beth and Hal could meet "Jim's girl." Mary Lou charmed them in a matter of minutes by saying, "How lucky Jim is to have people he loves living so near." As we were leaving, Beth whispered to me, "Jim, she's absolutely lovely."

On the drive to New Haven, we talked about being homesick for the West and laughed over our dancing class at the University Club. The warmth and friendliness of this natural Western girl reminded me of home. By the time we reached New Haven, I was asking myself why I had waited so long to invite Mary Lou for a weekend.

Friday had been carefully planned with an all-night series of events. Mary Lou and I joined the Saybrook group for dinner that evening at the family home of one of our New Haven members. Afterward, I drove Mary Lou to nearby Hamden to get dressed for the dance. It was a snowy evening. On my way back to the dorm, daydreaming about Mary Lou's warm smile, I drove through a red light, was sideswiped by a taxi, and skidded into a telephone pole. Hal's new car was heavily damaged, and I ended up on my head in the back seat, shaken but not hurt.

With the help of a kind campus cop, the taxi driver was pacified, and Hal's car was towed away. When I got back to Saybrook, J. G. came to the rescue and volunteered to drive Mary Lou and me to the dance. J. G. and I decided not to tell anyone about the accident so that Mary Lou's weekend would not be spoiled.

My guilty conscience prevented sleep that night and drove me out of bed to face the music on several fronts. Surprisingly, Hal was understanding when he heard the news. However, the rest of the morning was less successful. Campus cops, insurance agents, and the auto wreckers alerted me fully to my financial liability.

On Saturday, we saw a Yale swim meet, watched the Yale-Harvard hockey game, and attended another dance at Vernon Hall. After the dance, three couples went somewhere to eat. I don't remember much because I fell asleep in the car on Mary Lou's shoulder.

After church on Sunday, we took a long walk around the campus and the New Haven Green. I was thoroughly subdued and unusually quiet. Mary Lou said, "It's real friendship when you don't feel that you have to talk." We were comfortable together and I liked her a lot, but my mind kept coming back to how I could possibly pay for the costly car accident. After lunch we talked about getting together in New York during spring break and then we ran to make Mary Lou's train to Boston. She said goodbye with a kiss on the cheek. A picture of Mary Lou occupied a place of honor on my dresser after that weekend.

When Mary Lou returned to Pine Manor, she told Louie everything in detail, how perfect dinner had been, and what a good time she had. "Jim is the one I want. But, Louie, he is awfully reserved. If I'm the one who's going to get him, I'm going to have to take the initiative."

I was able to see Mary Lou briefly over spring break when Mary Lou and her friends, Louie and Eleanor Ferguson, joined Eleanor's mother for two days in New York. We arranged to meet after dinner by the clock in the Waldorf lobby. Mary Lou was right on time and once again looked like a fashion model. We window shopped along Fifth Avenue and stopped at Rockefeller Center to watch couples skating to the music of Jerome Kern. We held hands while walking to Central Park and talked about the excitement of New York. Along Park Avenue, she came up with the idea that we hopscotch the sidewalk squares. We acted like a couple of grade school kids and drew plenty of kibitzing from people on the street.

I called a cab after an hour of walking so we could safely see more of the city at night. Watching the meter whirling, I asked the driver to take us to Battery Park where the old Staten Island Ferry offered a bargain five-cent ride. Mary Lou had never ridden the ferry and was enthusiastic. When we got to the dock she said to the driver, "Why don't you come along?" Unfortunately, he did, and an opportunity to be alone was lost.

Nevertheless, it was a beautiful night, and the lights of New York were spectacular. The cab driver appreciated being invited. When we got back into the cab, he said, "I'm turning off the meter. The rest of the trip is on me." Then, with a running commentary on the city and its people, he drove us all over Manhattan, through the Bowery, Greenwich Village, Broadway, Times Square,

Mary Lou, circa 1941.

the slums of Harlem, and past Park Avenue's luxury apartments. It was nearly 2:00 a.m. when he finally dropped us off at the Waldorf Hotel.

We were both much later than expected and when I got back to the Barclay Hotel, my father was angry. "How could you take a girl to such risky places at such an ungodly hour?" Mary Lou was also warned by Eleanor Ferguson's mother that it was too late to be out in New York City.

Criticism did not dampen my feeling of a wonderful time. With no distracting auto accident, I found myself looking at Mary Lou through different eyes. The same girl who cast a spell over me at age sixteen had grown into a beautiful young woman. She was my kind of Western girl, and I felt sure that she liked me. In later years, we both wondered why I didn't kiss her that night. Maybe the ever-present taxi driver made me self-conscious.

On spring afternoons in New Haven, I daydreamed about brown eyes and warm smiles and confided to my roommate that maybe Mary Lou would be the girl for me. With no money for travel between Boston and New Haven, Mary Lou and I didn't see each other until June when I went home.

I telephoned her at the Women's University Club in Seattle where she was staying for a night's rest before flying home. She said, "I'm sort of under the weather and not very pretty, but I'd love to see you."

As we drove around downtown Seattle, fever showed in her eyes. I touched her hot forehead and said, "Mary Lou, you should be in bed, not flying to Alaska."

"I'll be okay once I get home," she replied. Then she changed the subject. "I'm going to the U (University of Washington) this fall and will probably go through sorority rushing."

As we approached the Women's University Club, I said, "I won't leave for Yale before rushing," and asked if we could see each other in September.

"Yes, be sure and call me, Jim. I don't want to wait another year and a half for you to look me up. I'm going to write letters this summer so you can't forget me just because I'm in Alaska."

"No guy is going to forget you," I replied. "I'll write as many letters as you write."

Mary Lou paused a moment, then turned to grab the club's brass doorknob. With uncharacteristic boldness I ventured, "You're the swellest girl I know, Mary Lou!" She smiled and winked as she closed the door behind her.

The next day, I started my summer job at the J. C. Penney Co. store on Second Avenue in downtown Seattle. I worked maximum hours that summer and earned some good Saturday sales bonuses. These earnings were carefully saved and sent to West Hartford. But the entire summer's work was barely enough to pay the insurance deductible for the car I had demolished.

After our brief meeting in Seattle, Mary Lou returned to Fairbanks, her family, and the little cabin at Harding Lake for the summer. There, she fell in love with Ernest Patty, the son of the president of the University of Alaska and a family friend whom the Earling girls had known since grade school. Ernest was a year older than Mary Lou and had visited her once while she was at Pine Manor.

Ernest became a licensed pilot at age sixteen and earned his commercial license at eighteen. He spent his summers working as a bush pilot while attending Cornell. During the summer of 1941, he invited Mary Lou to fly to some of the beautiful mountain lakes of Alaska and on those romantic dates he wasn't as bashful as I had been about kissing her. Their attraction grew and, by August, Mary Lou began thinking seriously about wanting to marry Ernest. Before they left Fairbanks to return to college, the young couple was going steady.

Mary Lou's letters to me stopped that August. She did not write about the seriousness of her relationship with Ernest. When I called for a date in September, she made it clear that the sorority rush timetable was more important than seeing me.

In September 1941, Ernest returned to Cornell for his senior year. He was in Ithaca, New York, and I was in New Haven, Connecticut, on Sunday afternoon December 7th when radio broadcasts told a shocked nation the Japanese had bombed Pearl Harbor. The attack killed 2,388 Americans and wounded 1,178 more. Thirty-one ships were sunk or damaged, 323 American aircraft were destroyed or damaged.

Almost instantly Americans were galvanized together. Never since those days of World War II have I seen the country so united. College students, including vocal pacifists like me, were swept up in a wave of patriotism.

Ernest in Ithaca, and I in New Haven, stood in long lines at recruiting offices to sign up to join the armed forces. I learned that my cabin building skills had no military value and was told to finish college. Ernest had a commercial pilot's license and was commissioned upon enlisting. He was immediately given two weeks of training and then six weeks of home leave in Seattle while his combat unit was being assembled. The Air Force desperately needed pilots to stem the Japanese advance in the South Pacific. Bataan was under siege and the Pacific Fleet had been crippled. Men with almost no training were being thrown into the breach!

Although letters from Mary Lou had been infrequent during the fall, I still thought of her as "my girl." When I came home for Christmas, I called to invite her to the Sunset Club Holiday Party. Her aunt answered the phone and told me Mary Lou already accepted another invitation. I was surprised to find out about "another guy" and decided to invite Mary Deming to the party.

Ida Mitsue Nakauchi
Internment: An American Injustice

IDA NAKAUCHI CAME TO WORK for our family in 1936. She had recently graduated from Kent High School and went to work for my mother at a modest salary with room and board in the big house on 50th Avenue South in Seattle. Ida worked continuously for our family until Pearl Harbor and by that time had become a part of the family.

Ida was born January 9, 1918, in a rural area of King County, Washington, called Cherry Valley, near present day Kent. She was one of eight children. Her father, Kazuma Nakauchi, and mother, Miyoju Yoneno, were both born and raised in Kumamoto Prefecture, Japan. Kazuma arrived in Seattle in 1905 and Miyoju arrived in 1913. Their arranged marriage was recognized in 1912 in a Buddhist ceremony in Japan and then by a certificate from King County in Seattle on February 17, 1913. The newly married couple settled on a vegetable farm in the White River Valley where Kazuma was a tenant farmer.

The shock of the Japanese attack on Pearl Harbor in 1941 was as much a surprise to Japanese Americans as it was to other Americans. Public fury against Japan was ignited across the nation and there was near-hysterical fear along parts of the Pacific Coast. With lightning speed, the Japanese armed forces followed-up Pearl Harbor by attacking and conquering a wide swath of the South Pacific and Southeast Asia. The effect on the American public of these initial sweeping Japanese victories was profound. Fear was high along the West Coast.

On February 19, 1942, President Franklin D. Roosevelt signed Executive Order 9066 authorizing the forced evacuation from the Pacific Coast of all people of Japanese ancestry even if they had been born in America and were US citizens. The Army was instructed to relocate everyone of Japanese descent away from the West Coast for the duration of the emergency. This was the largest forced relocation of American people since the Indian wars.

A few days after Pearl Harbor, the Ellis family was shocked to learn that the Nakauchi family, including Ida, was likely to be ordered to leave their home and any possessions they could not carry, and to report to a local military assembly center.

My father and I were incensed that an American citizen like Ida Nakauchi, who was born in the United States and had committed no crime, could be locked up for no reason other than having Japanese ancestry. A vast majority of American citizens were descendants of immigrants from other countries and no similar group of American citizens of German or Italian descent were included in the World War II internment order. We felt the West Coast Japanese American internment was an unwarranted violation of constitutional rights of citizenship.

Nevertheless, the action included all people of Japanese ancestry living along the West Coast of the United States. They were taken under armed guard to inland internment camps beginning in the spring of 1942. The fear of an invasion by Japan had largely dissipated by 1943. However, the harm was done. Movement of Japanese Americans on short notice caused huge losses of value in crops, homes, businesses, and property.

When President Roosevelt's announcement was made, Ida was 24 years old. She left our home in Seattle in response to the first notice to register and moved back to the family farm in Kent where she had grown up. The War Relocation Authority (WRA) required her father to gather his entire family and report to the nearest assembly center established in Puyallup. Beginning on April 28, 1942, the first people of Japanese American ancestry were transported by train from Puyallup, Washington, to the regional Pinedale Assembly Center near Fresno, California.

Ida's personal impressions from her forced relocation were seldom discussed. However, she did share these memories with her family in the following account:

We left by train on May 2, 1942, from Kent, Washington, to the Pinedale Assembly Camp located near Fresno, California. Upon arrival I could see guard towers posted on all corners of the camp. Guards inspected our belongings, and we were assigned living quarters. There were four sections within each Pinedale barrack. The men of our family had one room and the women another. The barracks were not fully completed when we arrived, and my family was directed to a bare unit with no plumbing and a dirt floor. A single light bulb hung from the ceiling and canvas Army cots were the only furnishings. [Each "family unit" consisted of two rooms with 7-foot-high walls. Toilets and showers were in separate common areas for men and women and served 200 to 250 people.]

After a few months, we were moved to the Tule Lake Internment Camp in Newell, California, near the Oregon border. Movies and dances were held and there were commissaries to buy personal necessities, along with a hospital inside the camp that was staffed with doctors and nurses. Jobs were available, but no evacuee could be paid more than an Army private (which was then $21 per month.) I got a job working in the mess hall earning $19 dollars a month. Laundry was done in the laundry area and there were always long lines, so doing laundry for the family often could take several hours. After being in

California for months, my family was relocated to the Heart Mountain Camp located in Park County, in northwest Wyoming.

There were people living in Tule Lake that had been born in Japan and wanted to go back to their homeland. In 1944, several thousand detainees (loyal to America) were allowed to go to Chicago, Detroit, and other cities in the East. I made the decision to go to Chicago, where I worked for several different families. After release from the Heart Mountain Camp, the rest of our family relocated to Sidney, Nebraska, where they lived for three years with my sister, Mable, and her husband. Eventually, I was able to return to Seattle and go back to work for Mrs. Ellis. I brought my mother, father, younger sisters Ruby and May with me, and found a house for the family to live in South Seattle near Boeing Plant #2. Ruby attended Cleveland High School and eventually graduated from there.

Ida's sister Ruby recalls that when the children asked their father why they were being sent away from their home, his response was, "Shikatai Ga Nai" which in English means "It can't be helped." Throughout their internment, Ruby remembers her father was loyal to America, patient, optimistic and always in good humor.

When I first saw Mary Lou that evening, she was proudly towing a tall, handsome young man across the dance floor toward us. He was wearing the uniform of an Air Force first lieutenant with pilot's wings. "This is my fiancé, Ernest Patty Jr.," she said. "Ernie, these are two of my best friends, Mary Deming and Jim Ellis." When Ernest and I shook hands she added, "I want very much for you two to like each other."

At Mary's suggestion we exchanged a dance. I couldn't conceal my surprise at the fact that my best girl was about to get married to someone else and asked, "When did you get engaged?"

"We started going together seriously last summer in Fairbanks," Mary Lou said. "He took me flying to some beautiful and remote places. We just got engaged last week, but we grew up together and our parents have been friends for years." Then, seeing the disappointment in my face, she quickly added with a wink, "You were always too elusive."

"I'll miss those midnight ferry rides, Mary Lou. I can easily see why Ernest fell in love with you, but are you sure you love him?"

"Yes, I'm very sure. We really know each other awfully well. He is a great guy and I'm positive that you would like him." She paused, "We're getting married next month and he's going overseas very soon. Please wish us luck."

I realized the dance was ending, along with any chance of getting her back, so I put my best face forward. "Sounds like 'Goodbye, Mary Lou Earling.' Ernest is a lucky guy. I hope you have the best luck in the world." She gave my hand a quick squeeze then turned toward Ernest with a radiant smile.

Upon returning to Yale in January, I removed Mary Lou's picture from the top of the bureau. I told my surprised roommate, "The girl you thought I was going to marry has fallen in love with somebody else. Mary Lou is getting married to an Air Force pilot this month."

However, when Mary Lou wired her parents that she was getting married and asked them to come to Seattle for the January wedding, Roy and Mary wired her back asking the couple to wait until both sets of parents could attend the wedding. While Mary Lou's desire to get married was very strong, she didn't want to hurt her parents' feelings and the wedding was put off.

During Ernest's six-week home leave before overseas duty, Ernest and Mary Lou spent most of their time together. But sometime in February 1942, after a long weekend at Paradise Lodge on Mount Rainier, Ernest and Mary Lou broke up. Most of her friends did not know she had been engaged and I thought she was married. A few weeks later Ernest left for the South Pacific. He called on Mary Lou when he returned, but they never went out together again.

In early June 1942, I came home for two weeks of vacation before starting an accelerated senior year at Yale. On a date with Mary Deming, I asked about Mary Lou's marriage to Ernest. Mary said the marriage had never happened. She believed their romance had ended and thought Mary Lou would like me to call her.

I telephoned the next morning to the home of her Aunt Ruth Haight where she was packing for a flight to Fairbanks the next day. "Are you still engaged?"

Ernest's Service

ERNEST PATTY SERVED FOR 14 MONTHS as squadron navigator for the first group of B-25's based in New Guinea. He flew 100 combat missions and was one of a very few to survive. During his tour of duty, the Philippines fell and there was fierce fighting on Guadalcanal. Ernest won the Distinguished Flying Cross among other decorations. He came home in April 1943 and, after a month's rest in Seattle, served as a flying instructor in Arizona for the remainder of the war.

"No. That's all over now."

"Could you go out with me tonight?"

"Yes, I'd love to see you again. I'm glad you called."

After a downtown movie, we drove along tree-lined Lake Washington Boulevard. "You know, I thought I'd never see Mary Lou Earling again. You were so sure about Ernest last Christmas. For the last six months I really thought you were married. What happened?"

"The engagement was a mistake. A few weeks later we both learned that we weren't right for each other."

When we neared the Genesee Slough, she moved to break the ice. "Bet I can climb a madrona tree higher than you can."

A challenge like this could not be ignored by a former builder of madrona tree houses. "Okay, it's a bet."

I parked my father's old Lincoln in a wide space along the road. We slipped off socks and shoes, ran down the grassy bank and shinnied up two slippery-barked madronas. Mary Lou was as quick and agile as a monkey. We were laughing and shouting at each other from halfway up those trees when a young neighbor, Hurley Ring, came by and called up, "Hym, is that you up in that tree?" "Hym" was my family nickname bestowed on me in high school for no apparent reason. He yelled. "What are you doing up there?"

As we climbed down, I was sure she had let me win and we walked back to the car. Mary Lou was laughing. "Hurley thinks he's really got something on you."

"Yes, my neighborhood reputation is probably ruined. Maybe it's all part of our jinx. When you decided to marry Ernest, I told myself that it hadn't been a fair fight because you and I were jinxed. It always seemed like we were at different places or riding different trains. When we did get together, we were never alone."

With one electric touch we were wrapped around each other kissing, longing, and holding on to one another. We came up for air a few minutes later. "I thought you were NEVER going to kiss me," said Mary Lou.

"I thought I was never going to get the chance."

Both of us were surprised at the intensity of our feelings and we were both afraid to let go because we might not come back together. I remember not wanting to take her home.

By the time we reached Mrs. Haight's front porch and held each other tight during a long goodnight kiss, it was getting late. Mary Lou gently pushed me away. With her hand on the doorknob, she stopped and looked straight at me. "Whether you believe me or not, tonight was the best time I've ever had in my life and that includes my time with Ernest or anyone else—ever."

"It was the best time for me, too, Mary Lou. Will you be around if I call you next Christmas?"

"Yes, I'll be here and that's a promise." Then she smiled a little, "I wish you hadn't waited so long to kiss me."

She fished out her key, opened the door, blew me a kiss, and was gone.

I skipped down the steps and sang "Mary Lou" all the way home.

CHAPTER 4

This is the Army

THE JAPANESE WERE STILL in the Aleutians in the summer of 1942 and Dutch Harbor had been bombed. Roy Earling began to worry about the safety of his family in Alaska. In July, Mary Earling and the girls flew to Seattle. They stayed at Pleasant Beach on Bainbridge Island in a small waterfront cottage owned by the Gazzam side of the family, then moved to a rented Seattle house in September.

Mary Lou worked at the Frederick & Nelson department store in Seattle and commuted by ferry to Bainbridge Island that August. In September, she enrolled in French language classes for her senior year at the University of Washington. She also began working with her mother as a volunteer aircraft monitor at the Aircraft Filter Board in downtown Seattle. The Filter Board was a control center where the location of aircraft flying in the area was plotted on a large table, or "board," for controlling aircraft movements and identifying any possible hostile presence.

I drove back to New Haven. Senior year at Yale had been accelerated to permit the class of 1943 to graduate in December of 1942. Most students had enlisted in a service branch and would be called to active duty upon graduation.

Gazzam family home on Bainbridge Island.

After an average scholastic and activity record for three years, I finally made the Dean's Honor List. I was surprised to be chosen from the varsity debate team to debate Harvard and, after the 150-pound varsity football league was cancelled for the duration due to its travel requirements, I became a "mainstay" of the Saybrook intramural football team. Finally, to the amazement of the faculty and all my friends except J. G., I won a Dickerman senior prize in economics. Probably because there wasn't time to loaf, everything started going my way.

After graduation ceremonies, several farewell parties, and a train trip across the snow-covered Northern Plains, I arrived in Seattle to find an invitation on the dining room table from Mary Lou to a New Year's dancing party. The invitation included a note with "you will accompany Miss Mary Lou Earling." However, any serious romance was going to have to wait until the war was won.

In the winter of 1943, Bob and I were super charged with patriotism and impatient for the Army to call us up. We read every scrap of information about the military campaigns, and I took a temporary job loading gas cans for the Pacific War. Mary Lou was equally impatient, dropping one of her classes at the university to increase her part-time work at the Aircraft Filter Board.

As I found myself liking Mary Lou more and more, I began searching for a nickname to replace "Tony," a nickname bestowed on Mary Lou by Bush and Pine Manor classmates. I wanted a name for Mary Lou which would belong especially to us and not be associated with her former boyfriends. During 1942 and 1943 millions of young men were in training. A small Army Air Corps was transformed into a tremendous Air Force with thousands of planes and millions of men. In typical American style, a new language emerged from this national effort. The term "G.I." was derived from "government issue" and meant "any soldier." A G.I. who never did anything right was "a sad sack." A G.I. who worked hard or volunteered for extra duty was "an eager beaver." Mary Lou's enthusiastic responsiveness and her creative ideas for getting the two of us together in spite of all obstacles, made her seem to me like the "eager beaver" of our romance. This name was soon shortened to "Beaver" and stuck for the rest of her life.

In early March 1943, my brother Bob and I both received our orders, reported to the Armory in Seattle, and were taken by truck to Fort Lewis, fifty miles south of Seattle. We were issued uniforms and, as army privates, we were given aptitude tests to classify us for assignment. After a few weeks, Bob was sent to Camp Hood, Texas, for tank destroyer basic training. As he waved goodbye from the back of an Army truck, I found myself brushing away an unexpected tear. Bob seemed much too young and vulnerable for tank-destroying. He was just out of high school and had never been away from home.

During tests at Fort Lewis, the Army decided I had the aptitude and background to be a scientific technician. They pointed out that a meteorology program was open, and I accepted because it could lead to an officer's commission. The trainees lived together in University of Washington dorms during weekdays learning the math and science necessary for meteorology and did a few hours of daily calisthenics and military drills. Those who lived nearby were given passes to go home on Saturday afternoons and Sundays.

Cadet James Reed Ellis, 1943.

Jim in the Army.

Mary Lou and I were walking past the Lakewood Boathouse on Lake Washington one sunny April afternoon when she said, "Let's rent a canoe." Unknown to me, she was an old hand with canoes from her summers at Harding Lake. I was a complete novice but insisted on taking charge of the stern paddle. We paddled to Mercer Island and back. As we came opposite the north point of Seward Park on the return leg, I was seized by an impulse to stir up some excitement by rocking the canoe. I hoped it would produce a few squeals or shrieks. Instead, Mary Lou warned quietly, "Jim, you could tip this thing over."

Not getting the expected reaction, I tried again and sure enough, over we went. I swallowed a mouthful of water while going under and came up coughing, sputtering, and struggled to hold on to the capsized canoe. At the same time, Mary Lou was calmly moving hand-over-hand along the canoe toward me. "Are you OK, Jim?" Then saying, "There go your glasses," she ducked underwater to retrieve them and immediately dove again to rescue my wallet.

Under Mary Lou's capable direction, we got the canoe righted and recovered the paddles. The water was cold. I was in a wool uniform, but Mary Lou was wearing a light spring dress. By the time she started shivering, I had begun to shape up a little.

"Swim to the point, Beaver, and borrow a coat from somebody. I'll push the canoe in."

Mary Lou swam strongly to shore. A crowd had gathered while her escort floundered slowly toward shore with a canoe. A Good Samaritan loaned her a coat, and we had plenty of help bailing out the canoe. Back at my parents' house with dry clothes on, we laughed about how I looked with my wallet floating away. From that day, I had a new respect for Mary Lou.

Near the end of May, Mary Lou flew home to be with her family in Fairbanks for the summer. We called it a "cooling off" period and agreed to continue dating other people. It was not easy to say goodbye.

Then in September, along with most of "Flight G" meteorology trainees, I was promoted to cadet and sent to the University of Chicago for training to be a weather officer in the Air Force.

Early in the war, a select group of women who had been trained as pilots were employed by the Air Force to ferry military airplanes. Mary Lou wanted to join this group, and with the encouragement of her father, she moved to Tulsa, Oklahoma, in August 1943 and entered Spartan School of Aeronautics. She lived with a Christian Science family in Tulsa and worked hard, often flying twice a day. Not many women were starting flying careers in 1943. Most of the students at the school were men, as were all the instructors. The five-month course was a thorough one, with classes in the morning and flying in the afternoons.

Mary Lou took more than a few risks and had some close calls while learning to fly—once almost failing to come out of a series of practice spins and another time stopping just short of the fence on a solo landing. She memorized a comforting, old church hymn and recited it when things got scary. She loved the feeling of flying by herself and was exhilarated by this experience. At Spartan, she gained self-confidence and enjoyed the easy camaraderie of other fliers.

In early November 1943, Mary Lou and I each took a long train ride to meet in St. Louis, arriving on a Saturday evening. I had carefully reserved a

Mary Lou's 1943 flight log and 1944 diploma for her training at Spartan School of Aeronautics.

room at The Chase Hotel, while Mary Lou had made no reservations. When I arrived, the clerk told me the hotel was full and gave me a room at an older hotel across the street. Mary Lou arrived later and told the same clerk that she was alone in St. Louis, a long way from her home in Alaska. Somehow the clerk found a nice room for her at The Chase.

On Sunday morning, we visited her famous "Cousin Joe Gazzam," an old South Africa gold miner, at his opulent apartment suite and had lunch with him. After a goodbye kiss in the railroad station, the date was over. It was the only time Mary Lou and I saw each other from May of 1943 until January of 1944.

In late January 1944, Mary Lou graduated from Spartan with high marks and a private pilot's license. Shortly before graduating she had been told by the Air Force that new entrants into the women's ferrying program were no longer being accepted because of a surplus of male pilots who needed flying time. She was very disappointed but hoped that conditions would change and permit her to fly in the future.

CHAPTER 5

"The Right Girl"

"I'll bring along a smile or a song for anyone, but only a rose for you."

—*1925 Broadway Operetta* The Vagabond King

ON A DECEMBER TRAIN TRIP back to Chicago after visiting a girl I'd been dating, I had an epiphany about my relationships. As I listened to the clicking of the train rails, the confusion of the last year began to clear. I thought, *Mary Lou would go to St. Louis, or Chicago, or to the end of the earth for that matter for me. Maybe that's what it's all about. Mary Lou isn't thinking about herself, or even about getting a fifty-fifty balance in careers or marriage or anything else. She is for us, whatever it takes.* As this awareness took hold, I could feel a growing excitement.

At Christmas, my brother Bob came up from Mississippi to spend three days with me. We got permission for him to sleep on the floor in my room in the tower section of the International House dormitory on the University of Chicago campus. It was Bob's first Christmas away from home and he was terribly homesick. If someone played *White Christmas* on the nickelodeon, Bob was soon wiping his eyes.

I told him that Mary Lou was the girl I was going to marry.

"I think she's terrific, Hym, but I hope being married doesn't mean we can't take anymore fishing trips together," Bob said. He saw this as the end of an era of closeness. I promised that we would still take trips and also agreed to give Mary Lou a thorough hiking and fishing test before getting married.

Jim carried this picture taken of Mary Lou in Chicago in his wallet for many years.

After our brief visit, Bob packed his duffel bag for the trip south on the Illinois Central. Our handshake on the train platform turned into a long bear hug with big lumps in the throat for each of us.

I was now thinking about Mary Lou constantly. After the guys needled me about drawing weather maps while she was flying planes, I started private flying lessons at Elmhurst Field on Sunday afternoons. My roommate, Sid Horrigan, kept reminding me Mary Lou had almost married another guy and she wouldn't wait long for me. I remember saying, "How can you be married with bed check every night?"

A plan finally evolved. I would invite Mary Lou to come to Chicago for the Cadet Ball and give her my fraternity pin the first time we were alone.

Mary Lou arrived at the Mayflower Hotel in Chicago on January 28, 1944, to attend the ball with me. She wrote to her family that she was going to stay in Chicago for two weekends. She was finished with Spartan and had tickets to Seattle and Fairbanks.

Mary Lou made up her mind to take the initiative. "I decided that I was going to marry Jim if it was humanly possible, and that meant staying in Chicago."

With her own plan in mind, she rented an apartment at the Blackstone Mansions a few blocks from the International House. She got a job selling girls' dresses at the Marshall Field's department store in downtown Chicago. Three days after the dance she telephoned me at the I House, "Hi, hi! It's me. Unless you don't want me to, I'm going to stay in Chicago. It's the only way for us to have a fighting chance. Long separations are impossible for people like you and me. The Army won't let you come to see me in Fairbanks and who knows how long the war will last."

I was ecstatic. "Beaver, that's absolutely the best news I've ever heard!

Years later Mary Lou said, "I knew my mother and dad wouldn't understand, and I didn't know how to tell them. I knew in my heart that this was the only way to marry you."

The regimented life of cadet training did not permit as much time together as we wanted. We were able to see each other only from 6:00 p.m. until midnight on Saturday and on Sunday afternoons.

One early spring night after dinner, I called Mary Lou on a sudden impulse to see if we could get together the next Saturday. Mary Lou's voice was flat and distant.

"Hi. Mother is here. We're going home together tonight. I'm sorry it's so sudden. I've written you a long letter which explains everything."

"Beaver, wait a minute! I'm coming over right now." Then I turned to my roommate. "Jesus, Sid, she's leaving! Help me get out of here."

Absence without permission during study hours was an automatic washout under cadet rules. Even helping another cadet to break this rule was a serious infraction. "Hym, after taking all that chicken (a derisive term for Army discipline) for thirteen months and wracking' our heads over vector mechanics, you're going to bust us both and blow our commissions? It's crazy."

I told him it was make it or break it for me and Mary Lou and I had to go. I said, "All you have to do is let me back in the door at 9:45 p.m. There's never a guard at the Tower door."

After a slow grimace, he agreed. "OK, but Jesus Christ, don't be late!"

I sneaked out the Tower door and ran to the nearest flower shop. I bought a single red rose and a gardenia corsage. I wrote "Only a Rose" on one card, the title of a song composed for the 1925 Broadway Operetta *The Vagabond King*: "I'll bring along a smile or a song for anyone, but only a rose for you." I wrote, "Yours in Phi Gamma Delta" on another, and attached my fraternity pin to the corsage. With a box in each hand, I ran the five blocks to the Blackstone, took the stairs two at a time, and was panting heavily when Mary Lou's mother opened the door.

The suitcases were packed and waiting in the middle of the room. Both women were wearing coats and preparing to catch the 11:30 p.m. *Milwaukee Hiawatha* train to Seattle. Mrs. Earling quickly disappeared saying she had to go downstairs and would be back in a few minutes. Mary Lou and I were left standing alone in the middle of the suitcases.

"Beaver, what has happened?"

"Mother has been talking some sense into me," she answered quietly. "My family is unhappy with me for chasing you. They thought I was coming home after flying school.

I could feel everything slipping away and took her arm. "Please sit down, Beaver. Just for a minute. I want to give you something." She sat down, still wearing her coat and I handed her the two boxes. She opened each one, read the two cards and began to cry.

I reached for her hands. "Beaver, I love you. You're my girl. There's no one else." Mary Lou knew I had never said those words to anyone before.

She was smiling and crying. "I need your handkerchief," Mary Lou said. Blowing her nose and wiping her eyes she stood up, took off her coat, and put it on the big chair. Her smile got bigger and bigger. "I thought this was going to be the worst night of my life—and it's the best!"

When her mother returned, Mary Lou showed her the flowers and the cards. "Mom, I'm not going with you. Jim has given me his pin. I'm staying as long as he is here." Mrs. Earling gave me a hug and kiss, "Why that's wonderful news," but her eyes were saying, "Please, God, watch over my headstrong daughter."

Mary Lou picked up her farewell letter from the table and tore it in half.

It was just ten minutes before bed check when Sid unlocked the Tower door.

Jim and Mary Lou enjoying the afternoon on the University of Chicago campus, April 1944.

Because of her Tulsa training, Mary Lou was able to leave Marshall Field's and get a job with the meteorology department at the University of Chicago. It came with a monthly salary of $100. She wrote love notes in secret codes on the weather maps she plotted for the cadets to analyze.

During a blizzard in late March, a serious case of pneumonia and a high fever put me in Gardiner General Hospital in Chicago where I was unable to talk and was under special care. Mary Lou took a train ride every day to visit the hospital, even though she wasn't allowed to see me. She sent daily progress reports to my father and mother, which totally won their hearts. Each day a nurse would deliver a letter, cartoon, card, or flower "From Mary Lou with love."

When I got well and the weather warmed, I spent every off-duty hour with Mary Lou. We joined other couples walking the shore of Lake Michigan and watched children play. We took our shoes off and waded along the beach. We took pictures of each other and asked a passerby to snap us together. We dined out, spent Saturday nights at the movies, and sang for hours at the piano bars and to each other. We talked about religion, careers, and children. We had one serious difference. I thought soldiers should not marry and start families when the war might leave a young widow and children without a father.

One afternoon sitting on the beach wall I said, "In a couple of weeks all of us are going to be shipped somewhere. I don't know where I'm going or how long I'll be gone." I slipped my arm around Mary Lou's waist. "I promise not to marry anyone else, Beaver. Will you promise not to get married until I get back?"

Mary Lou shook her head, "I think you're wrong about waiting to get married. Not being married to someone you love is just wasting precious days." Then she looked straight at me. "But I'm willing to wait until the war is over if that's what you want."

We agreed that after my cadet graduation she should go back to Alaska to spend the summer with her family who had returned to Fairbanks. This was a hard decision because the possibility of getting together again before the end of the war seemed painfully remote. Fighting was accelerating on all fronts, and the end was nowhere in sight. The cadets had been told they would be sent overseas immediately. My brother, Bob, was already in England waiting for Normandy.

On a sunny June day, the graduating cadets paraded the midway and received their professional certificates and military commissions in the cathedral. Afterwards, Mary Lou pinned the gold bars on my collar.

"You're an officer and a gentleman now. No more gigs and bed checks."

She gave me a long kiss and hugged me tight.

We spent the day packing my flight bag. At midnight, I left for Seattle. At the Chicago Railroad Station, I pressed my face against the car window to catch a last look at Mary Lou. She stayed on the platform until the lights of the train were long out of sight.

⚘

During the summer of 1944, Mary Lou resumed her old job as an instructor in the Link Trainer Facility at Eielson Air Force Base in Alaska.

News of the Normandy invasion was filling the papers. I was surprised to get orders sending me to McChord Field only about forty miles from Seattle, and after three days at home I reported for duty.

Practical weather forecasting turned out to be easier than solving University of Chicago vector equations. I kept my eyes open for local climate clues and found my forecasts becoming more and more accurate. Most of the Chicago cadet class had been sent to overseas staging areas, and many had been transferred out of weather service, which seemed like a tremendous waste of training. My commanding officer at McChord referred to the whole army business as a giant lottery and that you just had to roll with the punches.

Mary Lou and I wrote to each other faithfully, and our letters reflected a growing frustration at being apart. She noted pointedly that some second lieutenants at Eielson were getting extra pay allowances "just for being married."

One Friday a TWX military telegram came through transferring me to Gowan Field in Boise, Idaho. Gowan Field was known as a good duty station and was headquarters for the Northwest weather region. However, upon arrival I renewed a continuing request for overseas duty. With Bob in France, I felt a need to get into some kind of action. I got acquainted with the headquarters staff after a few days and discovered where to go fishing from an officer who shared that hobby.

Weather forecasting was becoming familiar now, and I was learning the tricks of the trade. The main problem was sleeping. Our barracks was located next to the airplane warm-up apron and every morning at 4 a.m. four-engine B-52 bombers fired up with a tremendous roar outside the window. After a few sleepless nights, I finally got used to the noise and slept.

Mary Lou had promised to come to Boise on her first break from the University of Washington in the fall. The bus from Seattle arrived in the evening while I was working. Mary Lou registered at the old Owyhee Hotel and telephoned the station. "Your bad penny, Jinx Earling, has shown up again. I can stay until Sunday."

"Hurray, Beaver, you made it. We're going fishing tomorrow."

The next morning, we left for an overnight trip to Lowman, located in the Boise National Forest. We went with my fishing partner and his wife. After a two-hour drive to the south fork of the Payette River, the four of us agreed on a meeting place for lunch. Mary Lou and I were dropped off to cross the canyon on a rickety hand-pulled cable operated by an old trapper.

The crossing was a single rusted logging cable stretched between two trees across a white-water canyon sixty feet below. From the cable, a flatbed box—four feet long and two feet wide, with sides six inches high—was suspended by wire from pulleys at each end. I was barely seated behind Mary Lou when the cable operator slipped the catch from below. We shot out over the deep canyon and halfway up the other side. The sensation was scary and wild. As the box slowed down, I tried to hook the iron puller around the cable and pump up to the landing, but Mary Lou's head was in the way. We rolled backward to the bottom of the cable sag, swaying unsteadily over the middle of the rapids. Mary Lou was surprisingly calm. Slowly I pulled us along the cable to the other bank. We tied the box to a tree for our partners to use and started fishing.

Everyone caught good-sized trout and had great fun. Mary Lou climbed rocky banks, fell in the river, saw two bears, and slept close to me that night in a tent at Lowman. The next morning, we hitchhiked back to Boise on a sheep truck. Mary Lou laughed about how much work it was chasing me all over the country.

The night we returned from the fishing trip, I lay in my bunk after work listening to the roar of B-24 engines and imagined talking to my brother Bob. Years earlier, I had given him the nickname "Roph." "Roph," I said, "she passed the hiking and fishing test with flying colors. This is the absolutely right girl."

Mary Lou and I walked around town the next afternoon talking about ideas for dream houses. In the evening, she wore a pretty, blue dress and we had dinner in the Owyhee Hotel dining room. I couldn't stop looking at her. Those big brown eyes were working their magic again.

Putting the menu down, she smiled. "The fishing trip was really fun, and I had a beautiful time today."

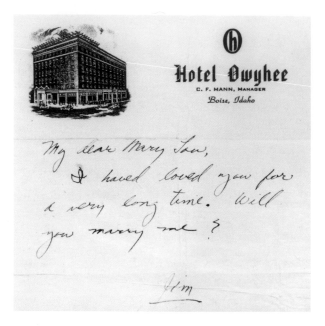

Jim's marriage proposal note to Mary Lou.

I handed a sealed envelope across the table, "You never know what's coming next, Beaver."

She opened the envelope with a wink. "I like funny letters and surprises." Unfolding the note, she read:

"My dear Mary Lou, I have loved you for a long time. Will you marry me?"

Mary Lou started to cry and people in the dining room stared at us.

"Jim!" Then, after a pause, "Yes, I'll marry you." She was sobbing and laughing and wiping her eyes with a napkin. "Yes. YES! I'm saying 'yes' before you change your mind!"

So many people in the dining room were now looking at us that I felt a need to explain. "I asked her to marry me, and she said 'yes.'" The other diners applauded.

"It's just like the movies," said Mary Lou.

We called my folks after dinner with the big news but couldn't get through to her parents in Fairbanks.

My fishing partner had taken my shift at the station so I could spend the night with Mary Lou. Lying in bed, we talked about the future.

"How many children do you want, darling?"

"Jesus, none right now, Beaver."

"No, silly, when we start a family."

"Well, two boys then, and two girls just like you," I replied. "How many do you want?"

"Oh, a dozen maybe. It's been a lot of work getting you. I want to make it count."

The next day, Mary Lou went back to Seattle to plan the wedding and I wrote her father asking permission to marry his daughter. A few days later a gracious consent came from Roy Earling.

In November 1944, I was transferred forty miles east to Mountain Home Air Force Base in Idaho, a combat training center for B-24 bomber groups. This was a signal that I probably would not be sent overseas for the next few months.

The airfield at Mountain Home had been hastily carved out of a sagebrush plateau above the Snake River. The station weather officer was an obsessive stickler for neatness who continually rearranged the pencils on the forecast desk. He never took a forecast shift and was disliked heartily by all, a feeling I quickly shared when he refused to approve more than a three-day pass for my wedding. This would have left no time for a honeymoon, so I flew down to Gowan Field headquarters and asked the commanding officer of the region to increase the pass by four days' travel time. He had met Mary Lou during her visit to Boise and happily signed a seven-day pass commenting that no man in his right mind would let *her* get away.

Back in Seattle, Mary Lou withdrew from the university and filled every day with preparations for our wedding. Mrs. Earling came down from Fairbanks to help with arrangements in November, The Earlings arranged a white-flowered wedding at Epiphany Church in Seattle and a reception at the Women's University Club where Mary Lou and I had bashfully exchanged glances many years before.

Even with the Earlings' help, many of the wedding details were rushed. The day of the wedding I had lunch with my father and grandfather at Manca's Restaurant. We then went to buy engagement and wedding rings at Hardy's

Wedding Day

Jewelry store on Fifth Avenue. Mary Lou was drying her hair over the floor register at her Aunt Ruth's house thirty minutes before the ceremony.

The wedding evening was a happy mixture of handshakes and kisses, laughter and excitement. The little church was crowded with family and friends. The matron of honor was Louie. My sixteen-year-old brother John was best man. My brother Bob was somewhere in France, and other than Sid Horrigan who came from Oregon to be our usher, my friends were scattered around the world at air bases, on ships, and fighting war fronts.

After the reception, John drove us down to the Canadian Pacific Pier in time to board the night boat to Victoria. The date was November 18, 1944. We walked the deck and watched a blacked-out Seattle disappear behind Fort Lawton. Mary Lou's smile was luminous.

The next morning our ship sailed into the inner harbor at Victoria, and newlyweds Lt. and Mrs. James Ellis disembarked to spend three days at the Empress Hotel. I had reserved a room with a double bed at the $6 military rate.

However, the room turned out to be small and dismal with a single window looking into a narrow light well. I went back to the desk clerk and asked for a room with a view, saying, "I don't care about the rate. This only happens once." The clerk thumbed through the hotel register, then gave me a different key. Our new room turned out to be the spacious Royal Suite with windows overlooking the inner harbor. The rate card on the bedside stand reminded me that $38 per day would consume a large chunk of my bank account.

These were beautiful rainy days. We swam in the indoor pool, walked through downtown shops, drank afternoon tea, and rode the streetcar to Oak Bay for dinner. Once in a while, we slept. We both wrote letters to my brother Bob who was then with the 376th Infantry Regiment of the Ninety-Fourth Division in France, to Mary Lou's sister Nancy who was serving as a Navy Wave in Florida, and to her sister Barbara who was in school on the East Coast. Both girls were heartsick that they had not been able to come west for the wedding. Bob wrote me, "I sure hope to heck that you don't get too home loving because we have to hit that backcountry for the real fishing." In her letter to Bob, Mary Lou asked if it would be okay to come along for *half* of the fishing trips with Jim.

When checkout time came, the bill had been figured at the $6 military rate instead of the expensive rate. The clerk looked directly at me and said, "There's been no mistake, Lieutenant. We hope you enjoyed your stay." It was a heart-lifting way to end a honeymoon at the Empress.

Both sets of parents met us at the dock in Seattle. That evening, the bride and groom boarded the Union Pacific for Mountain Home and their first home together.

Our train pulled into the small station at Mountain Home in the middle of an afternoon dust storm blowing sand and tumbleweed. Air base rules required that dependents have jobs before obtaining government housing. We walked a half mile to catch one of the olive drab buses running ten miles to the base where Mary Lou was immediately given a job in the parachute shop. By the time we got back to town and signed up for a room in the married personnel barracks it was 8 o'clock at night.

The lieutenant had retaliated for the seven-day pass by assigning me to a steady graveyard shift beginning at midnight on the day we arrived. Mary Lou's

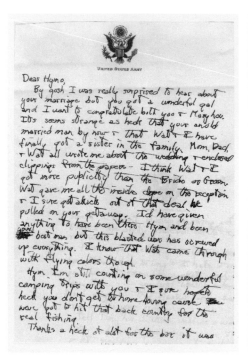
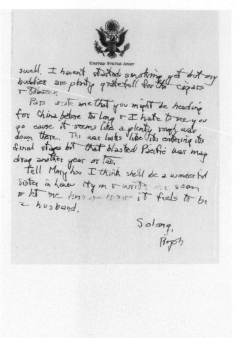

Unable to attend the wedding, Bob sent Jim a congratulatory letter.

job was a regular day shift starting the next morning. With careful planning, we could see each other for dinner and when we had the same day off. Mary Lou and I would meet for dinner at the officer's mess on the base, a twenty-minute bus ride from town. On some mornings, we passed each other on the way to and from work. I remember Mary Lou calling the shift assignment "a dirty trick." After about two weeks, my fellow officers successfully pressured the lieutenant into giving me a normal shift rotation.

Our first home was a single, small room containing a double bed and one chest. The single window looked out over a sheep-grazing pasture. In the center of the long building was a common washroom divided by seven-foot-high partitions for men and women.

Mary Lou was determined to get us moved from our tiny barracks room to one of the project apartments, but the waiting list was long. She discovered the waiting list changed as each combat group finished training, introduced

Mary Lou and Jim in front of the Mountain Home housing project.

herself to the manager, and got well-acquainted with his wife. Then one day, to my amazement, Mary Lou called me at work. "Our new home is number twenty-seven, next door to the manager's apartment. All our things have been moved. Dinner will be served at 6:30."

The new apartment had a living room-kitchen with a wood stove, a bedroom, a bathroom, and a small storeroom. After living in the barracks, the apartment seemed like a palace, even if the walls were not soundproof. Despite the hassles of our first months, our Mountain Home days were filled with happy times.

CHAPTER 6

Make Your Life Count for His

Private Robert Lee Ellis.

AFTER COMPLETING BASIC TRAINING at Camp Hood, Texas, in 1943, my brother Bob had been selected with several thousand soldiers for the *Army Specialized Training Program* (ASTP). The ASTP provided academic training for possible future officers and was drawn from army recruits who had finished basic training and had IQ scores of 125 or higher. Bob arrived at the University of Mississippi (Ole Miss) on September 1, 1943, and stayed until March 1, 1944. There he met Alan Howenstine from Indiana who became his good friend.

When the army made changes to the ASTP program structure, Bob and Alan were among the trainees transferred into the 15,000-man Ninety-Fourth Infantry Division at Camp McCain, Mississippi. Bob and Alan became part of Company H of the Second Battalion of the 376th Infantry Regiment. Some non-commissioned officers of the Ninety-Fourth saw the new ASTP men as "college boys" who could become threats to their rank. Others looked on them as "softies." Alan recalled:

> *. . . That's where our rigorous physical education program at Ole Miss really paid off. To the surprise of almost everyone in the Ninety-Fourth, we handled long marches, bivouacs, etc. just as well, if not better than them. . . we proved ourselves in combat, we were "the new men."*

In June of 1944, while we were still in Chicago, Bob had visited me during his two-week leave before the Ninety-Fourth shipped overseas. We had a great four-hour visit with sandwiches under the bright sun on the grass of the 1892 World's Fair Midway. Bob reported that Frank and Maude Noland were keeping a watchful eye on our Raging River cabin, that Tilly's cooking was as "fantastic" as ever, brother John was "growing like a weed," Pars was still "hard to beat" at dominos, and Walt Ring had gotten engaged to LaVon on his most recent leave as a navy pilot.

When I reported that I had given my fraternity pin to Mary Lou, Bob lamented half in jest, "The available girls back home are thinning out and the swell girls will all be taken by the time the war is over." We exchanged stories about camping trips and Granips Reed. Then before we knew it, our time was up. We walked quickly to the train station and after a couple big hugs Bob caught the southbound Illinois Central.

From the time Bob left for Europe, his letters were carefully written to avoid worrying his mother and father. He was conscious of how deeply they were involved in following the war and he never forgot how much they had invested in bringing him through his multi-year illness as a child. He was very careful not to indicate the conditions around him on the front lines that would put him at risk for illness or injury.

Bob's letters downplayed the record cold winter in which the Ninety-Fourth was moving back and forth within the deeply fortified western Germany. He never mentioned the difficulties of trying to sleep in the snow while under fire from enemy guns. He did not record any description of his day-to-day life on the front lines leading up to and during the Battles of the Siegfried Line and the Ardennes Bulge from December 1944 to February 1945.

I knew Bob was in a place where it was difficult to exist. Cold winter conditions made sleeping on the front lines difficult and fighting nearly impossible. While his letters emphasized the wonderful meals that men were getting from the battalion cooks, the truth was his normal daily routine on the line consisted of trying to stay alive in grindingly cold weather while eating frozen cans of 'K' rations. I knew this, but I don't know that my mother did. I'm quite sure Bob went to great pains to shield her from what would have only added to her existing high level of anxiety from knowing he was fighting at the front.

The Ninety-Fourth was deployed for two months in Brittany and charged with containing 30,000 German troops who had been bypassed during the initial Normandy push and were pinned down in two separate pockets near the towns of Lorient and St. Nazaire. Later, the Ninety-Fourth stretched across France to guard the allied army's rear from attack.

Alan Howenstine wrote about their journey:

. . . On September 8, 1944, we crossed the English Channel. Our ship departed from near Portsmouth and landed on Utah Beach. Interestingly enough, that was D+94 days. . . Some of the guys got so seasick they almost died and would not have cared if they had! Surprisingly enough, as soon as we stepped ashore, these same fellows within an hour were feeling fine. We marched eleven miles that night on muddy roads with full field packs, ammunition, rifles, etc. and very few dropped out.

The next day we boarded trucks. One night we bivouacked in an apple orchard near Rennes, France. Then we continued south and west, until we arrived at our destination . . .

Bob had kept in touch by writing letters to his family regularly and the Ellis family circle poured their love into a steady stream of letters and packages to Bob. Even Gramps Reed, who was not a letter writer, sent a letter to Bob every week that winter. Bob avidly devoured every incoming mail item. He shared each box of candy or cookies with his infantry squad and faithfully answered each letter whenever he was pulled back from the front line for rest, with glowing appreciation for every care package.

Bob Ellis (top right) and his fellow companions.

December 1944 was the beginning of the fourth year of war for the United States. Final victory was beginning to seem certain and there was even hope for an early end to the fighting in Europe after dramatic German losses and retreats on all fronts. This optimism was reinforced for me by the situation maps in the Mountain Home briefing room.

In early December, Bob had written to me, "The war over here seems to be winding down…" but he worried that the Pacific War where I could be headed was going to be "long and tough." Bob also wrote that his letters would be less frequent because, "We're going to be busy, but don't worry." I started to worry in January when our briefing maps showed the Third Army was stalled in hard fighting on the Siegfried Line, and Bob's letters were fewer.

In December, the division had been ordered to join General Patton's Third Army to face the German Siegfried Line. The weather that winter brought record cold and snow to the Ardennes Forest and the Saar-Moselle Triangle. Each morning back at Mountain Home, after giving a route weather forecast to the day's flight crews, I listened intently to intelligence briefings. The maps showed changing battle lines in Europe, but we couldn't tell exactly where the Ninety-Fourth Division was engaged.

The 376th and Company H took their turns in this bitter fighting and were engaged for weeks in a bloody back and forth struggle over tiny towns in the Siegfried Switch region which was a fortified defensive position. During rest rotations, Bob would write home with reassuring words like ". . . great turkey dinner the cooks were preparing for Christmas." We now know that in January and February, the 376th was one of three infantry regiments on point for the Ninety-Fourth Division attacking the flank of the Ardennes Bulge and cracking the Siegfried Switch to open the way to the Rhine.

Years later, I learned what Bob had withheld from us in his letters. Alan's account of this time reveals the difficult circumstances he and Bob faced that winter:

As temperatures across Germany and France hit record lows, our men simply weren't equipped for cold, snowy winter fighting. We each had long underwear, thin cotton socks, wool pants and shirt, a field jacket, overcoat, and wool cap to wear under our helmet. Each man carried a half of a pup tent and a wool blanket. We also had shoes and leggings and it wasn't until later in the war, that we were issued four buckle arctic combat boots. However, most infantry men felt they could move quicker during an attack without their boots. Each squad would leave their arctic boots behind, hoping to come back after an attack and retrieve them. Unfortunately, due to the required digging-in and the inevitable German counterattacks, those arctic boots were often never retrieved. The fact was soldiers spent the night with nothing but shoes on their feet and foxholes were often muddy or full of water.

The Associated Press reported that it took just three days for "Patton's Hard-Hitting Veterans" to mop up the triangle and that "it was the Ninety-Fourth Infantry Division which was the first to cross the Saar near the apex of the triangle."

One morning in early March 1945 while I was working at the forecast table in the Mountain Home weather station, a long-distance call came from my father. "Jim, the worst has happened!" Then he broke down and couldn't speak. My brother John came on the line. "We just got a wire that Bob has been killed in action. Hym, you'd better come home." I could only say, "No, no, no," in disbelief, and then, "I'll be home right away."

Lt. Fowler, overhearing, said, "You can leave in two days," I replied, "I'm leaving now," walked to the Red Cross office, and received approval for immediate emergency leave with train tickets to Seattle.

I cried on the bus all the way back to the apartment and kept repeating, "No, no, no." Once in the apartment, I started pounding the walls and shouting that it wasn't true. When Mary Lou heard the news, she rushed home. "I *know* it's wrong, Beaver," I said desperately. "They've made a mistake. But we have to go home."

"You've got to help your mother and dad over this hump. They will be crushed," said Mary Lou, trying to pull me together.

"Yes. Dad can't talk and hasn't told my mother. He wants *me* to do that."

We caught the Union Pacific that afternoon and were in Seattle the following evening. My father's face showed the impact of the news. My mother knew something was wrong.

"Why are you home? What's happened?"

I told her as gently as possible, but she still collapsed.

The family was shaken to its core but was held together by performing the customary rituals—notifying the newspapers, arranging for a memorial service, and responding to visits and phone calls. My father told me Bob would have liked for me to give the eulogy. I gave an emotional tribute at the Mount Baker Presbyterian Church where Bob and I had attended as children. The church was full, and taps was played by one of Bob's friends in uniform.

In a phone call from Spokane, Gramps Reed had confessed, "We're pretty shook up over here." After the memorial service, the family agreed that Mary Lou and I should stop in Spokane on our way back to Mountain Home and comfort the grandparents. Mary Lou retrieved her old Chevy coupe, The Green Dragon, from her uncle's garage. We drove through some snowy weather to the Reed home in Spokane and spent the night with the desolate grandparents. As we were leaving the next morning Grandmother Reed said, "Jim, you're going to be all right. You have such a wonderful girl."

Yes, I thought to myself, *but Mary Lou can't replace my brother. I hardly know her.*

While driving back to Mountain Home I became obsessed with the idea that Bob was still alive. I convinced myself that the Army had goofed, and we would get some word from him any day. I dreamed that he was being held in a German POW camp. I told myself that God would not permit the loss of such a good life. Of all the young men I had known, Bob was the kindest at heart, and the one least deserving of dying young.

Mary Lou was sympathetic, understanding, and unobtrusively helpful during these emotional days, but I could not accept her sympathy any more than I could accept the reality of Bob's death.

Finality arrived in April, in the form of a letter from the Company to inform the family written by Alan Howenstine. He later recalled:

> *... I remember agonizing over every word. I had never met any of Bob's family. That was probably the most difficult letter I ever wrote. . . I tried to express my sorrow. I know I told them Bob died instantly. His death was the result of a German mortar shell which landed very close to him. A large piece of shrapnel hit him just under his helmet on the back of his neck. I didn't tell the family of that last detail. Neither did I tell them of Bob being hit by shrapnel earlier in the day. It just grazed his wrist. I wasn't there when that happened. Instead of going back to the aid station and having it dressed, Bob just had the medic bandage it. I told him he should have gone back, at least he would have received a Purple Heart. But Bob wasn't that kind of a guy, he wouldn't make a fuss over such a slight wound. I can remember seeing that piece of tape on his wrist after he was dead. I have always felt one of the experiences which changed me from a boy to a man, was the sad letter to Bob's grieving family.*

Yes, Bob was dead. God had allowed this terrible thing to happen. After those summers when Bob and I lived together sharing all kinds of conditions, somehow, I felt I had not been there for him when it counted the most.

My first experience with death of a family member proved to be devastating. When the full reality of that terrible event in Germany sank in, I found I was not prepared to handle the loss of the closest person in my life. Mary Lou was understanding and supportive during the days of shock and disbelief, but now she watched with growing concern as I became depressed, disoriented, and even self-destructive. I tried every device to get transferred overseas—to get into some kind of fighting. I volunteered to perform assignments for which I was not qualified. To her gentle sympathy my standard response was, "You don't understand." Instead of taking walks with her, I sat in the room and looked at the walls.

One day I walked in unannounced to the Base Commander's office and asked to be transferred to the unit then finishing its training and about to head overseas. The Colonel reacted sharply, "How did you get in here, Lieutenant? I've heard about you. You're not worth shit right now. I wouldn't make you part of any unit going into harm's way. Go back to the station and do your job."

Word of this latest episode passed around and when I came back to the unit that evening, Mary Lou grabbed my shoulders, "You've got to get hold of yourself. You're trying to throw your life after his. It won't do any good to lose two lives. Why not make your life COUNT for his?"

I reacted with the usual, "You don't understand," and walked away resenting her interference. But during a solitary hike through snowy fields, I began thinking about what she had said. *Make my life count for his?* Surely Bob's life should count for something more than bravery in the line of duty. I came back to the apartment.

"What did you mean, Beaver?"

"Well, you have a gift for speaking and leading. What about community work, or conservation, or anything you and Bob believed in? We could take part of our life and give something to others for Bob."

As the idea took hold, I began to think positively. There were many things Bob would have wanted to do for others if he had lived.

"That's a heck of a good idea, Beaver. We could devote part of our time to public service for Bob."

"I would like to help you do that," Mary Lou answered quietly. This conversation planted the seed of what was to become a life-long commitment of our time to the community which Bob loved.

Bob Ellis, circa 1943.

The Germans surrendered in May, and Mary Lou announced another initiative. "Your folks need a grandchild. We should have one as soon as possible."

"But, honey, we agreed no children till after the war. What if I should get killed?"

"Even more important then that we have a baby. Besides, we're going to have one anyway, so you'd better get used to the idea."

Love came over us like a warm sea wave. Her intuitive magic was at work again.

Although sadness and occasional tears remained for months, almost overnight my darkest corner was turned. The news they might be grandparents was an immediate tonic for my mother and father, and Mary Lou and I began to plan with purpose for the time when the war would finally end. How would we make it through law school? Where would we live? How would we feed the family, plan to space the ages of our children, and begin to perform our commitment to Bob—all with almost no money?

Alan Howenstine Visits Hazel

ALAN HOWENSTINE never forgot his friends in the Ninety-Fourth. He served with Bob as part of a mortar platoon and wrote the following letter from Europe to his Aunt Mabel shortly after V-E Day on May 8, 1945.

May 20, 1945

Dear Aunt Mabel:

. . . V-E Day I spent very quietly. In fact, if you would have told me that a group of average American soldiers like ours in this Company would take the peace so quietly, I would have just laughed. There was no furor whatsoever. I think one big reason I took it easy was that I thought so much about my best pal. He was killed at the Saar. I met him at L.S.U., ran around a lot with him at Ole Miss, and when we came to the 94th we were in the same section. Until we came overseas, we always lunched together, went to shows together, shared packages from home—and everything. . . Fifteen minutes before he was killed, I was talking with him about what good times we would have after the war. Just as I left him, he said, "Yes if we ever get home." We both laughed about that. . . You just don't forget as good a boy as Bob was. I think that was the way with the rest of the fellows. . .

Yours,

Alan

Shortly after my father died in 1970, Alan made a point coming out west and visiting my mother. His conversation with her was most comforting to her. When the conversation ended, I said to my mother, "This sort of ties a ribbon around it don't you think, Tilly?" She nodded and expressed her appreciation to Alan for coming. His trip to Seattle was a way of saying goodbye to Bob and finding a sense of closure surrounding his death. We will always be grateful to Alan for his acts of kindness to our family over the years.

BOOK TWO

*Law and the Happy,
Hungry Years*

✦

CHAPTER 7

New Baby, New Start

THERE WAS NO LETUP in the Pacific War after V-E Day, May 8, 1945. Although no one doubted the outcome, the Japanese Army fought tenaciously in the battle for each Pacific Island. Casualties were heavy and "kamikaze" tactics showed an enemy willing to perform suicide attacks on a regular basis. A major invasion of the home islands of Japan seemed inevitable and the Japanese military showed a willingness to fight to the last in each battle. It was generally expected that the war could last another two years. Our work at Mountain Home was now directed to the Pacific fronts.

Our old friends Betty Lou and Dolph had married May 4, 1944, not long after Mary Lou had arranged their meeting on a blind date. Shortly after V-E Day, we received a wire saying they were ordered to Mountain Home for combat training and would be arriving the following week. Dolph was a pilot of B-24s, and Mountain Home was a combat training base for the crews of these planes. My principal job had become route forecasting for bomber groups undergoing training. This meant working in the station from 11:00 p.m. to about 4:00 a.m. developing a forecast, then briefing the pilots on expected weather conditions, and flying with them on their practice mission.

Dolph and Betty Lou Hoyt, and Jim and Mary Lou near Anderson Ranch at Mountain Home, 1945.

These flights ended around noon and you could sleep till dinner. The shift rotation was four nights on, then three nights off.

Military personnel lucky enough to have a car carefully hoarded their gas ration coupons for use on the days off. Mary Lou and I rode the base bus all week so we could explore nearby mountains in The Green Dragon on our days off. In May, we shared a couple of picnics in the hills with Dolph and Betty Lou. We once squeezed 6'4" Lt. Henry Brainard into the rear seat of the little coupe with 5'4" Lt. Sid Law lying across the back shelf and drove to Sun Valley and back.

The Earling and Ellis families also came to Mountain Home for short stays in the extra room of our project apartment. During one of these visits, my brother John and I drove The Green Dragon over a steep and rutted wagon road to the famous ghost town of Silver City. When the Earlings came, Mary Lou's sister Barbara, then seventeen, joined us for a fishing trip on the Malad River where we climbed steep cliffs and walked through a nest of rattlesnakes.

After Dolph's training group was shipped to the Pacific War theatre and the weather in the hills turned warmer, Mary Lou and I sometimes went fishing in the Boise River on days off. The river was ice cold in the morning, but hot sun on the boulders turned the water lukewarm by afternoon. Mary Lou was now pregnant, but the baby did not yet really show, and she was so beautiful and graceful that I would tease her to take her clothes off and go swimming with me. She would always demur with, "Some old prospector may come along," or, "I'm not supposed to go swimming now."

In anticipation of the new baby, we began saving every extra dollar for the future. Mary Lou got better-paying jobs, first in a drugstore, and then in a combination restaurant-bar in Mountain Home. The latter turned out to be a bad idea because working in the kitchen made her sick and working as a bar waitress resulted in unwanted passes and pawing. Mary Lou didn't complain, but one day I dropped in and saw what she was putting up with. When she quit, the boss objected. "You didn't give notice. You don't have any money coming." Mary Lou stiffened.

"You're going to pay me in full and right now!"

Seeing the look in her eye, Mary Lou's boss decided that wisdom was the better part of valor, and he paid her on the spot.

After V-E Day, most of those who had not already seen action in Europe or were not required for occupation were added to the forces for the invasion of Japan. In late June, orders arrived sending me to gunnery school in Florida to be trained as a flight crew weather officer for air groups being assembled on Guam. Their role would be to support an attack on the main island of Japan and travel was not authorized for military dependents.

Before daylight on a warm morning, we packed our possessions in The Green Dragon, left Mountain Home sleeping in the sagebrush, and headed for Seattle. The day turned into a scorcher and wartime recapped tires were notoriously vulnerable to heat. We drove the whole way at thirty-five miles per hour, stopping now and then to cool the tires and finally pulled into my parents' driveway late that night.

Our plan was for Mary Lou to get a job in Seattle until the baby came. She would live either with her parents, with her aunt and uncle, or with my folks while I was overseas. We figured if we kept Mary Lou's expenses down for the next couple of years, and watched our pennies, we could save most of our Army pay and allowances to pay for the baby and our expenses while I worked my way through law school. When the war was over, we intended to live at Raging River and add to the one room log cabin. After Bob's death, his half interest in the cabin property had been transferred to me by my father. This would permit us to live there during what I saw as several "lean years" ahead.

During the two days of home leave in Seattle, family conversations were focused on the coming baby, but the shadow of my brother's recent death was still present. All of us expected that the war in the Pacific would continue to inflict heavy casualties and last for at least two years. It was a tearful goodbye at Seattle's Union Station and Mary Lou later recalled that, like my parents, she spent a restless night dreaming that another "regret to inform you" wire came to 4016 50th Avenue South.

The train ride from Seattle to Panama City, Florida, took me into the Deep South for the first time and the gunnery school at Tyndall Field brought me together with several old friends from cadet days. We paid close attention to the training program for machine gun firing and parachute practice jumps, knowing that survival might hinge on these skills. The trainees were told that after the short gunnery course we would be sent to the Pacific where we would serve to support the invasion of Japan. Our veteran instructors reported that America's war effort was "paving the Pacific with ships," but they believed that the Japanese would make the final campaign difficult. Then, as my fellow trainees and I were preparing for combat, US President Harry Truman startled the world with the news of our dropping the atomic bomb in Hiroshima and Nagasaki.

The Japanese surrendered within days, and the long and bloody war was suddenly over. An emotional V-J Day celebration erupted when all personnel were assembled on the tarmac at Tyndall Field to hear the Colonel take the microphone and say "The Japanese have surrendered. The war is over." It was August 15, 1945. Everybody began calling home and the lines were all jammed. I finally got through and heard Mary Lou's happy voice. "Darling, my prayers were answered! Everything's coming up roses. You might be home for the baby."

"How about that, Beaver! It's a whole new ball game for us!"

Later, lying on my cot, I realized that the unexpected end of the war also meant that we would be on our own sooner than we had planned. My pay would stop and the Army would no longer take care of us.

While we were homesick for each other and each avidly devoured one another's letters, I never expected to answer the phone in the Tyndall BOQ (Bachelor Officers Quarters) two weeks later and hear Mary Lou's voice, "I'm here at the bus station in Panama City. I love you and I want to be with you."

"Why didn't you call me?" I asked, feeling dumbfounded.

No one in the family had known about Mary Lou's trip. She had conspired to stay "for a few nights" at Louie's house so no one would discover that she was leaving, then caught a transcontinental bus for the four-day trip to Florida.

"This is a dumb thing for you to do," Louie told her before they parted. "Here you are, four months pregnant. You could lose the baby on such a long bus ride."

"We've been separated too much," Mary Lou replied. "It's just no fun without Jim, and I'm not going to lose this baby."

Louie later remembered, "Mary Lou made me promise not to tell anybody. I felt terribly guilty, but I drove her to the bus station anyway. Mary Lou later admitted to me that she was exhausted when she got to Panama City."

Mary Lou's unexpected arrival was the beginning of the most difficult time of our married life. Mary Lou felt that we should be together "with our baby coming," but hadn't called ahead because she feared I would try to talk her out of coming to Florida. After she arrived, she was disappointed and hurt that she was not welcomed with open arms following a long, hard trip. I was angry that Mary Lou had decided to come without first talking it over and believed she was spending the money we needed to make our future possible. I saw her bus fare across the country and apartment rent eating up our small savings.

Despite our differences, we were as hungry for each other as ever and we had good times together. Everyone loved Beaver, but she and I began to argue more every day. My determination to be independent and not to take help from our parents intensified these arguments. I worried that our long-range plans would have to be postponed in favor of a job for cash. It might be necessary to stay in the Army for another year or two. I was frustrated and Mary Lou was heartsick. She tried patiently to change the subject. But the closest thing to a complaint about my behavior was to say once, "Why am I always the one who has to make up?"

In September, orders came assigning me to Meridian, Mississippi, with the provision that no dependents would be permitted there. It was the beginning of a series of assignments to close weather stations at airfields which were shutting down. Mary Lou had no choice but to take the train home. The depth of our arguments had shaken us both, and when she arrived back in Seattle our bank account had been used up.

During October, November, and December the Air Force closed airfields in Meridian, Mississippi, and Stuttgart, Arkansas. Each base was nearly deserted by the time I arrived, and with the war over, most civilian soldiers were just "putting in time." Since only two or three flights were cleared each day, most of my time was spent playing cards, writing letters, and drawing plans for enlarging the cabin at Raging River. Bit by bit, I started saving money again.

The Stuttgart base was then serving as a stockade for 10,000 German POWs. When they were repatriated, the field was shut down and in December I was transferred to Craig Field, an active air base near Selma, Alabama.

Mary Lou and I exchanged letters at least every other day but our words had lost buoyancy. Both of us had been hurt during "The Battle of Panama City." She was impatient for the baby to come, and I was impatient to be discharged and sent home.

In December, Mary Lou wrote that she was becoming "as big as a freighter." Although she felt wonderful throughout her entire pregnancy, I insisted that she be attended by a doctor. She did consult with the Ellis family doctor but was never happy with him or the army doctors. I attributed this reaction to her Christian Science background and her skepticism about doctors in general. When her checkups indicated that everything was normal, my worrying gave way to anticipation.

Mary Lou's mother, father, and sister Barbara came down from Fairbanks and squeezed into Pierce and Ruth Haight's home in the Denny Blaine neighborhood. Happy expectation filled the house. After all, the new baby would be the first arrival in a new Gazzam-Earling generation.

At Christmas, Mary Lou mailed a wonderful box of many packages to me at Selma with clever drawings of "The Freighter" and her "cargo." R. B. even composed a clever poem about the family vigil for the new arrival.

On the morning of January 2, 1946, Mary Lou experienced the strange and scary atmosphere of a hospital for the first time in her life, anesthetic and all. However, when she woke up and saw a healthy baby boy, all her misgivings about doctors and hospitals were dissolved in the thrill of the moment. "I was happier than I thought I could ever be," she told me later.

R. B. immediately sent the following wire to Selma. A giggling operator read it over the phone and I exploded with joy.

I just came today at 2:33 p.m. and weigh 6 lbs. 14 oz.
Mother and I both feel fine. Lots of love,

Your son

I wired back:

Beaver, you did it! Hubba! A boy! I love you very much sweetheart. We're proud of that Freighter and no foolin'.

Jim

The next day we got a call through and agreed to name the baby Robert Lee Ellis II, after my brother Bob.

The new baby gave everyone a big lift, but our old enemy, separation, was still working against Mary Lou and me.

For the next few months Mary Lou alternated between the Haight and Ellis homes in Seattle. Ruth Haight was a Christian Science practitioner and differences arose over the doctor's instructions on caring for the baby. My parents were very possessive of "Bobby" and my father wrote that the baby

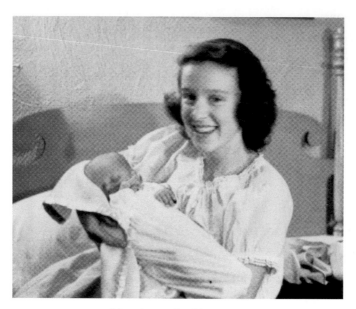

Mary Lou and Bobby, 1946.

was "not getting his vitamins." This renewed my concerns about Christian Science. I wrote Mary Lou that she was breaking our agreement not to apply Christian Science to the care of Bobby. When her answer was ambiguous, I answered with criticism and withheld the loving words she wanted to hear.

Mary Lou cried herself to sleep more than once, but again, never responded in kind. Her writing was always upbeat, loving, and encouraging. She sometimes wrote twice a day and at one mail call, four of her letters arrived.

During the winter of 1946, Mary Earling took a long train and bus trip to visit Nancy in Florida and stopped off in Alabama to find out what was wrong between Mary Lou and me. "She cries in her room every time she gets a letter and she won't talk about it."

After dinner we talked for hours in her Selma hotel room, sitting on an old brass bed with a worn-out spread. The visit brought us close for the first time, and we found that we liked each other very much.

Mary cleared the air on Christian Science saying, "Mary Lou and you should do things your way."

Mary took the blame for not teaching her daughter to be more careful about money, and she reminded me to keep this weakness in perspective. "Mary Lou has big virtues and big faults, and both come from her generous and loving nature."

She also urged me to be reasonable about parental help. "Let us pay for her trip to Florida."

"No one else should pay for our mistakes," I said defensively.

Finally, I let my guard down and poured out my feelings. I told Mary how important it was for me to be able to take care of my wife and child and that I couldn't see a way to do that and still complete law school. As our conversation continued, my side of the story became more embarrassing for me to tell. I realized that my goal of independence was self-centered. Why didn't I think as much about what Mary Lou wanted or needed? And my jealousy seemed out of date. Why couldn't I forget and forgive the same way Mary Lou did?

That night in a tiny hotel room in Selma, Alabama, changed the direction of our marriage. I can still see Mary's earnest face lit by one small lamp and hear us talking intensely while the old ceiling fan turned and squeaked. When I caught the last bus to the base in the early morning darkness the world seemed better.

When Mary returned to Seattle, Mary Lou and Bobby joined her at the little Pleasant Beach house on Bainbridge Island. Mary Lou was breathless to know about the visit.

"Does he still love me?"

Mary shared that, yes, he loved her very much and he wanted to get home to see Mary Lou and Bobby. Mary went on to explain Mary Lou had married a very stubborn and independent young man. He was taught to support himself, and when Mary Lou had spent all their money going to Florida, he lost his independence. It was going to be a hard few years ahead. Mary Lou would have to learn to get by on very little and make him believe that what they have is all she'd need or want. Jim would work hard, and Mary felt everything would be fine if Mary Lou worked hard too.

After that time the course of our marriage was never in doubt, and April at Pleasant Beach was a happy time.

In Alabama, spring comes early. The trees leafed out in February and I took long walks on my days off. Many signs of the Old South were still plainly visible in 1946. The Southern Railroad still used some cars from post-Civil War days. I walked side roads which often carried mule carts and passed near log cabins where outdoor fires were heating iron cooking pots and laundry was hanging from clothes lines. A Saturday mule auction in Selma attracted people of all colors and ages. I heard sounds of country banter that must have changed little over many years.

Segregation by race in the town of Selma was hard for me to accept as a young Westerner. I was not accustomed to seeing places marked "For Whites Only" or "For Colored Only."

One soft spring evening while waiting in town for a military bus to take me back to the base, I began talking to a Black staff sergeant who had just returned from eighteen months in the China-Burma-India theatre. He was a friendly and articulate teller of war stories and was waiting to be discharged and sent home to his wife and children in Ohio. When a city bus came by, I suggested we grab it to save time. There was one empty double seat and we sat down together. As we took our seats, the chatter in the back of the bus quieted down, and the driver made no attempt to start the vehicle. After a few minutes he said loudly, "This bus doesn't move until people take their proper seats." My friend looked at me. "He means us, Lieutenant. He won't move because we're sitting together." I felt a surge of anger and shame.

"To hell with him. Let's get off!" We got up and walked out. The bus driver shrugged his shoulders and drove off. Back on our bench my friend said, "Thank you for that, Lieutenant."

The South never seemed quite the same to me after that night. I found myself becoming more aware of the many forms discrimination took in the daily life of Selma and resolved to work against such things when I got out of uniform.

As spring unfolded its warm and muggy days, good news came in bunches. Congress passed amendments to the G.I. Bill allowing veterans to receive subsistence benefits in addition to school costs. In March, a promotion came through for this "oldest living second lieutenant," bringing a modest increase in pay. Future plans began to look more hopeful.

In May, the much-anticipated order for the discharge of No. 085995—First Lieutenant James R. Ellis—arrived at the Craig Field Weather Station. In two days of whirlwind activity, station properties and papers were signed over to my successor and one of the Craig Field pilots flew me to Atlanta for official separation procedures. Three years of Army life were coming to an end. The next afternoon I started a cross-country railroad trip for the last time.

The Empire Builder screeched to a stop at Seattle's Union Station. I knew the people I loved would be on the platform and when the porter pulled out the footstep, my father and mother were coming toward me. We grabbed each other with happy hugs. Then behind me, John said in a deep voice, "Daddy," and I turned to see Mary Lou holding the baby. It was a moment of pure joy—hugs and tears and laughter and everybody talking at once.

John carried my bag and we climbed into the family car for the ride along familiar streets to Lake Washington Boulevard, past the madrona trees where Mary Lou and I first kissed, to the big brick house at 4016 50th Avenue South. Home, at last.

✦

CHAPTER 8

Law School *and* Raging River

Man should be able to walk in his cities, to find peace as well as excitement,
to find rest as well as work, to make easier contacts with his fellow man, and
to gain inspiration from nature.

—*Jim Ellis, "Human Environment and Public Investment," remarks,*
Seattle Junior Chamber of Commerce Luncheon, January 21, 1966

THE MORNING AFTER homecoming, Mary Lou woke up early. She lay quietly with her head on my chest listening to the "heart that makes my world whole." When I noticed how quiet the baby was, Mary Lou gave another hint of how she would spoil me in years to come. "I slipped out and fed him while you were asleep. He's talking and playing as good as gold."

After a big family breakfast filled with excited conversation, the waves of activity began to build. Summer term at the University of Washington Law School began in less than a month. In the weeks before my discharge from the Air Force, the whole family had exchanged ideas for an addition to the one-room log cabin at Raging River and I had instructed my dad to place an order with the Preston Mill Company for building materials within my budget. My terminal leave pay from the Air Force was enough to purchase the materials for a bathroom, bedroom, and kitchen addition.

A stack of lumber was waiting when we drove down the narrow dirt road which neighbors had recently built to their river properties. Rusty door locks yielded slowly to the key and the damp air of three rainy winters had allowed ivy to grow inside the log walls. Cabinets that Bob had built in grade school shop class brought twinges of memories, but now the May sunshine was pouring into the clearing and the river whispered anticipation.

My brother John had generously offered to help enlarge the cabin after his graduation from Franklin High School and he was as good as his word. Soon, two *different* brothers, John and I, were working like horses: cutting trees, skidding them onto the rack, and stretching a steel cable across the river to carry a rolling chain block. Housewarming presents for the cabin included an electric table saw from my parents and an electric washing machine from Mary Lou's parents. There was no telephone until cell telephones came along later, but electricity had been installed during the war while both Bob and I were away in the service.

Our plan was to live with my folks in Seattle until the addition was finished. In the meantime, we would work at Raging River on weekends and during school breaks. We hoped to make the cabin livable by the beginning of fall quarter. Mary Lou worked as hard as the young men, caring for Bobby, making meals, doing dishes, building fires, cutting wood, running errands, and giving an extra hand wherever it was needed. We were often still working at 9:00 p.m. Green logs are heavy and the handwork is slow; the project just took longer than planned.

When classes started in June, I got a job shelving books in the law library to add a few dollars to our income. Mary Lou typed the class notes, kept Bobby healthy and happy, and drove across town to the Fort Lawton PX each week for low-cost groceries. The library job gave us a financial boost and wonderful new friends, but also took time away from studying.

The unfamiliar legal concepts proved to be more difficult than expected. One evening I confessed to feeling lost in Professor Harry Cross' real property law course. I lamented to Mary Lou, "Maybe I'm not cut out to be a lawyer."

"That's crazy," she answered. "You're as smart as anybody." Then she winked. "Maybe you ought to study in Ida's old room so Bobby and I don't distract you so much."

One afternoon I came home from school to find my desk, lamp and books had been moved to the empty room above the garage. Sure enough, the quiet location increased my concentration and by exam time in August I had begun to get a feel for the language of law. My first term ended with good grades.

Living with my parents while building the cabin addition gave us a generous home with loving grandparents and family bridge games. However, it was not entirely a bed of roses. By the middle of summer my mother was beginning to resent Mary Lou's presence in the house that had long been her exclusive domain. The loss of one of her sons made her more possessive of the other two. Hazel's meticulous housekeeping differed from Mary Lou's casual approach, and my father observed, "It's hard to have two women in the same kitchen." When we moved to Raging River during the four-week break between summer and fall semesters, I was determined to finish the cabin and create our own home.

Construction of the cabin addition took on a frenzied pace. Still, no matter how hard we worked the chances grew slim that we could complete a cabin warm enough for a baby by winter. However, I refused to admit this apparent fact and began to work harder and later.

On a warm afternoon in early September, I was standing inside the rising enclosure straining to slide a freshly peeled log into position on top of the wall. The heavy timber slid across the wall like a greased pig, crashing down inside the cabin wall. Mary Lou was watching from the window as the falling log narrowly missed me. She ran outside, ducked under the new wall, and grabbed my arm.

"You're going to kill yourself! This cabin is just not worth getting yourself hurt. Bart Douglas almost lost his leg because he tried to work when he was tired. No matter how hard you try, you won't be able to finish before school starts. Let's face it! Please, for Bobby's and my sake, take the afternoon off and rest."

I was tired, frustrated, and feeling the pressure of time running out. An unfinished cabin meant staying at 4016. I pulled my arm away.

"Look, Beaver, we've got to get three more logs up before dark. You're just slowing me down. Leave me alone!"

Mary Lou shook her head and disappeared into the cabin. I turned to pry the fallen log out of the dirt, re-chained and hoisted it into position on the wall, loosened the chains, climbed the scaffold, and measured the notch.

Then, as I worked, I heard Mary Lou's voice, "Hi, hi! Let's go swimming. Come on! Be a sport! Slide down the rapids with me."

Jim mixes mortar for construction of the kitchen chimney, 1947.

Setting the walls in place was a dangerous job.

I looked up to see her standing on the back porch, naked in the sunshine, and then watched as she moved gracefully toward the river. The sight of this beautiful girl walking away was just too enticing. I dropped the axe to the ground muttering, "Oh, well, what the hell!"

A half hour later, we were lying in the sun on an Army blanket. My urgent project no longer seemed urgent. In a quiet moment I conceded, "You were right, Beaver. There's no chance of finishing. I wanted you to have your own house, but the job is a lot bigger than we figured."

"You've knocked yourself out, darling. I love you for trying, but one man can only do so much. We'll manage okay at 4016."

When fall term began in October, the doors and windows had been installed in the new addition, but there was no chimney for the wood-burning heater and the bathroom wasn't finished. Sitting in the bathtub you could feel the wind whistle through the cracks in the logs. It was time to think about moving.

Mary Lou's father R. B. was a master at figuring out ways to help a proud but impoverished law student. Just before I was discharged from the Army, he had suggested that we buy his low-mileage 1941 Mercury for the same price he had originally paid. Cars had greatly appreciated in value during the war and were very scarce. Mary Lou sold her 1936 Green Dragon Chevrolet and by paying a few hundred dollars more we ended up with reliable transportation for the thirty-minute commutes to Raging River.

In July of the same year, R. B. wrote to me that he would be retiring and moving to Bainbridge Island in a few years and wanted to shift his investments from Alaska to Seattle. He asked if I would "do a favor" for him by finding a "rental property in the north end of the city" which would yield an annual return of approximately 10 percent. Mary Lou looked around and reported several possibilities, including a tiny house located close to the university on NE 37th Street which could be purchased for six thousand dollars. R. B. answered that the small house sounded just right, and the sale was closed. A couple of weeks later he requested that I manage the property for him, with the goal of obtaining $50 or $60 a month in rental income.

Jim reading to Bobby in the home rented from Roy in the University District.

As you may have guessed, when Mary Lou and I left Raging River in late October, we became the first tenants of R B.'s little "investment house." This pattern was repeated during the winter months for each year of law school. From May through September, we lived in the log cabin while the little house was rented to others at a high "summer rate." Under R. B.'s formula, this permitted us to pay a lower "winter rate" and still return 10 percent a year on his investment. Our low shelter cost made it just possible to live on an income of about $120 per month.

R. B. refused to accept any more than a 10 percent return. Mary Lou and I knew that his real return was a comfortable home for his daughter and her children and a face-saving boost for his son-in-law.

Most G.I. Bill families lived in small apartments in a temporary housing project near the campus next to the Montlake garbage fill. These spartan units made our little University District house and the unfinished cabin at Raging River seem like luxury housing and these became gathering spots for potluck dinners, poker parties, and Independence Day picnics complete with small children, fireworks, wiener roasts, wading in the river, cases of beer, and lots of laughter.

Mary Lou, Bobby, and Jim at Raging River, circa 1947.

By 1948, Mary Lou was expecting our second child. One morning in June she came running from the cabin to the nearby bunk house where I was studying. Her voice was full of excitement with news that her water had broken. "We don't have a lot of time to spare, darling," she said, and we made a record run from Raging River across the Lake Washington Bridge to Seattle. Mary Lou's labor was short and both of us were ecstatic when a baby girl was born that afternoon. The happy mother came out of the delivery room smiling. "Now we've got one of each, darling. It doesn't matter what we get next." In a few days, we brought baby Judith Anne home to the cabin. My childhood bassinet and crib were returned to active duty again, and the washing machine got a good workout that summer.

As soon as Bobby had begun to crawl, Mary Lou had pressed me to build a fenced outdoor space to keep children safely away from the river. On nice days Bobby, and later Judi, played in an eight-foot square playpen, and Mary Lou was free to work on an endless list of projects to make the cabin more livable and pitched in on some of the heavy construction work as well.

The Raging River cabin was a retreat not only for Jim and Mary Lou, but for extended family and friends as well. Circa 1940s.

For most of the years we lived at Raging River, there were no other children within walking distance of the cabin. In this quiet setting, Bobby and Judi learned to play by themselves. They were anxious to "help" Mom and Dad on building projects and took special delight in hunting for periwinkle snails under river rocks or making minnow ponds in the shallows. Mary Lou was determined to teach the children to swim and as they reached the age of three years, they were enrolled in Seattle Parks Department classes at Mount Baker Beach.

On long summer evenings when Bobby was old enough to walk, he and I often went fishing up or down river from the cabin. I remember late one evening we went farther than usual to a deep fishing hole below Brown's farm and Bobby caught a big trout. As we hiked back in deepening dusk, Bobby was a little worried about getting lost, but nothing would stop him from carrying his 14-inch trophy in both hands. When we reached the clearing, Mary Lou came running to meet us, just as proud and excited over Bobby's fish as he was.

Jim, Bobby, Mary Lou, and Judi in front of the cabin fireplace, circa 1948.

The combination of law school, outside work, cabin building, and two small children left very few quiet times together. Among our most precious times were late evenings after the children fell asleep and Mary Lou and I sat under the stars watching the flames of a roaring fire in one of the many tree stumps which had been cut to make cabin logs and to bring sunlight into the clearing. The fir spruce and hemlock stumps burned almost continuously for several summers to remove them from the clearing.

One evening we sat together listening to the crackle of burning wood. Mary Lou leaned close saying, "Darling, watch the sparks. They look like they're joining the stars. I believe Bob is watching those same stars. It's so peaceful and I'm so full of love. I wish this night could last forever."

"Sometimes I want the clock to stop, too, Beaver. Like now, when you look so pretty in the firelight. When Bob and I lived here, we also felt the peace of this place. Gramps Reed spent many hours tending stump fires when he stayed here with us. He would poke at the coals with his cane, smoke those big cigars, and tell stories."

"Bobby's going to be a chip off the same old block, Jim," she replied. "He's always wanting to go fishing and to help you with the fires. It's fun to watch habits that bring happiness pass down the family."

For six years after World War II, we lived in the log cabin at Raging River from March until November. During law school we spent the winter months in R. B.'s little University District house. The first few winters of law practice we rented an apartment on Capitol Hill, an apartment on nearby Mercer Island, and finally purchased a white frame house on Roanoke Street in Seattle's Montlake District. During each migration we squeezed our worldly goods and growing number of children into our car that was bursting at the seams and riding low on the axles.

These were happy, hungry years. Mary Lou bought no clothing for herself. I used my Army uniforms until they wore out. On public occasions, Mary Lou wore dresses acquired before our marriage. For housework and odd jobs, she rolled up the cuffs on my Army fatigues. Budgeting for a family of four on an income of $120 a month was a constant struggle, especially for a young woman who had been raised in a family where there was always enough money.

River trout were a big part of our diet in the summer months. We also ate lamb burgers, the lowest-cost meat product of that time, and Mary Lou cooked lots of spaghetti, which became a family favorite. For years, Mary Lou made brown bag lunches for me. My lunches were always the best of anyone on the law library work crew and I took a lot of kidding about the surprises she included, and the love notes I often found inside.

Judi playing in the "yard" dotted with tree stumps at Raging River.

In 1949, I passed the bar exam and was hired as an associate by the pioneer Seattle law firm of Preston, Thorgrimson & Horowitz. The firm was highly regarded and consisted of four partners and two associates. The original law firm was located in Seattle's Boston Block, and in later years moved successively to the Pioneer Building, the Lowman Building, the Northern Life Tower, the IBM Building, and occupied offices in the Columbia Center in Seattle in my last years of law practice.

As the youngest lawyer in the firm, I researched issues, prepared memoranda, ran errands, set cases for trial, kept the office docket, checked transcripts, interviewed witnesses, served legal papers, maintained the library, and tried a few small cases.

I commuted six days a week from Raging River to a small office in the Northern Life Tower at Third and University Streets. My salary of $250 per month almost doubled our previous family income, but the new job required an immediate cash outlay for a second business suit. My father remarked that this suit looked like it had come from "the bargain counter." His next birthday gift to me was a well-fitted suit from Littler's in downtown Seattle.

Even with the larger income, we still worked hard to get by—sometimes with unexpected results. Each summer we grew fresh vegetables for the table at Raging River. One night I arrived home after dark and fertilized the vegetable garden from a sack in the woodshed. The next morning, we discovered that I had grabbed a sack of cement instead of fertilizer!

One of Mary Lou's weaknesses was forgetting to enter checks in her checkbook. This caused trouble when we were barely making enough to pay our bills. A missed check could—and sometimes did—result in an overdraft. Notices of overdrafts came to the law office and were embarrassing. We could probably trace two-thirds of our arguments during those hungry years to bank overdrafts; the other third to over disciplining our children. I tended to be stricter than Mary Lou until I saw that her system of encouragement was more effective.

Despite constant shortages of money and struggles with her checkbook, Mary Lou remembered those years as "beautiful times," and poured her energies into the "pure joy of little children." She never saw them as work, but rather "the most fun I've had in my life." I marveled at her patience and her ability to divert the children's attention away from activities which could become destructive or dangerous.

Mary Lou worked like a horse wherever we lived. However, there were early signs that her body might not be able to keep pace with her determination to get things done and her indomitable spirit. During the winter of 1949–50, we lived in a third-floor apartment of an old house on Capitol Hill. The washing machine was in the basement. With two small children, Mary Lou climbed those four flights of stairs several times a day. One afternoon I received a frantic phone call from the landlady who reported that Mary Lou had fainted and fallen down the stairway. I called the doctor, left work, and ran the six blocks from the bus stop.

Mary Lou was lying on the landlady's downstairs couch. Two scared children were holding on to her. Bobby piped up, "The doctor says those stairs are too hard for Mommy to climb, and she's 'sposed to stay in bed for two days."

I was worried to see Mary Lou so pale. "We're going back to Raging River the first of the month! From now on, Bobby, you and I will haul the laundry up and down those stairs. Okay?" Our four-year-old nodded his head, determined to help.

"It sure is nice to have two strong men around the house," Mary Lou observed with a smile.

In response to my concern about Mary Lou's condition, the doctor explained it was not a life-threatening condition, but that she wasn't as strong as she looked and advised us that Mary Lou should have yearly checkups and not 'overdo.' The best treatment would be rest.

I thought to myself that telling Mary Lou not to overdo was like telling water not to run downhill. In the next few years, she didn't really change her habits, but the fainting spell did not occur again. Gradually our worries disappeared. At the time, there was no hint of the diabetes that would strike so suddenly 12 years later.

My first years with Preston, 1949-1950, included the first year of the Korean War and reservists were being called to active duty. During discharge processing from the Air Force in 1946, I had signed up for the Reserve but did not elect to receive the part-time pay and retirement benefits offered for active reserve status.

The door to my office looked out through bookshelves to the entry elevators. One afternoon in the autumn of 1950, I was surprised to see my cadet school roommate, Sid Horrigan, walking out of an elevator —in uniform! I ran out to ask, "Sid what happened?" He grimaced and said he had been called up and was heading out to Fort Lawton to be sent somewhere, maybe Japan. He explained it had happened quickly and hoped it wouldn't be Korea. As we talked in my office, my mind raced. We had been in the same cadet graduating class and served the same length of time on active duty in WWII. I might also get called. Sid didn't think so. Unlike me, he had participated in one-day-a-month active duty for several years and was "on their radar."

The very next day, Mary Lou, who was now pregnant with our third child, called from home in tears to say we had received a wire from Air Force Weather Service Headquarters assigning me to a new unit in San Francisco. She said, "You're being transferred to San Francisco."

I reacted, "You're kidding!"

"Well, that's what it says," she answered.

I hurried home to see the telegram. The telegram *did* read like it was transferring me to San Francisco. Remembering the years of service required in World War II, it seemed like a similar interruption could throw my law career way off course.

The next morning, I showed the wire to Charles Horowitz. He read it and was instantly outraged. "They can't do that! We haven't finished the Dulien brief!" This reaction brought a well-hidden smile.

Fortunately, calls to San Francisco revealed that the wire was merely Army jargon for a paper transfer between inactive units. I was not going anywhere. The senior officer who took my call remarked that I had children and shouldn't worry as they weren't looking for people like me, yet. The potential call-up blew away and Charlie, Mary Lou, and I all relaxed.

The following winter we lived in a ground-floor apartment on Mercer Island. Mary Lou was pregnant with Lynn and spent her spare time house-hunting with Bobby and Judi in the back seat of the car. On one of these trips, she found a white frame house in Seattle on a corner of Roanoke Street near the Arboretum. The price was $12,250. We paid the down payment with my first big fee earned for the legal work I did to build a sewer system in a small district south of Seattle.

The former owners of our new house on the corner gave a warm neighborhood welcome dinner, and the Ellis family quickly became a part of the Montlake community. As the youngest of the fathers, I was drafted to coach a football team of 120-pound boys in the Seattle Parks Department league, while Mary Lou began a year of den mother duties for the Cub Scouts. The community was closely knit with lots of dropping in between neighbors and casual parties.

Our daughter, Lynn, was born March 26, 1951, shortly after moving to the Roanoke house. Our planned family was complete.

After spending quiet months in the woods at Raging River, the busy city seemed filled with action. Autumn was a particularly exciting time, when festive University of Washington football crowds flowed through our Montlake neighborhood on Saturday afternoons. On these game days, Bobby and Judi took advantage of the opportunity to earn spending money by selling reserved parking spaces in our driveway.

In the fall of 1952, Bobby started first grade at Montlake Elementary School. He had lived most of his childhood on the upper Raging River where there were no other families with children. He had learned a lot about nature, but little that prepared him for a crowded first day at school. When I let him out of the car on the edge of the playground, he looked lost, and after a few days he didn't want to go to school. No amount of coaxing would change his mind and Mary Lou began to accompany him to class.

One evening Mary Lou said to me, "The problem is simple. Bobby could adjust, but his teacher is mimicking his shyness and he is withdrawing further. She says he is a slow learner, but we know differently. She rewards cleanliness inspections with a spray of perfume! Things will just get worse if we don't change teachers right away."

Mary Lou began talking to the principal and I talked to school district officials. At the time, the district had an ironclad rule against changing room assignments and thus changing teachers. I was willing to drop the matter, but Mary Lou was not.

"No rule should be ironclad," Mary Lou insisted, her eyes flashing. "There *have* to be exceptions.

Mary Lou talked to teachers, to PTA leaders, and finally confronted the principal. "I'm going to be here every day until you move Bobby to Mrs. Nygreen's room."

After a few days of Mary Lou's relentless presence, the system found a way to transfer Bobby to Mrs. Nygreen's class. He responded immediately and became a high achiever throughout his school years and adult life. Beverly Nygreen and Mary Lou became long-time friends. The incident taught me that bureaucracies respond to persistent pressure *and* that nothing could stop Mary Lou when she knew she was right!

To avoid the month-end "battle of the checkbook," Mary Lou tried several ways to earn extra money at home. Her friend Pat Way remembers that these amazing schemes were not exactly practical, and I know that they uniformly operated at a loss. For example, when Mary Lou started a small preschool group, the parents were delighted. However, the fees were quickly consumed by the expensive learning materials she purchased for the kids.

Mary Lou did make real savings in our budget by doing her own home improvements: hanging wallpaper, painting a ceiling, or fixing something on the roof. She was dauntless and discouraged by nothing.

Once a month Mary Lou and I budgeted money for a babysitter and saw a movie together. Our only other entertainment was an occasional low-budget homemade dinner with friends. As my law practice grew, we could afford a babysitter more often. This gave us the chance for an occasional weekend alone, which we usually spent at Raging River or in the Earling's cottage at Pleasant Beach on Bainbridge Island. However, having more income also meant less time to enjoy it. As my night meetings increased, it became more difficult to commute the twenty miles to Raging River. Faced with the choice of the beautiful river or saving time to be together, we often chose time.

✿

CHAPTER 9

Apprentice

THE ROOTS OF THE PRESTON firm were planted in 1883 when 25-year-old Harold Preston arrived from Iowa to practice law. Seattle was little more than a booming village and Washington was still a US territory. In the last two decades of the 19th century, gold strikes in the North Cascades and the Klondike sparked several waves of migration to the Puget Sound area by gold seekers and providers of their supplies and services. The poplation of Seattle in 1860 was about 150 and is estimated to have reached 285,000 by 1916 when Preston and his law partner Oliver Thorgrimson were operating their firmly established law practice. Well after Mr. Preston's death in 1938, his presence was still felt in the law firm he had started. His son Frank was practicing at his father's desk and brass cuspidors sat on the floor of each lawyer's office for cigar smokers to spit into.

When I came to work at Preston, Thorgrimson & Horowitz in March 1949, it was a six-lawyer firm with offices in the Northern Life Tower at Third and University. The firm was the first tenant in the Northern Life Tower because the Northern Life Insurance Company was a client. The firm occupied the small 20th floor where the building tapers. Four elevators opened onto a long row of

Jim's Preston office in the Northern Life Tower Building in Seattle, early 1950s.

THE LAW FIRM OF

PRESTON, THORGRIMSON AND HOROWITZ

ANNOUNCE THE ASSOCIATION OF

JAMES REED ELLIS

WITH THE FIRM

FOR THE GENERAL PRACTICE OF LAW

2000 NORTHERN LIFE TOWER

SEATTLE, WASHINGTON

MARCH 10, 1949   ELIOT 7580

Jim's Preston announcement, 1949.

metal bookshelves ending in a one-chair reception area with a high counter at one end. Behind the counter was a metal safe and back-to-back desks for three secretaries and a bookkeeper-receptionist. The attorney office doors opened onto rows of steel bookcases. A visitor to the 20th floor in 1949 saw busy typists and a wall of bookshelves. I saw lawyers solving the problems of society. No lettered doorway was needed to say this was a working law office.

The 20th floor and its wonderful occupants proved to be just the right combination of place and people to help an idealistic and naïve young lawyer learn the practice of law. It was my great good fortune to be exposed to the professional lives of Harold Preston, O. B. Thorgrimson, and Charles Horowitz. They became guiding beacons for a lifetime of law practice and public service.

When I arrived, the bookkeeper showed me to an empty office last used by a former partner. When I sat down in the chair, my attention was caught by a large pair of wide-bottomed pants hanging by suspenders from a coat rack in the corner. They belonged to the former occupant, eighty-five-year-old Leander T. Turner. Turner had joined the Preston firm in 1917 and had left a record of successful trial work.

The bookkeeper smiled and said Mr. Turner would come by soon to pick up the pants. Sure enough, a week later he knocked on the door and I was treated to an hour of great stories. After he left, I noticed the pants were still on the rack. Three visits later they were still there. L. T., as he was known, missed his friends in the office and leaving his pants behind gave him a reason to come back and chat.

On one of his visits, L. T. shared some personal advice. He had practiced with Harold Preston and O. B. Thorgrimson for many years and during that time they shared a number of good fees. Both Preston and Thorgrimson owned fine homes and acquired good investment incomes. In sharp contrast, L. T. was living in a rented upstairs room and possessed only modest resources. He leaned forward in his chair to say, "The moral of this story, young man, is never grubstake miners or invest in dairy farms."

Among the first things I observed on my new job was the near reverence with which everyone in the office spoke of the firm's founder, Harold Preston. At the time of his death, H. P., as he was known, was widely regarded as the "Dean of the Seattle Bar" with a record of integrity, professional success, and progressive public achievement. He was clearly the most widely respected lawyer of his time within the legal profession in Washington State. His capacity to bring people together and achieve progressive results was recognized by all. His integrity was unchallenged. The affection felt by colleagues in his law firm was genuine. The senior associate in the firm, Fred Sansom, swore to the truth of a legend that when Harold Preston was called to testify in a case and was about to be sworn in by the bailiff, the judge interrupted the bailiff and said he didn't need to swear Mr. Preston in this court. It was not surprising that his death landed on the front page of the *Seattle Daily Times* on January 1, 1938. The story was headlined, "Harold Preston, Dean of Bar, Dead of Stroke."

My father, Floyd Ellis, and Harold Preston's son Frank had graduated from University of Washington Law School in 1919 and remained life-long friends. I took advantage of my father's long friendship with Frank to gather pieces of the life story of Harold and to understand his rare capacity to create consensus.

OLIVER B. THORGRIMSON'S PIVOTAL ROLE

Harold Preston's longest law partnership was with Oliver B. Thorgrimson who joined the firm as an associate in 1910 and became a partner two years later. Mr. Thorgrimson was still practicing when I arrived in 1949, and he soon became a living role model and teacher for me. He opened doors, gave advice, and proved to be a guiding influence for our twin goals of practicing law and performing public service.

O. B. not only gained a national reputation for his knowledge of the law of municipal financial obligations, but he also became a respected legal advisor to the Seattle business community. It was significant to me that while he was a partner in the law firm, O. B. was also active in civic affairs, serving as a member or leader for many area organizations. I wondered at the time how O. B. managed to find the time to successfully carry out these various responsibilities and still meet the demands of the practice of law.

When applying for work in the fall of 1948, I had shared with Mr. Thorgrimson that Mary Lou and I had made a covenant to devote part of our life to public service work in honor of my brother who had been killed in the war. O. B. responded that the law firm's partners were pleased we would make such a commitment; however, I should understand that working for the Preston firm would require my full-time attention because, "The business of law demands it." I got a clear message not to overdo my public service activity during work hours. Over the next few years, this impression gradually changed with O. B.'s growing support for our civic effort to create Metro.

More than anyone else, O. B. provided advice and encouragement during my early law practice and public service work. He opened doors to the business establishment and mentored me on community service. In about 1950, six or seven months after I joined the Municipal League and its Committee on County Government, the president of the League, Paul Green, came to the office to discuss with O. B. the possibility of my becoming legal counsel for the League. Mr. Green had watched me in committee meetings and believed this appointment would be good for the League and for the firm. O. B. was a former League president and responded with enthusiasm. In fact, he called me into his office the next day and told me that the invitation had been extended and that the firm very much wanted me to accept the job. He added the League would pay $100 a month for this work and the firm had agreed I should keep this as my personal income which would add substantially to our $250 monthly salary from the firm.

Mary Lou and I were ecstatic. The League job was the beginning of our commitment to honor my brother Bob. It resulted in a 1952 appointment as Deputy King County Prosecutor to assist a board of freeholders (county residents elected to serve on the board) preparing a proposed charter for King County. In fact, it launched much of the public service activity that followed. The firm also encouraged the huge amount of unpaid work that eventually led to the creation of Metro.

Some of the experience from my early Thorgrimson years opened doors to a growing municipal practice. O. B. was an admirer of Harold Preston and frequently used examples from Harold's life experience as guidance on civic and legal issues as well. O. B. gave me advice that turned out to be career-saving.

During our few short years of working together, O. B. emphasized the importance of caution in practicing municipal finance law. He once told me you can't afford to be wrong if you're giving opinions on bonds because your opinion will be treated as a virtual warranty of payment by most bond purchasers. On another occasion, he sternly told me to never risk my integrity as

O. B.'s Trees

When I told Mary Lou about Oliver B. Thorgrimson's initial cautious response to our public service commitment, she said, "I'd like to meet O. B. and his wife Myrtle. I hear they are avid gardeners. This may be a stronger common interest than you think."

A few weeks later, I asked O. B. if it would be all right for us to visit his garden. He said to absolutely come by any weekend.

On a sunny day, Mary Lou and I drove to their beautiful home south of Seward Park on Lake Washington. O. B. was working in the garden. They invited us in for tea and during the conversation Mary Lou expressed her desire to see their greenhouse.

"Jim tells me you are growing trees from cuttings, and I'd like to see how this is done."

O. B. led the way to the greenhouse where he explained the cutting process and showed us five small pots containing new cuttings from his prized Chinese dogwood tree. He explained that Chinese dogwood trees were covered with white flowers in late June and were rare around here, with only one or two of them in Seattle. I told him we would sure like to start one. He said he could do better than that and would give us one of his starts after it had grown good roots.

Mary Lou and I did not then have a place to plant such a tree, but a few years later when we bought a house in Bellevue, O. B. and Myrtle brought us a healthy young Chinese dogwood in a large five gallon can. He said the tree was small, but it would grow into a fine addition to our entry.

Over the years, Mary Lou and I watched as O. B.'s dogwood grew into a 30-foot-high tree covered with beautiful white bracts every June. His kind gesture showed us he was a caring and purposeful, man. He wanted to leave his garden and his community better than he found them. We often remarked that he would be happy to see what grew from his gift.

you only lose your integrity once. I remember these words of guidance because they came from such a respected source and because they fit my own instincts.

O. B. Thorgrimson had pioneered the law of municipal revenue bonds in Washington. He would look at me seriously and tell me a bond lawyer cannot afford to be wrong once. If there is any reasonable doubt of validity, we don't approve without a test case. If a bond issue is large and lacks clear guiding precedent, we may need to establish *res judicata* before giving our approving opinion. *Res judicata*, or law of the case, means that parties to litigation are bound by the decision and cannot subsequently challenge it even if change has occurred in the case law since the decision.

He also counseled me to look closely at bonds where user revenues are the sole source of payment and to understand the fallibility of officers and employees of public borrowers. Defaults in payment can occur when all procedures are legal. Economic conditions can interrupt the flow of revenues. Local officials can become sloppy and make unintended mistakes. Financial houses or advisors can "stretch" to sell a deal. Sea changes in economic conditions or political tides can affect judges. O. B. urged that I never be afraid to ask questions, inspect facilities, and do my own arithmetic. He encouraged me to apply common sense caution when assessing risk and to fully use appropriate "rate coverage" or other protective covenants in making revenue pledges or establishing reserves and standards of operating practice. His teachings still ring in my ears.

CHARLES HOROWITZ

Both O. B. and his son Richard, as well as Charles Horowitz, strongly encouraged my instinct to back up crucial promises to construct and operate facilities with careful analysis. We called this "belt and suspenders" and it served me well more than once in the years that followed. I learned from one of the best. Charles Horowitz was a prolific producer of questions of fact to be answered under oath by anyone asserting a claim in Court against his client. Among my first jobs as an apprentice was to serve legal papers for him which needed proof of the time of receipt. He usually dictated these lengthy "interrogatories" to his secretary early in the morning and they were notoriously detailed. One afternoon I served upon an unsuspecting lawyer, a thick set of Charlie's questions. The poor man actually began to shake as he angrily thumbed through this pile of paper, asking "How many people in your big office worked on these?" I answered that Charlie did this by himself. As I closed the door behind me, I heard him mutter "No man could do this. Horowitz isn't human, he's a machine!"

Horowitz's reached his legal career goal in 1974 when he ran for an open seat on the State Supreme Court and was elected statewide by more than 121,000 votes! Charlie wrote 270 opinions during the six years he served. He retired from the high court in 1980 because of statutory age limitation and returned to the Preston firm where he became a senior statesman in the office.

Richard and O. B. encouraged me to visit issuing cities and districts to explain bond procedures. Dick avoided "unnecessary" trips when the mail could serve as well and he disliked night meetings. For me, long drives and night meetings seemed a small price for gaining a good understanding of the grassroots elements of municipal law and practice. Trips to Soap Lake, Ephrata, Yakima, Wenatchee, Longview, and Port Angeles were time-consuming but resulted in lasting friendships and greater knowledge of the real world of local public finance. Some law school classmates who became part-time city attorneys around the state began to refer municipal law cases to me when they encountered conflicts of interest with their private clients.

This resulted in Dick turning over to me the legal work for a small sewer district at the south end of Lake Washington, Bryn Mawr-Lake Ridge. He generously offered to let me treat this client as if I had originated it for the purpose of fee sharing. This district was the beginning of my awareness of sewer system construction and operating practices, and it led to my early understanding of the effects of discharging treated sanitary sewage effluent into the lake. This work also connected me with people with whom I would develop long relationships over the years.

Our firm founder, Harold Preston, once said that any success he had in his law practice came from his determination to uncover all facts and to explore all facets of law until he found the combination of facts and precedent needed to win. His resulting "dig, dig, dig" work habit became an ethic of the Preston firm and proved itself dramatically in one of my early assignments from Charles Horowitz.

Charlie had been retained to take an appeal to the Ninth Circuit Court of Appeals from a Federal District Court judgment against Dulien Steel Company in a contract dispute. He asked Ed Starin and me "as a matter of highest priority" to research all cases on the subject from California where the contract was made. We first worked through the Reporter System and after reading over piles of books and spending a fruitless Friday and Saturday, the two of us returned to a quiet building on Sunday. It seemed to me that we must have exhausted every possible key subject in the reporter system. We began a laborious search through volumes of incompletely indexed California state reports of decisions made prior to the creation of the National Reporter System.

Late Sunday afternoon with piles of books off the shelves, I heard a shout from the library table.

"Jim! Come here!"

I ran in to see Ed grinning from ear to ear and holding up an old California State Reports volume. "Look at this!"

I read the short opinion of an 1870's California supreme court and exploded, "Ed! You did it. This is a total 'white cow!'" A white cow case is one where the facts before the court presented a question essentially identical to that presented by your case. We danced around the table like kids. When we ran the citator, we found with great satisfaction that the case had *not* been overruled.

We showed Ed's case to Charlie on Monday morning and received a rare "Excellent!" Believe it or not, this old decision was the *only* case cited in a unanimous two-page opinion of the Ninth Circuit Court of Appeals reversing the trial court and ruling in favor of Dulien!

It was common practice when I came to work for successful lawyers to actively practice into their 80s and for name partners to bring their sons into the law firm. This was the case for both Frank Preston and Dick Thorgrimson.

FRANK PRESTON

Frank Manley Preston was the eldest son of Harold Preston and Augusta Morgenstern Preston and was in the same graduating class from law school as my father. When I came to the Preston firm, Frank was a successful trial lawyer for firm clients, including the Traveler's Insurance Company and Metropolitan Life Insurance Company.

One afternoon, Frank came into my office to say that he and Tracy Griffin were defending a medical malpractice case brought by a prominent plaintiff attorney. We were defending a doctor sued for injuries to a woman allegedly caused by malpractice during childbirth. He asked if I would like to come down when they brought their expert witness on to testify that the procedures used by our doctor followed the customary and appropriate best practice of obstetrics. I jumped at the chance to watch experienced trial lawyers perform.

I met Frank's witness, a very congenial and soft-spoken man who was a highly regarded specialist in obstetrics and gynecology. He had carefully prepared himself and had sat through the trial. When Frank called him to the stand, he revealed extensive experience and national recognition as an expert in gynecology. I was impressed by his qualifications, but Frank told me before we came to court that he believed the modest, understated manner of the witness would convey crucial credibility to the jury and was equally important as his expertise.

The plaintiff's counsel first attempted to belittle the witness' qualifications and discredit his background. He had brought several authoritative books to the counsel table and examined our expert about the opinions in these books referencing small excerpts. Our witness repeatedly insisted it was important to consider the larger context from which the questions were taken and suggested he be given the books to read before responding. Counsel refused and was argumentative, while the witness remained reserved and modest in his responses, never wavering in his testimony.

Finally, the witness repeated an answer and counsel exclaimed the witness had already said that! The doctor responded that he knew he had repeated his answer, but that counsel had asked same question three times previously. The jury was now on the side of the witness.

Frank just sat quietly behind our counsel table, never interrupting the questioning. Finally, he leaned over to me and whispered that the witness was doing better for himself than Frank could ever do for him. It became increasingly apparent that the witness had the jury with him.

After about two hours, the plaintiff's counsel asked the doctor if he believed men were descended from monkeys? Frank did not object to the question, he wanted the witness to handle it on his own. The question was argumentative, and counsel was angry when he posed it. The witness leaned forward looking at counsel and said he did not believe he was descended from a monkey, then paused and added he wasn't so sure about the counsel. The entire court room burst into laughter.

A juror in the back row stood up and clasped his hands over his head, as if to say, "way to go." It was something to see. Frank sat there like a cat that had swallowed a canary. The judge watched the whole thing unfold and could be seen smiling. The plaintiff's lawyer was visibly disturbed by the jury's reaction but couldn't do anything about it. He finally pulled himself together and told the judge he had no further questions, and the judge declared a recess. The verdict came down in favor of the defendant two days after the jury had been sequestered.

When the case was over Frank said to me that sometimes we do our best work when we say nothing. If you can keep quiet and not interrupt what is unfolding in the court room, it may turn out to give you a ten strike. What I learned from Frank that day was that a lawyer can sometimes do his best work when he sees that his expert witness is thoroughly prepared and allows him to defend himself.

RICHARD "DICK" THORGRIMSON

In 1950, the Municipal bond business was growing fast. The end of World War II saw Europe in shambles. The US manufacturing capacity was intact and quickly expanding. A sharp increase in babies in the United States as families settled into a post-war climate created a pending need for more public schools and classrooms across the state, especially in areas of high employment like King County.

Dick Thorgrimson and his father were swamped with requests for proceedings to authorize and issue bonds. Dick realized early on that I would be needed to take some of this overload and spent time showing me how to deal with school districts. Dick had prepared detailed checklists and carefully developed forms and familiarized me with our prescribed procedures. He insisted on my reading and rereading the statutes and cases that governed the requirements for authorization and issuance of debt. He was very good at drafting clear instructions. I learned a great deal from his clarity of language. He pointed out that public officials are often not experienced in debt issuance, and they treat letters from us like gospel.

Working with Dick was extremely good for me. I had not developed his meticulous methods or learned a complete knowledge of applicable statutes and practices. I studied his documents thoroughly and submitted my work to Dick before I mailed it out. I tried especially hard to get into his rhythm and we functioned smoothly together. It helped that his secretary served us both for my first two years. Once I got the hang of using his templates and clearly written letters, I started turning out a significant amount of work and we became an efficient machine for authorizing and issuing school debt throughout Washington, Oregon, Alaska, and Montana

Most large issues were handled by Dick. I focused on smaller and simpler issues. He saw the wisdom of assigning certain districts to my attention to assure continuity of service to our clients. He preferred to manage the workload from his office for greater productivity, but I wanted to visit districts and cities, see whom I was working with, and directly answer their questions. Dick assigned to me more than a dozen small districts, cities, and towns with instructions for me to start visiting and working with them.

The important lesson learned from this part of my apprenticeship was the value of being clearly understood by our clients, especially when they were not educated in the complexities of municipal finance instruments. On my visits to small towns and districts, I noticed copies of my letters were posted on bulletin boards in district offices, allowing everyone to see what was being done. I found the real payoff was the enjoyment of working with people who looked to us for safe-harbor guidance.

The most useful thing I learned was to organize my work, to do a number of things in a short time, and not to jump around between projects. On a rare occasion, I would come up with an idea that was new and useful. However, the more time I spent with districts, the more value I saw in the high degree of detailed wording that the firm had already developed. This was admired by our clients and encouraged them to be equally meticulous.

Most districts were not close to their debt limits in the beginning of the baby boom, but it didn't take long for a huge surge in borrowing to take them close to their limits. We managed to keep up with the first wave of need for new schools, but growth continued and very soon Dick and I were looking for another person to help us.

EDWARD STARIN

My all-purpose mentor in the office was Edward Starin. Ed was about eighteen years older than I and had developed a general practice of his own before associating with Preston and becoming a partner in 1953. He was a fine lawyer, a leader in the Jewish community, and a kind and wise man. Best of all, he was a trusted friend and patient teacher.

Some of my lessons at the Preston firm came from asking Ed to include me in the routine tasks of his general practice. One day Ed dropped by my office to say he was doing a sheriff's sale in the morning of some bar furniture for a tavern that failed to pay for the furnishings it purchased. He said we have the unpleasant duty of collecting the furniture, that probably no one else would bid on it, so we'd make a bid of $100 and haul away the furniture. I went to the sale with him the next morning and was surprised to see how quick and routine the procedure was. But it also left an impression.

The tavern was closed. Inside, the bar sections, stools, and chairs were piled together. I met the operator of the tavern and Ed introduced the deputy sheriff when he arrived. The deputy announced he had a duly prepared Order of Sale and was going to conduct the sale, and anyone gathered could make a cash bid to buy the furnishings. He asked us to identify ourselves and state our bid for the bar, stools, chairs, and tables. The tavern operator stood there not saying anything. Ed expressed we were there representing the creditor and would bid $100. The tavern operator shouted that was outright robbery! Ed said it wasn't and that the tavern operator had purchased the items with our money. That was the only verbal exchange. The sheriff then asked if there were any other bids? The operator had the right to bid but didn't have any money. So, the sheriff pounded his fist on the bar and said, "The sale is closed. The furniture now belongs to "XYZ" company, and I authorize the purchaser's agent to remove it."

Ed had arranged for a truck for the furniture. While it was being loaded, the tavern operator continued to complain. Ed reminded him he got the money from our client to buy this furniture and he now owns these items.

Ed said, "You can't blame him for collecting on a bad debt."

The tavern operator responded, "The rich always end up with everything." It was apparent that he was bitter, and I thought about this as we were driving back to the office.

I looked at Ed, "The system does work, but it isn't painless."

Ed nodded his head and said, "You're right."

He explained the system doesn't work without pain and wouldn't work at all if people who borrow money don't pay it back. Collecting it is unpleasant because the guy is broke and now won't be able to operate his business, but if debt isn't collected no one will lend money to people who want to start a business. I knew that repossessions had to be done but it was a reality check to watch first-hand. The legal system only works if you can enforce it and, that day, I saw the pain in that process.

Young lawyer salaries were notoriously low in 1950 when apprentice working conditions still prevailed. We brought lunch from home on most days. One of the enjoyable fringe benefits of these first years was meeting law school friends for lunch at a café which would let us bring homemade sandwiches if we purchased soup. On a sunny day we would sometimes walk to the end of a waterfront dock with our brown-bag lunches and soak up the spectacular view of ferries crossing a blue Puget Sound in front of snowcapped Olympic Mountains.

On my first lunchtime walk along Seattle's waterfront sidewalk, I discovered that the view was not as pristine as it appeared from the windows of downtown office buildings. Up close along the sidewalk, it was shocking to see outfalls of raw sewage and toilet paper from Downtown and First Hill sewers splashing into Elliott Bay at every street end. The sewage solids formed floating mats in full view from the sidewalk. I was appalled by the fact that rivers of untreated and disease-carrying human waste from residential, commercial, manufacturing, industrial, and hospital sources were still being dumped 24/7 into Elliott Bay and the Duwamish Estuary in our "modern" society.

Seattle was a city that had found a way to bring tap water from the mountains to half a million people, to fireproof commercial buildings, to re-grade downtown streets and level Denny Hill, and to sweep and wash streets and sidewalks every Wednesday. Yet, Seattle could still not see the need to treat its raw sewage. The simple explanation was that what is out of sight is out of mind for people in homes, stores, and offices. It was, of course, cheaper for the city to dump its waste into the nearest water course and rely on treatment by dilution in Puget Sound. The deep-water dilution idea had been given long-standing currency by nationally recognized engineer Abel Wolman and, for years, was accepted procedure of the City of Seattle. The same practice was followed by Victoria, B.C. and surrounding municipalities until 2010.

One Sunday afternoon, I took Mary Lou on this waterfront walk. She reacted at first sight, "What a shame to spoil our waterfront with this horrible floating sewage!"

I remember asking myself what Harold Preston would do. I was sure he would find a way to combine consensus public action with the tools of municipal finance to cure a public health menace as glaring as dumping raw sewage on Seattle's Puget Sound doorstep and restore clean water to this glorious landscape.

✦

CHAPTER 10

Growing with Preston

I WAS IMPRESSED by the patterns of work that had been set by the principal founders of the firm. Harold Preston and Oliver B. Thorgrimson left for their successors a spotless reputation, valuable customs, and important client relationships. When I ran into difficult situations, I asked myself what H. P. or O. B. would do if faced with the same problem. I came to believe that it was wise to follow their example. The legacy of H. P. and O. B. became a source of inspiration and caution that guided the lawyers of the firm for many years.

I, myself, had been taught by family and teachers the value of managing personal expenses with caution and building trust in human relationships. My father's business reputation for integrity was strongly reinforced by my mentors at the firm. My father also set a business example of promising less than you believe you can deliver. These influences were the source of the "better than promised" performance goals we later set for our civic projects.

On February 1, 1953, Edward Starin and I became partners in the law firm. The firm's practice grew rapidly in the immediate post-war period and senior partners began asking me to handle management details of the law office. As a result, I began to devote time to keeping the office running smoothly, subject to their approval of major decisions.

It was also becoming apparent that the firm would need to grow more if it was to retain its established position in the profession during years of rapid population growth for Seattle and the Puget Sound area. Hiring decisions over the next ten years formed the future core of the new firm of Preston, Thorgrimson, Horowitz, Starin & Ellis.

Early hires who became important building blocks of the firm were Donald Holman, Gordon Conger, John Gose, Gerry Grinstein, and Betty Fletcher. Not long thereafter, Kent Carlson, Bill Burkhart, Forrest Walls, Joel Starin, Cynthia Weed, and Michael Crutcher joined our growing firm. Other early hires made significant contributions but chose to strike out on their own.

DONALD HOLMAN

During my first years with the law firm, it was clear that post-war growth in the Northwest was going to dramatically increase requirements for new schools, roads, and municipal improvements. Dick and I were soon swamped. I asked my brother John, who had graduated from UW law school shortly after I had, if he knew anyone in his law class who might make a good municipal bond lawyer. John believed Don L. Holman had the right combination of smarts and attention to detail.

Don was working in the State Attorney General's office at the time. I called him for an interview, and he was excited about a long-term, private sector opportunity. The partners quickly approved him, and Don joined the firm.

Don soon showed his skill at drafting, understanding, and creating quality documents for our municipal clients. He was effectively holding his own in no time at all and his success within the firm was immediate. Dick and I took advantage of Don's availability and quick acceptance by local financial houses and municipal clients. It didn't take long for Dick to give him large responsibilities—just as he had given me. Don preferred working on the document side of the municipal practice and did not enjoy the demands for argument and debate that came with controversial situations or trial practice.

Over the next several years Don became an important part of our practice and was elevated to partner in a relatively short time. Don had a quiet manner

Portrait of Jim for the Preston law firm, circa 1951.

that projected confidence and helped him develop strong working relationships with local officials and his ability to effectively communicate with the financial industry contributed to his success. He became highly regarded by others in the American Bar Local Government Committee and within the finance industry. Together, we grew a very substantial volume of business and became the volume leader among Northwest law firms in this field, building on the reputation O. B. Thorgrimson had established for the firm locally and across the country.

Sadly, stresses began to play a role in Don's family and professional life, leading to his early death in 1986.

BETTY BIMMS FLETCHER

One of our greatest good fortunes was to have practiced law with Betty Fletcher. Betty graduated Phi Beta Kappa with honors from Stanford University in 1943, with a BA in History and Pre-Law.

While at Stanford, Betty married Robert (Bob) Fletcher who graduated from Stanford University Law School in 1945. The couple returned home to Tacoma, where Bob became a partner at Betty's father's law firm. He later became a popular professor at the University of Washington Law School, and eventually a full professor of law and associate dean of the Law School.

After a family was underway, Betty enrolled in the University of Washington Law School. With a long commute from Tacoma, her parents' help with two children, and her endless determination, Betty graduated first in her law school class in 1956. She was awarded the *Order of the Coif*, an honor society for United States law school graduates.

I was acting as the firm's interviewing partner when she interviewed at Preston, Thorgrimson & Horwitz. We were interviewing for a lawyer with full participation in our practice serving other lawyers in the office, but also learning and eventually performing all facets of law practice. I expressed a strong interest in hiring her immediately because she possessed a winning personality and was the number one in her class. It would be a real coup for a small firm like ours to hire a top woman lawyer and the honor graduate of the UW Law School. We would one-up the firms in town that weren't lucky enough to hire her. Women were not being hired by law firms as lawyers at that time unless they had special connections, but Betty had shown initiative and determination in pursuit of a

Betty Fletcher:
First Woman to Join the Rainier Club

CEBERT (BILL) BAILLARGEON, president of Seattle Trust and Savings Bank said to me one day he thought Betty Fletcher would be a great first woman member of the Rainier Club and asked if I would join him in nominating her. I said, "It's a great idea, Bill. I'll be happy to join you. Now that I'm on the board of the club, maybe we can steer it a little bit."

One evening prior to the nomination, I had asked Mary Lou whether women should be able to be members of the Rainier Club. Mary Lou's consistent support for what she called "common sense" women's rights sometimes came as a surprise to me because she was so completely absorbed in the nurturing and support of her own family.

"Absolutely." Mary Lou answered. "She is so outstanding that even those old men in leather chairs will be hard put to turn her down." She had heard me talk about deals that were done over lunch tables in the club and about the access to business opportunities gained through networks of business and professional people. Mary Lou added with a conspiratorial smile that the admission of Betty to the Rainier Club would be "a real game changer for other women."

"Betty has chosen a career in law, and she is as good as any man in that profession. This club is part of an old boy network that gives men an advantage. Women lawyers should not be shut out of that part of the system." I applauded in mock approval, but Mary Lou was just getting started. "I chose to give myself full time to raising children because that was what I most wanted to do with my life. I'm glad I made that choice. But if our daughters want to practice law or be commercial pilots, or whatever, they should have the same opportunity to prove their ability as men have. Fair is fair."

Questions that arose during consideration of Betty's application by the board then would bring laughter in today's world. One member commented, "I suppose she'll want to go into the men's bar?" I responded, "That is absolutely the first place she'll go." There were more than a few heads shaking over this change in a long habit of male privilege. I argued, "You know, sooner or later this is going to happen. I can't imagine a better person to be the first woman admitted to our club than Mrs. Betty Fletcher."

It passed the board but was hotly debated in the membership meeting. More than thirty members formally resigned in protest!

The Rainier Club takes pride in being the first of Seattle's "Men's Clubs" to admit women. That man's world has changed dramatically by recognizing a growing breadth of roles for women in society. Betty became a national leader in this evolution. Now you can't find Rainier Club members who admit to having voted "no."

---

job with our firm. After discussion and wide agreement, we hired Betty Binns Fletcher as the first woman lawyer in the historic Preston firm.

Betty was quickly recognized in the law firm as an excellent lawyer and Charles Horwitz made her his indispensable associate. The rest of us had difficulty getting access to her outstanding talent. Charlie was president of the Seattle Bar Association and asked Betty to start a newspaper for the association. This was the beginning of the present-day *Bar Bulletin*. The role provided Betty high visibility among Seattle lawyers and the high quality of the publication was soon noticed by the membership.

Betty served first as a practicing associate lawyer and later as a partner in the Preston law firm for 23 years. She was a high producer. When Charlie was appointed to the State Court of Appeals, he gave Betty all of his clients, including Justice William O. Douglas of the United States Supreme Court, which helped build her reputation.

My relationship with Betty was a rewarding partnership. Any work Betty did with me always demonstrated a first-rate legal mind and I was impressed that Betty wasn't willing to give up easily when she thought she was right. She was a tough negotiator. She was also supportive over many years of the civic goals that Mary Lou and I pursued for local government reforms and activities. We very much enjoyed our civic relationship and personal friendship we shared with Betty and her husband Bob.

Some of the most important issues of my time were those involving the rights of women. It was clear Betty was going to be an ardent advocate of women's rights. Among Betty's many pioneering achievements were being tapped in 1972 by Governor Evans to serve as a member of a new advisory Women's Commission and then drafting and receiving legislative approval and state ratification of an Equal Rights Amendment to the state constitution; becoming president of the Seattle King County Bar Association in 1972, a first for a major city bar association in the United States; and advancing rapidly in the Washington State and American Bar Associations.

From an early date, I was sure that at some point in time, Betty would become a judge. It happened with meteoric speed. In 1979, President Carter nominated her to the Ninth Circuit Court of Appeals, the second highest level in the federal judiciary below the US Supreme Court.

She soon established herself as "The Angel of the EPA." She became an enforcer of strict construction and interpretations of the seminal *Environmental Protection Act* during the controversial development of law surrounding environmental impact statements and other key procedural safeguards of the environment. She pursued her judicial scholarship with persistence, led by her scholarship and clarity of expression, and eventually was recognized as a leading authority on environmental issues of great importance.

FORREST WALLS

Forrest Walls, known as "Forry" to his friends, attended Seattle Pacific University in 1960 and graduated from the University of Washington Law School in 1963. Forry was well respected and honored by his clients and colleagues throughout his law career. He was a responsible leader of our municipal bond department and became widely known in the profession as an able, meticulous, and highly respected bond attorney. He practiced law at Preston, Gates & Ellis, and later K&L Gates, for 37 years, serving in the role of managing partner of the Preston municipal finance practice until his retirement in 2001.

Forry and I became close confidants throughout our years of working together. In fact, of all the lawyers working in what became the Municipal Department, Forry was the one attorney who assisted me the most after he became an experienced bond lawyer in his own right. Forry was able and willing to fill in for me if I was unable to attend the closing of a bond issue. He once even closed a bond delivery for me in New York when he discovered one of the required certificates in the transcript was missing. He verified the original then prepared a new certificate, the closing continued as if nothing was amiss, and the purchaser was never aware of the potential problem. I came to rely on his judgment and careful attention to detail.

Outside of the office and the practice of law, the two of us shared a strong personal interest in the environment and in the native history of our area. Forry's great love was the outdoors. We shared an intense common interest in supporting the creation of the Mountains to Sound Greenway and the designation of the Alpine Lakes Wilderness Area around Snoqualmie Pass.

Years of increasing civic commitments required me to be absent from the office frequently. I will never be able to repay Forry for always being there to cover for me. I came to trust his integrity and sound judgment.

When Forry was diagnosed with symptoms of Parkinson's, he didn't quit working. He chose to stay active and remain involved in the law practice as long as he was able. He and his wife, Vi, continued to host firm outings at their Puget Sound waterfront vacation home near Shelton and travel until his death in 2009.

CASES AND CLIENTS: THE DEVIL IS IN THE DETAILS

NOTATION: Jim carefully outlined people, projects, and cases in his manuscript outline that he felt were important to his early professional growth and to the Preston firm. He did not complete his writing but fortunately we have two stories in his words about his bond work with the Pacific Natural Gas Company as a client and the lessons he learned from his work on the case of the sinking of the vessel the Barbara Lee.

NORTHWEST NATURAL GAS PIPELINE COMPANY

Through the 1950s, my work for the firm consisted of preparing or reviewing bond ordinances and resolutions for cities, counties, and special districts. In the course of doing bond work, I developed friendships with businesspeople in banking and securities firms. As I began to handle larger issues, I found myself occasionally doing bond deliveries in New York City where major financial firms maintained offices and large bond issues were often designated for closing and delivery. It wasn't long before this work came to the attention of people in the local banking and investment community. Their new work was usually, but not always, related to the financial needs of cities, counties, and districts.

Sherman Ellsworth of the Seattle investment firm of Harper & Son referred to me the construction company Pacific Natural Gas Company. This company had been formed to build systems for the distribution of natural gas in cities and towns of Washington. These locations were places expected to receive natural gas that would soon be delivered by the large Northwest Natural Gas Pipeline Company. Washington communities were eager to have access to this new fuel. It was safer and cleaner than manufactured gas or coal and would stimulate business growth. I helped Pacific Natural Gas negotiate franchise rights to build local delivery systems in several cities and to negotiate their supply contracts with the pipeline company.

In the summer of 1957, I made several trips to New York to work on drafts of financing documents for the construction of the Pacific Natural Gas distribution systems. These trips were my first experience with regulated private loan and public stock financing. We put together the documents for the mortgage loans and the public sale of common stock to finance the Pacific Natural Gas construction program.

As I spent more and more time away from home, Mary Lou began to accompany me occasionally. On one of these New York trips, our Pacific Gas financing deal was closed at the J.P. Morgan Bank on Wall Street with more than two dozen parties bringing shopping carts for the exchange of lengthy documents. In accordance with custom, the participants and spouses were invited to celebrate after at a party hosted by the underwriting lenders at a Long Island Beach Club. Attendees representing the East and West coasts broke just about even in the humorous toasting competition. However, Mary Lou, the intelligent, good listener, clearly was the sought-after conversation partner.

The trip culminated in one of the guys daring the group to a Coney Island parachute jump, one that Mary Lou aced! The Pacific Natural Gas financing was successful, as was the winning performance by the lady from Seattle.

LESSONS FROM A GRAYS HARBOR TRAGEDY

Roy Furfiord was a client of mine on matters affecting his crab fishing business in Grays Harbor. I had gotten to know him during one of my local government bond trips to Hoquiam in the 1950s.

On January 28, 1960, Roy's fishing vessel, the *Barbara Lee,* met tragedy. The *Barbara Lee* made a valiant effort to tow a Coast Guard rescue vessel, *Invincible*, to safety but capsized in the heavy seas off the Grays Harbor Bar. The *Invincible* had been disabled by a large wave while attempting to cross the treacherous Grays Harbor Bar. The *Barbara Lee*'s skipper, Robert Bolam, and crew member Ted Sigurdson drowned. Crew member Harold Pernula and the crew of the self-righting *Invincible* survived after a harrowing night. Bolam and Sigurdson received posthumous medals from the Coast Guard and praise from the local fishing community. A small collection of about $200.00 was taken up by Coast Guard personnel for the widows and children of the deceased.

Roy came to Seattle to ask if I thought he or the widows of the drowned crew members had any legal recourse against the Coast Guard, and whether we would be willing to pursue the case on a contingent fee basis. I agreed to explore the matter with the firm.

A young partner, John Gose, and I visited Hoquiam to examine the Coast Guard station logbook and to interview the widows. The pages describing the *Barbara Lee/Invincible* incident were surprisingly clean for January 28, 1960, the day of the accident. This fact, along with an undercurrent of suspicion among the Grays Harbor fishing community, left us feeling that something wasn't right about the official version of the tragedy and deserved pursuit. There would be a risk of failure and the high cost of representing Roy and the widows, but the Preston partners decided unanimously to undertake this case on a contingent fee basis as a wrongful death action.

The Coast Guard crew had been transferred out of the area, which made taking a deposition too expensive in advance of trial. Fortunately, our interviews with the two widows left us with positive impressions. Mary Louise, the widow of crew member Ted Sigurdson, was in her early twenties, sweet mannered, and completely devoted to her husband and their two small children. We felt she would make a promising witness. Onalue Bolam, the widow of Robert Bolam, had a straightforward likeable manner, but she was

The Seattle Times 11
Saturday, January 30, 1960

Hearing Called In Sinking Of Fishing Boat

A Coast Guard hearing was scheduled at Neah Bay this afternoon into the capsizing of a Coast Guard boat and the sinking of a fishing vessel that went to its aid.

Two of the three men aboard the fishing boat Barbara Lee drowned when the vessel tried to aid the 52-foot patrol boat Invincible, disabled in the storm-lashed waters off Westport Thursday night.

Lost when a wave engulfed the Barbara Lee were Robert Bolam, Westport, and Ted Sigardson, 28, Grayland. Harold Pernula, Westport, was taken aboard the Invincible.

The Invincible's engines went dead when she capsized in the rough waters, then righted herself. She was taken in tow by the Coast Guard tug Yacona. Unable to cross the bar at Westport because of high seas, the vessels headed for Neah Bay. They were expected there this afternoon.

Coast Guard officials here said Comdr. W. K. Earle, 13th Coast Guard District legal officer, and Lieut. Comdr. J. M. Austin, chief investigating officer, would conduct the hearing.

Scheduled to appear at the hearing were Warrant Officer Peter Lindquist, commander of the Coast Guard's Grays Harbor Station; Richard H. Miller, coxswain of the Invincible, and Roy C. Furfiord, Seattle, owner of the Barbara Lee.

The hull of the Barbara Lee washed toward shore yesterday north of Grays Harbor.

Court Grants Awards In Sea Deaths

PORTLAND, Ore., Dec. 24. — (U.P.I.) — Two widows whose husbands perished in attempt to rescue a Coast Guard vessel in 1960 were awarded a total of $31,600 in a Federal Court decision yesterday.

Federal Judge John F. Kilkenny awarded Onalve Bolam of Aberdeen, Wash., $16,900, and Mary Louise Sigurdson, also of Aberdeen, $9,700.

The judge also allowed each widow a $2,500 special award in compensation for loss of their husbands.

The men, Robert Bolam and Ted Sigurdson, were aboard the fishing boat Barbara Lee, which capsized and sank January 28, 1960, after twice trying to tow the Coast Guard vessel Invincible to safety during a storm off Westport, Wash.

The decision also awarded $9,700 and a $2,500 special award to Roy C. Furfiord of Westport, the Barbara Lee's owner.

a risky witness because of her history of frequent employment changes that could be used against her in court.

Each time I dug deeper into the case, the more convinced I was that we could not stand by and see justice denied because we didn't pursue tort damage recovery for two surviving spouses. The first issue was immediate and clear. If we prepared our claim on the grounds of maritime salvage, we would be severely limited in the amount that could be recovered. On the other hand, if we successfully maintained a tort action for wrongful death by proving negligent causation, there could be a substantial recovery for the surviving widows and their children. Charlie, O. B., Richard, and Frank supported my desire to pursue the tort theory despite the risks.

This would be a first admiralty-related case for both of us.

Roy Furfiord brought Harold Pernula, the only surviving *Barbara Lee* crew member, to one of our early meetings to discuss the case. Harold's testimony was absolutely critical to our case because Coast Guard personnel were unlikely to admit any mistakes.

Pernula's story was riveting. He had found himself in the water after a big wave capsized the *Barbara Lee* during the act of towing the *Invincible*. He was able to rescue an injured and semi-conscious Bolam by pushing a piece of floating plywood under him and swimming them both to the *Invincible*. Once there, Richard Miller, the coxswain/skipper of the *Invincible*, his engineer, and Pernula tried to lift Bolam on deck, but another wave pulled the unconscious Bolam back into the sea. Pernula finally got on board and as the more experienced seaman on hand, he suggested that with the radio down they try to get the *Invincible* to drift in the right direction to carry it away from the reef. He and Miller steered them away from the reef, anchored, and huddled in darkness awaiting the arrival of help.

It wasn't until late that night that the cutters *Yokona* and *McClain*, found the *Invincible* and towed it to Neah Bay.

Everyone agreed the primary objective should be to get an adequate recovery for the two widows and three children. The potential recovery for a wrongful death case would be many times greater than any possible salvage award. We proceeded on that premise and did not represent Harold Pernula throughout the preparation and trial of the wrongful death suit.

The trial was held in the Federal Court House in Portland, Oregon. The last night before the trial, the government made the *Invincible*'s skipper Richard Miller, available for our examination. We hastily arranged for a court reporter and met this key witness for the first time. He turned out to be an honest witness with a clear memory of the event. To our happy surprise his testimony supported key facts as we had hoped. This information was critical to our case and contradicted the deposed testimony of the Coast Guard station personnel.

The court room was packed, and the high-profile case attracted press coverage. I found myself very nervous and tense knowing that we now had a shot at making our case. I had asked the two widows to bring the children of the deceased to sit in the front row for Kilkenny to see, but he announced in a strong voice to remove them immediately! I realized we were in the presence of a take-charge judge who was going to follow all rules strictly.

We then proceeded to introduce our case briefly and to call as our first witness, Richard Miller, the skipper of the *Invincible*. The candor of this witness and the strength of his testimony were convincing. I could sense that Judge Kilkenny also thought this eyewitness was telling the truth about what he saw and heard. We called the Coast Guard station personnel who repeated their deposition testimony almost verbatim and in direct conflict with the eye-witness testimony of the skipper of the *Invincible*.

I had hoped that the obvious sincerity and grief of Mrs. Sigurdson would evoke a sympathetic response from the court. However, Mary Louise froze with fear when she took the stand and Kilkenny asked me to have her step down. I was shaken by this gap in our case. Without Mrs. Sigurdson, I knew that the other surviving widow, Onalue Bolam, would have to be our entire emotional case. Mrs. Bolam proceeded, however, to astonish me with the power and sincerity of her testimony. By the end of her story, I was crying, Judge Kilkenny was crying, and I don't think there was a dry eye in the house, with maybe the exception of Doug Fryer, counsel for the government. It was the most powerful conclusion for our case that I could have hoped for and had come from an unexpected source.

As I have explained, we had waived our clients' claims for salvage to enable us to focus the court solely on the issues of negligence and causation within the damage framework of a tort action. I was sure that Judge Kilkenny clearly saw what we were trying to prove and felt that he agreed with it. The trial was now over, and we had to wait for the judge to hand down his decision. We were completely convinced we had won the case.

When Judge Kilkenny provided his opinion on the case March 26, 1963, he did not find negligent causation by either the seafaring personnel or the station personnel of the Coast Guard. He saw what happened as "solely caused" by a freak ocean wave of nature and ruled against any recovery on the grounds of negligent causation. He did, however, close his opinion with the statement that the evidence presented by the facts brought out in the trial formed the basis for a salvage claim. He indicated he would consider reframing the issues under a new pre-trial order.

We were crushed by this decision. We had worked hard to find negligence and thought we had proved it. Nevertheless, I seized on the last sentence of Kilkenny's ruling and prepared a motion for a salvage award based on the evidence already presented. Before ruling on this newly framed claim, Judge Kilkenny asked Douglas Fryer, the principal counsel for the government, and me to meet him in his courtroom. He expressed his belief that this was a case that should be settled and instructed us to reach a fair and generous settlement. The court wrote and published a second opinion, dated December 20, 1963, in which Kilkenny described his reasoning for reframing the issues from the trial under the rules of salvage.

The final result of losing the negligence lawsuit was a generous settlement reached under the Court's second opinion confirming the critical heroic behavior of the private salvers. However, a claim on behalf of Harold Pernula was never filed nor included in the second pre-trial order. This was not the firm's legal duty because we were not representing him, but it was my moral duty, and the failure to get it done was mine and no one else's. Once I realized the oversight, it was too late to change the award. To this day, I deeply regret not seeing that Pernula filed a claim to collect from the government his share of the approved salvage award. Harold Preston would have been chagrined. This mistake of omission was a painful lesson that the devil resides in overlooked details. It was caused by my being overworked on too many matters at the same time.

BOOK THREE

Public Service

✦

CHAPTER 11

Home Rule Charter

The city of tomorrow can open doors to a better way of life, or it can strangle in its own haphazard growth.

—*"The Shape of Things to Come," Municipal League of Seattle and King County, 1956*

EVEN BEFORE GRADUATING from law school, Mary Lou and I talked about how we would perform our public service commitment to Bob. One of my early role models was Seattle lawyer John T. Rupp who had served two terms as president of the Municipal League of Seattle while I was in law school. After being hired by the Preston firm, my first civic step was to join the League, and I did so with the firm's backing.

The Municipal League had a long history and was a respected 2,500-member, voluntary, citizen organization dedicated to the improvement of local government. It had a small paid staff consisting of secretary C. A. "Tad" Crosser, a membership director, and a publications officer. Paul Siebert was the editor of the League's monthly *Municipal News* and was an engaging and energetic young leader about my age. I enjoyed every staff meeting and found it interesting that Preston law firm partners had long been active members. In fact, Harold Preston had once served as head of a successful City Charter effort for the City of Seattle. I signed up for the County Operations Committee and attended meetings faithfully and this led to my hiring as part-time legal counsel for the League as a supplement to my firm work.

At the time, King County's government structure was a hold-over from the early days of sparse population where the county was divided into three districts. Each district was ruled by a commissioner residing in that district. This produced a difficult situation for key county employees, like the county engineer, responding to regional issues but unable to act on anything other than directions from the county commissioner of each district. The inefficiency of this system, with its numerous separately elected county officers, seemed to cry out for change. This was Tad Crosser's field. He had studied local government, had been active in civic organizations for years. He pressed for restructuring.

The League's long-range goal was to have nonpartisan, efficient, and responsive local government. When I joined, it was engaged in planning for a local Home Rule Charter for the government of King County and the organization had sponsored a constitutional amendment to permit the creation of a charter. If approved by voters, the charter would replace the three-member Board of County Commissioners with a new form of government. The League board had approved a slate of candidates for the board of freeholders who would be tasked with preparing a charter for submission to the voters of King County. Since no other organization offered a slate of candidates, the League was the source of the ideas that went into the creation of the proposed charter.

When the freeholders were elected, they requested that the county prosecuting attorney, Charles O. Carroll, appoint me as a special assistant to help them draft the new charter. When the prosecutor's offer arrived, the law firm asked me to take a leave of absence to avoid conflicts of interest. The next night, after the children had gone to bed, Mary Lou and I probed this new opportunity. The chance to perform our first significant public service, to learn basic principles of municipal law, and to be paid for such work, seemed almost too good to be true.

However, events don't always work out as planned. In April 1952, I had no sooner settled behind a desk in the courthouse when opponents of charter reform brought a lawsuit challenging appointment of the new special assistant. The county auditor, Bobby Morris, refused to approve salary vouchers while the suit was pending, and we suddenly found ourselves without a salary of any kind. Opponents hoped their lawsuit would stop the drafting of the charter, but Mary Lou and I agreed that we should not quit.

"They're just trying to scare us away," said Mary Lou. "We can get along for a while, if the prosecutor will let you keep working."

The prosecutor was known to be a public opponent of charter reform, so he directed his chief civil deputy, Kenneth Smiles, to make this decision. Ken believed that drafting a constitutionally authorized charter for the county was a legitimate duty of the county attorney's office. He directed me to continue the work and vigorously defended the suit.

Less than a year after Mary Lou had settled our children into the freshly painted rooms of our house on Roanoke Street, she moved them back to Raging River. By renting out the Roanoke house, using our small savings, catching river trout for dinner, and holding down our expenses, she managed to keep all of us eating for more than four months while the salary lawsuit went through a trial in Superior Court and an appeal to the State Supreme Court. Ken won the Superior Court decision, but opponents knew that their appeal would continue to stop payment of our salary and believed that a few more months might wear us out.

One evening in July, while I was working at the cabin on a memorandum of legal issues facing the freeholders, Mary Lou leaned over my shoulder to remind me that we were down to our last twenty dollars.

"We're going to have to borrow from somebody, darling. Bills are piling up and the children have to eat."

Both sets of parents were strong supporters of our civic activity throughout their lives and would have been happy to help with a loan, but from the beginning of our marriage, we had agreed not to borrow from parents. So, I started looking elsewhere for a personal loan. Luckily, the Supreme Court announced its decision upholding my appointment just two days later before any loan was taken! Ken Smiles triumphantly marched me into the auditor's office and all back salary was paid on the spot. When I reported the good news to an ecstatic Mary Lou, we celebrated with a steak dinner. The net result of the lawsuit turned out to be an increase in our savings and a lasting aversion to trout for dinner.

When the charter was completed, I went back to work with the law firm and joined the public campaign for voter approval. Mary Lou and I met many people who cared deeply about their community during the charter reform effort. Al and Mary King of Kirkland, John "Jack" and Jean Henry of Bellevue, John and Libby Rupp of Seattle, and C. Carey and Mardie Donworth of Medina were among those who became lifelong friends. We listened to stories of early city reform campaigns told by Tad Crosser, who had become our civics teacher and good friend.

The freeholders showed courage in adopting a strong, nonpartisan, council-manager charter.

I learned a little about local politics during the campaign for voter approval of the charter. Money for reform was hard to find but flowed freely to maintain the status quo in the Court House. Both political parties used their treasuries to attack the charter with its proposed nonpartisan elections. County employees raised more than $20,000 at one meeting in the courthouse because they feared for their jobs under the proposed merit system for public employment and promotion and the council-manager system of decision making. The prosecuting attorney and the sheriff were leaders in the local Republican Party and became public spokesmen for the opposition. In one heated public debate, the prosecutor threw a copy of the charter across the podium at me!

The campaign tactics of charter opponents often strayed from substantive issues. An airplane dropped leaflets over the city asking, "Is this Moscow or Seattle?" When I appeared at public meetings, the same deputy sheriffs in civilian clothing were always there to laugh loudly at the wrong times and lead the applause for my opponent.

The total raised to pass the proposed charter ballot measure was less than $6,000 and in the general election of November 1952, it was defeated by more than a two-to-one margin. The loss was very disappointing, but young reformers do not stay discouraged for very long.

During evening chats after the kids were in bed, Mary Lou wondered whether action on public needs would really result from simply reorganizing the internal structure of county government. She was skeptical of the value of restructuring for its own sake. She reminded me of Tad Crosser's story about Kansas City where similar city-manager reform resulted in replacing a national model with one where corruption became commonplace.

During the charter campaign, I crisscrossed the county and saw that some of the most serious public problems were being caused by sprawling urban development outside of Seattle. Polluted waters crossed the boundaries between cities and county and seemed to cry out for a regional solution. Commercial warehouses and factories were discharging untreated industrial waste into a Green-Duwamish River which ran through the county and several cities. In new residential subdivisions, septic tanks leaked into creeks and drainage ditches. If sewers were built, the effluent from a sewage treatment plant would discharge into the nearest lake or stream. The combined sanitary and storm sewer system of the City of Seattle was discharging large quantities of raw sewage into Elliot Bay every day and large amounts into Lake Washington on rainy days. The city of Renton, The Boeing Company, and the Bryn Mawr Sewer District were each operating their own sewage treatment plants. From Lake Ridge Sewer District Chairman Sam Kenney's house in unincorporated Bryn Mawr, you could see three different treatment plants pouring treated effluent into the south end of Lake Washington.

During the charter campaign, I also saw hundreds of acres of deep black, loam, farmland being covered by pavement and buildings. Fully developed suburban areas were without any public bus service.

Mary Lou saw open space, clean water, and bus service as the kind of public needs people can understand and work for. "Why don't you give a talk to the Municipal League about your metropolitan planning and service ideas," she suggested. "Your charter friends might like a new crusade to work for."

THE "SHAPE" REPORTS

In November of 1953, I gave a prepared speech to a joint meeting of Municipal League committees. My father Floyd, Mary Lou and her father Roy, her uncle Pierce Haight, League President Ben Ehrlichman, and friends who had worked on the county charter campaign attended. They climbed a well-worn stairway to a room in the old YMCA Annex to hear me advocate area-wide performance of several public services.

The speech was well received and a few weeks later the League created a special committee to study the feasibility of metropolitan government. Men and women who would become lifelong allies in our battles for regional improvements joined the new Municipal League Metropolitan Problems Committee. In a sign of 1950s culture, this committee consisted of 52 men and three women.

Over the next two years this league committee published two studies that attracted attention. The first was called "The Shape We're In" and outlined the causes and effects of problems like water pollution and traffic congestion which were spreading across the Seattle metropolitan area. The second report, called "The Shape of Things to Come," proposed a new metropolitan government to provide area-wide action on sewage disposal, public transportation, and comprehensive planning. The "Shape" reports and the new Lake Washington pollution findings of higher concentrations of phosphorus and algae due to sewage in the lake by UW Professor W. T. Edmondson attracted publicity.

Earlier, in 1952, our Montlake precinct neighbors had elected me a delegate to the Republican County Convention pledged to Eisenhower. This activity in the Republican Party had increased my acquaintance among business and community leaders. Now, with this new public attention, a few downtown businessmen suggested I run for mayor. Mary Lou and I did some serious soul-searching about the nature of our commitment to community service. She was concerned that a career in public office would disrupt a normal life for our children. She urged me to pursue our pledge to Bob in ways that would be more compatible with family goals.

I believed that restoring and conserving water resources, preserving parklands, farms, and forests, and helping the disadvantaged were the kind of activities my brother Bob would have wanted us to pursue. However, it was becoming clear that significant progress toward any of these goals would take sustained effort over a long time. A mayor's tenure is uncertain. Each day the newspaper headlines reminded us that political rivalries, crime, and other crisis issues constantly demand the Mayor's attention and could distract us from the long-term goals we wanted to pursue. For these reasons, I declined the invitation to run for mayor and later joined a group working for the nomination and election of Gordon Clinton, an able and unselfish young lawyer who became an excellent progressive mayor. The strategy of working for the election of good citizens who would support our goals for the metropolitan community became a pattern. If our candidate lost, we offered to help the winner.

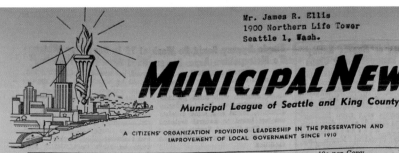

Mr. James R. Ellis
1900 Northern Life Tower
Seattle 1, Wash.

MUNICIPAL NEWS

Municipal League of Seattle and King County

A CITIZENS' ORGANIZATION PROVIDING LEADERSHIP IN THE PRESERVATION AND
IMPROVEMENT OF LOCAL GOVERNMENT SINCE 1910

| Vol. XLV No. 18 | SATURDAY, APRIL 30, 1955 | 10c per Copy | Page 69 |

Metropolitan Seattle

The Shape We're In-What To Do About It!

In our sprawling metropolitan area everyday problems of living have become vastly complicated and costly. Young people and middle-income families are leaving Seattle for the suburbs by the tens of thousands. Traffic and transportation tie-ups already threaten to strangle the development of our area. More than 100 separate special districts and municipalities wield governmental powers within King County at the present time and this number is growing every year.

These are the causes of this malady of "suburbanitis":

1. A demand for larger living space.

2. An increasing use of private transportation.

3. An increasing demand for a high standard of urban services even in low-density population areas.

4. A demand for modern industrial plant locations of adequate size and with proper facilities and a lack of space therefore inside the city.

5. An increasing exodus from existing built-up city areas caused by obsolescence of older buildings and the undesirability of compact platting.

6. A demand for major city improvements of benefit beyond the city boundaries, particularly in costly express highways.

7. An increasing economic interdependence of all parts of the area as the local economy grows and becomes more complex.

Growth Not New, But——
The health of thousands of families
(Continued on third page)

League Committee's General Conclusion

"The City of Seattle and its surrounding area is rapidly becoming a single metropolitan community. The area is physically, socially and economically integrated. The committee recommends that a more unified government be established for this metropolitan area."

Background to League's Metropolitan Area Study

This study of Metropolitan Seattle and its problems was launched in November, 1953, at a joint meeting of League's City Planning, County Planning, City Budget and Finance, City Utilties and Services, and the County Budget committees. At that meeting, Attorney James R. Ellis set forth the functional and governmental problems plaguing the Seattle metropolitan area.

As a result of Ellis' speech the Board of Trustees formed the **Metropolitan Problems Committee**—a specially selected group of men from other committees—to explore the problems in detail.

To analyze the problems of Metropolitan Seattle the committee was **divided into subcommittees.** Each subcommittee investigated a particular part of the over-all problem. For example, one subcommittee studied water supply and sewage disposal, another police and fire protection, etc.

(Continued on fourth page)

To solve the multiplicity of problems which plague our metropolitan area the League committee recommended "a more unified government be established." While there are at least seven possible forms which such a government could take, the League committee did not explore these alternatives in detail. Although the League recommends greater governmental integration, no attempt has been made to develop this conclusion into a detailed plan. That will be the subject of another report.

Here are the seven possible forms of government:

1. Direct annexation of substantially all of the metropolitan area by the City of Seattle.

2. **Performance of metropolitan functions and services** by the City of Seattle throughout the metropolitan area with only limited direct annexation.

3. Creation of a series of **metropolitan special districts** to handle certain problems common to the metropolitan area.

4. Creation of a **single metropolitan government** charged with the duty of handling common problems within the area while leaving local functions to the individual cities and towns.

5. **Consolidation of the city and county governments** within the metropolitan area and the performance of all governmental functions within that area by the consolidated government.

6. **Performance of a limited number of functions** by combined city-
(Continued on second page)

In the early 1950s, we did not yet have a clear concept of all our civic goals. Only a rough outline of the most obvious ideas was included in the YMCA speech. However, as circumstances changed and new opportunities arose, these goals became clearer. It was increasingly apparent that we should frame a bigger picture where projects close to our hearts could complement each other and could also serve to strengthen the fabric of community. We hoped to see:

- The natural beauty of the Puget Sound region preserved.
- Cities of manageable size separated by lakes, farms, forest lands, and parks.
- Patterns of development that conserved open land, encouraged affordable housing, and supported transit use.
- Safer roads, better transit service, and more pedestrian and bicycle paths.
- Water bodies cleaned up and managed as a renewable resource.
- A smorgasbord of recreational and cultural facilities serving a cosmopolitan population.
- Local governments united to tackle those tasks which were regional in nature.

We saw a balanced transportation system as one of the most difficult and basic needs if cities were to preserve air quality and open space, remain socially cohesive, and be economically competitive. Balance meant facilities to move cars, trucks, transit vehicles, bicycles, and pedestrians. In the Seattle metropolitan area, transit/pedestrian/bicycle facilities were becoming the underdeveloped parts of a balanced system.

I believed that a two-level system of metropolitan government would better help us reach our environmental and social goals. In a two-level system, a local level (usually a city) performs general government functions, and a second level (some form of metropolitan government) performs those special functions which cross city boundaries and require area wide funding. A two-level system would give public officials the tools they needed to protect the natural environment, relieve congestion, and provide the public services needed for an urban population which was rapidly growing and changing. I also hoped to keep purely local functions of government as close as possible to the people governed so they could better respond to community concerns.

Gradually, Mary Lou's thinking about human needs and my desire to create better structural methods were molded by the creative work of other co-authors and took shape as a series of action programs and projects. Early co-authors came primarily from the Municipal League of Seattle and King County, and the Seattle League of Women Voters. They included Albert A. King, Carey Donworth, Madeline Lemere, Dorothy Block, Robert Beach, Ray Ogden, Jr., Alec Bayless, Paul Seibert, Jack Henry, Dan Evans, Slade Gorton, Richard Riddell, Joel and Frank Pritchard, David Sprague, Lewis Johnson, and John Blankenship. Many of these reformers were young lawyers who participated with us in later projects.

One emerging theme of this work was the belief that effective responses to urban problems required area-wide planning and that our effort as citizens could ignite that response. Following Mary Lou's intuitive hunches, we concentrated on pursuing special projects that were consistent with our commitment to family.

✓

CHAPTER 12

Citizens Save Lake Washington

. . . Here, we watch a welcome turning point in the story of our lakes and rivers and inland sea. Here, we mark some proof that urban man can live and work in a beautiful land without destroying beauty.

—*Jim Ellis, dedication speech at West Point Treatment Plant, July 20, 1966*

THE METROPOLITAN SEATTLE population had surged to over 900,000 by 1955. Communities like Bellevue and Mercer Island were expanding around Lake Washington. Lake Washington is a large and deep lowland lake stretching 22 miles from Bothell to Renton. Before 1916, all water came into the lake from a low-elevation drainage basin. The only outflow was the Black River at the south end of the lake. In 1916, the lake level was permanently lowered almost ten feet to permit the operation of a ship canal and locks to Puget Sound. The Cedar River was concurrently diverted into Lake Washington upstream from its former junction with the Black River. This brought a sufficient flow of water from the Cascade Mountains into the lake to permit the operation of the Hiram Chittenden Locks. Thereafter, about two years were required for the volume of water in the lake to be replaced by fresh water from its river sources.

In the 1950's, dozens of combined sanitary-storm sewer outfalls, thousands of septic tanks, and ten sewage treatment plants serving more than twenty cities, towns, and districts were placing this vital, local resource at risk. The population growth, urban development, and effluents from ten treatment plants around Lake Washington all steadily increased and poured more phosphorus into the lake. This phosphorus nourished a heavy growth of algae which fouled swimming beaches and depleted dissolved oxygen in deep water. Awareness was growing among the average citizenry that something needed to be done to prevent their lake from becoming seriously polluted.

Professor Robert O. Sylvester of the University of Washington had reported in 1952 that some Lake Washington bathing beaches were contaminated by bacteria from sewage and algae from treatment plant effluent. In 1956, Professor W.T. Edmondson and his colleagues at the University of Washington identified the nutrients in sewage as the primary cause of higher concentrations of phosphorus and algae in the lake. Studies revealed that a new form of blue-green algae, *Oscillatoria rubescens*, was gradually making the water murky and they warned that "nuisance conditions" would follow in a few years.

The "Shape" reports called for a federated system of local governments to manage area-wide problems like water pollution. However, a new state law would be required to create the legal machinery necessary to make the federation possible.

JACK HENRY

I first met commercial banker John F. "Jack" Henry sometime in the early 1950s at a League committee meeting. Jack was a vice president at Pacific National Bank, which later became part of Wells Fargo Bank. He and his wife Jean had built a home in the newly platted area of Vue Crest near Old Bellevue where Jack also served as a commissioner of the Bellevue Sewer District. We found a shared interests in hands-on house building and Northwest Native American culture.

Jack was committed to protecting the natural Northwest environment. When Jack heard of my legal work for Bryn Mawr-Lake Ridge Sewer District, he asked the Bellevue Sewer District attorney, Pearce Haight, to invite me to an evening meeting of the Bellevue Commissioners to discuss financing the expansion of their overloaded Meydenbauer Bay sewage treatment plant. Henry knew that the growing Bellevue area could not continue to discharge the effluent from its treatment plant into tiny Meydenbauer Bay. The primitive Bellevue Treatment Plant looked like a leaky barrel and its outfall was only a few hundred feet from the intake of the Bellevue Water District's domestic water supply. When concerns were raised over the long-term effects of putting more treated sewage effluent into Lake Washington, Henry and his fellow commissioners began looking for alternatives. Jack became an early advocate for taking the sewage from all eastside cities and districts out of the lake and transporting it around the south end for treatment and disposal in Puget Sound. Bellevue Sewer District formally asked their engineers to assess the feasibility of this idea.

As the negative effects of treated effluent on lake water became better known, Jack became a pied piper for his "eastside trunk" sewer concept. He and fellow commissioners met with state officials. They explored the possible interest of other districts in joining to plan such a project. His idea for a voluntary joint contract to build the common facilities was something that could have been implemented without new state legislation. However, Jack ran into a stone wall when his engineers reported back that all the homes and businesses then served by the eastside cities and sewer districts, taken together, were not sufficient to pay the interest on revenue bonds needed to finance such a huge undertaking.

In 1955, a small group of Municipal League members met informally to hammer out possible legislation. We gathered around our family kitchen table, which I referred to as Mary Lou's kitchen table. This group included Albert A. King, Carey Donworth, Alec Bayless, Raymond Ogden, Jr., and Robert Beach. Occasionally others would join us. We called ourselves the "Kitchen Group" and this name stuck. Al King brought his typewriter to these evening sessions. I brought a copy of the Municipality of Metropolitan Toronto Act which had been enacted by the province of Ontario, Canada, in 1953 to address a similar problem. Carey Donworth and Bob Beach brought the perspectives of a small city and a large sewer district. Donworth was a councilman of the small City of Medina and Beach was a commissioner of the large Lake City Sewer District. Mary Lou contributed coffee, cookies, encouragement, and an uncharacteristically quiet house.

The federation idea appealed to us as a means of pulling twenty different districts and cities together, and the Toronto legislation formed a basis for the first several drafts during a two-year effort to write a bill for the Washington legislature. However, adapting Toronto to Seattle was challenging. Canada had a parliamentary system with few restraints by public votes. Washington State, on the other hand, had a Jacksonian tradition of public "brakes" on its elected representative initiatives and referendums, in addition to constitutional limits on taxes, and a history of special districts for special purposes, from schools to utilities to ports.

When Gordon Clinton was elected mayor of Seattle in 1956, he asked me to chair a citizen's advisory committee, the City-County Committee (Metropolitan Problems Advisory Committee), to study and make recommendations on the full range of Seattle-King County urban growth problems. The King County Commissioners joined Mayor Clinton in appointing the forty-eight members of this committee. It was broadly representative with a core of informed Municipal League members, League of Women Voters activists, and all of the Kitchen Group. This was one of a series of breakthroughs for women in Seattle. Only five of the forty-eight members of the committee were women, but they became an important part of the clean lake movement. Ruth Itner of the UW Bureau of Governmental Research served as the Secretary of the Committee and as a resource for the members. The Committee held the meetings at the Bureau. Ruth became a life-long activist for government reform and in later years was instrumental in developing the Iron Goat Trail at historic Stevens Pass.

The challenge for the City-County Committee was to find a way for many different cities and special districts to agree upon a common course of action. Each sewer system was separately owned and operated. Private engineering firms protected the territory of their contracts. There were different public and private bus systems. Most local agencies jealously watched over their planning territories. Even when they were next door neighbors, their separate plans didn't always mesh.

An effort by Bellevue's Jack Henry to get voluntary cooperation among Eastside sewer districts had failed to produce agreement. However, this effort helped convince Governor Langley to join Seattle mayor Clinton and the King

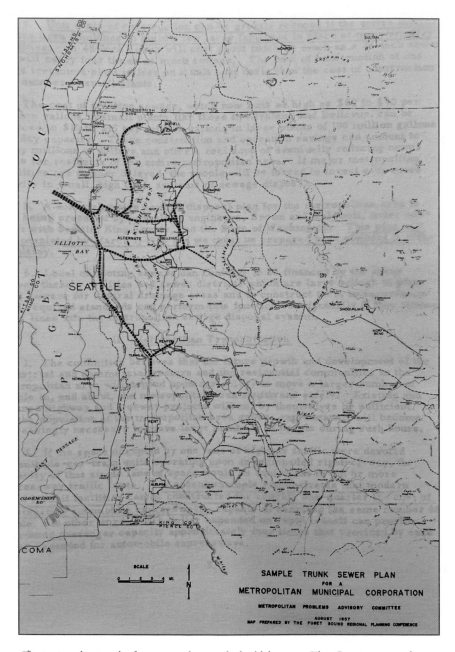

The proposed network of sewer trunks stretched widely across King County, east and west.

County Commissioners in hiring an independent outside engineering firm, Brown & Caldwell, to analyze Henry's Eastside Interceptor concept among other possibilities for an area-wide sewage disposal system.

After carefully reviewing structural alternatives, the City-County Committee recommended that a special, multi-purpose federated metropolitan council be authorized by state statute to perform one or more of six metropolitan area-wide functions. The six functions were water pollution abatement, water supply, public transportation, garbage disposal, parks and parkways, and comprehensive planning. The council was named Metro.

One of Metro's functions would be the construction and operation of metropolitan interceptor sewers and sewage treatment plants. To ensure that no sewage would enter the lake, each city or district would be required to connect its local sewers to the metropolitan interceptor system for transport, treatment, and disposal. Each facility would remain in city or sewer district ownership and control.

The keys to reaching committee agreement on recommended forms of special purpose legislation proved to be dividing the functions between regional interception and treatment facilities (wholesale), and local collection facilities (retail). This was coupled with management of the new Metropolitan Municipal Corporation by a federated council of elected local officials whose powers were limited to specific regional functions. Seattle City Council members became supportive when they saw that the governing council of the new regional agency would be composed of elected city and county officials, including of course, Seattle's own mayor and members of its council. The Kitchen Group draft became the City-County Committee recommendation.

In-depth newspaper reporting of the Lake Washington pollution problem and accurate reporting of the proposed federated council solution helped move Seattle public opinion behind the new legislation. A "Metro Bill" was introduced in the 1957 legislative session by two law school classmates who had been elected to the State Senate. The sponsors were State Senators Bob Greive (D) and Bill Goodloe (R). First-term representative (later governor) Daniel J. Evans was the floor leader in the House. Former Representative Floyd Miller (later mayor) was the City of Seattle lobbyist. House Speaker John O'Brien pushed the bill through a hostile committee chairman and pulled it out of Rules. Representative Ed Munro (later county commissioner) cast the deciding House vote and Governor Al Rosellini signed the bill into law. All of these leaders were from King County.

This legislation was the first of its kind in the state of Washington and many experienced observers were surprised when, after lengthy debate, the bill was actually passed by the Senate. When the bill reached its assigned committee in the House, the chairman from Snohomish County refused to permit action. A substantial number of Snohomish County residents had developed a fear of Seattle domination which could not be overcome within the urgent timeline for action on Lake Washington. Sewers from much of the area were later connected by contract, and fears were mitigated by the example of Metro performance.

Since the legislative session was nearing adjournment, Floyd Miller and I appealed for help from Speaker of the House John O'Brien of Seattle. O'Brien called the foot-dragging committee chairman out of a meeting into the hall and said in effect that no bill from this committee would be taken up by the Rules Committee unless the committee chairman took action immediately to release his hold on the Metro Bill. We then successfully circulated committee members, got the signatures needed for a "do-pass" committee motion, and the chairman formally transmitted this to Rules. O'Brien made sure the Metro Bill moved promptly through Rules to the floor.

On the last day of the 1957 Session, with floor leadership from Dan Evans, O'Brien ordered a roll call vote. A constitutional majority of "yes" votes—a majority of all House members, not just a majority of those voting on the bill—was needed for passage. A new electronic vote counter projected the voting on a screen for all to see. After several hair-raising minutes of back-and-forth vote switching, the total "yes" votes settled at one short. Seattle Republican representative Zeke Clark, thinking that the "no" votes were going to defeat the Metro Bill, switched from "yes" to "no" so he would be in a position to move for reconsideration. Evans saw this and frantically persuaded Zeke to switch back to "yes" while the machine was still open. In a matter of seconds, the stage was set for Seattle Democrat Ed Munro's dramatic return to the floor to cast the last vote needed for a constitutional majority. O'Brien held the counter open until Ed Munro came marching down the aisle to his desk and cast what became the deciding vote. The speaker immediately slammed the counter closed and declared the bill passed. It was a very close call for Lake Washington.

During this sometimes-stormy legislative process, supporters of the Metro Bill had been forced to accept an amendment requiring that the formation election for Metro obtain a majority "yes" vote from both the citizens residing inside Seattle *and* from those living outside Seattle, with the votes in each area to be counted separately.

Meanwhile back home, the Bellevue Sewer District Commissioners had persuaded the State to join the City of Seattle and King County in hiring the engineering firm Brown & Caldwell of San Francisco to prepare a feasibility study for a specific system of pipes and pumping stations.

This system could intercept all sewage going into the lake and transport it for treatment and disposal in Puget Sound. Completed in early 1958, the resulting six-hundred-page *Brown & Caldwell Report* recommended a variation of Jack Henry's Eastside Trunk sewer concept and confirmed that the interception and treatment of the sewage effluent then going into Lake Washington was feasible under the following condition: It must be funded by an *area-wide* sewer service charge of $2.50 per month for each single-family residence served by a sewer line and an equivalent amount for commercial users. A general tax on property would *not* be required to support the Metro revenue bond financing.

The recommended plan proposed construction, in stages, of a system of large trunk sewers which would intercept twenty-one different local systems and deliver the sewage to large treatment plants for ultimate disposal in salt water. This core plan would be sized to accept future connections from towns and districts in the Sammamish and Green River Valleys. Brown & Caldwell also concluded that a new "Metro Municipality," or something like it, should be created to manage construction and operation of the recommended system.

Metro activists were eager to put their hard-won state legislation to work. With encouragement from Mayor Clinton, a ballot proposal was recommended by the City-County Citizens Committee. A few months later the special election preparations were underway in several cities. They

Municipal News

THE MUNICIPAL LEAGUE OF SEATTLE AND KING COUNTY

A NON-PARTISAN, FORCE OF 5000 CONSTRUCTIVE CITIZENS
WORKING WITH YOU FOR A BETTER LOCAL GOVERNMENT

Vol. XLVII, No. 26   SATURDAY, NOVEMBER 30, 1957   25c per Copy   Page 153

GIGANTIC SEWER PROGRAM IS UNVEILED

Engineers make Lake Washington sewer plan for year 2030. 26 treatment plants cut to 2. No sewage in lake permitted

With a degree of awe, recently we heard about an ambitious plan for the most suitable and economical disposal of sewage in our metropolitan area up to the distant year *2030 A.D.* It would involve (1) diminishing of the present 26 treatment plants to one or two to which all the sewage from this huge drainage basin would be conveyed, and (2) the total elimiation from Lake Washington of raw sewage and effluent from treatment plants in order to save that beautiful body of water.

1895 Plans Was Success

The success of this prodigious future plan may be anticipated from the success of the little-known 1895 sewage plan prepared for the City of Seattle by an engineer named Williams from which came the huge North Trunk sewer which still is and will be the back-bone of the city's sewage system. Mr. Williams cannot be held responsible for the Ravenna cave-in.

The above information recently was brought to the League's Metropolitan Problems Committee, Carey Donworth, chairman, by Harold Miller, project engineer for Brown and Caldwell. This San Francisco firm of consulting engineers has been employed by the city, county and state to make a survey of the Lake Washington Drainage area and lay out a plan for its future development. Miller says that the cost estimates will be disclosed in January and the complete report will be issued in March.

High-lights of Progress Report

Here were the high-lights of Miller's report not only to the League committee but also to the Metropolitan Problems Advisory Committee and several other groups:

Boundary of area — Includes 575 square miles (over five times Seattle's area) of which 350 are in the Greater Lake Washington Basin and 145 square miles in the Green-Duwamish Basin.

Population Forecast—

Year	Pop. Est.
1957	800,000
1980	1,257,000
2030	2,238,000

Present Sewer System — Only 90 of 575 square miles in area are sewered. When Alki and Lake City Plants are completed, two-thirds of 75 million gallons daily will be treated in 26 treatment plants. Thirty per cent of 800,000 population is not served by public sewers. Thousands use septic tanks. By 2030, total will increase to 265 million gallons per day.

*Types of Treatment—Primary Treatment—*solids are settled out and put into digestor where gas is carried off and inert sludge remains. Effluent water is chlorinated. *Secondard treatment—*The former plus effluent subjected to biological treatment in filters.

Condition of Lake Washington—No raw sewage or effluent from a treatment plant should go into Lake Washington. Two hundred seventy thousand pounds of phosphorus a year from treatment plants and rivers are nourishing algae whose successive crops will eventually spoil Lake Washington. Only 4 per cent of sewage disposal into Lake Washington at present comes from Seattle's sewer system. In the city there are 32 storm water overflows which discharge into lake only in rainy weather.

Salt Water Intrusion into Lake — Increasing intrusion of salt water into Lake Washington prevents turn-over in lake water, tending to make it septic from decaying matter. This might be overcome by locating large sewage treatment plant above locks, using its effluent to operate locks. This would cost $7 or $8 million more.

Possible Treatment Plant Sites—

1. Convey all sewage in Lake Washington and Green-Duwamish Basins to one huge sewage treatment plant at *West Point* at the outfall of the North Trunk sewer.

2. Sewage from Bothell, Lake City and other northern areas would go to *West Point Plant* while sewage from southern concentration points would go to new plant near *Renton* which would discharge effluent into Duwamish.

3. *Three Plants—*West Point, Harbor Island and Renton.

Several other alternatives were proposed by Miller.

requested that 'Metro' be established with power to perform the functions of sewage disposal, public transportation, and comprehensive planning for a large area of King and Southern Snohomish Counties.

After a series of public hearings, the King County Commissioners deleted the Snohomish area from the proposal. Snohomish County residents and officials, fearing Seattle, had strongly protested their inclusion. South King County residents also protested, but their able county commissioner, William Moshier, believed the people of his district should not be left out of a metropolitan program he saw as necessary for their future development.

An election was called for March 1958.

By the summer of 1957, these exciting legislative and engineering events seemed to Mary Lou and me like a promising beginning for our public service goal of projects to make life better for people. If only the voters would approve the new "Metro" government.

When the King County charter had been defeated by the voters five years earlier, Mary Lou and I had spent many evenings rehashing the battle. It was her strong belief that we hadn't done enough of what she called 'neighboring.' "You guys were this tiny band of faithful. Where were all the people who should have been helping?" she asked, "Where were all the women? And you were so darn serious. If you were having any fun nobody could see it." She recalled what a big thing neighboring had been in Alaska. "Sourdough" dances in winter and midnight baseball games in summer were ways people could have fun while getting to know each other.

Earlier, I had watched the basics of neighboring in action in 1952 alongside Tony Kusak, owner of Kusak Cut Glass Works in Rainier Valley. Tony and his wife Neva lived across the street from us in Montlake. He had led our Montlake neighbors to elect me a precinct delegate for Eisenhower at the Republican County Convention. From the County Charter defeat, I had learned that neighboring was even more important when seeking to unite people of *different* neighborhoods behind a regional governmental reform. With new suburban developments springing up everywhere, more people had to learn to know new neighbors. They also had to reach across boundaries and join other neighborhoods in thinking about the impacts of growing pollution and congestion in their larger urban community.

The Municipal League

MUNICIPAL LEAGUE
of seattle and king county
LYON BUILDING, SEATTLE 4, WASHINGTON, MAin 8333

BECAUSE MARY LOU'S AND MY involvement in the League was anchored by our pledge to perform civic work, I participated as a League committee member more than most others. That ultimately led to my serving as president of the Municipal League. John Rupp and Ben Ehrlichman had been role models of mine in law school. I had read about John's work as president of the League and had seen how he and the League had functioned to influence action on local public issues. John and I became good friends in the course of our working together. He had a great sense of humor and became a strong supporter of my later civic activities and projects.

I attribute much of my rise within the League to Ben Ehrlichman, a leading businessman and a past-president of the League. When Gordon Clinton appointed me to chair his Metropolitan Problems Advisory Committee. Ben hosted a luncheon at the Rainier Club to introduce Gordon and me to a sizable group of downtown business leaders, giving us a glowing introduction and an opportunity to explain the Metro Plan to the business community and the reasons why we believed that Metro had the potential for leading the cleanup of Lake Washington. We also explained how Metro could manage other important activities necessary to the proper growth of the city and that it could be the solution of many of Seattle's area-wide problems. Following the luncheon, we received ongoing business support which helped create Metro in the September 1958 election.

Ben was also important in introducing me to the National Municipal League. He encouraged me to attend their annual National Conference on Government meetings. I began going and found them informative and exciting. The meetings also connected me with people in other parts of the country involved in civic reform work.

During my Municipal League leadership, I became absorbed in strengthening the League as a force in local affairs. The League had a long and honorable history as a civic reformer, but its membership had hovered between 2,000 to 3,000 people. I believed it was important to grow our membership base to 4,000 or 5,000 members. Once I became president, I mounted a campaign to increase the League's membership to 5,000. This goal was actually achieved for a two-year period when there was great public interest in the successful campaigns creating Metro to clean up Lake Washington, and later during in what would be come Forward Thrust efforts to extend area-wide efforts to other functions. Unfortunately, League membership began to fall back once the efforts were authorized.

The process of getting lots of people involved became a central part of our civic work. Both Mary Lou and I came to believe that wide participation was more than half the battle in local public elections. This was intuitive for most old hands, but we learned the basics of citizen action through trial and error.

After the 1957 legislative victory in Olympia, I asked Mary Lou how she would win the upcoming Metro election.

"I'd have more block parties and coffee hours," she answered. "I'd put more people on campaign committees, hold more meetings in homes, and get more speakers and doorbellers out. Focus more on children in your ads. Most of all, let more women take charge of organizing these things. Madeline Lemere, Dorothy Block, and Fam Bayless would be great."

A substantial grass roots campaign was organized in the winter of 1957–58. Hundreds of men, women, and children actively participated. Neighboring was working and a campaign budget of $15,000 was fully subscribed to by business firms. The measure was endorsed by most newspapers and civic organizations.

> *I'd have more block parties and coffee hours.*
>
> — Mary Lou Ellis

However, Campaign Chairman Richard Riddell and I wrongly assumed that the health and safety reasons for cleaning up sewage were compelling and obvious. Most of our campaign brochure was devoted to detailed descriptions of how the Metro Act and the ballot proposal would operate. Few readers got past the first page. Our advertising had little emotional appeal. On the other side, anti-Metro campaigners stirred emotional taxpayer suspicions about government and deep rural-city biases surfaced. They published exaggerated cartoons portraying Metro as a "Seattle Octopus" swallowing up helpless farmers, small towns, and taxpayers.

On March 11, 1958, when the votes were counted, a majority of the suburban-rural electorate said "no." Election returns inside the City of Seattle were 79,365 "yes" and 55,614 "no." For the area outside Seattle the vote was 22,793 "yes" and 29,352 "no." Although an overall majority of voters were in favor of Metro, the separate majorities required by the new Metro Act did us in. Mary Lou and I had lost our second election.

The March election was a stunning defeat. The next morning a gloomy postmortem breakfast meeting was attended by a subdued, small core of the faithful. Seattle mayor Gordon Clinton observed that many people believed cleaning up the lake was the most critical need, and that transit and planning reforms could be deferred. He also believed some castside areas had been persuaded to vote against the March ballot measure because it seemed unfair to them to be asked to pay for their own sewage treatment plants and *also* pay for the Metro System which would replace them. He suggested that these "white elephant" facilities be purchased by Metro along with any other existing facilities which would be needed for the Metro System. The cost of purchasing and operating these facilities could be paid as part of the cost of the proposed metropolitan sewer system. Temporarily operating these small treatment plants could provide job continuity for existing suburban employees until new job opportunities were created in the large Metro treatment facilities.

Those present responded with enthusiasm to Clinton's idea for a "sewers only" election and a buy-out of existing "white elephant" sewage disposal facilities. The new ballot measure would be sufficiently different from the March proposal to justify going back to voters at an early date.

That evening, when I got home and told Mary Lou about Gordon's idea, her face lit up. "That's a terrific idea! Gordon understands the power of giving." Then after a pause, "Do you think he would go one more step and let the suburban mayors make that announcement? It would be a big thing for them." I realized this would be a great tactic but said, "I don't know, Honey. That's asking Clinton to do a lot. Last week he was accused by *The Argus* of being a weak mayor. Now he has a chance to show strong leadership." *The Argus* was an independent weekly newspaper published in Seattle and circulated primarily in the downtown business community. Mary Lou countered, "It could make a Metro-fan out of Byron Baggaley." Baggaley was then the mayor of Kirkland and had co-chaired the anti-Metro campaign in the March election.

The following day, at a private meeting in the mayor's office, I made a gutsy suggestion, "Gordon, *Mary Lou* thinks you should let the suburban mayors make this purchase proposal, and then agree to it on behalf of the City." He swung slowly around in his swivel chair, and I heard him mutter, "Weak mayor." Then, as he turned back and looked at me, he said, "But she's

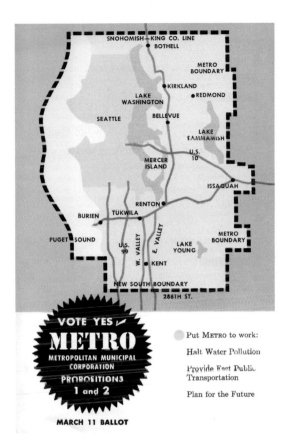

*Early Metro map promoting transit and water
projects in advance of the March 1958 vote.*

right, isn't she?" I nodded my agreement and Gordon called Council President
David Levine. They quickly agreed they could get the approval of the City
Council if such a proposal came from the suburban mayors.

David Levine was president of the Jewelers Union and a very bright City
Council member. He had a gift of using few words and caustic humor. In
those days, most differences were thrashed out in closed meetings before
taking council action. If he couldn't get a colleague to agree with him, Dave
would often say "Alright let's go outside," meaning in front of the press. This
practice usually brought unanimous votes.

Jack Henry and I were asked to inform the Eastside mayors. They promptly called reporters to attend a public announcement of their request for purchase. *The Seattle Times* reported this (with picture) and included at the end of their story a brief favorable response from Mayor Clinton and Council President Levine.

At the next Seattle City Council meeting, Levine asked me to brief the members. We met in a conference room behind the public Council Chamber where I described the effects of the new Metro Act and the "sewers only" ballot compromise. The new Metro Council would have the ability to compel local sewer systems to connect to new interceptors and would effectively ensure that sewage effluent from the growing suburban population would no longer be discharged into the lake. I emphasized that the City of Seattle contained a large majority of the population and under the new Metro Act would have a majority of votes on the new Metro Council.

Levine gave a characteristic terse summary for his colleagues that emphasized it wouldn't do any good to stop putting sewage in one side of the lake if the other side keeps dumping. Metro will take both sides out.

There were no questions. Everyone filed through the door into the public chamber and took their chairs. The "yes" vote was unanimous.

A short time later, Kirkland mayor Byron Baggaley was pictured on the front page of the *Eastside Journal* saying he would co-chair a new committee to clean up the lake right this time.

Following their election defeat in March, the true believers had never really thought of giving up. Our small, core group of eight pushed on: Gordon Clinton, Jack Henry, Bryon Baggaley, Madeline Lemere, Dorothy Block, Clayton Wangeman, and Mary Lou Ellis.

After all, a majority of the people who voted had approved of the idea and there were clear signs of where our strengths and weaknesses lay. There was a consensus among activists, politicians, and media people that the controversial transit and planning functions, which required general tax support, should not be included in the new ballot measure. The campaign committee was reinforced by adding influential women and doctors, the County Medical Association became a formal supporter, and Dr. Clayton Wangeman was appointed to chair the new campaign committee. Efforts were focused on the urgent issue of water pollution abatement financed by a monthly sewer service charge, and we went back to the drawing board to develop a new election measure which could pass muster in the suburbs.

Madeline Lemere was a determined member of the League of Women Voters. She was smart, enthusiastic, and willing to devote seemingly endless hours to her passion for Metro. She had been on the City-County Metropolitan Problems Advisory Committee. She often offered her home to entertain committee members and spouses. Madeline and her friend Williamena Peck, "Willy," spent many days in the courthouse carefully analyzing the votes cast by each precinct in the March election. Both women became convinced that a majority of voters living in precincts south of Renton would continue to vote "no" even for a "sewers only" measure. County Commissioner Bill Moshier reluctantly agreed that areas south of Renton were too remote from Lake Washington to be won over by a "sewers only" Metro. These changes made passage more likely, but some voters outside Seattle would still have to switch from "no" to "yes." Under the Metro Act, any incorporated city was required to be wholly included or wholly excluded in forming the boundaries of Metro.

Madeline argued forcefully before the City-County Committee and the board of King County Commissioners that the areas south of Renton and east of Bellevue should be deleted from the area voting in the new election. Brown & Caldwell engineers gave assurances that the Metro interceptor sewers leading into the proposed new Metro treatment plants could be *initially* sized to accept a *future* connection of Issaquah, Redmond, Kent, and Auburn. They also believed that effluent from a state-of-the-art secondary treatment plant would *not, by itself,* have a negative effect on Duwamish River water. They assured us that the water of the Duwamish River would be carefully monitored. In the future, if effluent from the new Renton plant *did* in fact have a negative effect on river water, an outfall line from Renton to Puget Sound could be feasibly financed and built at that time.

Postponing this expensive part of the longer-term Metro project would help to hold down the amount of the monthly sewage disposal charge. The initial burden of the sewer service charge would fall heavily on Seattle residents because Seattle contained more than 90 percent of the sewer customers of Metro. It would take many years before reasonable equity of burden sharing was achieved by strong growth in the suburban population served by sewers.

Madeline also argued forcefully to the Committee that the areas in question had already voted "no" on Metro by large margins in March and that "we should not bite off too much because we can't afford to lose twice." The new boundaries and the concept of development at a later stage of a new outfall to Puget Sound were accepted by the City-County Committee. At the formal request of the cities of Bellevue and Kirkland, the Board of King County Commissioners placed a "sewers only" measure on the regular September 9, 1958, primary election ballot. The boundaries of the proposed Metro were set to include only the cities and unincorporated areas draining directly into Lake Washington.

The summer of 1958 turned out to be unusually sunny and warm. Additional sunlight produced a record bloom of algae on the lake. Prevailing winds pushed the surface algae into green mats and clumps in shallow water and piles along the beaches. The offensive odor from decaying algae could be smelled by residents around the lake. The State and County Health Departments posted "NO BATHING" signs on Lake Washington swimming beaches. The large crowds that gathered along the lakeshore that August for the annual Sea Fair celebration could not ignore the smell of decaying algae.

At the first meetings of the enlarged campaign committee, led by Dr. Clayton Wangeman, Richard Riddell, and Dorothy Block, Mrs. Block brought more than her usual knitting and suggested she take her kids down to the lake and get their picture in front of a 'NO BATHING' sign. The committee was enthusiastic. The resulting photo of her children spoke a universal language and packed an emotional punch. It replaced the detailed technical explanation we had used in the campaign brochure for the March election. The new picture and its caption "Clean up our filthy waters" conveyed the single purpose of the September ballot measure and became the heart of the campaign. Newspaper ads, billboards, store window posters, and campaign brochures featured the Block children in bathing suits in front of a "No Bathing" sign. The press widely and correctly reported that many Lake Washington beaches were closed to swimming by the State and County health departments for public health protection. Most voters who crossed the Mercer Island floating bridge or lived on the hills around the lake could smell decaying algae that summer. Everyone understood the basic question they were voting on in this election.

Both of us worked long hours in the campaign and our son Bob became actively involved carrying literature door-to-door in our Bellevue neighborhood. The campaign committee organized neighborhood campaigning with a "Mother's March for Metro." Mary Lou strongly supported the change in campaign strategy. "That's more like it! People can't understand a complicated

The poster featuring the Block children on the closed Lake Washington swimming beach successfully captured the attention of voters.

federation of governments, but they can understand that NO BATHING picture." Hundreds of women and children participated in this doorbelling effort.

The roster of Metro campaign speakers became a "who's who" of future Washington State leaders. These included future three-term Governor and US Senator Daniel J. Evans; future State Representative, State Attorney General, and US Senator Slade Gorton; future State Senator, six-term US Congressman and Lt. Governor Joel Pritchard; and future US Congressman, US Secretary of Transportation, and US Senator Brock Adams.

The result of the September 9, 1958, election on Metro was a convincing victory for Lake Washington both outside and inside the City of Seattle. The vote outside Seattle was 15,693 "yes" to 7,860 "no." The vote inside Seattle was 58,617 "yes" to 41,703 "no." The turn-around by eastside voters was striking. The people of Kirkland, who had voted 2-1 against Metro in March, voted 2-1 in favor of the revised measure in September. Only the voters of Renton at the south end of the Lake continued to vote "no" as they had in March.

In retrospect it's hard to believe that the campaign to clean up Lake Washington could have become so controversial. We expected opposition from a few professionals who would lose their fees for financing and building suburban sewage treatment plants since the new plan would eliminate the need for these plants. We also expected that some local officials would resist giving up direct control of their sewage treatment operations. Sewer district and city officials are sometimes reluctant to give up powers to appoint employees and operate facilities which they have been accustomed to controlling and are often urged not to "abandon" their loyal employees to a less certain future. However, the opposition of conservative citizens to this single purpose ballot proposal was hard for me to understand. They still called the new federation an "octopus" which would become a "super government." There were even a few who believed the whole thing was part of an underground communist conspiracy.

In fairness, the 1958 Lake Washington clean water elections occurred when the national environmental conscience was only beginning to stir. The US Environmental Protection Agency would not exist for another fourteen years. There were no federal appropriations for water pollution abatement grants. The entire cost of the Metro plan was proposed to be borne by local sewer rate payers, many of whom had never before paid a sewer service charge. By latter-day standards, and with the advantage of hindsight, the program was a great bargain. However, a project of this scale was almost without precedent and the proposed $2.50 per month sewer charge seemed excessive to some cost-conscious residents.

After Metro had been approved by the voters, a letter was sent from members of the League of Women Voters of Seattle to the National Municipal League nominating Metro for an All-America City Award. These national awards had been given each year since 1949. Written nominations were publicly solicited from thousands of cities, towns, and counties across America. Finalists were invited to make oral presentations to a distinguished jury at the annual November meeting of the League. Each year eleven cities were finally named "All-America."

The Kitchen Group was featured in Look *magazine*
when Metro received the All-America City Award.

In their letter of nomination, our friends from the Seattle League of Women Voters cited five years of extraordinary citizen action, including passage of major state legislation and leadership in two metropolitan area-wide elections. When Metro was named a finalist, the nominators traveled east to make their presentation to the All-America City jury. The Municipality of Metropolitan Seattle was the first nominee to encompass a large city and eleven other cities in a metropolitan area. Metro's nomination was presented on behalf of all its component cities.

When winners were announced in the January 1960 issue of *Look* magazine, the citizen effort which created Metro had won an *All-America City* award!

This prestigious prize was a good excuse for general celebrating. It was a "first" for Seattle and a vice president of the National League came out to take part in the ceremony. *Look* magazine published a picture of the Kitchen Group clasping hands in victory around Mary Lou's kitchen table. In recognition of the collaborative nature of the federation campaign All-America City banners were given to *each* component city and to King County as well as the named winner, Municipality of Metropolitan Seattle.

Businesses in the metropolitan area sponsored a banquet in Seattle's Olympic Hotel to honor the cities and citizens from all parts of Metro. These towns didn't usually celebrate together, and the political parties usually had separate gatherings. The atmosphere was especially warm because there was a shared feeling of accomplishment in getting Metro started. The evening was a warm-hearted mix of all kinds of people who had found lofty inspiration in the lowly cause of sewers. The parade of "All-America" banners was thrilling to watch.

Of course, it remained to be seen whether the experiment would work. Would Metro finally clean up pollution which had been tolerated for so long? Would our children actually get to swim at the beaches we had worked so hard to open? On celebration nights, however, nobody thinks about possible failure. They are happily caught up in the joy of victory and its magical mood of optimism. After the clear-cut election victory, and with "All-America" banners to show for their efforts, the citizens of Metro passed the ball to their elected officials on the new Metro Council with a burst of emotional momentum and a prayer to get the job done right.

✸

CHAPTER 13

Metro: Laying a Foundation

Without exception, they spurned the short-term cash, looked well into the distance, and set their sights for the next generations.

—Jim Ellis, dedication speech at West Point Treatment Plant, July 20, 1966

AFTER THE SEPTEMBER 1958 election victory, our friend Morrell "Mo" Sharp, the mayor of nearby Beaux Arts Village, was chosen by the small cities to represent them on the new Metro Council. One evening Mo came by to tell me that most members of the Council believed the chairman should be someone who was known to share the goals of the Metropolitan Reform effort. The statute required that the chairman be selected by the members of the council and "could not hold any public office or be an employee of any component city or component county of the Metropolitan Municipal Corporation." He had been asked to find out if I would accept the job on a part-time basis. Over cookies and coffee, I asked him how the federated council was working. He thought the "clean lake goal" was strongly shared and it helped that everyone was accustomed to local council procedures. If capable executive leadership were found, Mo believed the Metro Council would play its part very well. I promised to talk with my partners and get back to him promptly.

Mary Lou and I were excited by the visit. After Mo left, we talked intensely about this new possibility. For several months it had seemed to us that I would be most useful to the clean-water cause in the role of Metro's legal counsel.

This collage series of headlines, articles, and imagery covering Ellis' Metro work was put together for the Ellis family with help from Linda Mickel.

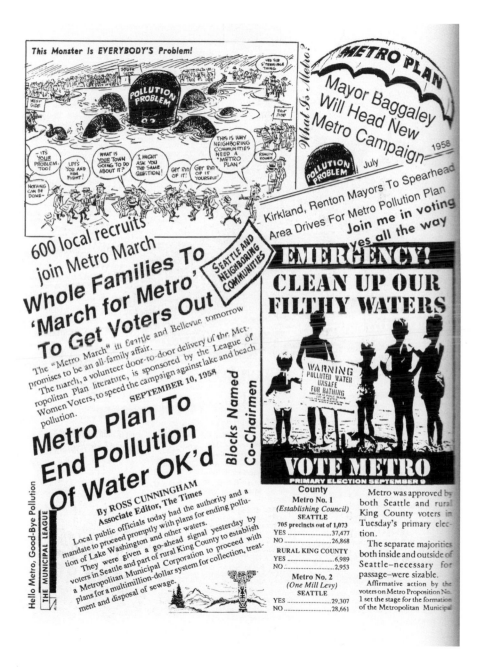

Tough legal issues were sure to confront the financing and construction of such a large project. The Preston law firm was widely known as specializing in municipal finance law, and I had worked for eight years learning this part of the practice.

Mary Lou also reminded me that I was much younger than my partners and that rumors kept circulating that I would run for public office. She correctly sensed that the partners would see the job of "chairman" as signaling a career change away from law and toward politics. Our good friend and co-reformer Carey Donworth was a successful labor-management consultant with a calm temperament and good judgment. He had shown leadership ability in working with people holding different views during the five-year citizen effort to create Metro. If Carey were chairman and I were legal counsel, Metro would have *two* people in key positions who were dedicated to serving the clean water mission. When Mo Sharp reported this response, it was quickly accepted by Carey and the Council.

The first official meeting of the Metro Council was held on October 1, 1958, about three weeks after the voters had said "yes." On October 6th, Donworth was elected chairman of the Council, where he served on a part-time basis for twenty-one years. On October 22nd, I was appointed legal counsel for the Municipality and performed this part-time job for the next twenty years. The Preston firm was retained as Bond Counsel shortly after my appointment and would be able to provide valuable counsel and assistance in regulatory, condemnation, and damage claim matters.

Harold (Hal) Miller was serving as director of the Washington State Pollution Control Commission (PCC) after completing the Brown & Caldwell study. During the winter of 1958–59, he was actively recruited by Carey and key council members, and on March 1, 1959, resigned from the PCC to become Metro's first executive director. He was a graduate of Purdue University with degrees in engineering and psychology. Hal and Carey persuaded Maralyn Sullivan to leave her position with United States Steel Corporation in San Francisco to become clerk of the Council and administrative assistant to Miller. Hal and Maralyn proved to be pure "ten-strikes" for Metro.

The voter-approved mission of Metro was limited to the single function of abating water pollution. All debt service, construction, and operating costs of the necessary metropolitan sewage disposal facilities were to be paid from sewer service charges. As federal and state grants were authorized, they were applied for and used. However, only repayable loans or advances were available in the beginning. For the First Stage project, the total of federal and state grants received by Metro was less than the amount of state sales taxes paid by Metro on its construction contracts.

The Metro Council unanimously adopted its official Comprehensive Plan that Brown & Caldwell had prepared for the September 1958 election. The First Stage project of this plan became the first action program for the new municipality. Long-term funding for this project became "Job One" for all of us.

In the spring of 1959, Metro rented its first office space on the second floor of a building at 152 Denny Way, above a tailor shop. Soon the small Metro staff of four employees was joined by employees of Metropolitan Engineers, a joint venture of four engineering firms. They were tasked to design the vast web of new sewage disposal facilities that made up the First Stage project. The joint venture consortium gave us instant skills and familiarity with the territory and eliminated what might otherwise have been destructive professional competition to get the work. The four firms were Brown & Caldwell, R.W. Beck and Associates, Hill & Ingman, and Carey & Kramer. The engineers crowded into small work areas where they set up drafting tables and unpacked their slide rules and pencils.

Miller had brought a young PCC engineer, Charles V. (Tom) Gibbs, in as Metro's third employee. Initially, Tom worked four days a week for Metropolitan Engineers and one day for Metro. Within a few months he would be working full time at Metro developing a remote water-quality monitoring program for the Duwamish River and learning from Miller a leadership style that soon defined the agency.

The process of building a complex Metropolitan sewage disposal system now began to take shape. It was immediately necessary to find a source of preliminary funding because the voters who approved the creation of Metro had not yet approved a tax levy to pay its start-up costs.

We received a welcome phone call from L.R. Durkee. Durkee was a long-time Mercer Island resident who was then serving as the regional representative for a new federal pollution-abatement loan program. He suggested Metro could apply for a federal planning advance of up to a million dollars to be repaid with interest when Metro bonds were issued, saying this was just what the new federal legislation had been created to do. Working with the engineers, we prepared an application for a $1 million loan to pay preliminary costs. We didn't know whether or when the application would be approved, but the Council was eager to pursue this channel rather than squeeze cash out of an already tight City of Seattle budget. Everyone was delighted when the loan request was quickly approved. This source was used to cover costs of engineering design, negotiate sewage disposal contracts with eleven different agencies, and pursue a test case that the Preston law firm would require to be decided by the State Supreme Court before approving the validity of any Metro bonds.

There was an immediate need for a qualified financial advisor. I suggested that the Council send out a Request for Proposal (RFP) to potential advisors who would be asked to "prepare a revenue bond issue for competitive public sale." Metro received several responses to its RFP including one from Wainwright & Ramsey, a New York firm, whose work was limited to advising and assisting issuers. Everyone thought that Sonny Wainwright of Wainwright & Ramsey was the most impressive, their fees for advisory services were reasonable, and their references were strong. The Council hired Wainwright & Ramsey.

The Metro Council now had in place the Council chair and clerk, executive director, engineers, financial advisor, and legal counsel needed to develop a long-range financing plan for the First Stage project.

From the beginning, extreme right-wing opponents of Metro had asserted that this new form of government was "unconstitutional" and predicted that courts would throw it out. Most lawyers believed our statute was constitutional, but the Corporation Counsel of Seattle did not share this view. Other officials worried problems would emerge in practice that had not been considered in drafting the new law. Senior partners O. B. Thorgrimson and his son Richard suggested that contracts be entered into with local agencies delivering sewage to the Metro system, and strongly urged that the legality of these contracts and the constitutionality of the Metro Act be tested in court. The size of the public borrowing, the scale of the project, and the precedent-setting nature of the Metro governmental structure had convinced us that the prudent course of action was a test case.

O. B. Thorgrimson used a "brick house" analogy to explain his view that the Metro system was like a brick house born out of political compromise between separate utilities. Each brick was a separate city or district operating its own sewer collection system. Metro provided the mortar and foundation for the whole house by providing sewage disposal facilities for everyone. The collection systems and the disposal system each depended on the other. Enforceable contracts with each local entity were needed to make sure that changes in local personnel or local voter attitudes would not result in failure to perform the promises made to Metro. Initial financial planning contemplated issuing forty-year bonds from time to time during the ten-year First Stage project to pay for metropolitan disposal facilities. Each city or district participant contract would run for fifty years to assure revenue throughout the life of the Metro bonds.

The key to enforcing these long-term promises was the validity of the participant contracts and the constitutionality of the Metro statute. If both were tested and found valid, Metro could build a strong brick house. If either were found to be invalid, the house could collapse. A favorable Supreme Court decision would ensure that the legal mortar and foundation provided by the metropolitan sewage disposal system would be solid and lasting.

During the Metro campaigns, I had been personally angered by persistent accusations that Metro was a communist conspiracy. After the election these unsupported charges continued to appear in pamphlets and brochures emanating from Texas and were distributed at public meetings and political caucuses which I attended. We needed an authoritative response to these charges or our ability to obtain future public support could be undercut. All things considered, I believed that bringing *and winning* a test case was both a legal *and political* necessity. I will confess that I was also eager to use whatever skill I had learned to trump the name-callers and to win one for the citizen volunteers who believed in the political integrity of our effort.

When I first suggested to the Metro Council that it would be a good precaution to have a test case, Councilman Dave Levine gave me a piercing look and said I was becoming the client, lawyer, judge, and jury for this entire project. I responded, "Councilman, that's one reason why we need a test case. My partners and I are convinced that everything is legal, but we could be wrong, and this is the largest project I have ever done, and one of the largest projects the City has done. If we are wrong, and the statute is found at some future date to be unconstitutional, our Metro bonds would go into default. Financial losses for thousands of people would cause all hell to break loose, and the City's credit would be damaged. I believe the statute and contracts are valid, but we should have a test case." Levine thought a moment and then agreed. He knew the stakes were high and he was financially conservative by nature.

In preparing the contract with the City of Seattle and planning the legal test case, several long-term policy decisions were developed around contracting. The time consumed by these efforts turned out to be well spent. Metro charges could not begin until we had received a favorable decision from the Supreme Court and that would be months away. In the meantime, engineering work could proceed on schedule with funds from the federal planning loan.

Ed Starin and I worked on these contract issues and received cooperation from everyone. Seattle Mayor Clinton and Council President Levine had promised during the earlier Metro campaign that if existing sewage treatment facilities owned by any participant were by-passed by the new project, they would be purchased by Metro. Seattle's North Trunk Sewer was one facility that would need to be acquired and improved.

Contract discussions and negotiations with Sewer District Commissioners and with officials of smaller cities gave us an opportunity to build local understanding of the coming Metro sewage disposal charge which we aimed to be uniform for all entities served by Metro. There were also carrots in each contract. We knew that the people in Renton had not voted for Metro, but their City Council wanted to get cash for their soon-to-be by-passed treatment plant and to make taxable use of the valuable site.

Working with city staff, we drafted the first "pilot" contract between Metro and the City of Seattle. The City of Seattle was the logical subject of a pilot contract, because it was Metro's largest customer and the heart of Metro's credit worthiness.

The formula for determining sewage disposal charges provided that each single-family residence would pay a flat monthly amount and other users would pay an equivalent amount. The average single-family house consumed 600 cubic feet of water each month and this was considered a fair measure of the sewage produced. Therefore, any apartment or business establishment would be charged for each 600 cubic feet of water consumed. This was "equivalent" to the average single-family home and was generally considered fair and widely, if not happily, accepted.

The rate formula portion of the pilot draft was also reviewed with Bellevue Sewer District where Jack Henry was a commissioner, with Lake City Sewer District where Bob Beach was a commissioner, with Al King of Kirkland, and with other lawyers from the City-County Metropolitan Problems Advisory Committee. Each of these legal building blocks were developed in consultation with Hal Miller, Carey Donworth, the Metro engineers, key members of the Metro Council, and attorneys for other participants.

Businessman Dorm Braman, the able and energetic chair of the Metro Council Finance Committee, David Levine, the intelligent and strong president of the Seattle City Council, and Ed Munro, a forceful leader on the King County Commission, were closely involved with each policy step in the financing program and made contributions to the final product.

The participant contracts between Metro and its cities and districts, together with the test case decision, would be the foundation of the Metro revenue stream. All participant contracts would use the same formula for determining sewage disposal charges, contain the same effective start date for these charges, and provide that Metro would operate all treatment facilities on the start date. This was a key point because no one wanted Metro to begin billing participants for service charges until it was disposing of their sewage.

We discussed drafts of key parts of the contract with Sonny Wainwright. He contributed ideas for language that would be understood and accepted by bond buyers.

After multiple legal reviews and advertised public hearings, the Metro Council and the Seattle City Council each unanimously approved their sewage disposal contract. However, the mayor and city clerk did not sign the contract stating they were advised by the City's Corporation Counsel that there may be a question as to its legality. Metro then sued the City requesting that the Court declare the contract and statute to be valid.

The participant contract with Seattle was essential to carry out the ten-year First Stage portion of Metro's comprehensive plan. Metro would immediately purchase $6.285 million dollars of permanent facilities from the City of Seattle which were needed for the First Stage plan. At the same time, necessary existing facilities would also be purchased from other participants. Metro would take over the sewage disposal operations of all participants on the first of July 1962. By that time, Metro would have in place its Comprehensive Plan and financing resolution, its system-wide rate resolution, and its first bond sale resolution. The latter would authorize Metro to issue bonds from time to time as funds were needed in a total amount of $125 million. All of these actions *and* a favorable Supreme Court decision would need to be in effect *before* any bonds were issued or construction contracts signed.

In order to have a decision which would be binding on the successors of the parties in the case, it was necessary for the Court to appoint an attorney representing the holders of outstanding sewer revenue bonds which had been previously issued by the City of Seattle. The city treasurer found a bond holder who understood the Metro case and was willing to participate. We asked the presiding superior court judge to appoint a lawyer who would represent all holders of outstanding city sewer revenue bonds, someone who would do a good job but not charge an arm and a leg. Lloyd Shorett, then presiding judge of King County Superior Court, understood what we were trying to do and asked if we had anyone in mind. I said, "Yes. I know a young lawyer who was a classmate of mine, his name is Griffith Way. Mr. Way is very bright, will do a good job, and charge a reasonable fee." The judge approved this arrangement and Griff was appointed.

The City of Seattle was represented by its veteran Corporation Counsel, A.C. Van Soelen, and assistants Al Newbould and Arthur Schramm.

Nicholas Maffeo, a Renton lawyer, resident, taxpayer, and leader of the group which opposed Metro in the elections, would be a defendant in the case and represent himself. We had expected he was going to sue us anyway and he was willing to do so as a defendant.

Al Newbould worked hard and performed very well, and Griff Way also did an expert professional job. In fact, when I read his brief and the cases cited, I was temporarily shaken, thinking we might just *not* win this thing. However, by the time of trial my confidence had fully returned.

Griff argued strongly that contracting with Metro to operate part of a system which the bond holder thought was going to be operated entirely by the City amounted to unlawfully changing the form of management from that which he expected in his bond contract.

We had anticipated this argument and provided in the contract that any payments required to be made by the City to Metro would be *junior* in their lien on City sewer revenues to the lien of the City's outstanding sewer revenue bonds. The trial judge understood this issue immediately and supported our approach. This was an experienced judge who believed that a city utility should be able to contract reasonably with another agency, to add expertise, or to make joint arrangements so long as the City bonds retained their prior right to receive utility revenues.

The trial was completed in less than two and a half days. At the judge's request, we prepared, and he signed a Declaratory Judgment that the statute was constitutional, and the contract was valid. The City, the bondholder, and the Renton taxpayer then filed appeals to the State Supreme Court.

Ed Starin, Gene Sage, and I worked together on this case through Superior Court trial and Supreme Court appeal. The test case would have to be decided before any construction contracts could be awarded. The engineers were concerned that the case might delay them at first. As it turned out, our interim federal loan assured us that the start of construction would not be delayed in any significant way.

On December 22, 1960, I first heard the result when Hal Miller saw me across Third Avenue and hollered, "You Won!" He made a zero with the fingers of one hand to show it was unanimous. I rushed into the office to read our official copy from the court clerk.

The opinion covered each issue in plain English and on all points was a clear-cut victory for Metro. One welcome effect of this unanimous decision from the state's highest Court was quieting most "Communist conspiracy" critics and reassuring Metro participants and supporters. Sonny Wainwright was delighted with the Court's opinion and cited it in the official statement for every subsequent Metro sewer revenue bond issue.

O. B. Thorgrimson was actually smiling when he shook my hand! For this Icelander of few words, it was a major display of emotion.

The ensuing sale of Metro's first bond issue drew active bidding. The bids were opened by the county treasurer in the Council Chambers and the sale was approved that day by the Metro Council at an attractive net-effective interest rate. Wainwright told the Metro Council that the strong Supreme Court decision contributed to the successful sale.

$$\maltese$$

CHAPTER 14

Metro: The First Stage

. . . a federation of cities can perform a common task well and without swallowing each other.

—*Jim Ellis, dedication speech at West Point Treatment Plant, July 20, 1966*

WITH METRO'S VALIDITY confirmed by the state's highest court, 50-year sewage disposal contracts signed by local sewer providers, and long-term revenue bonds issued, the table was set for construction of the First Stage of the Comprehensive Sewage Disposal plan. The plan adopted by the Metro Council had been prepared for the area within the boundaries of Metro as fixed for the September 1958 election. The facilities of the comprehensive plan were to be developed in stages with the worst pollution problems addressed in the First Stage. This ten-year project included miles of interceptor sewers and tunnels along the east side of Lake Washington to a new secondary treatment plant at Renton; another group of similar facilities along the northwest side of the lake to a new primary treatment plant at West Point; and a third group located along the lower Duwamish River and the Elliott Bay waterfront leading to the new West Point Plant. A small treatment plant was also constrcuted at Piper's Creek, adjacent to Carkeek Park in Seattle.

Comprehensive Plan facilities to serve areas outside of Metro's original boundaries, like Kent, Auburn, Issaquah, and Redmond, and an expensive effluent line from the Secondary Renton Treatment Plant to Puget Sound were planned to either be parts of later stage construction projects as annexations to Metro or contracts for service were completed for these areas.

In our first private conference in my office, Carey Donworth, Hal Miller, and I made a three-hand-shake pledge to achieve Hal's vision of building a First Stage project that would make Metro and Lake Washington "a clean water model for the nation." I asked Hal if we could complete the planned ten-year construction program in nine years. He thought we could, and this started a tradition of "better than promised" performance targets. As we progressed, this short-hand slogan caught on and invigorated everyone in the new organization with pride.

Hal proved to be an extraordinary leader of Metro and its consultant team. He focused on the "big picture," engaged the best people, and gave them wide discretion. He focused his effort like a hawk on issues of schedule and cost. Hal could track "critical path" threads through a maze of different contracts and actors. He placed great confidence in the lead design engineer of Metropolitan Engineers, Frank Kersnar, and the two of them met weekly. Frank was a brilliant technical designer and a stickler for high standards in preparing contract documents.

Hal was respected by his colleagues, idolized by Metro office staff, and completely dedicated to his challenging mission. When appearing before the Council or any public group, he projected a calm and confident demeanor. Hal was a hard man not to believe. In private conversations, he listened carefully and posed perceptive questions. I found myself relying more and more upon his technical knowledge and leadership instincts when major issues arose during the First Stage project.

Maralyn Sullivan came on as the clerk-secretary to the Council and administrative assistant to Hal. Maralyn was raised on Vashon Island, and lived most of her life there, but she had varied private-sector work experience from California to Hawaii, becoming an experienced and sought-after executive secretary. In our initial interview, I saw a combination of intelligence, natural grace, intuitive courtesy, and a genuine affection for the Puget Sound environment. Maralyn was responsible for hiring the office staff and became the hub of communication within Metro. She was also responsible for assembling and certifying official transcripts of proceedings, was a conscientious stickler for detail, and quickly learned the special requirements of public agencies.

The clerk of the council was the point of contact for most people dealing with Metro, and Maralyn proved to be a responsive keeper of the public gate. Her professionalism and personality set a tone for the whole agency.

The new Metro statute required that all legislative actions be authorized by resolutions of the Metro Council. Carey and Hal understood the need for Council members to be fully and timely informed on future action being considered by Hal, and to be the first to hear each bit of actual First Stage progress. Carey believed that a council whose members served Metro on a part-time basis should be confronted with as few surprises as possible.

Hal asked the chairman, legal counsel, and clerk to join him for early discussion of any Council action he was considering as executive and wanted to be promptly informed of any legal issue that might arise.

After the bond sale in 1961, all efforts turned to building. With a cadre of engineers working full speed to maintain construction schedules, prepare bidding specifications and award contracts, it was important for Metro's attorneys to prioritize legal work for timely support. One of the first contracts let was for the end section of the South Interceptor, Metro's name for Jack Henry's Eastside Trunk sewer, which passed through the City of Renton on its way from Bellevue and Kirkland to the site of Metro's Renton Treatment Plant.

An underground water aquifer existed beneath the surface of the City of Renton. Contractors digging a ditch for the new South Interceptor cut into this aquifer and the ditch quickly filled with water. Contractors were required to pump any water out of the ditch and to keep it dry until their new pipe was properly laid and backfilled. During this continuous pumping, the water table under a large part of the City of Renton was lowered. Buildings began to settle, some roofs sagged, brick walls began to crumble, and some foundations cracked or broke as did street and sidewalk paving.

This unexpected disaster produced consternation among the residents and business owners of Renton. Temporary injunctions were obtained, and claims poured in for damages. We advised Metro and informed the contractor that ultimately there was no defense to claims for fair compensation by owners of property damaged by this sewer construction. The fact that Metro was a public body didn't mean it had a right to damage private property. Claims were settled and insurance paid quickly, but Metro's first entry into Renton had made us public enemy number one in Nicholas Maffeo's hometown.

Unfortunately, there was more trouble ahead. The next segment of the crucial interceptor had to be built through an adjoining developed industrial area where the same water table existed. By now all potential contractors were fully alerted and adjusted their bids to allow for high insurance premiums, high dewatering expenses, and costly interruptions of work schedules. Metro might be able to prevent permanent injunctions, but it could not prevent property owners from seeking temporary restraints and the Metro Engineers could not compromise pipe laying specifications.

What followed was a demonstration of private ingenuity. When bids were opened to construct the second section of the South Interceptor, all proposals came in much higher except for one bidder, Scheumann & Johnson. We worried that this bidder might not fully understand what he was getting into. However, we were treated to the pleasant experience of watching inventive expertise at work.

The contractor constructed the line in 300-foot sections by driving steel sheets into the ground around one section at a time. Each section was then excavated, and water was pumped out. When the ditch was dry, pipe was installed, connected to the completed section, and back filled as required. The steel sheets were then pulled out and used to build the dewatering wall for the next section of pipe. By dewatering quickly and having the pipe and select fill materials on site when each section of ditch was pumped dry, his crew could lay bedding gravel, set pipe, make tight joints, back fill, and get out. The new process *did not* draw down the water table beyond the ditch. The second contract for the South Interceptor was finished in a fraction of the time it took to complete the first contract and *there were no claims*! The residents and business firms along the route were greatly relieved.

This experience was a dramatic lesson on the value of allowing alternate methods to reveal better ways of doing a job. Unique construction challenges arose, and innovative efforts were applied throughout the project. From pipes and materials, to processes and equipment, ingenuity was applied, often to great savings in time, money, and lives.

A significant engineering achievement took place where the Northwest Lake Washington interceptor was planned to be connected by a three-mile-long tunnel to the existing north trunk sewer of the City of Seattle. This tunnel would intercept the Lake City Sewer Treatment Plant (the largest on Lake Washington) and other plants along the north shore of the lake. It was as much as 125 feet below the surface and there was so much water in the ground that higher than normal atmospheric pressure was needed to keep the work site dry. Construction unions and contractors were properly worried about their people working under this heavy pressure.

The "bends" is a life-threatening disease caused when high pressure outside the body creates nitrogen gas bubbles in body fluids. These bubbles seek to escape when the exterior pressure is reduced to normal upon return to the surface. If bubbles escape suddenly, they can cause serious injuries and death. State workplace regulations were based on the premise that the degree of risk for "bends" depended on the length of time people worked under higher-than-normal air pressure. Accordingly, unions insisted, and regulations required, that periodic rest breaks be provided at the surface.

John S. (Jack) Smith, the Metro engineer in charge of Westside pipelines and tunnels, initiated his *own* extensive research and found that the ill effects of "bends" were not caused by the *amount* of time worked under high pressure, but rather by the *number of times* the body was subjected to sharp drops in pressure on returning to the surface.

A special hyperbaric chamber gradually adjusts people to the high pressure below, and most importantly, back down to the normal pressure encountered on returning to the surface. Jack learned that if the number of controlled decompressions were reduced, the risk of bends would be correspondingly lower. He started working to change statutes and regulations to permit longer working periods and reduce the number of trips to the surface in each working shift from two to one decompression.

Hyperbaric chambers were tested to secure the best available technology and all tunnel construction workers and engineers were educated in the new, safer work rules. Metro constructed a number of major tunnel projects under the new rules with no fatalities and no serious incident of decompression requiring off-site medical attention. Jack Smith led the entire effort, with doctors and lawyers providing backup, to get the changes through the state legislature and the Department of Labor and Industry. The new practice significantly lowered costs and was an unqualified lifesaving success.

The Renton Treatment Plant (later renamed the South Treatment Plant) location gave Metro the opportunity to acquire a large site in an industrial growth area before industrial and commercial development consumed most of the valley's farmland. The plan called for a site of twenty-five acres. Former Governor Al Rosellini was acting as an advisor for the Great Northern Railroad and other local landowners at this logical location for the new treatment plant. He suggested that Metro buy a larger area than had been planned because public utilities in a growing area usually needed room for expansion sooner than they expected. We were successful in getting Council approval to purchase 53 acres for $250,000. This acquisition proved to be a Godsend later when the plant was expanded twice to serve rapid development and annexations.

People often think that no one wants to live or work next to a sewage treatment plant, but well designed and well-operated modern plants can be good neighbors. Metro obtained the site without condemnation because Rosellini knew the value of land and wanted to avoid wasting time and money in condemnation.

The intent of the First Stage project of the Comprehensive Plan was to clean up the worst pollution conditions inside the boundaries approved by voters. Obvious examples were the Lake Washington algae crisis and the gross raw sewage pollution at West Point, Shilshole Bay, Elliott Bay, and the lower Duwamish Waterway and estuary.

For almost a century, a growing concentration of downtown Seattle buildings had poured their entire volumes of raw sewage into Elliott Bay through dozens of street-end pipes emerging in front of a waterfront sidewalk. People came to board ships and ferries, access waterfront businesses, or simply watch the ships and smell the salt water. They also saw and smelled the disgusting flow of millions of gallons of raw sewage and toilet paper spewing out at their feet. The waterfront, the waterway, and the estuary had long been used as open sewers and carried increasing amounts of industrial waste. It was satisfying to watch this gross pollution being systematically attacked.

The plan for interceptors and pumping stations to clean up Elliott Bay and the lower Duwamish hinged on a major tunnel under Second Avenue which could deliver huge quantities of wastewater through the Interbay and Magnolia neighborhoods of the city to a new treatment plant at West Point. This tunnel had to be large enough to intercept more than ninety raw sewage outfalls, including 73 located in street ends between each block along the downtown waterfront. The same tunnel would also intercept raw and partly treated sewage flowing through Seattle's old and failing Diagonal Avenue Treatment Plant, as well as the raw sewage to be collected by a new Marginal Way trunk being built by Metro to intercept outfalls dumping raw sewage and industrial waste into the lower Duwamish River waterway and estuary.

The Second Avenue tunnel was critical to cleaning up this heavily polluted water, but construction of such a large tunnel was difficult because of requirements to control ground water so close to the Sound, to protect adjoining buildings, and to relocate utilities.

In the early 1900s, filling the natural tide lands and regrading hilly streets had been necessary to build the modern city and culminated in R.H. Thompson's effort of sluicing most of Denny Hill into Elliott Bay. Fortunately, these regradings and fillings were done before the construction of the Metro tunnel under Second Avenue. New reforms in underground work rules also helped to make construction of the Second Avenue Tunnel a less costly and much safer project. This tunnel became one of the most difficult and important steps in building Metro's First Stage water cleanup project.

The Second Avenue tunnel and the Marginal Way interceptors removed huge quantities of raw sewage and industrial waste from Elliott Bay and the Duwamish waterway and estuary. Dissolved oxygen in the lower river improved tenfold when this tunnel and these interceptor lines were connected to the new West Point Treatment Plant.

I was shocked one afternoon in 1964 when Maralyn phoned me in the middle of a Mercer Island Water District meeting to say that Hal had just died. Tom Gibbs found him slumped over his desk and he didn't recover consciousness. We believe that among the contributing causes of this sudden stroke were Hal's intense work habits and the unceasing pressure of striving for difficult goals.

River Water vs. River Sediment

E. COLI COUNTS in the water of the Duwamish estuary and Elliott Bay went from more than 10,000 units per sample in 1960, to less than 100 units in 1990, which is considered a safe level. It is important to distinguish between the quality of the water in the river and the solid sediments on the river bottom. High toxic levels were accumulated in these bottom sediments during more than a century of waste discharges. The water column in the river, the estuary, and Elliott Bay was cleaned by Metro, but years of constant vigilance and continuing action will be required to remove toxic deposits accumulated in bottom sediments and to prevent new pollutants from entering the water in this industrial area.

It was hard for us to adjust to the loss of such an important team leader and so dedicated a missionary for the Clean Water cause. When the Renton Treatment Plant was completed the dedication of the plant to Harold E. Miller was an easy call. It would have greatly pleased Hal that his successors Fred Lange and Tom Gibbs finished the First Stage project construction ten months ahead of schedule and within two percent of estimated cost.

From his hiring as Metro's third employee in 1959, Tom Gibbs had been groomed by Hal to be his eventual successor and to help establish disciplined research practices and state-of-the-art technology. Tom's subsequent tenure as executive director covered critical years of new Metro achievements. He became a trusted leadership voice for Metro and a role model for its employees. I watched him work and saw how his patient, low-key style avoided one pitfall after another for the new agency. Tom didn't just listen. He absorbed and processed what he heard, and was sensitive to personal issues, in ways which inspired staff trust. Integrity stamped everything Metro did during his tenure. He was particularly effective in taking measured steps within severe constraints to meet permit requirements at the Renton Treatment Plant and to build the public confidence that would be needed for approval of future annexations. The quality of early executive leadership established Metro as an exciting and fulfilling place to work and as an agency that could be relied on to keep its commitments.

Two generations of Seattle sewer system engineers and employees had been trained that sewage treatment was not needed for saltwater outfalls. In the early days Seattle operated under the construction guideline: "If you get sewers to water, you're okay." However, as public demand for clean waterways grew, it became apparent that Seattle's combined sewer overflows (CSOs) were in fact a big problem. Tom Gibbs worked to find affordable ways of reducing combined sewer overflows during periods of heavy rains by temporarily holding them in their largest pipes and releasing them gradually to Metro Treatment Plants. This would reduce the frequency of sewage overflows to water courses. City Engineer Roy Morse was also challenged by this problem and recognized the handwriting on the wall that the City would have to separate portions of its combined storm and sanitary sewer system at very high cost. Additionally, the City of Seattle faced local sewer backup problems in homes and businesses caused by the same peak storm flows. Fortunately, the subsequent Forward Thrust program was able to create public support for addressing this problem.

During Metro's first years, 1960–65, while new facilities were being designed, financed, and built, the algae problem in Lake Washington grew sharply worse. However, by 1967, after the West Point plant began to receive sewage formerly treated by the large Lake City Sewer District Treatment Plant, there was visible improvement in lake water clarity, and by 1970 the resulting improvement was better than originally forecast. This was an exciting process to watch and, as Lake Washington gradually improved, public opinion began shifting in favor of Metro even in places where people had voted against it.

Also, Dr. Edmondson's accurate predictions for the recovery of Lake Washington were dramatically confirmed and widely publicized. He became influential on the world scientific stage.

People in the Green River Valley began to watch the wave of new development surging in the valley and recognized Kent needed to replace its open sewage lagoons located near downtown that were discharging into the

Green River. When Isabel Hogan was elected Mayor of Kent in 1970, she led a successful public vote to annex Kent to Metro. A South Valley interceptor was then built to pick up Kent's sewage and permit their downtown sewage lagoon property to be converted to other uses. This new interceptor was designed to be large enough to also accept the sewage from Auburn.

East of Lake Washington, the city of Issaquah was discharging into Lake Sammamish which connects via the Sammamish River to Lake Washington. This was another area where the voters had rejected Metro in the first election but had been accounted for in the Comprehensive Plan. Actual connections were achieved ahead of schedule by contracts with the City of Issaquah, the Lake Hills Sewer District, and the City of Redmond.

Most of the people living in the Green-Duwamish basin had voted to stay out of the original Metropolitan effort. This fact delayed Metro's capacity to finance its planned goal of removing the Renton Secondary Treatment Plant outfall from the stressed river to a point in 400-foot-deep salt water off Duwamish Head in Puget Sound.

After the Secondary Treatment plant at Renton was built in 1965, and later the South Interceptor and the Valley Interceptor to Kent and Auburn were connected to the new plant, Metro's water quality monitoring showed a marginal condition for ammonia and dissolved oxygen in the Duwamish River below the plant. When the Second Avenue Tunnel was connected to a new West Point Treatment Plant, drawing off stormwater and untreated sewage from the area, huge improvements occurred in the quality of the Duwamish Waterway, the estuary, and Elliott Bay, but not in the river just below the Renton Plant. Rapid growth and development in the tributary area increased the volume of effluent from the Renton plant to approach the volume of the natural summertime flow in the river, thereby reducing the dilution of the effluent. Careful operation of the treatment process was required to meet permit conditions. Construction of the planned outfall from the Renton Treatment Plant to Puget Sound was delayed by disputes over location and cost issues. However, when it was eventually built in 1987, the deep saltwater off Duwamish Head and the river responded well.

The work of dedicated and capable public servants is needed to make the public improvement dreams of citizen activists come true. Harold Miller had been hired as the first executive director of Metro because he had directed the Brown & Caldwell studies and believed deeply in the plan. Maralyn Sullivan served as clerk of the council because she believed that government did not need to act like a mechanical bureaucracy but could function more efficiently with warmth and courtesy. Hal's successors, Fred Lange and Tom Gibbs, followed in Hal's footsteps. Metro engineers, contractors, and employees gave 110 percent to a successful effort to achieve better-than-promised results.

The high standards set by Miller for public management inspired his successors. Donworth, Lange, Gibbs and Sullivan informed the Metro Council fully before each policy decision and Hal's "model" goals continued to guide employees and contractors to perform successfully. Citizen reformers could point with pride to their part in a civic effort which "cleaned up our lake." Leading by example showed that officials and professionals can consistently

"Better than promised" had become the hallmark of Metro.

perform at the top of their games and that a generation of citizen activists could leave their lakes, streams, and saltwater harbor cleaner than they found them.

"Better than promised" had become the hallmark of Metro. Everyone worked to complete the First Stage Project and to clean up Lake Washington, Seattle's Elliott Bay, Shilshole Bay and Duwamish estuary *sooner than projected*, and with a sewer rate *lower than promised*. The extension of the Renton Treatment Plant outfall to Puget Sound and the conversion of West Point from primary to secondary treatment were accomplished in the Second and Third Stage Projects. It was satisfying for those who wanted to show that democratic institutions can deliver on their election promise

✿

CHAPTER 15

Metro: Home Stretch

This is not the dedication of a project for its own sake, nor simply the honoring of deserving men and women. Rather it is a dedication to a quality in man – the quality of the long look and the will to serve.

—*Jim Ellis, dedication speech at West Point Treatment Plant, July 20, 1966*

FROM THE BEGINNING, Harold Miller had staunchly maintained that when Metro's First Stage project was completed, the quality of the water and beaches along Elliott and Shilshole Bays would be transformed in summer from filthy dirty to clean and safe. Dr. Edmondson and his UW colleagues had determined that the same project would gradually return the year-round quality of Lake Washington water to its natural clarity.

By the summer of 1966, it was clear to those of us watching daily that the project was holding close to its schedule and budget. For most Metro residents, however, the underground construction was out-of-sight and out-of-mind. Publicly visible water quality improvements had to await completing the crucial West Point Treatment Plant and connecting the new tunnels and interceptors to the new plant.

From 1961 to 1962, however, there had been one widely felt impact of the First Stage project: collection of the Metro sewage disposal charges. It was the job of legal counsel to oversee enforcement of regulations requiring that all local sewer systems connect to the Metropolitan treatment and disposal system, and that Metro collect sewage disposal charges for this service. In fact, these rules were the financial and operating backbone of Metro's comprehensive water pollution abatement program.

Private industries with high water usage were stunned when they received bills for their Metro sewer charges. Eventually most of these industries accepted suggestions for process changes which lowered charges by reducing the water consumed in their manufacturing processes, and local lawyers were aware of the State Supreme Court's decision upholding Metro's sewage disposal contracts.

However, a federal-state conflict was raised by lawyers for the navy which owned and operated the Naval Air Station at Sand Point on Lake Washington and the Pier 91 ship terminal on Elliott Bay. Local personnel refused Metro's repeated requests to connect navy sewage facilities to the Metropolitan disposal system. Tom Gibbs remembers coming with me to the navy offices at Pier 91 and receiving the off-putting comment that higher Naval authority could not approve connection costs. We became very concerned when they did not request Congress to appropriate the money to pay connection costs. I flew to Washington, D.C., to discuss the matter with the Navy's legal counsel in the Pentagon.

A maze of corridors led to the office of a civilian lawyer. After listening politely, he delivered a detailed lecture in a patronizing tone, to the effect:

"You should know that the United States Navy cannot reasonably be expected to comply with all the different local rules and ordinances in each of the dozens of places where we operate facilities in this country. This subject has been litigated before and there is a long line of cases going back through early English common law which has held that 'The King can do no wrong.' There is a similar precedent in American cases that the federal military cannot be compelled to connect their facilities to local systems."

I explained that Metro was completing a regional system that would remove all sewage treatment plant effluent from Lake Washington at great cost. Of the ten treatment plants which had caused the pollution of the lake, the navy would be the only public or private plant continuing to discharge effluent into the lake if they refused to connect to the regional. He responded, "We are often an exception."

I left the Pentagon frustrated and determined to ask Washington's Senator Henry M. "Scoop" Jackson for political help. He was a member of an important appropriations subcommittee and I figured he would know what to do. The next day, I met Senator Jackson for the first time and was greatly impressed by this intelligent and personable first-generation son of Norwegian immigrants. He shook my hand warmly and congratulated us on the successful passage of Metro's clean water program. I poured out that the navy installations at Sand Point and Pier 91 were threatening that success.

I remember Scoop smiling, leaning forward in his chair, and saying in effect, "Well, you know, next week we will find out if the King's crap is any different from anyone else's. I am pretty sure we will solve this problem, Jim. I will let you know."

The following week, I received a call from one of the Senator's assistants exclaiming I should have been there to listen as Scoop blew them away. At the budget appropriation meeting the day before, Scoop asked if there was any provision in the proposed budget for connecting navy facilities in Seattle to the new water pollution abatement system for Lake Washington and Elliott Bay. The answer from the navy representative was 'No, there is not.' The assistant said Scoop suggested the navy representative check that out because Scoop planned to defer acting on the budget matter at hand until he heard a positive answer to his question.

Three days after Scoop's warning, a uniformed navy captain appeared at the Preston reception desk and was escorted to my office. He introduced himself and explained he understood that Metro would like the navy sewer facilities to connect to Metro's new treatment plant. He explained that the navy had not understood the situation but had now learned what was needed and would get it done and that an appropriation would be included in a bill then before the Senate. We shook hands and I thanked him for coming. A sufficient appropriation *was* added during the continued committee hearing and the overall navy budget was approved.

The navy connections to Metro were timely made. Our elected representative system of government functioned. The son of first-generation immigrants showed the way. Somehow, all the King's men, in good order, moved in the right direction.

A public call for bids was made to construct the new 3,400-foot-long outfall line for the West Point Treatment Plant with an effluent dispersal section in water 240 feet deep. I remember asking Fred Lange and Tom Gibbs whether Metro would be able to find a contractor in the Northwest who could undertake such a difficult job. The outfall would require deep-sea divers to work with huge pipes under high pressure in strong tidal currents. We were reassured when the chief diver for the low bidder was announced to be John Lindbergh, the son of Col. Charles A. Lindbergh. "Lucky Lindy" had been a boyhood idol since our family listened to radio broadcasts of his solo flight across the Atlantic in 1926. Like his father, John Lindbergh was essentially fearless. He loved the underwater environment and supervised installation of this huge concrete pipe and its effluent dispersal section in a place where it has been successfully maintained ever since.

Ground had been broken for the First Stage project at Renton on July 20, 1961. By November 1970, the planned ten-year project would be in place. Employment on Metro construction reached a thousand per day from 1963 to 1965. Most of this work was started before the Boeing boom of 1965 to 1968 hit full stride, resulting in some bids below estimate. More than ten miles of major tunnels were built in various lengths of up to three miles, and in diameters of up to eight-and-a-half feet. The first of these tunnels pioneered new safety procedures. By 1970, the tunnels under Second Avenue and the University District were completed and connected to the West Point Treatment Plant. The entire First Stage project was finished ten months *ahead* of schedule. Costs were within two percent of original cost estimates made before the first contract was let.

The West Point Treatment Plant was located within the Fort Lawton military reservation on a sand spit just steps from Puget Sound. On the sunny afternoon of July 20, 1966, the brand-new sewage treatment buildings were ready for visual inspection by the press and public.

It was an awesome sight to drive down the tree-covered Fort Lawton hillside and see a sweeping view over the Coast Guard Lighthouse to the blue water of Puget Sound with its background of Olympic Mountains. For more

West Point Treatment Plant, circa 1966.

than sixty years this approach to West Point had been overwhelmed by the stench of raw sewage rotting on the beach and the view of Puget Sound had been spoiled by a huge grey slick of floating raw sewage larger than several football fields.

Puget Sound water was blue, and the new plant was spotlessly clean on dedication day. The entire Metro organization was busting its buttons. Measured against its contemporaries around the nation, the First Stage Project was, indeed, a significant step toward a better environment. In fairness, the actions of people at any time need to be judged against the conditions and prevailing knowledge of their time. Metro was well ahead of its peers in the 1960s.

The dedication of Metro's West Point Treatment Plant was a memorable celebration. You could feel the excitement of the crowd. Everyone looked out on the sparkling clear water of Puget Sound and knew they were taking part in a moment of local history. It seemed like they had worked and waited a long time for this day and the words of my dedication speech rang especially true for them.

During the ten-year construction period, the population of the Seattle metropolitan area increased from 750,000 to 875,000. The Metro sewer service area increased from 230 to 290 square miles and the volume of sewage receiving treatment increased by 50 million gallons per day. By 1970, effluent discharges into Lake Washington from ten treatment plants had been reduced from 20 million gallons per day to zero. All dry weather raw sewage flows into Elliott Bay and the lower Duwamish River waterway and estuary were intercepted by new Metro trunk sewers. The intercepted wastewater flows were taken through the Interbay and Magnolia neighborhoods to West Point for treatment in the new plant. The new plant immediately eliminated the old raw sewage outfall on the low tide beaches of West Point. This large treatment plant was the lynchpin of the entire First Stage project.

In addition to treatment plants on Lake Washington, the old Issaquah treatment plant on Lake Sammamish, and the old Diagonal Avenue plant on the lower Duwamish River would be abandoned. Wet weather overflows of combined sewers would remain. This problem required priority action for years.

In sharp contrast to the years required to turn over the water in Lake Washington, the tides of Puget Sound flushed water in and out of Elliott Bay and Shilshole Bay every day. Dramatic improvement in the summer season water quality of these saltwater bays occurred almost immediately after the huge raw sewage flow from the North Truck Sewer was removed from West Point beaches by completion of the new Metro Treatment Plant and its deepwater outfall.

Word got out that something besides a World's Fair and Boeing airplanes were happening in the Northwest corner of the nation. Reporters, authors, and commentators from national media began to check out Metro. By the 1970s, these newspapers included *The New York Times*, *The Los Angeles Times*, and the *Christian Science Monitor*. The magazines included *Harper's*, *Time*, *U.S. News & World Report*, *National Geographic*, and *Today's Health*. CBS television produced a Walter Cronkite network news segment. All these stories described Metro as an exciting example of urban water pollution abatement in a beautiful setting.

The clean waters in Lake Washington and Elliott Bay came too late for Harold Miller to see, but he knew they were coming. The rest of us saw construction of the First Stage projects finish ahead of schedule and turn out cleaner water than promised. We like to think that somehow Hal knew his "model for the nation" was born to wide praise and in time to help spark the movement for national clean water legislation. The seminal "Clean Water Act" was passed by the Congress and signed by President Nixon in 1972. National conservation organizations increased their focus on water resources. The effects of pioneer authors like Rachel Carson took root in national thinking. The President's Council on Environmental Quality, the US Environmental Protection Agency (EPA), and the National Water Commission were created. And Lake Washington became a well-known grassroots success story.

BOOK FOUR

Camelot
with Children

✸

CHAPTER 16

Family Life on Shoreland Drive

She created a place in the heart for her children, a planning headquarters for our community dreams, and a refuge of friendship for everyone who came.

—*Jim Ellis*

ONE OF MARY LOU'S and my earliest shared goals had been for her to be a full-time mother while our children were growing up. This goal was never compromised and neither of us ever regretted it. A single income meant less money to spend in the early years of marriage than we might have wished but was never a real hardship. We were in good health and knew that our parents would help us in any crisis beyond our financial capacity.

However, our decision to do civic work at times created conflicts between law practice, civic tasks, and family. If the practice of law is a demanding mistress, then public service can be an insatiable one. Even with encouragement from law firm partners, large chunks of time could not be taken away from the practice of law without damage. This meant that each civic cause became an additional job. Working at two jobs meant ten- to fourteen-hour days, as well as many nights and weekends. Looking back, it is obvious that this level of public activity could not have been sustained over so many years without the steady, creative, and most importantly, enthusiastic participation by Mary Lou.

In the early years, we had to learn the hard way about the tricks of balancing two jobs. We found that we could undertake more projects and achieve better results if some civic work was combined with compensated law practice, i.e., serving as a special deputy for the county freeholders or later as legal counsel to Metro. Still, the working hours were long, and I had too little time to spend with Mary Lou and the children. Arguments and tears arose over the frequency of late-night meetings and family events that I missed. Even when I showed up, I was often too tired to participate fully in family activities.

When preoccupied with legal work or public causes, I sometimes missed pieces of family conversations. "Dad has his filter up" was the children's creative label for my "deafness." Mary Lou reminded me once, "We would like your undivided attention for a few minutes. Your filter may be sifting some good ideas out for saving, but it's letting too much of life pass through."

Mary Lou drew upon every ounce of her large reservoir of ingenuity to find methods of easing conflicts between family, civic, and professional activities. Part of the story of our life together is a collection of the ways she found to make my multi-task career not only bearable but exhilarating. The bad news is that she had to fight so hard to give family its appropriate place in our lives. The good news is that most of the time, she won.

Just as Seattle was growing and changing, so was the Ellis family. We had received notice in 1954 from the City of Seattle that our Montlake house was in the area to be condemned for the Empire Expressway and the planned approaches to a new Evergreen Point Bridge across Lake Washington. Mary Lou immediately began searching for a new house. She was about seven months pregnant with our unplanned fourth child but managed to visit dozens of properties with different real estate agents, making a list of possibilities and showing the best ones to me on weekends.

During a week when I was in New York with business clients, she previewed several properties on the east side of Lake Washington and was shown a house under construction in Bellevue located right on the lake. She

Formal portrait of the Ellis children overlooking Lake Washington from their Shoreland Drive yard, circa 1961.

knew at once that this was the place for us—if only she could persuade me to spend all our savings and borrow beyond our current capacity.

On the morning when I came home after an all-night flight, Mary Lou met me at the front porch with a big hug. Her voice was full of excitement. "Put your bag down and come with me right now. We've found the perfect place!"

"Honey, I'm beat. I'm going right to bed. I'll see it tomorrow." These were the days of propeller airplanes and long flight times.

"No. You have to see it right now."

"How much does it cost?"

"I won't tell you until you see it."

"I won't go unless you tell me what it costs."

This domestic discussion continued in front of our neighbors for five minutes until, desperate for sleep, I finally gave up and got in the car. Mary Lou drove us to Bellevue while I sat in the front seat with arms folded, wearing one of my best pained expressions.

The trip ended in a small, undeveloped area south of Meydenbauer Bay. As we turned onto a gravel road through the madrona trees, we saw a striking view of Seattle across Lake Washington. I was instantly hooked, just as she had expected.

The $35,000 asking price was more than we could afford, but after maneuvering and compromising the owner kept the back half of the lot and a deal was struck at $29,250. The price included 100 feet of waterfront, and completion of the house, then under construction, with changes which divided the daylight basement into rooms for Bob (age 8), Judi (age 6), and Lynn (age 3). For the down payment we sold the stock Mary Lou's father had given her, cashed in our few savings bonds, and even withdrew the small balances in the children's bank accounts. It was a close squeeze.

In the last month of her pregnancy, Mary Lou arranged many of the details of this purchase, took part in road easement and water line negotiations, and saw to house modifications with the contractor.

On January 11, 1955, while we were still living at Montlake, Mary Lou called me at work. "Honey, I think the baby's coming." I raced home and drove her to Swedish Hospital. Mary Lou was determined that I see the birth of one of our children. However, the labor was slow in starting and the doctor sent me back to work for a few hours.

That day I was scheduled to make a luncheon speech at the Seattle Chamber of Commerce. Before the end of the speech, our office messenger walked into the auditorium, and my talk came to a sudden close. I reached the hospital in time to be with Mary Lou during her hard labor and to watch in wonder when Steve was born. The nurses then excused the rest of us while they cleaned up and I found myself standing outside the delivery room feeling faint. Fortunately, a bench was handy.

I soon saw Mary Earling emerge from the elevator. She never failed to be on hand for the birth of grandchildren and after R. B.'s retirement we were together frequently. She noticed my weakened state and laughed and said I looked as pale as a sheet. The nurse invited us into the delivery room where Mary Lou was holding the baby and smiling. She said, "You know, darling, our planned babies were girls, and our unplanned babies were boys. Now we have just the family we wanted, two boys and two girls."

John Ellis and Doris Steams

DORIS STEAMS AND JOHN ELLIS had been Franklin High School sweethearts and were married in the Mount Baker Presbyterian Church in Seattle on August 1, 1953. Our daughter Judi was the flower girl, and I was the best man. The reception was held on a beautiful summer evening on the spacious grounds at my parents' home. Four children were born of this marriage, Thomas Reed, John Robert, Barbara Christine, and James Floyd. My brother John went on to become a partner in the law firm of Holman, Mickelwait, Marion, Black & Perkins (now Perkins Coie) and later became the chairman and chief executive officer of Puget Sound Power & Light Company.

During the next few weeks Mary Lou and I made frequent trips with the children to watch the construction of the new house. Once, as we drove over the little knoll where the lake suddenly bursts into view, Mary Lou leaned against me. "It's our Shangri-La, Jim, darling. Could any place be more beautiful?" Indeed, it proved to be our home for the rest of her life. Our children grew up in this house on Shoreland Drive, built tree forts in the madronas, learned to swim in the lake, and kept pigeons, rabbits, dogs, and even a horse.

We moved in before the house was finished, and the whole family planned paths, plantings, and rockeries for the raw dirt yard. Landscaping had been cut from the contract to save money. Mary Lou painted animals and flowers on unfinished walls in the children's rooms. In the fall, Bob and Judi entered Enatai Elementary School.

When Mary Lou learned that the owner of the old farmhouse next door might be willing to sell, we called my brother John and his wife, Doris. They were enthusiastic and in a short time bought the property and moved next door. After living for a few years in the farmhouse, John and Doris built a new home on the site. They raised their family of three boys and a girl in this home.

Family projects to improve our new house may not have matched the backbreaking efforts at Raging River ten years earlier, but they came close. Under a basic division of natural interest, Mary Lou became Mrs. Inside, and I was Mr. Outside. During the next twenty-five years, the house would be remodeled twice to meet the needs of a growing and changing family. Mary Lou's design goals were to encourage each child's individuality, to give me a quiet sanctuary for homework, to provide at least one "warning door" for untimely invasions of our bedroom by children, and, of course, to reduce the morning bathroom lineup. Her style was to bring a range of design choices to the family (all of which she had pre-screened) and to let us decide which color, which piece of furniture, or which arrangement we liked best. Not surprisingly, there were few arguments under this system.

My exterior design goal was a modest house in an eye-catching garden. The first outside project was to excavate the hillside behind us and eliminate the steep thirty-foot path from the parking area to the house. This meant that thousands of yards of earth had to be moved. We hired a loader dozer and began calling people and offering free fill dirt if they would haul it away.

During the first three days, the dozer loaded two or three trucks and idled the rest of the day. I was ready to give up, but Mary Lou kept making calls and late one afternoon emerged from the house with a yell, "We hit the jackpot!" She had reached a Snohomish County contractor who offered to take all the dirt. The next morning a line of six empty trucks was waiting, and our dozer operator had his hands full all day. By night, a new driveway and parking area had been excavated and graded.

The yard was still a raw hillside scraped bare. We wanted to bring home something of the mountains with waterfalls, rocks, and native plantings. Over the next ten years we hand-picked rocks from a quarry near Monroe, and collected native alpine plants, rounded river stones, and weathered snags and stumps. Plants and trees came from Bampa Gazzam's property at Stavis Bay on Hood Canal, and from the Forest Service digging site at Corral Pass in the Cascades. Most of the smooth river rocks and weathered stumps came from the south fork of the Snoqualmie River.

Our faithful 1956 Chevrolet wagon, "The Old Yellow Beast," hauled heroic loads of rocks, stumps, and dwarf trees over rugged mountain roads. On one of our stump-searching expeditions, we spotted a gnarled cedar stump across the Snoqualmie River. We crossed a foot bridge downstream and walked back along the riverbank. The plan was to roll the stump into the water and start it across with a big push. It took all of us to pry one end of the stump up to

Landscaping the 903 Shoreland Drive yard involved the whole family and brought great adventures as well as treasured quiet moments.

a tipping position. Fearing that it would roll back on the children, Mary Lou held on to it a moment too long. She was still on top of the stump as it tipped over, splashed into the river, and quickly floated beyond reach. The kids began yelling, but Mary Lou reassured them, "I'm OK. I can ride this thing across. Get on the other side and throw me a rope."

While we ran back to the bridge and crossed the river, the stump and its captain somehow drifted through the deep water without turning over and landed on a gravel beach a few feet from the campers' road where our wagon was parked. This same stump still decorated our entry years later!

Many of the rocks in our rockeries and waterfalls were literally placed with our own sweat and blood. On one occasion, a rock we were prying into position slipped off my iron pry bar onto Mary Lou.

In a matter-of-fact tone, she said, "Jim, my hand is caught under this thing."

After a minute of frantic digging, the rock was lifted off her hand. Two fingers were badly smashed, and blood was

Mary Lou's drawings depicting the strenuous family landscaping efforts.

everywhere, her hand an ugly mess of bone and flesh. Neither then, nor later in the emergency room, did Mary Lou cry or complain, but assured everyone that her hand would be fine. It took weeks for the wounds and breaks to heal, and she was left with a permanently crooked joint in one finger.

If Mary Lou was pretty good at dreaming up family projects, she was a veritable master at motivating her crew. Her approach could be summed up in one phrase: increase their enjoyment of the work. She watched each of us, found what parts of the work we liked the least, and then proceeded to do those parts herself. For example, I loved to work in the garden or to build things, and this outdoor effort provided release from the tensions of downtown competition. I found it frustrating, however, to interrupt gardening or carpentry to find misplaced tools or to shop for fertilizer, hardware, or lumber. Mary Lou either foresaw these needs and supplied them in advance or interrupted her own activity to run errands. If a bottleneck slowed our progress, it seldom lasted long.

Her trips to buy nails or lumber always produced fringe benefits for the workers in the form of popcorn, fruit, candy, or a favorite-flavor ice cream cone. She found every excuse to praise progress, no matter how spotty. And at least for this crew, one compliment was worth a dozen criticisms.

Any house gradually takes on character from those who live there. Mary Lou led the "character building" process with her special formula of optimism, love, and family participation. She created a place in the heart for her children, a planning headquarters for our community dreams, and a refuge of friendship for everyone who came. In no time at all, her free spirit transformed the shell of stone and wood into a "castle in Camelot."

I remember how warmly everyone who came into our home was received, how easy the laughter. Everyday routines were made special. When I drove out of the driveway each morning there were always two good-bye waves—the first as the car started up the hill, and the second at the hilltop just before turning out of sight. These were not absent-minded lifts of the arm, but vigorous, two-handed, over-the-head waves, complete with blowing kisses and victory signs.

Every time our barking dogs announced a family car's arrival, the front door would swing open and Mary Lou's smile would light up the entry—arms held wide for a homecoming hug. This was her way no matter how tired she was or how worn out and discouraged the returning student or worker.

Camelot was not always spotlessly clean. She once confided, "When I have to choose what to do with my time, the house always seems to come last, and the dishes get a quick shuffle. I like to have nice things and a neat home, but I want a happy family more. There never seems to be enough time for everyone and everything. Family should get the most, then friends, then civic work, and if there's time left over, I'll do the house."

Mary Lou and I grew up in extended families. We watched our parents, grandparents, aunts, and uncles make conscious efforts to "keep in touch with," "gather together," and "watch over" each other no matter how distant. Our families were the touchstone that made us feel comfortable as human beings in a world that sometimes seemed alien. As children we spent considerable time with grandparents and these experiences were "good times" that stuck in our memories. Mary Lou wanted our children to know their grandparents as well as she had known hers.

When the Earlings moved from Fairbanks to Bainbridge Island they purchased a vintage 1930s cabin cruiser and used it for summer sailing in the San Juan Islands. When we were asked to come along, Mary Lou usually managed to dovetail schedules so we could accept. The children loved those cruises.

My parents were also anxious to have quality time with their grandchildren but, except for Christmas or Seafair parties, they usually invited a select and more manageable number of children—sometimes Bobby, sometimes "the girls," or a particular child for a special event. This meant that Mary Lou had to deliver the chosen ones and babysit the remainder. Still, she jumped at every chance for grandparent visits.

The children remembered staying in the big Ellis house with its St. Bernard watchdog and playing all kinds of games with "Tilly" and "Pars" (my kids' nicknames for their grandparents). There were exciting shopping trips downtown with Tilly and baseball games with Pars. There were trips to University of Washington football games and a Disneyland vacation. Steve remembers lawn bowling on a grassy court and many conversations with grandparents. In September, the Puyallup Fair with its prize farm animals and circus-like atmosphere was Tilly's tour de force and the children looked forward to it all year long.

Perhaps the biggest effort to fit her children into the separate worlds of their grandparents was Mary Lou's annual "Christmas crash." The "crash" consisted of three different celebrations accomplished on the same day. In later years, everyone also went to a candlelight church service on Christmas Eve at Bob's urging.

The family getting ready for Christmas, circa 1955.

Preparations began months ahead with only token assistance from me until the last weekend when our friends, the Ways, joined us to cut trees in a clearing near Raging River. Our trees were usually scrubby and topped with a cardboard flag which was prepared by Lynn and bore the insignia "Charlie Brown's Christmas Tree" from the comic strip character for whom things never went right.

Of course, the children had to be dressed in their best clothes for Christmas Day. The morning started early at Camelot with plenty of fanfare, stockings, and present opening. About mid-morning everybody squeezed into an overloaded station wagon for a trip to the Ellis grandparents. Their house was always beautifully decorated, gifts were wrapped exquisitely, brunch was delicious and bountiful, and my father served champagne in the afternoon as friends came to call.

Mid-afternoon we caught a ferry to Bainbridge Island for the last stage of the holiday. In their secluded Pleasant Beach cottage, Roy and Mary Earling traditionally trimmed a small tree with carefully preserved heirloom ornaments. "Grandmom" and "Grandpop" handed out still more presents, a big Christmas dinner was shared with Mary Lou's sister Barbara and her family, and the children collapsed exhausted into bunks in the Earling guest house.

Mary Lou never considered the possibility of celebrating with different grandparents on alternate years, saying, "We're lucky that our families live so close. Who knows whether everyone will still be here next year."

Most days were not dull around Camelot. To the casual observer the place must have looked like a four-ring circus with no one in charge. In fact, of course, the circus had its purposes and Mary Lou was the ring master. The rest of us were comfortable with the conductor.

On rare occasions, I could be seen coming or going from somewhere else, seeking refuge to do homework, or waging a losing struggle to protect the furniture. Moments of reflection told me that I was beginning to fall behind the four young mysteries who were unfolding before us. One evening after quiet had mercifully descended, I asked Mary Lou how she managed to find out so much about each child.

"You need to spend more time one-on-one with your kids, darling," she answered, "especially when *they* want you to. The secret is discovering something that is really important to them. Once you find that something, they will talk about it, and you can learn."

In the years that followed I tried to find these openings, helped by occasional prompting from Mary Lou. One chance occurred when Bob entered high school and he decided to turn out for the wrestling team. He made this decision entirely on his own. When Mary Lou found out, she was worried.

"Can't he do something that is less dangerous?" she asked one evening.

I thought wrestling would be an ideal physical activity for Bob because he could compete with boys his own size and his innate determination would make him successful. After some discussion, Mary Lou finally acquiesced, and we encouraged this new activity.

Mary Lou and I attended most of the meets for the next two years. It was sheer agony for her to watch these young wrestlers pin each other or put their opponent in a predicament. Much of the time, Mary Lou closed her eyes or found a way of covering her face as if in thought. She confessed that in every match she was "worried sick" that Bob would be hurt.

In his senior year, Bob was a member of Bellevue's surprising state championship team. For the first elimination tournament he was matched against the top seeded wrestler in his weight class. When Bob's opponent was introduced, Mary Lou leaned over to say, "He looks twice as big as Bob. It's not a fair contest." In fact, however, Bob astonished the crowd by pinning his opponent in the second round of the match. Mary Lou had not actually seen the victory because her eyes were closed tight. For her, however, the importance of these events was that I had found something important to Bob that he and I could share.

From her early childhood, I had felt an intuitive rapport with Lynn. We often sang and danced and clowned around. However, when she reached high school age, it was hard for me to understand some of the erratic behavior of my youngest daughter. Lynn was always trying something new and doing the unexpected. Mary Lou stayed close to Lynn during this period, but I seemed to be losing touch with her.

It had been our practice to take each child on one of my trips to Washington, D.C., so they could learn about the nation's history. When Lynn's turn came, Mary Lou suggested that I add a side trip to New York and take Lynn to a Broadway musical play.

"Lynn is interested in theatre. She likes singing and feeling the excitement of something new. If you add a little New York entertainment to the D.C. history, you will have a real chance to share with your daughter."

Lynn was ecstatic when we added New York to our itinerary and the big hit of the trip was the Broadway musical play *Promises, Promises*. Her eyes were wide as saucers and she bubbled over with enthusiasm. When we returned to Seattle, she purchased an original cast recording and memorized the songs. The trip gave us a chance to share something special, and briefly let me inside her world.

When Steve was about ten years old, I promised him that we would plant a vegetable garden on the first warm Sunday in April. In preparation, Mary

Lou took Steve to the nursery to purchase seeds, small tomato plants, and a sack of fertilizer. The next Sunday turned out sunny and warm, but I had brought work home. After breakfast I closed the study doors saying, "I need one hour of quiet, Steve, to finish this draft, then we'll plant the garden."

The work proved more difficult than expected; three hours later I was still struggling with it. About noon Mary Lou quietly came into the study, closed the door behind her and whispered, "Come over here for a second. There's something you should see."

I objected, "Beaver, I'll never get this damn thing done if you interrupt me."

"It'll just take a second. You have to see this."

I got up and followed her to the door, then looked through a small crack to see Steve sitting patiently on the couch in the living room.

"He's been sitting like that for two hours waiting for you to come out! Why don't you finish that thing tonight?" asked Mary Lou. "We don't have many Sundays as nice as this. Remember, darling, there's only one spring when your boy is ten years old."

I felt a lump rising in my throat as I looked through the door at Steve, then turned and folded the papers away.

The afternoon was glorious. Mary Lou brought a picnic lunch up to the garden. We sat on the grass and watched the paths of sunshine sparkle on the lake. Steve and I shared the ancient thrill of farmers planting seeds. When the neat rows were tamped down, fertilized, and watered, father and son surveyed their effort. Steve complimented our work.

"Not bad at all," I agreed. "Do you think we'll get your mother's Good Housekeeping Seal of Approval?" referencing the popular phrase derived from *Good Housekeeping* women's magazine, which sometimes awarded a "Seal of Approval" to good consumer products.

Steve brought Mary Lou up from the house, and after enthusiastically admiring each row, she put her arms around her husband and son. "You guys do good work together."

The indenture draft was finished that night, after Steve had gone to bed.

⼗

CHAPTER 17

A Ragged and Funny Crew

DURING THE EARLY years of our marriage, we spent most vacation times at Raging River, working on the cabin, but a year after moving into the Montlake house, Mary Lou saw the need for some "no-work" vacations. With a growing family, increased law office responsibility, and our civic commitment to Bob, we were both working 12 to 14 hours a day. And some of our civic projects were proving to be controversial and stressful. Mary Lou and I needed more rest and the whole family needed more quality time together.

This was the beginning of a continuing effort by Mary Lou to set aside time for real vacations. We sometimes managed to squeeze out two or three days occasionally, but each year she insisted that we take the authorized two-week vacation at some place out of reach from the office. These vacations covered the full range of Northwest recreational treasures from Lake Chelan to the San Juan Islands, but our favorite place became the Washington and Oregon coasts, no matter the season.

*Jim joins friends for some fishing at Lena Lake in the Olympic
Mountains for a break from cabin construction and law studies.*

THE COAST

The whole family was fascinated by the romance of lighthouses, the rusty
hulks of shipwrecks and the possibility of finding a green glass fish net float
which had been carried for years on the Japan Current across the Pacific.
Adventures included clam digging and camp cooking, rockhounding and
antique shopping. The ocean came to symbolize excitement, togetherness,
discovery, freedom, and fun for our entire family. Because of our small
clothing budget, Mary Lou dubbed her motley group the "Ragged and Funny
Crew," drawing from the words of one of the songs we sang at the top of our
lungs while driving.

Mary Lou made these beach vacations enjoyable for everyone by being
sensitive to our different desires. Each person's favorite activity was somehow
accommodated in a crowded agenda. When Lynn became restless in the agate
mines, Mary Lou would take her to explore a nearby town while the rest of
us looked for agates to our heart's content. Picnic lunches were magically
delivered by Mary Lou to "keep you guys on the beach and having fun."

Jim and Lynn digging a "mine" in their quest for agates.

Jim and Steve sort and rub oil on agates
during a later trip to Yachats, Oregon.

Judi and Jim agate hunting.

RIVERS AND RASPBERRIES

As the children grew older and sought activities with excitement, we bought two-man rubber life rafts for floating Cascade Mountain rivers. Mary Lou concurrently purchased a number of life jackets. After Bob and I tried rafting the Yakima River, everyone wanted to have a piece of the fun. Soon, raft trips became the high point of summer weekends for our teenage children and their friends. Our rafting rivers were usually picked to permit a one-day trip. They included the Yakima and Cle Elum on the east slope of the Cascades, or the Stillaguamish, the Snoqualmie and, our favorite, the Skykomish, on the west slope of the Cascades.

Mary Lou's worrying about "dangerous rapids" brought howls of laughter from children who felt safely immortal. Nevertheless, Mary Lou checked the rafts for leaks, purchased new ones at any sign of weakness, kept all life jackets in a state of readiness, and informed us of the latest safety procedures.

After joining us for several runs on the Skykomish River, Mary Lou said, "It's too scary for me. Let me be the car driver and pick you guys up at the end of the run." It had always seemed like a long hike back to the car after a wet float down the river. I am absolutely sure that her motive was fun for the group because she was essentially without fear for herself. In any event, Mary Lou insisted on being the driver and dozens of trips were more enjoyable for the rafters because she waited and worried at the bottom of the run. She would often pick us up with a box of fresh raspberries for her hungry crew.

Our family rafting adventures occurred a few years before this form of recreation became popular and before safety rules were widely circulated. Mary Lou and I insisted that rafters walk or drive along the route of each run before putting the rafts in the water. The children were generally reckless and looked at these precautions as ways to keep Mom from worrying. However, they thought differently after a Sunday afternoon when Lynn and Steve rafted the South Fork of the Snoqualmie with me.

The river had been deceptively easy until we rounded a bend to see a pile of trees that had fallen across part of the stream. In an instant, we were pushed against the logjam and tipped over. Lynn was thrown up onto the logs, but eight-year-old Steve and I were thrown downward and under the jam. When I came up thirty feet down river, I could see Lynn, but not Steve.

I felt a wave of panic! I frantically scanned the deep pool and there was Steve, swimming in the clear water about six feet under the surface. With a few frenzied strokes I swam toward the eddy holding him down, dove under and grabbed his jacket. A few minutes later we were gasping for breath on the gravel bank. Steve had swallowed water and after he began breathing normally said, "Dad, we're lucky to be alive."

We all thanked God and rested awhile. Then Lynn saw that our means of transportation was stuck tight in the jam. Removing the raft required three exhausting swimming efforts and lasted half an hour. When we finally floated down to the bridge where the car was parked, we poured out the story to a relieved Mary Lou.

Kathy Fletcher Develops a Passion for the Environment

Our family rafting adventures sometimes included friends. To reciprocate Betty and Bob Fletchers' hospitality for inviting me to dinner one evening while Mary Lou was traveling, I asked if they would like to take a river raft trip with me on the Skykomish River. We shared a deep interest in Northwest flora and fauna and they and their daughter Kathy were delighted with the idea. I packed up our family's two rafts and the four of us drove up to the Skykomish River

With quick instructions and life jackets on, the four of us set out on an adventure. Kathy and I were in the first raft with Betty and Bob following close behind us. I knew the first stretch would be particularly exciting for first timers. I could tell that Kathy was really enjoying the ride. I took the opportunity to point out to her just how much better one can see the natural environment by traveling along the way.

From the outset, Kathy was enthusiastic. After the first section of rapids, the remaining section of the run was smooth and uneventful, and we had the opportunity to enjoy the beauty of the river. Everyone was impressed with the incredible view of the natural surroundings and the beautiful river valley.

As we stood on the riverbank ringing out our wet clothes at the end of the trip, Kathy looked at me and said, "That is the most fun I've had in my life!"

I could tell she had been moved by the sound and feel of the river in this natural environment. Years later, Kathy became an active environmental leader as an employee of the Carter Administration, serving on the White House Domestic Policy Staff. She handled environmental and natural resource issues during the time I was on the National Water Commission. I sometimes heard people on the Commission staff refer to her as the *"Femme Terrible"* of water project development. I smiled to remember that she inherited the intelligence and determination of her mother and father, and maybe a little of her dedication stemmed from her first river rafting trip.

Later, Kathy founded and directed People for Puget Sound, a citizens' organization formed in 1991 to protect and restore Puget Sound and the Northwest Straits. She also served on the Northwest Straits Commission and the Puget Sound Partnership's Ecosystem Coordination Board.

THE HAWAII SURPRISE

In the spring of 1968, Bob was graduating from Yale University. Mary Lou suggested that he might enjoy a family vacation in Hawaii more than our flying to New Haven for graduation. Predictably, I reacted that a trip to Hawaii for a large family would be too expensive, and that I could not get away from the office for that long a time.

After a few skirmishes on the subject, Mary Lou appeared to abandon the idea. However, unknown to me, she found that Bob *would* much prefer a family vacation to a graduation ceremony. Mary Lou then quietly conspired with my secretary to block out a week on my calendar in June and made excursion-rate airplane and hotel reservations for Hawaii.

A couple weeks before the graduation date, I noticed that the week of June 15th was almost free of appointments on my calendar. One evening when Mary Lou and I were alone in the den I said, "You know, honey, it's too bad I didn't go for your Hawaii idea. It might be possible to get away for a week after all."

Mary Lou disappeared into the bedroom, then reappeared with an ear-to-ear grin and a handful of tickets and reservations. "Just in case you changed your mind, I thought I'd get these. I haven't told the children where we're going, so you can make it a surprise."

"Beaver, you are something else! Would you take a big hug from a crow-eating goat?"

(I had bestowed the nickname "Old Goat" or "O.G." on myself to call attention to the fact that some fathers seem to end up paying the bills.)

SUNDAYS IN THE MOUNTAINS

As soon as the children were old enough to hike and the warm weather arrived in Puget Sound, Mary Lou began to pack lunches for Sundays in the mountains. If we left Bellevue in early daylight, we could reach most trailheads by mid-morning, walk to rocky vistas, lakes, and meadows, and be home in time for dinner. Our much-loved dog, Trixie, was a regular member of our Sunday crew.

We hiked for the simple joy of it. Each of us took turns carrying a single backpack, which held lunch treats on the way up and trail litter on the way down. No telephones broke the circle of communion with family and nature. We took pictures of things we liked and left flowers where they grew. Mary Lou taught us the names of most of the mountain flowers that greeted us. Recalling the neatly labeled geology specimens in R. B.'s study, we were challenged to find lava from volcanic eruptions, bedrock polished by glaciers, shells from sea beds thrust up when ridges were formed, and pieces of trees that had turned to stone by the chemistry of time.

One Sunday in July, we hiked to a small lake in a mountain meadow. After lunch, Mary Lou and I leaned against each other back-to-back, soaking up the peace and warmth, while the children fished for trout from the shallow shoreline under the watchful eyes of Trixie. The afternoon sun cast long shafts of amber light between the peaks, filling the basin around us.

"Aren't these mountains something special, Beaver?" I asked. "They seem to be saying, 'Come home to the wonder of creation.'"

"Yes, Jim darling," Mary Lou responded, reaching out to put her hand on mine. "There's something about sunlight on the mountains that makes me glow inside." After a moment of quiet she took my hand in both of hers. "If we believe in a God of this creation, why don't we declare ourselves and join a church?"

I turned around to look at her. A love of nature was one of our strongly shared feelings, but church participation had always been left in a kind of limbo between us. "Honey, most churches are too bound up in doctrine for me," I replied. "Each doctrine claims to have the only path to God's kingdom. Church leaders too easily turn secular events into God's will. Minute differences become chasms. Do we want to be defined by such an idea?" My own feeling was that the Golden Rule was a pretty good Bible for practicing honesty, generosity, and kindness in daily life and better than listening to church sermons. I knew Mary Lou saw all of these as parts of a whole. "Isn't there more than one way to keep the Sabbath well?" I asked, hoping to keep our "church" experience in the mountains I had loved since boyhood.

Mary Lou did not enjoy listening to repetitive litanies of doctrine any more than I did, but she believed that church services could also be an experience in discovery.

"A good church should encourage us to think more about God," she answered, listening to me intently, far from ready to drop the subject. "A good

Mary Lou enjoying a mountain hike.

minister should stimulate your mind, not shut it down. Church services should be more like people of good will reaching toward God together. Remember how your brother Bob wrote that he seldom missed church services while he was in combat? He needed shared prayers then."

It was now clear to me that Mary Lou had been thinking about this subject and waiting for this moment for some time.

"Natural beauty is a wonderful reminder of God's presence, but it isn't the only one," she continued. "Is the creation of mountains any greater miracle than a baby being born?"

I was beginning to feel defensive. "Maybe we're both right, Beaver. Who knows for absolute sure? Ever since grade school the mountains have been my temple. John Muir once said, 'The devil never hunts above the timberline.' Millions of people have been killed in the name of different holy writs by the armies of intolerant religions. There are no wars between mountains. It's always been easier for me to pray in this temple."

"I'm not talking about holy wars, Jim, or about intolerant religions. I'm talking about you and me and our children, about the universal love that Jesus taught, and about choosing a Christian church that will be right for us. I know human institutions are fallible, but that's a reason for us to support the good ones. Joining a church doesn't say that we have the *only* way to understand God. It just says that we think Jesus showed one path that we can take and that we want our children to know about this way."

We were facing each other by this time, sitting with hands clasped over knees. As Mary Lou spoke intensely, I began to look for an honorable retreat.

"Which of the different churches of Christ do you want us to join, honey? Would you accept a tolerant minister like Dale Turner? Would you still listen to other religious views? Rabbi Levine comes close to many of our shared ideals. And how much time would we have for family hikes in the mountains, if we spend Sunday mornings in church?"

"I love Rabbi Levine, and Dale Turner would be perfect for us, but I have an even better idea," replied Mary Lou, sensing that this was the time for her punch line. "Why don't we join Bob's church? You admired Lincoln Reed's sermon when we attended Easter service with Bob. Why not be together in the same church?"

It was now clear that I had fallen into another tender trap from which escape was useless. Our son Bob had read the Bible from cover to cover on his own initiative in the ninth grade and had joined the Bellevue Congregational Youth Group with friends. Mary Lou and I had both seen the positive effects of this program. And, after all, I believed in the teachings of Jesus Christ as much as she did.

"We don't need to be in church every Sunday," said Mary Lou, reaching for a touch of compromise, "We can still hike in the mountains when the weather is right."

"OK, Beaver, let's do it!" I knew she had hit upon the right course and decided it was time to join the winning side. "Let's tell Bob first so he can get credit for new church members."

We stood up and walked hand-in-hand toward the children on the lake shore. Why hadn't I thought of Bellevue Congregational myself? The fact was that my son was leading me! Albeit with a little help from his mother.

The children had given up fishing after many unsuccessful casts from the shore. I made a few tries and couldn't get a strike. "It doesn't look like trout for dinner tonight," I said. "We may need a raft to fish this lake." Bob later packed in a small rubber raft on hikes and seldom failed to catch fish.

The years that followed didn't bring a major change in our activity pattern. To Bob's great delight we joined his church, but our attendance was slim; most summer Sundays were still spent hiking mountain trails, rafting rivers, or cultivating gardens. There was a subtle difference, however, in the unspoken unity of the family, in the religious grace of celebrations and in the circle of friends when losses were too hard to bear alone.

The mountains remained our summer temple. If anything, the sun shone more brightly along the peaks as we hunted for agates on Red Top and the flowers seemed to open more fully as we walked through high mountain meadows. And for Mary Lou and me, a growing consciousness of the meaning in life and the teaching of Jesus Christ meant longer pauses to reflect upon nature and humanity as gifts from the mystery of creation.

BOOK FIVE

Vision of the People

CHAPTER 18

Dorm's Transit Dream

Transportation is only one of the physical elements which shape a city. To achieve a satisfactory total design, the relationship between all of the shaping forces must be recognized . . . Just as a system of sewage disposal is necessary for the enjoyment of beaches or waterfront parks so each of the basic sinews of the city has a direct relation to the more familiar projects for city beautification and human fulfillment.

—*Jim Ellis, "Transportation and the Shape of the City" speech to the Seattle Rotary Club, November 3, 1965*

METROPOLITAN PUBLIC transportation proved to be the most stubborn challenge facing Mary Lou and me in our post-war commitment to make life better for people in the place where my brother Bob grew up. The Kitchen Group of crusaders knew that public transit was essential for the mobility of young, elderly, low-income, and handicapped residents of cities. We also believed that a major investment in rapid transit facilities would eventually be needed to efficiently carry a reasonable share of working commuters through limited main corridors during peak hours. After our election defeat in March 1958, we struggled for a way to bring metropolitan public transportation back on the regional political screen.

The war years of gas rationing and scarce cars had produced jam-packed buses and trolleys but, after 1950, public transit patronage in Seattle and across the nation began a sharp decline. As urban portions of the Interstate

"National System of Interstate and Defense Highways Act"

When Dwight Eisenhower became President, he applied his memory of German "Autobahns" to propose and build a national system of limited-access express highways to and through the major urban centers of the United States. Eisenhower signed the "National System of Interstate and Defense Highways Act" on June 29, 1956. It originally provided eighty percent federal funding needed for a national network of highways. These highways included I-5 running north and south through Seattle, and I-90 running east and west. The interstate freeways soon became the new backbone of American surface transportation.

As freeway construction spread across the country, city planners pointed out the large amount of space required to carry people by automobile and the surprising amount of space needed to park these vehicles. One freeway lane of space has the capacity to carry five times more people per hour by train than the same lane of space can carry people by car.

Highway system launched by President Eisenhower were opened for use, the share of public transit trips declined further, while auto trips surged.

The post-war years brought Seattle a rapid growth in population, personal incomes, cars, trucks, as well as industrial, commercial, and residential development. World War II had destroyed the factories of Europe and Japan, while factories in the United States were unharmed. This fact enabled United States companies to supply a pent-up global demand for cars, trucks, and manufacturing equipment. Aircraft production shifted toward commercial planes and Boeing became a world leader. The Marshall Plan created by Truman poured dollars into Europe to pay for reconstruction. Per capita real incomes grew and federal debt per capita declined.

Also, after years of war-time separation, young men and women were focused on building their lives and formed new families at a record pace. The children born in the fifties and sixties became the huge "baby boom" generation. These families wanted houses with big windows and new developments with open space, so developers built new housing in the suburbs where ample land was available at lower prices. These new homes needed roads, schools, and utilities. And, as soon as cars became available, more workers wanted to drive to work, and the rural county roads were soon overloaded each weekday morning and evening.

One consequence of building the interstate freeway system was the clearing of wide paths for limited-access highway lanes through existing cities. In the process, tens of thousands of homes and businesses were demolished. Seattle was no exception. The I-5 freeway cut through the city from north to south, displacing more than 12,000 families and business establishments. Throughout the nation, business and labor pushed to have new freeway capacity completed quickly, but the displacement of tens of thousands of families produced a significant public backlash.

At first, new freeways provided greatly improved travel times. However, traffic built up quickly as more cars used the improved routes. It wasn't long before peak hour congestion became as bad on these new freeways as it had been on the old roads they replaced.

Public transit buses were moving in the same crowded traffic lanes. A need for rapid public transit on separate rights-of-way became apparent to those who had seen fast and efficient subways and elevated structures in many eastern cities.

It was, of course, very expensive to build new freeways. But it was also expensive to build new rapid transit lines, particularly if they were built underground. A few big cities had inherited complete subway systems from the pre-freeway era, and a few succeeded in putting transit trains in the center lanes of new freeways. This latter idea was shot down for I-5 in Seattle by State Highway Director William Bugge who said it was an interesting idea if people could wait five years longer for the freeway to be redesigned. Bugge knew business leaders were not willing to wait any time at all to get existing congestion unplugged by new freeways which were funded and ready to be built.

Thus began a growing struggle between pro-highway and pro-transit advocates nationwide. A "highway lobby" of automobile manufacturers, petroleum producers, tire companies, and other ancillary business and user organizations raised large amounts of money to lobby for additional fuel-tax funding for federal and state freeways. On the other side, federal, state, and local tax financing for public transportation facilities was virtually non-existent. A heroic exception was the San Francisco Bay Area which voted for taxes and built a rapid transit system (BART) that became an inspiration for people like then-Councilman Dorm Braman.

This benign neglect of transit began to change as citizen protests grew in the urban neighborhoods through which new freeways were proposed to run.

Regional transportation planning was largely in the hands of state highway directors until creation of the Puget Sound Council of Governments (PSCG), a new regional planning body authorized by the state to approve plans by local governments for state and federal grant eligibility.

The 1957 state legislation that had led to the successful election for the Lake Washington cleanup had also authorized that voters could later use the same Metro Council to perform other functions. Proponents of the failed election for sewers and transit in March 1958 had not given up their public transportation vision. Dedicated and determined, Seattle mayor Gordon Clinton appointed Dorm to a new City-County transit committee that would explore the next steps needed to move the transit issue forward. Transit planning was authorized by the legislature to be performed by Metro and by the PSCG.

The new committee and the PSCG consultants saw a need for additional highway capacity to take some of the general traffic load off I-5 by building a parallel expressway on the eastside of the lake. However, they also saw the need to divert part of the I-5 peak-hour commuter travel load from the freeway to a new rapid rail transit line located either in the I-5 median, or in a subway adjacent to I-5. They found that rail rapid transit trains could carry more than five times more people during a peak hour than automobiles using an equal amount of space. If new electric transit facilities were built in subways under existing streets, building density could be supported, surface noise from trains would be avoided, and air quality would be improved. Scarce street space would remain available to service vehicles and local automobile access.

The big challenge for rail subways was the high cost of underground construction. Financing the large capital costs of long-lived public facilities was customarily met by borrowing the construction cost and repaying the amount borrowed in manageable installments. However, in the Metro example, even with a lengthy repayment period of forty years, the amount of local bonds which could be issued under Constitutional limits would be less than half the estimated cost of a rail rapid transit system with substantial subway segments. The regional consultant study confirmed that a *large* amount of either state or federal funding would be needed to pay for underground rail rapid transit facilities that could serve the growing Seattle King County Metropolitan area and eventually the central Puget Sound region.

In 1962, President John F. Kennedy sent a major transportation message to Congress. He called for the establishment of a program of federal capital assistance for mass transportation. In his message President Kennedy said, "To conserve and enhance values in existing urban areas is essential. But at least as important are steps to promote economic efficiency and livability in areas of future development. Our national welfare therefore requires the provision of good urban transportation, with the properly balanced use of private vehicles and modern mass transport to help shape, as well as serve, urban growth."

DORM BRAMAN AND WARREN G. MAGNUSON

In the years before the Seattle World's Fair of 1962, national press attention was seldom drawn to Seattle. A few national news stories focused on the start-up of Boeing's commercial jet transport program and the first phase of Metro's pace-setting water pollution abatement plan which had just begun to produce visible improvements. However, this quiet curtain was opened wide when Seattle business and city leaders staged a splashy and surprisingly successful World's Fair in the summer of 1962.

Washington State Senator Warren G. "Maggie" Magnuson was Chairman of the Senate Commerce Committee and an influential member of the Appropriations Committee. He was instrumental in securing federal funding for the World's Fair, including the strikingly beautiful Pacific Science Center building. He also encouraged organized labor to give a "no strike" pledge while the fair was being built. The fair illustrated the local impact of his national influence. Seattleites enjoyed the fair and it surprised everyone by operating in the black.

Many pundits had forecast that the Seattle World's Fair would fail because of its location at the Northwest corner of the nation and the saturation of national interest by prior world's fairs in New York and San Francisco. However, the Seattle promoters were not discouraged. Eddie Carlson, Joe Gandy, Bill Street, and others overcame many challenges and pulled off a successful fair. The privately built Space Needle became a symbol of the fair and a long-lasting icon of the city. The monorail built to take people from downtown to the world's fair site became an instant success and fare revenues provided enough net cash to pay the cost of construction.

Dorm Braman was attracted to and excited by the fair project. It appealed to his instinct to build large things which people could use and enjoy. The monorail intensified Dorm's and the community's interest in mass transit. He brought the monorail concept to the Metro Study Committee and used his membership on the World's Fair Committee to learn firsthand about other cities' rapid transit systems. The Seattle Monorail was suggested as the solution for rapid public transit in the Seattle area. It was a time of great optimism and it propelled Braman to begin seriously considering a run for mayor.

The fair had also been a personal victory for Maggie, but it contributed to over confidence in his re-election campaign of November 1962. The closeness of the 1962 election came as a shock to Magnuson and his close advisors and resulted in a complete reorganization of his Senatorial staff. Magnuson made the brilliant young Senate Commerce Committee Counsel, Gerald Grinstein, his new chief of staff. Raised in Seattle and a graduate of Yale and Harvard Law, Grinstein believed the campaign had not understood the rising baby boom generation. He suggested a strategy for Magnuson to become the Senate leader on consumer protection. Maggie shifted his new platform to issues of public health protection and removal of obstructions to the flow of commerce between states. His new focus came with a heightened profile at a national level, further deepening his clout.

Dorm Braman understood the capabilities of rail rapid transit and the challenging double hurdle of high subway construction cost and the sixty percent "Yes" vote required for the approval of local bonds to finance such high costs. He called me to come to his office one morning shortly after his March 1964 election as mayor. Leaning forward in his new chair, he said he had concluded that getting *state* support would be "hopeless" in the face of opposition by State Highway Director Bill Bugge and the automobile lobby. However, he believed *federal* support might be achieved with leadership from the growing seniority of Magnuson as an influential member of the Appropriations Committee. While I was sitting in his office, Braman telephoned Maggie in his Seattle office and asked for a meeting. The Senator agreed to meet with us the following morning.

After listening intently to Dorm, Maggie asked one question, "Mr. Mayor, if you know, do your people want this program?" Dorm responded that he was convinced that the people of Seattle would vote for rapid transit bonds if they could get sufficient federal funds to ensure that the system would actually be built. Magnuson was intrigued by the idea of a big project that could have real benefits for the largest city in his state. He pointed out that a national program would first have to be authorized. He knew that President Kennedy had proposed such a program and believed that President Johnson would support it. He told us that a bill along these lines had once passed the House, and another had recently been introduced by Senator Williams of New Jersey but was stalled in committee. From his close relationship with Lyndon Johnson, Maggie was confident that the new President would support Federal Transit Financing legislation as a part of his "Great Society" vision for the country.

Dorm Braman and I also sensed during our meetings with Magnuson, that if anyone could get the Public Transportation Bill through the Senate, it was Maggie. We knew that this bill was the crucial key to giving Metro a fighting chance of obtaining the sixty percent "Yes" vote needed to pass rapid transit bonds in the Seattle Metropolitan area.

Maggie suggested that Dorm and I come to D.C. with a draft of appropriate changes to Senator Williams' bill which Magnuson could offer to support. The "Williams" bill was better than we had hoped for with sixty-six and two-thirds percent of the cost to be paid by the federal government. This was more than the fifty-fifty split we had hoped for. (In 1973, the federal share would be raised to eighty percent to make the federal transit share equal to the highway share.) After minor changes in language, Dorm and I flew to Washington, D.C., where Maggie would introduce us to Senator Williams.

Looking back, I recall the differences between the offices of Magnuson and Williams. Maggie's office was buzzing with activity when we arrived. It took a few minutes for his staff to clear the decks for Braman before we were led in. When we got to Senator Williams' office, the place was almost empty, and we were ushered in immediately. After Maggie introduced us, he took charge of the meeting in a low gravelly voice, explaining our changes to the bill were "very minor" and suggested he would be willing to support Senator Williams' bill if they were acceptable. Williams took all of two minutes to digest the changes we had suggested and said, "They *are* minor and will be improvements, Senator." Maggie then offered that "Seattle and San Francisco" might be willing to do the "dog and pony" show for the Committee hearing. Senator Williams expressed delight at this suggestion.

Shortly after leaving Washington, D.C., Dorm and I brainstormed at length about how best to build our team for the upcoming "dog and pony" show. He would get the Puget Sound Council of Governments consultants to join us in making a presentation of the metropolitan area transportation plan, emphasizing the rail rapid transit component. These consultants were already under contract and were eager to participate in developing the presentation.

Dorm believed that rapid transit was the most important project that could be undertaken during his tenure as mayor, and he was optimistic about Maggie's chances for passage of the Williams legislation. Dorm confided to me that once he got his teeth into something as important as this his instinct was to see it through no matter what. I watched this growing commitment become more intense each week as Williams' transit bill moved closer to passage.

We flew back to Washington, D.C., for the "dog and pony" and it was well received. A large group of people attended. Not many Senators, but a good number of key staffers. Our presentation of slides and maps was delivered to a packed room and followed by a wide range of questions. Before we left Washington for home, Maggie was pleased and indicated that a few Senators might need "work" but that he would pursue them personally.

The legislative process for this potentially huge new federal program was lubricated and accelerated by Magnuson's adroit handling and President Johnson's overt support. To the surprise of some, the Urban Mass

Figure 12

Bus Stations
Rapid Transit Route & Stations
METRO AREA PERSPECTIVE

Dorm's and Maggie's transit map.

Transportation Act of 1964 (the Williams bill) was passed by the Senate 52 to 41 and by the House 212 to 129.

In addition to the authorizing legislation, future appropriations would of course be needed. But Magnuson was confident that with administration support he could get an amount appropriated which would be sufficient to fund the full federal share of Metro's plan. Of course, approval by the yet-to-be-created federal transportation department would be required and the local share of costs would have to be approved by Metro voters. The new act permitted appropriation of the full federal share of the cost of construction upon federal approval of the local plan. This federal appropriation would become immediately available for expenditure by the local agency. Metro would be able to invest the full approved federal share of capital funds until required to pay construction costs. This would provide a cushion of interest income to offset any increase in construction occurring after local bonds were issued.

We were greatly energized by this major congressional action. It was the sea-change in an ocean of challenge that we had been desperate to get. If signed by the President, it meant that we could usefully pursue ways and means of gaining the sixty percent majority vote required for Metro general obligation bonds. Dorm believed from the outset that Metro was the appropriate local agency to plan, build, and operate the metropolitan transit system. He had watched the progress of the Metro Sewer program and knew that Metro could successfully manage a large project.

By 1964, the joint City-County Committee on rapid transit had worked for two years with PSGC consultants on the nature and extent of the basic system. It had become clear to all members of the committee that rapid rail transit with its grade separated right-of-way was the key part of a long-range solution.

Braman was elated by passage of the new act. He had inspected new rail rapid transit systems in Montreal and Toronto, Canada, and the Bay Area of California. He had watched the Metro Council build a model sewage disposal system in the Seattle metropolitan area and was convinced that the same Council could successfully build a rail rapid transit system.

Dorm approached City of Seattle problems very much as he had approached his scout troop. A devoted six-year scout master of Troop 511 and former president of the Chief Seattle Council of Boy Scouts, Dorm was experienced at helping others through strong leadership, encouraging teamwork, and inspiring others to believe. He wanted his city to build something that would improve people's lives and he deeply wanted to share the excitement of this achievement with his fellow citizens.

On July 2, 1964, President Johnson signed into law, the historic Civil Rights Act of 1964. Senator Magnuson had led this Bill to final Senate passage with a masterful four-hour speech, personally delivered from the Senate floor. The Act was generally acknowledged to be primarily the work of Magnuson, and specifically Title 2, a portion of the act addressing a wide range of race-based restrictions placed by states on people of color to exclude them from public accommodations and services used in interstate travel. Grinstein has said that he thought the passage of Title 2 was the "greatest achievement of Maggie's political career."

Just days later, on July 9, 1964, President Johnson signed into law the landmark Urban Mass Transportation Act of 1964. For the metropolitan areas of the country and for Warren Magnuson, the new transit legislation was a striking act of national leadership. For Dorm Braman, it turned a far-out dream into a practical possibility.

Now it was our job to make the vision a reality.

✦

CHAPTER 19

Réveillé for Forward Thrust

Each of us knows intuitively that personal liberty begins with self-discipline and grows with love and work. Citizenship begins with thinking about the needs of others whether they live in the same neighborhood, city, metropolitan area, state, or nation.

—Jim Ellis, "Remembering Forward Thrust Forty Years Later" remarks, delivered October 27, 2008, at a Seattle Park Department party celebrating the payment of the last of the Forward Thrust bonds issued in 1968.

THE MID-1960S saw good times in King County. Boeing was hiring. Populations were growing. Real per capita disposable incomes were rising. Recent public investment decisions were turning out better than promised. Newly elected Governor Daniel J. Evans, a young veteran, symbolized the future. Public confidence in government and business leadership was high.

It was becoming apparent that the initial Metro water cleanup was going to be a success, possibly a stunning success. New treatment plants and interceptor sewers were being constructed on schedule and within budget. Metro was proving to be a conservative and effective way for the cities, sewer districts, and the county to get things done. The progressive civic leadership that created Metro gained credibility in the eyes of the public. National awards for citizenship became shared sources of local pride. At the same, time business and government leaders were on a promotional roll.

Selected Population Comparisons
1950 – 1960

Municipality	Census 1950	Census 1960
King County	732,992	935,014
Auburn	6,497	11,933
Bellevue	1,548	12,809
Issaquah	995	1,870
Kirkland	4,713	6,025
Kent	3,278	9,017
Medina	*	2,285
Mercer Island	*	*
North Bend	787	945
Redmond	573	1,426
Renton	16,039	18,453
Seattle	467,591	** 557,087
Snoqualmie	806	1,216

The December 1960 decision by the Washington State Supreme Court unanimously upholding the constitutionality of Metro, had shown most informed Seattle residents that this new government was not some sort of foreign idea. Rather, Metro was a "Made-in-Washington" product in the American tradition of change aimed at improving the ability of local governments to meet public needs. The 1960 All-America City Award for the citizens who created Metro, confirmed that they had done good work for their neighbors in the Seattle Metropolitan area. I believe these public "pats on the back," contributed to our desire to tackle problems, and our ability to gain support for more civic crusades.

As 1965 got underway, Mary Lou and I sensed that the voters of the metropolitan Seattle area might be ready for another civic challenge. One evening, I tested a new idea on her. "Why not try for a whole basket of public projects in one big election? What if rapid transit, better arterials, a covered stadium, new parks and recreation facilities, a modern airport, *and* a world trade and convention center were all offered at one time and supported by a coalition? If a green light could be given to all these public improvements in a single election, this area could see a renaissance."

Mary Lou reacted with contagious enthusiasm. "The idea is brilliant! It could really capture people's imagination. It would be great to find a catchy slogan that makes the whole thing simple." Drawing on her love of flying and public awareness of the new world of powerful jet engines, Mary Lou came up with the name "Forward Thrust" and it stuck.

As we talked into the evening with increasing intensity, she began to sense that this new dream might also become an obsession. "Don't stretch yourself too far, darling," she warned. "You are already working too hard. The children and I need to see you once in a while. And what about Paul Seibert? Have you talked with him about this new idea?"

PAUL SEIBERT

Paul Seibert was a close friend and a born spark plug of activity. Paul and his wife Betty had become our good friends during work together at the Municipal League and in the Lake Washington clean-up crusade. Paul had moved to Seattle from Oregon in 1945 to work for the Municipal League. In addition to being a public relations expert, Paul served as the editor of the *Municipal News* from 1945 to 1952, when he joined Frederick E. Baker and Associates of Seattle as public relations director. In 1958, Joe Gandy, the founding president of the Central Association of Seattle, persuaded Paul to manage that organization as executive vice president. Joe said that finding Paul Siebert for this job was his "Gift to Seattle."

Our friendship continued through his years with the Central Association, later called the Downtown Seattle Association. We talked frequently about the work of Mayor Clinton's committee on rapid transit. Downtown leaders had been looking for a way to reverse declining transit ridership and the mayor's committee believed that frequent downtown service by rail rapid transit could do the job. However, they also realized that expensive subway construction would be needed in the city's narrow waist between Lake

Washington and Puget Sound. Such a system could not be financed entirely by local funds.

By the summer of 1964, with the authorization of federal funding by the Urban Mass Transportation Act of 1964, Maggie was confident that the Congress would appropriate sufficient funds to pay two-thirds of the cost of building a federally approved rapid transit system for the Seattle Metropolitan Area. Dorm and I believed that his dream of rapid transit had now become possible *if* we could achieve the state-required 60 percent "Yes" vote for the General Obligation Bonds needed to finance the local share of construction costs.

When I first mentioned the idea of a multi-purpose capital crusade to Paul, he had been intrigued, but after the news of available federal financial assistance made rapid transit feasible, he jumped on board with both feet. He said our idea for a major capital improvement program just went from good to fantastic! He recognized our most vital need was transportation and the obvious missing link is rapid transit. He suggested that transportation be the center piece of our "capital crusade" and would be the perfect subject for a major speech to Downtown Rotary. And soon. Public information strategy was Paul's special talent. Mary Lou and I listened intently and then followed his lead.

Paul thought we should first talk to media management on a confidential basis and see if they would hold off public comment until after the speech was made. In October, we met with the managers of the large radio and television stations and the county newspapers to see if they would be willing to support such a huge civic effort. Every reaction was positive! John Fournier of the *Valley* newspapers was enthusiastic, as was Bruce Helberg of the *Bellevue Journal American*. The conservative president of KIRO, Lloyd Cooney, became very excited and offered to simulcast it. Although this was never actually done, it did reflect the encouraging enthusiasm we needed. Attitudes had changed in Renton, Kent, and Auburn during the years following their rejection of Metro transit authority in 1958. The population was growing rapidly. Metro had become familiar and was no longer thought of as a "monster."

Paul wanted to keep the idea confidential until members of the public could all hear it at the same time. In a later era, this might not have been possible but, in 1965, it was accepted by our local media.

Paul and I presented our vision separately to Seattle's two metropolitan newspapers. We met first with Dan Starr, the publisher and CEO of the Hearst owned *Seattle Post-Intelligencer* (*P-I*) and its editor, Lou Guzzo. We were escorted up to Starr's office where he met us at the door, shook hands, and pointed us toward a large, overstuffed couch, opposite Lou. Then, taking a seat behind his desk, he did not say another word throughout our presentation. As we explained our plan, Lou Guzzo interrupted frequently with comments like, "What a super idea!" and "Just what Seattle needs!" When we finished, I asked if the *P-I* would support us, and our eyes turned to Dan. I was concerned that he had not asked any questions. He leaned forward in his chair, looked me straight in the eye and with a rising voice said, "I'll tell you what the *P-I* will do. We'll go balls out for this thing!" I replied with a huge grin, "That's terrific, that's great!" Both men were as good as their word.

The following day, Paul and I met with Ross Cunningham, editorial editor of *The Seattle Times*. Ross was the voice of the paper on things political, subject to onsite approval by a member of the Blethen family who owned the paper. We were escorted into Ross' spartan office. After cordial greetings, Ross sat down, began puffing on his pipe, and now and then asked a question. After maybe twenty-five minutes, we finished and waited for his reaction. He tapped his pipe a couple of times on the side of the ash tray, looked at us and said, "I'll be back in a minute." Ross walked a couple doors down the hall to Mr. Blethen's office. After not more than three or four minutes he returned, sat down, leaned back in his swivel chair and said, "Jim, this is a magnificent idea!" He continued to share they thought it would be a wonderful thing for the city and *The Seattle Times* was prepared to give us "one hell of a kick-off." He assigned Walt Woodward to cover my speech and follow me for a week afterward, and every day the paper would print a story about unrolling the project. The paper would decide what to oppose and to support once the committee was finally appointed, had done its job, and made its recommendations to voters. This was better than we had hoped for, and I reacted with, "Thank you, Ross! This really gives us a boost!" Ross Cunningham and *The Seattle Times* were also as good as their word.

Paul and I agreed from our first conversation that we should talk one-on-one with key business leaders to see if they liked the idea well enough to pledge start-up funds. Such a pledge would make credible our call for a new committee to develop the program. Eddie Carlson immediately came to mind as the organizer of business support, someone who could gain the community's acceptance of change as dramatic and costly as Forward Thrust.

EDDIE CARLSON

Eddie Carlson's role in the success of the 1962 Century 21 World's Fair Expo at the Seattle Center had been significant and his rise from bellhop to CEO of a major international company was better than fiction. In 1965, it was a natural for us to ask this remarkable man to lead the business community into the visionary future of Forward Thrust.

Carlson had been the lynchpin behind the five horsemen of private leadership for the successful World's Fair. Along with Harold Shefelman, Joe Gandy, Ned Skinner, and Bill Street, Carlson quietly made the fair into a strong and vibrant contribution to the cultural development of the city. Carlson's credibility persuaded Senators Magnuson and Jackson to become principal advocates for federal participation. Just about every Seattle area resident was impressed when the fair outperformed public expectations and left a beautiful, lasting, legacy at Seattle Center.

In the fall of 1965, when I called Eddie Carlson to discuss his potential involvement in helping us gather seed money for Forward Thrust, he invited me over to his office at the [Olympic] hotel for lunch. Paul and I had figured Eddie would be a strong supporter and he didn't disappoint. After hearing a description of the concept, he said we were on to something big and it was just what the city needed. The timing couldn't have been better! The World's Fair was a success, Metro was making progress every day, and public confidence in business was high. He was sure he could raise $50,000 for the committee with help from some key people. He said he'd call me back when he had done that and pledged to keep it quiet until my speech.

I sat in on a luncheon to watch Eddie Carlson solicit pledges of money from about a dozen business leaders. Bill Woods, the chief executive officer of Washington Natural Gas Company, expressed concern and asked if Eddie wasn't simply asking them to drive the nails into their own coffins. He was referring to the additional property tax that would be levied on business properties to pay principal and interest on Forward Thrust bonds. Eddie paused only a second and let Bill know this thing was going to happen. Forward Thrust was for real, and he'd rather be in it than out of it. He believed every businessman who thought about it would want to be involved in the process. He said we needed to help guide Forward Thrust, rather than sit on the outside and be unable to affect it. When Carlson finished, Bill smiled and said he understood, agreed, and to count them in.

Eddie knew how most Seattle businessmen viewed civic activity. They would rather be in the driver's seat than in the passenger's seat. Looking back in fairness, the Seattle of 1965 was a smaller community of business and civic leaders. They knew each other. Eddie's leadership of the World's Fair and his early decision to support Metro had bolstered confidence in his judgment. The pledge list of Eddie's initial contributors to Forward Thrust reads like a Who's Who of Seattle business in the 1960s.

I had wanted to tell Dorm Braman what we were planning and why, but Paul believed strongly that we should not take any political figure into our confidence before the speech. He reasoned that the idea would become known as the political property of that person and his opponents would then have to oppose it.

ROTARY KICKOFF SPEECH, NOVEMBER 3, 1965

Finally, on November 3, 1965, it was time for the kickoff speech. A full house was signed in for the Downtown Seattle Rotary Club lunch when I walked into the Olympic Ballroom. By the time the thirty-minute speech ended, the audience was on its feet applauding and Mary Lou's catchy slogan "Forward Thrust" had been publicly launched.

When the luncheon ended, Mort Frayn came up to the podium to get a marked-up draft of the speech and later printed a thousand copies as a pamphlet with the picture of a jet engine on the cover. Frank Pritchard was with Mort and offered $1,500 of free printing to get us started! It was an exciting day and Paul's carefully planned launch of Forward Thrust had just begun. *The Times* released its afternoon edition with a front-page story by Walt Woodward summarizing the speech and describing a positive reception. The paper was already on street corner stands as people came out of the Olympic Hotel!

ELLIS SEES 'GOLDEN AGE'
United Plan for Seattle

(For editorial comment, see Page 8)

By WALT WOODWARD

A massive, united program with "World's Fair zip and area-wide effort" to usher in "a golden age for Seattle" was called for today.

In a speech at the Seattle Rotary Club luncheon meeting in the Olympic Hotel, James R. Ellis said the formation of a 100-person "Forward Thrust Committee" and the financial "partnership" of all governments in the area could result in:

1. A basic-rapid-transit system.
2. A major-league sports stadium.
3. Necessary major arterial-street improvements.
4. Sufficient parks, plazas and green belts "to permanently eliminate urban sprawl."
5. A world trade center.
6. Matching funds for urban redevelopment.

The local cost? Ellis—43-year-old civic leader and attorney known as the "father" of Metro—said it all could be accomplished at a Seattle-King County per capita cost "about equal to the price of a carton of cigarets each month."

NOTING THAT "we often miss the big picture" in separate community programs, Ellis asked:

"Why not take a giant step in capital programming by developing an area-wide program involving our several governments and all interested private groups in a united effort to achieve major capital purposes within our lifetime?"

His program called for a $500 million total in capital improvements in the Seattle metropolitan area at a local investment of $200 million. The balance would come from state and federal funds.

"If each unit of (local) government were to use its financial capacities to carry out a portion of this unified program, we could take a step into the future that would transform the city," Ellis said.

He did not specify the various governments. But it was obvious he was talking about the City of Seattle, the Seattle Port District, King County and Metro.

THE PROGRAM WOULD REQUIRE various bond-approval votes by the people.

"With concerted work," Ellis said, "the plan of financing could be presented to the people in 1967."

Rotarians, including many who led the community effort for a successful World's Fair, were asked by Ellis:

"Can we focus the interests of different civic groups, can we challenge our government officials to accept partnership roles in a total effort?"

Answering his own question, Ellis said the Forward Thrust Committee would not labor singly for rapid transit, a stadium or parks, but would be "a joint effort to weld all of these elements into a total project substantial enough to challenge a great community effort."

The speaker warned his listeners that membership on the committee would "require a binding commitment in time" and "money . . . donated in substantial amounts."

Equally plain-spoken to governmental units, Ellis said "cooperation without rivalry would have to be unstintingly given by public officials."

EARLIER IN HIS SPEECH, Ellis, a tireless advocate of rapid transit, explained why the area's future depends on an integrated transportation system that would preserve Seattle's Central Business District.

Declaring that "downtown and suburban centers are more complementary than competitive," Ellis said that for every $10 earned in the city's core, $8 is spent "in the residential suburbs."

But, he said, "the volume of movement needed to serve 120,000 jobs downtown cannot be met by existing freeway lanes." He added this warning:

"If sole reliance is placed on these existing freeway lanes, congestion will throttle growth."

The only way to permit open space in the core and to meet large peak-hour transportation demands, Ellis said, "is the use of high-rise structures and rapid transit."

He declared for "electric" rapid-transit facilities. They "do not pollute the air," he said.

THE CITY'S CORE is worth preserving for eight reasons, Ellis told his audience. They are:

1. The core generates "primary employment" by becoming "the principal management headquarters for the Northwest quarter of the United States."

2. It is a tourist "terminal attraction."

3. Its Seattle Center and complex of hotels and restaurants make it a "major convention center."

4. It contains the "essential ingredients" for a "great world and regional trade center."

5. It is the "financial center of the Northwest."

6. It offers "unique opportunities" for regional and specialized retailing.

7. It contains the "major administrative activities" of many government subdivisions.

8. It has "some of the nation's finest facilities" for higher education and research.

The Seattle Times had a detailed story about the Rotary speech and the Forward Thrust ideas ready for the newsstands.

Walt Woodward stayed close for a week, reporting public reactions from well-known people. He knew that a follow-up speech would come later with more detail for those who might want to help the new committee. Each day he interviewed a community leader who was in support of the program. This repeated attention from Seattle's largest newspaper was the best kickoff we could have hoped for.

Mayor Braman had been sitting next to me on the speaker's platform during the speech and was hurt that I had not shared the vision of Forward Thrust with him. When I sat down, he asked me why I hadn't. I was embarrassed and mumbled, "It was the way to get Rapid Transit." Dorm agreed but reiterated I should have told him. When the luncheon ended, he didn't join the well-wishers, but walked away silently. I remember not feeling very proud of myself.

However, Paul Seibert's instinct proved to be prophetic. The surge of publicity following the speech caused Democrat County Commissioner Scott Wallace to announce publicly that he would lead an effort to do the program. Dorm knew that joint leadership was crucial and within a week, he was on the phone to me saying that he understood where we were coming from and wanted to talk. In his office, I explained that to pass any tax-supported bond issue for a large service area, the voters of that area would have to participate. The boundaries of Metro and the county were larger than the City of Seattle. Those voters would need to understand that this was not a "Seattle Deal," or they could be turned off. Dorm saw this point and began to put his enormous energy and drive into building a joint effort with other cities and King County.

Before local governments in Washington State could issue general obligation bonds, the State Constitution required an election in which 60 percent voted "Yes" and the number of persons voting on the bond proposal was at least 40 percent of the number of voters of the issuing entity who participated in the last preceding state General Election.

It was difficult to prevent others from trying to take charge of what was becoming a "good idea" news story. Three days after the Rotary kickoff, Seattle Chamber President John Fluke Sr. invited Paul and me to breakfast at the Rainier Club to propose that the Chamber lead the program and manage the fundraising effort. Paul explained that if we did that, we would lose support in the cities outside Seattle. This had to be a county-wide effort in order to pass the crucial issues. If people outside of Seattle believed this was a downtown Seattle project, they wouldn't go for it. John saw this right away and offered his personal endorsement and whatever help the Chamber could appropriately give.

At first, I was worried when Commissioner Scott Wallace spent weeks trying to organize the program as a King County project. Paul Seibert had been right in expecting such a reaction and his advance preparation kept the press on the side of shared city-county leadership during the time Scott was pushing a solo effort. Eddie's informal pledges from business leaders had beaten Scott to the punch for sources of money and local Chambers had already committed to a joint effort. Two months after the speech was delivered, Scott came by my office and agreed he couldn't do it alone and asked how he could help. I answered, "We've got to have breakfast with Dorm Braman. Let's call him." Dorm was eager to meet us the following morning. At 7:30 a.m. in the Olympic Grill both men agreed to jointly appoint a nominating committee of about twenty people. These community leaders would be charged with the duty of naming the Forward Thrust Committee of 200. A majority of the nominating group roster was agreed to that morning.

A few days after our breakfast, Mayor Braman and the three King County Commissioners publicly announced the members of a nominating committee. This group in turn worked for two months to select the 200 members of the Forward Thrust Committee. The people selected in this slow process were broadly representative of both public officials and citizens from all sections of the county and all parts of the economy. The press provided continuing support for this approach.

A COMMITTEE OF 200

The "Committee of 200" as it became known, was our way of building an area-wide base for the wide-ranging recommendations that needed to be developed. Paul and I had planned a follow-up speech to spell out areas the Forward Thrust Committee of 200 would explore. The speech, *"Human Environment and Public Investment,"* was given at a Junior Chamber of Commerce anniversary celebration lunch in January 1966 to members from around the metropolitan area.

By late spring of 1966, the Committee of 200 had been officially appointed by the mayor and city council of Seattle and the commissioners of King County. Everyone who accepted positions on this new committee agreed in writing *to make a personal commitment of between two and four hours a week, for 18 months, and not to assign this responsibility to a subordinate or alternate.* The county-wide nature of the committee was apparent when the 200 names were publicly announced. It was clear from the beginning that Forward Thrust would be an unusually broad and potentially strong civic force.

All members received a copy of the January speech. Eddie Carlson's business leaders raised more than $100,000 in initial seed money for committee expenses, double what Carlson had promised. More importantly, they had agreed to become part of a permanent finance team which would raise the private money needed to pay committee costs. A not-for-profit 501c3 corporation, "Forward Thrust, Inc." was formed to administer the committee effort and took responsibility for fundraising, meeting arrangements, minutes, and committee records, as well as assembling the extensive background information that would be needed by the study subcommittees.

Looking back, it was almost as if the Preston law firm and Metro experiences had been designed to train us for Forward Thrust. Mary Lou and I knew many members of the Committee of 200 and I knew the nuts-and-bolts of many issues they would face. I believe the success that followed was due in large part to the painstaking time and effort that went into building area-wide acceptance for the goals and broad membership of the Committee of 200!

Serving as chairman of the Forward Thrust Committee and president of Forward Thrust, Inc., required much more than a quarter of my time. In fact, it became a full-time, unpaid job. At this point it became as consuming as Mary Lou had feared. For a while the excitement of new ideas kept energy and optimism high. But this was followed by troughs of fatigue or conflict when it became a struggle to keep one foot ahead of the other.

Absences from the office raised old concerns by senior partners that I would become almost unavailable for law firm work.

Other side effects of this high-profile cause began to surface. Lou Guzzo wrote a column in the *P-I* with the heading, "Jim Ellis for Mayor." A few local officials expressed suspicion that Forward Thrust was a steppingstone for secret political ambitions. Other rumors circulated that my real motive was to make a ton of money from legal opinions on the issuance of the large amount of bonds that would be needed. Some good friends noticed that I was becoming over-worked. They worried that I might not be able to maintain the level of effort needed to ride herd on this huge program for two years. There were nights when Mary Lou volunteered long backrubs just to put me to sleep.

One night, I was not feeling well and had just gotten into bed when a sharp pain sent me bolting upright with a howl. These pains repeated every few minutes. Mary Lou called Dr. Jim Haviland at home, and I soon found myself in Swedish Hospital with a perforated ulcer and strict orders to stay quiet for a couple of weeks. Under the watchful eyes of my wife and family, I undertook a routine of exercise and rest and was able to return to work in time to prepare for the crucial 1977 legislative session.

One day, Walter Straley, the president of Pacific Northwest Bell (PNB), called to ask if we could meet for breakfast. The next morning, he explained that PNB would like to hire me full-time for two years with an annual salary of thirty-five thousand dollars to work *solely* on the Forward Thrust program. He said the program was the kind of development effort the telephone company would like to lead if they would be publicly accepted. They recognized the momentum behind it had a real chance to make the program happen but were worried I wouldn't survive physically or financially for the next two years if I was trying to maintain my law practice. He gave his word that there would be no influence from PNB. They would pay my salary and provide me with an office and a secretary. I would take a leave of absence from my law firm and focus solely on Forward Thrust. This was a possibility that had not occurred to me. The salary they were offering was generous and the arrangement would permit full concentration on the Forward Thrust effort.

When I came home that evening, I couldn't wait to share the good news with Mary Lou. Her reaction was a surprise: "You can't do that! You simply cannot go to work for the telephone company and be paid big money. People will say that's why you are doing this." She reminded me that we would have to ask a great many people to volunteer their time and effort if Forward Thrust was going to have any chance of success. "How can you ask volunteers to work for nothing, when you are making good money?" As usual her intuition was right. Common sense reminded me that volunteer crusades require some citizens to make sacrifices in order to credibly lead others. I thanked Walt Straley and declined his offer.

Another time, Joel Pritchard, my friend and debate partner from Young Republicans, came to the office to discuss the need to clear the concerns about our firm offering opinions on future Forward Thrust bonds if I was involved. After pointing out that I couldn't give away my partners' work or income, I suggested that I could donate to charity *my share* of any income generated by the firm for opinions on future Forward Thrust bonds. Joel thought this was a good solution and the issue was defused.

As the committee membership began to take shape, public expectations grew in scale and complexity, and an excellent small staff was hired by Forward Thrust, Inc. Donald J. "Bud" Donahue retired from the Seattle Chamber and came to serve as executive secretary.

Richard S. "Dick" Page, a personable and bright young member of Senator Henry M. "Scoop" Jackson's staff, was suggested as a possible candidate for a program development officer. I asked Senator Jackson, who was following Metro, if he would consider releasing Dick Page for a couple of years to do this important job. Scoop agreed to talk with Dick. I received a call the following day from Dick. He was enthusiastic about taking a leadership role. With Dick, Forward Thrust got more than an excellent program coordinator; it got a sensitive and diplomatic leader for this complex project with its potentially challenging Committee of 200 citizens, each with strong ideas. Dick would later go on to be executive director of Metro, head the Federal Mass Transportation Agency, and then became the manager of the Washington, D.C., Regional Rapid Transit System.

The stage was set. It was time to move Forward Thrust from the inspiring excitement of possibility to the challenging puzzles of reality.

A Committee of 200

By the summer of 1966, more than 200 men and women had been officially appointed by Seattle mayor Dorm Braman and the Board of King County Commissioners to become the Forward Thrust Committee of 200. The actual number started at 220 and fluctuated slightly during the life of the committee as vacancies occurred and were filled. The individuals came from different communities and interest groups in the county, eventually totally 220 men and women. All members of the Committee of 200 served without any compensation.

James R. Ellis	George Bartell, Jr.	David M. Checkley
President	J.W. Barton	Ark G. Chin
Lowell P. Mickelwait	Fred Bassetti	K.A. Cole
Vice President	Alec Bayless	Norton Clapp
Dottie Smith	Walter Berg	David Cohn
Vice President	Ted Best	Ernest Conrad
John M. Fluke	Noel Bicknell	Harold W. Cooper
Vice President	Lyman J. Black	Elliott N. Couden
Phyllis Lamphere	Joan Blaisdell	C.A. Crosser
Vice President	John D. Blankenship	James A. Crutchfield
Thomas E. Bolger	John W. Bolenbaugh	Charles P. Curran
Treasurer	J. Dorm Braman	John H. Current
Marvin B. Durning	Leon Bridges	John L. Curry
Secretary	T. N. Buchanan	Don Custer
Harold Abramson	Robert F. Buck	Joseph Davis
Norman Ackley	Dorothy Bullitt	Louis Demattea
William Adams II	Peter Bush	Dr. Brewster C. Denny
Dr. Harold L. Amoss	Willis Camp	Jean DeSpain
Arthur B. Andersen	Ernest Campbell	L.R. Durkee
Cleveland Anschell	Lee Campbell	Myrtle Edwards
John Aram	Edward E. Carlson	A. Sherman Ellsworth
Robert D. Ashley	Harry L. Carr	Patricia Emerson
Patricia M. Baillargeon	Jack E. Chambers	Anthony I. Eyring
Bruce F. Baker	Joe Chandler	Jerome Farris
Miner H. Baker	William Chatalas	Bennett Feigenbaum

Betty Fletcher

Paul S. Ford

John Fournier

R. Mort Frayn

Paul S. Friedlander

John M. Frodesen

Joseph E. Gandy

Avery Garrett

Mary Gates

J. Wilson Gaw

Gary D. Gayton

Arthur Gerbel

Charles V. Gibbs

J. Harry Goldie

Slade Gorton

R.R. Greive

Jennings Hanseth

Dorothy Harper

Dyron V. Hartley

Frank Hattori

John H. Hauberg

John M. Haydon

Frederick W. Hayes

J.F. Hayward

Bruce Helberg

Jack F. Henry

M. Perry Hobbs

Harry Holloway

Dr. Brantley Holt, Jr.

James E. Hussey

Ruth Ittner

Archie Iverson

William M. Jenkins

William L. Jennings

Allan R. Johnson

Bruce W. Johnson

William L. Johnson, Sr.

David A. Johnston

Norman J. Johnston

Rex D. Jones

Rev. Mineo Katagiri

James I. Kimbrough

Albert A. King

Robert King

Paul Hayden Kirk

Ralph Klein

Jack Kniskern

H. Dewayne Kreager

Madeline Lemere

Allen Locke

Kenneth M. Lowthian

George M. Mack

Annamarie Mann, Jr.

Clarence F. Massart

C.M. McCune

Joseph L. McGavick

Ron Meeker

J. Reginald Miller

L. Joe Miller

Lynn B. Miller

Dr. Rosalie Miller

William A. Millington

David A. Mitchell

J.R. Mitchell

John S. Murray

James E. Navarre

Ibsen Nelson

John M. Nelson

Mechlin D. Moore

Allen B. Morgan

Ilsa Morris

Roy W. Morse

Ed Munro

Kenneth Munson

E.J. Nist

Everett Nordstrom

Charles H. Norris

John T. O'Brien

Robert D. O'Brien

Ray Olsen

Don Olson

Frances Owen

Warren J. Pease

Williamena Peck

W.J. Pennington

Dr. Richard Philbrick

John N. Porter

Catherine Prince

Frank A. Pritchard, Jr.

Joel M. Pritchard

Harry A. Pryde

Donald A. Schmechel

Robert H. Schulman

Morrell Sharp

Harold Shefelman

Jeannette Rathfelder

Marjorie Redman

Elizabeth Rivily

Jack B. Robertson

Charles W. Ross

Jack Rottler

John N. Rupp

James M. Ryan

John L. Salter

Edward B. Sand

Paul F. Sanders

B.L. Sherrill

Langdon S. Simons, Jr.

W. Hunter Simpson

Hugh A. Smith

John D. Spaeth

Charles Sparling
John D. Spellman
Dan Starr
Victor Steinbrueck
William S. Street
Helen Stickland
Dr. Walter Sundstrom
M. J.R. Williams
Walter B. Williams
Dr. James L. Wilson
Robert W. Witter

Buckie Taft
Joan Thomas
Jack C. Thompson
James H. Todd
Gordon Tongue
Wes Ulhman
Robert E. Van Devanter
Victor Van Valin
Jeannette Veasey
Donald Voorhees
William E. Wall

Scott Wallace
Richard Weisfield
Charles West
Ann Widditsch
Andrew M. Williams
J. Vernon Williams
William P. Woods
A. Dean Worthington
Bagley Wright
Howard S. Wright
John L. Wright

✦

CHAPTER 20

Time Builds Trust and Friends

Participants at any level in our system of self-government will find that success is carried on a tide of patience and persistence.

Jim

FROM THE EARLIEST effort to fulfill our commitment to my brother Bob, Mary Lou and I realized that the possibility of achieving any large public goals would hinge upon finding many friends who shared our ideas. By 1965, it looked like this was beginning to happen. In 1953, The Metro Clean Water effort had started with a speech to perhaps thirty Municipal League members in an upstairs room of the old YMCA Annex building and was publicly reported in a League members' newsletter. In 1965, the Forward Thrust crusade began with a speech to more than three hundred Seattle Rotary members in the ballroom of the Olympic Hotel and was reported in a week of daily news stories by the metropolitan area newspapers.

I believe the primary reason for this increase in public interest was the successful track record of the Kitchen Group of friends who founded Metro and brought local governments together to build a better-than-promised sewage disposal system. That success story allowed us to later suggest a multi-purpose capital facilities program like Forward Thrust. The positive Rotary reaction to the "Thrust" kickoff was saying, in effect: "We'd like to have these good things. Jim was right about Metro; maybe he's right about Forward Thrust."

I admire the tremendous leap we attempted with the Committee of 200. This diverse group of citizens was asked to create a coherent capital improvement program which would be acceptable to voters in more than 50 cities and meet the public facility needs of a growing metropolitan area in an uncertain future. The committee struggled for months with a wide range of project challenges before finding the key pieces to the puzzle. The phrase "vision of the people" was used by committee members and reporters to describe the consensus process of this broad group. From the beginning, the Committee of 200 hoped to bring all local capital facility proposals to a vote on the same day.

VISION STUDY COMMITTEES

The mechanics of functioning with 200 members demanded that working groups be created with strong chairs. The result was the development of Vision Study Committees which became the heart of Forward Thrust. An Economic Analysis Committee was also established to provide overall guidance in monitoring economic guidelines for all Vision Study Committees to make sure the vital question of affordability would not get lost in the push by various groups advocating for their projects.

John F. "Jack" Henry and John H. Current co-chaired the Economic Analysis Committee. They clearly understood the importance of property-taxpayer acceptance of the burden of paying the tax bills for capital facilities. They were accepted by the tax conscious business community, and they demonstrated a responsive leadership style in working to implement the ideas of the Vision Study Committees. Jack Henry, as respected vice president and senior loan officer of Pacific National Bank, had a knack for making financial subjects understandable, never dominating meetings, and bringing out the best in colleagues. His manner kept everyone on track. John Current, executive director of the Washington Research Council, had a special reputation as an authority on the business impacts of local government taxation. John possessed an encyclopedic knowledge of the tax and debt histories of cities with which Seattle was most often compared.

The three of us sat together for long discussions of the existing legal limits on local government debt and its ability to build and operate a large

Vision Study Committee Chairs (three phases)

Campaign (1)
Thomas E. Bolger, Chairman
Community Centers (2)
Mechlin D. Moore, Chairman
Carl Jensen, Vice Chairman
Culture & Entertainment (1)
Joseph E. Gandy, Co-Chairman
Langdon S. Simons, Jr., Co-Chairman
Economic Analysis (1) (2) (3)
John F. Henry, Co-Chairman
John H. Current, Co-Chairman
Health-Safety-Welfare
Rex D. Jones, Chairman
Dottie Smith, Vice Chairman
Housing (1)
Alec Bayless, Chairman
William S. Leckenby, Vice Chairman
Legal (1)
Andrew M. Williams, Chairman
Legislative (2)
Frank A. Pritchard, Jr., Co-Chairman
C. Peter Curran, Co-Chairman
Multiple-Use
Richard Page, Co-Chairman
Calhoun Dickinson, Co-Chairman
Parks & Recreation (1)
Calhoun Dickinson, Co-Chairman
J. Vernon Williams, Co-Chairman
Public Health & Safety (2)
Alfred J. Schweppe, Chairman
Larry M. Carter, Vice Chairman
Public Relations
Bruce F. Baker, Chairman (1)
Eliot C. Read, Chairman (2)
Public Schools
Ernest W. Campbell, Chairman (1)
David E. Wagoner, Chairman (2)

Quality in Environmental Design
Paul Hayden Kirk, Chairman
John L. Wright, Vice Chairman
Speakers-Listeners Bureau
Bennett Feigenbaum, Co-Chairman
Donald A. Olson, Co-Chairman
Storm Water Control
J. Harold Abramson, Chairman
Andre Gay, Vice Chairman
Transportation-Highways (1)
Robert F. Buck, Chairman
Noel B. Bicknell, Vice Chairman
Transportation-Transit (1)
Warren J. Pease, Chairman
Bruce F. Helberg, Vice Chairman
Transportation-Transit (2)
J. Harry Goldie, Chairman
James H. Todd, Vice Chairman
Transportation-Transit (3)
Joel Pritchard, Co-Chairman
David Sprague, Co-Chairman
Urban Redevelopment (1)
Lyman J. Black, Chairman
Judge Jerome Farris, Vice-Chairman
Public Utilities (1)
J. Harold Abramson, Co-Chairman
B. L. Sherrill, Co-Chairman

(1) Participated in the 1968 phase of the program.
(2) Participated in the 1970 phase of the program.
(3) Appointed by the Metro Council in 1971 to advise on planning for a new county-wide bus-only transit system with the new consulting firm, Daniel, Mann, Johnson & Mendenhall (DMJM). See Chapter 33.

project and to pay its other debt obligations. We speculated on the amount of the annual debt payments that taxpayers could safely agree to pay each year over the life of bonds issued to build large projects. Jack Henry reminded me that an individual taxpayer was less interested in total project costs than in knowing what *his share* of that cost would be. We needed to get people to talk about *relevant average* taxpayer costs instead of the *total cost* of each project considered to get our arms around the real challenge of public fear.

The state constitution restricted the purpose of voted general obligation bonds of local governments to "capital purposes only," not operating costs. Forward Thrust bonds would be issued to pay for voted capital purposes only, not operating deficits, and none would mature beyond the life of the improvement. Transferring the function of public transit to Metro would remove existing transit operating deficits from future city and county general fund budgets, and a new sales tax revenue was recommended to help cities with general operating costs.

John Current was particularly worried that people would put off these projects that would be far more expensive in thirty or forty years, leaving the next generation facing a more costly financial situation. He knew that without any of the new project facilities, we were the *lowest* property tax city of all the comparable examples and believed that even after we built the projects in our vision—and he emphasized this— "The local share of such cost to be borne by the average taxpayers of this county will still be below the average property taxpayer in comparable cities." This became the overall test which the Economic Analysis Committee would apply in reviewing Vision Study Committee recommendations and comparing alternate project proposals.

Initially, Forward Thrust's focus on "environmental quality" simply meant locating and designing new facilities to fit the natural environment. Committee members later agreed that new public capital facilities should also be compatible with the adjacent existing "built environment" as far as practicable. Designs should also meet high architectural standards and provide operating efficiency. This led eventually to establishing official design committees by the City of Seattle and King County to approve construction plans of Forward Thrust facilities.

Stages of Vision Study Committee Work

Background Studies of human and environmental needs.

Economic Analysis of practical limits for an affordable public capital improvement program.

Legislative Action to create better ways and means for state and local governments to achieve environmental protection and public capital purposes.

Specific Ballot Measures to finance feasible public capital projects in King County using new legislative authority.

Public Progress Reports for voter approved projects.

The Committee was preparing its vital state legislative pieces for the 1967 legislative session. From May to December 1966, the Vision Study Committees separately explored possible projects. They reached out to get advice from officials of local, state, and federal governments as well as citizens, associations, community clubs and individuals. Project proposals were reviewed for affordability, operating feasibility, and duplication to ensure that each project contributed to a balanced total program and stayed within financial guidelines. Each Vision Study Committee estimated the costs of acquiring and building recommended improvements for the new or expanded capital facilities, as well as future operating costs, and sources of payment were explored. Supporting the work of the Vision Study Committees became Job One for Dick Page and me.

While studying the possible projects, the Culture and Entertainment Committee actively considered possible state legislation that would enable the county to charge an excise sales tax on the sale of hotel room lodging. This tax would be credited against the state sales tax for half of the stadium cost. One morning, Joe Gandy, co-chair of the Culture and Entertainment Committee, called to disclose that a Major League baseball franchise group wanted to "go the stadium alone" and submit a stadium proposal to King County voters in the fall of 1966. The group recognized Forward Thrust wanted to submit all of its projects in a single election but felt the stadium couldn't wait another year or two. An opportunity to obtain an American League franchise in Seattle was

Forward Thrust Mission and Process

Over the life of the Committee of 200, the Forward Thrust mission became the following public capital facilities:

- Balanced and integrated highway and public transportation systems, to provide convenient, safe mobility for people of all income levels and to encourage desirable patterns of urban development
- Park facilities and open spaces to provide opportunities for rest, recreation, environmental education, and enjoyment of leisure time for all age and income levels, including zoo improvements and a marine aquarium
- Public facilities and regulations to help ensure clean air and clean water by reducing existing and potential sources of pollution
- Public facilities required to support economic development and provide public services for a rapidly growing population
- Public improvements required to prevent deterioration of older neighborhoods and to support attractive new residential environments
- Culture and entertainment facilities sufficient to provide opportunities for both participant and spectator activity for all interests and ages, including a new all-weather stadium
- Public airport and seaport facilities required to support strong industry, trade, and commerce
- Public facilities required to prevent major flood and storm water damage
- Public facilities needed to protect scenic views including, where feasible, the undergrounding of utilities

available if the stadium could be voted on in a special election the coming fall. I told Joe I understood the necessity for a franchise, and we wouldn't do anything to damage Seattle's chances. When Joe left, I called Eddie Carlson to tell him. Eddie didn't think we could do anything about it. He also didn't think they would be able to pass a stadium vote. So Forward Thrust stood aside.

The county commissioners put a stadium bond issue on the September 20, 1966, primary election ballot. This was the second submission for stadium bonds. This time it received a majority "Yes" vote, but not enough to pass the constitutional 60 percent approval hurdle.

The loss of this election was a downer. Any future stadium vote by Forward Thrust would now become a "third try." I remembered from an ill-fated freshman track year in college, that after two false starts, a third disqualifies the runner. From the beginning, I hoped the Forward Thrust election would include a big-league sports stadium. Mary Lou was not a stadium fan. "This stadium plan is going to be your albatross," she pronounced. "Public taxes should be used for low-income housing or neighborhood parks." I felt that a new stadium would help to bring the metropolitan community together in support of their own major league teams. I wanted sports fans to be part of our "all-for-one" Forward Thrust crusade.

A few days after the election defeat, Joe Gandy came back to my office and passionately pleaded that the stadium proponents be allowed to rejoin the Forward Thrust process. He said the group would support the entire Forward Thrust program and contribute financially to the whole election campaign, *if* we'd include the stadium during the study and legislative phase of Forward Thrust. The Committee agreed. Eddie then helped secure hotel owners' support for a Forward Thrust-sponsored bill that would authorize King County to levy and pledge to the payment of stadium bonds a two percent excise tax on the sale of hotel room lodging. This new county hotel room tax would be credited against the state sales tax charged on the transaction. Hotel guests would not see higher costs on their rooms, and, in net effect, "state" funds would become a source of partial funding for the stadium bond issue!

In September and October 1966, the Committee of 200 convened a series of "committee of the whole" meetings to make it possible for everyone to listen together to a wide range of subjects and opinions. Professional experts and consultants, public officials, staffers, representatives from business, finance, academia, and citizen groups gave the Committee of 200 their views on needed public facilities along with estimated costs. Fortunately, professional consultants had been employed by the Puget Sound Council of Governments to develop long-range regional plans for highways, transit, parks, and open space.

It was apparent from the fall meetings that the dreams of King County citizens were big dreams, even beyond anything that the founders of Forward

Thrust had imagined. I was shocked to read one morning a *Post-Intelligencer* front-page banner headline: *"Puget Sound 'Slurb' War to Cost Billion."* The *Post-Intelligencer* was a strong editorial supporter, and my instant reaction was "Good grief, our friends could kill us with this kind of publicity!"

When I got back to the house, the telephone was ringing with a call from my father. "People are going to wonder what your folks have been drinking." I responded, "I know. It is scary. I'll try to get an explanation printed." He feared the whole program could be prematurely characterized as reckless and excessive. Subsequent disclaimers seldom erase the sound of a bell that has been rung so loudly. Five days later, a *P-I* editorial explained that the covered meeting was simply a "brainstorming" session to "come up with a program which the people of the area would support." As events unfolded, the headline proved to be prophetic. I knew that transportation projects could reach this number, but still felt surprised. It was a shrill wake-up call with the effect of an emergency alarm.

Many community and business leaders in the 1950s and '60s were drawn from my parents' generation that was deeply scarred by the Great Depression of the 1930s and this deep-seated feeling could be a high hurdle in the path of any visionary action by the Committee of 200. We required all Vision Study Committees to follow common sense economic guidelines to address fundamental issues of economic value and affordability for all proposed capital facilities, but with major annexations to Seattle, Bellevue, Kent and Auburn, population growth was spreading further into unincorporated areas of King County. From the start, school districts were excluded from our mission at their request, but the mounting backlog of roads, utilities, and the capital facilities needed to serve a growing population was more costly than we had expected.

It had been apparent to most people who heard the first Forward Thrust speeches, that money would have to be borrowed to pay for the long-range capital improvements needed by the City of Seattle, King County and its smaller cities, Metro, and the Port of Seattle. There was of course no magic in borrowing. Interest costs were paid to lenders. Borrowing was simply a practical way of paying contractors selected in a bidding process. It permitted affordable taxpayer payments by spreading repayment in specific dollar amounts over time. It was also an equitable way for public issuers to spread costs among those who would benefit from a public facility during its long useful life.

Both statutory and constitutional restraints existed on the amounts that could be borrowed by local governments to be repaid from their general tax base, and local public borrowing was limited to five percent of the actual value of the taxable property. State legislation can be enacted by a majority of state legislators, but constitutional change requires approval by the people in a statewide election. Legislative changes affecting taxes would require the support of leadership from political parties, as well as local governments, business, labor, and civic organizations.

There was consensus of the Committee on the need to increase the statutory authority of local governments to issue bonds with a vote of the people. This would require amending several state statutes. Henry and Current suggested that the City of Seattle could pay the cost of combined sewer separation by using the special constitutional borrowing capacity available only for sewer systems. They also suggested that King County could finance county-wide systems of arterial highways and parks, whether located inside or outside of cities, by increasing the statutory borrowing limit of the county to equal the statutory borrowing limit for cities. These statutory changes would permit a large amount of voter-approved borrowing without the need for statewide constitutional amendments.

Dick Page and I worked with Vision Study Committee chairs and members of the Executive Committee to recommend new state statutory debt limits. We warned it would not be easy to win legislative approval for such an ambitious agenda. Prematurely announcing costly projects could doom the possibility of passing these new legislative limits.

A practical limit on any voted bonds is the amount of taxes that would be *accepted* by voters to pay annual interest and principal installments. It was clear to committee members that local governments would have to issue long-term bonds to pay large acquisition and construction and spread the payment of that cost over many years to reduce the amount paid in any one year by taxpayers.

We determined the best way to fund the local share of flood control, covered stadium, arterial highways, and large park projects (including zoo improvements and a new aquarium) was to issue general obligation bonds out of an enlarged general borrowing capacity of King County. The federal grants authorized by the 1964 federal Mass Transportation Act, and the unused general obligation borrowing capacity of Metro, could together cover the huge cost of a metropolitan rail-bus rapid transit system. Airport expansion needs could be met by the Port of Seattle bonds payable from airport user charges without voter approval.

As 1966 came to a close, the Committee recommended what had become a nineteen-bill program for introduction in the coming January session of the state legislature. The Legal Committee was asked to prepare the legislation needed to permit the full plate of capital projects for presentation to the voters. These Forward Thrust bills included submitting, to *state* voters, two bond issues funding state grants for water pollution abatement and public park purposes. The proposed stadium legislation for King County was also a matter of statewide interest because of its regional recreational draw. No local program this large had been presented to the Washington Legislature. However, we came loaded with enthusiasm, broad public support in King County, and extraordinary legislative leadership. Hold on to your hat!

CHAPTER 21

Climbing the Legislative Plateau

Positive civic action of any consequence requires more sustained work than most people are willing to commit.

—*Jim Ellis, "The Chance of Our Lifetime," speech, 1968*

IN REFLECTING ON THE AMBITIOUS 1967 legislative program, it is significant that we did not consider hiring a lobbyist. It was a minor miracle at this stage of our effort that we were not actively opposed by at least some powerful interests. But Forward Thrust was just such a miracle.

In the winter of 1967, the buzz under the Capitol Dome was curious conversation about the Forward Thrust legislation and what was happening to it. Statewide positive interest was spurred by the recent history of Seattle's successful World's Fair and Metro's successful clean-up of Lake Washington. Within the broad membership of the Committee of 200, there were executives of some of the largest state-wide private employers.

The known public icons of the new program were a possible big-league sports stadium and strong emphasis on transportation, pollution abatement, and park improvements. As the result of Paul Seibert's successful public launching and the bi-partisan appointment of the Committee of 200, there was not a rush of partisan opponents willing to tell the Legislature to kill these bills. Forward Thrust continued to be favorably treated by the state press and was

Monitoring the progress of the Vision Committee propositions.

endorsed by both political parties. Well-known leaders in the capitol included Governor Evans and the majority leaders of the Senate and the House.

The same political realities and practical logic that moved the Committee of 200 to focus on existing local governments with sufficient territorial reach and unused constitutional borrowing capacity sounded reasonable in Olympia. Arterial highways and public park projects serving the needs of *both* cities and unincorporated areas seemed like logical functions to be assigned to King County with its largely unused borrowing capacity.

It was notable that all legislative borrowing authorizations proposed by Forward Thrust for local governments would require submission to their voters for approval.

The Legal Committee drafted, and the Board had approved, nineteen proposed Forward Thrust bills for legislative introduction. Two of the bills would authorize *state* bonds to be voted on in November 1968 to assist local governments with grants for public parks and water pollution abatement projects. The other bills would primarily increase the ability of King County, Metro, and Seattle to issue bonds for different parts of the Forward Thrust capital program.

Republican Governor Dan Evans, House of Representatives Republican Majority Leader Slade Gorton, and Senate Democratic Majority Leader Bob Greive were either Forward Thrust committee members or strong public supporters. We discussed our program privately with each of them before the session. Governor Evans enthusiastically endorsed and encouraged the whole process. He believed it would be "difficult but doable" if we had bipartisan leadership in the legislature.

...difficult but doable...

Slade had been elected to the Washington state House of Representatives every two years after 1958. He had earned the high regard of his colleagues by the time he was elected majority leader in the House in 1967. If we were able to get our bills through the Senate, Slade believed he could successfully manage them through the House. Slade pointed out we would have a more difficult problem in the Senate where personality differences among the leaders were great. In the House, he believed they were sufficiently organized to deal effectively with the whole program. Slade's assessment of both chambers proved accurate.

The Senate was a unique problem. Bob Greive was the Democrat majority leader and an old friend of Metro. He had attended Forward Thrust meetings in the fall of 1966 and was an enthusiastic supporter of the program. It was natural for me to take our proposed legislation to him in the Senate. Unfortunately, he was harassed by the determined political opposition of rival Senator August Mardesich from Snohomish County. "Augie," as he was known, had been defeated by Bob for the position of majority leader and they became in Bob's words, "blood enemies." Augie was very intelligent and made trouble for Bob throughout the session. Bob's challenge was to pass our bills without Augie killing or crippling any of them.

Bob made political allies with adroit use of favors and raising campaign funds for colleagues. I knew he had intense differences with House Republican Slade Gorton, the new majority leader, over the politically charged issues of redistricting. Nevertheless, neither of them allowed these differences to interfere with their work on the Forward Thrust bills.

In the House, the choice of a sponsor was even easier because Slade Gorton was a good friend from Metro campaign days, as well as an active

Forward Thrust leader and member of the Committee of 200. We had worked together as Young Republicans. I knew Slade to be brilliant and honest. He suggested we introduce all our bills in the Senate, get them all through that Chamber, and then bring them to him for final passage in the House.

We followed this advice and all nineteen Forward Thrust supported bills were introduced in the Senate early in the 1967 session. Greive planned to take the bills up one at a time when the time was right and made sure that none of the bills would be assigned to a committee chaired by Mardesich. Once our bills worked their way through their respective committees of origin and the Rules Committee, and were ready for Senate passage, Bob would take up one or two bills whenever Mardesich was not present. He usually called me at home from the floor of the Senate. These calls always seemed to come during the dinner hour. I usually picked up the telephone and remember Greive saying, "He's gone" (meaning Mardesich had left for the day). "I'm going to take up this bill. Tell me what I should say about it." I would give him a short recap of the measure. Bob would then hang up and go to work. Later he would call back to say the bill had either passed the Senate, or he had moved it back to Rules so he could do more persuading. Usually, when he called back, the bill had successfully passed the Senate.

Greive plugged along carefully. The process was painfully slow and there was growing concern that after many weeks several of our bills had not yet moved through the Senate. Bob had managed with remarkably good results, getting all but one of our bills through the Senate just three days before the end of the session! The nineteenth bill would have authorized "tax increment revenue financing." We dropped it because it was complicated to explain and was being portrayed as a means of avoiding voter consent for levies on taxable property.

On the morning after the last of our Senate Bills was delivered to the House, I went down to Olympia to talk with Slade. "We have passed eighteen Forward Thrust bills in the Senate. They are now in the House, what do we do now?" He responded that he had told me to bring them all over to him but hadn't said to wait until the last three days of the session! Nonetheless, Slade immediately went to work that morning in a masterful way. In a matter of minutes, he had assembled the chairmen of the relevant House committees and the Speaker of the House in his office. He proceeded to give this group an explicit and impressive summary of the actions that were needed and reminded them that the state Republican Party had taken a position *in support* of the whole Forward Thrust program. A schedule was set for each committee to report its bills out to the Rules Committee and a timeline for the Rules Committee to move each bill for floor action. I have never seen a better job of organizing and inspiring people to perform such a large and complex set of legislative tasks in such a short period of time. Unbelievably, all of those committee chairmen did their jobs on schedule. However, the end of the session was fast approaching. On the last day, I went down to the House Chamber to watch the action because a number of the bills still remained to be passed and adjournment of the legislature was set for midnight.

I remember sitting in the balcony of the House Chamber during the tense last day of the session. There was not enough time left in the session for the House to consider and act on all the bills then on its calendar. Many House members were worried that their particular legislation would be lost in the backlog if lengthy speeches were not curtailed. One by one our bills began to come through, but I noticed that three of our bills were not even on the calendar. About 9:00 p.m. that evening, with a huge backlog of bills yet to be considered, a five-minute recess was called by the Speaker to take up a special calendar of bills. When the session reconvened, only the three remaining Forward Thrust measures were up for consideration! These included the controversial stadium financing bill which we had worked hard to make more acceptable to the public. I thought, surely, they would get hung up by somebody. Then I watched Slade take the floor. He remarked that they had a lot of bills to consider, and he told the Speaker they wanted to do this expeditiously. Slade moved to take our three measures up and implored the other members of the House to be considerate of their colleagues in the length of their remarks. Sure enough, the pressure to get action on remaining bills encouraged the three measures to be minimally debated and quickly passed. I felt at the time that we were witnessing a legislative miracle.

It was a great relief and thrill when the 1967 legislature finally adjourned. Throughout the process, we kept Governor Dan Evans informed about the status of the bills. He signed all eighteen bills into law with a flourish. The final Olympia outcome was a smashing victory for Forward Thrust. The most important eighteen of our nineteen bills were enacted into law. The two state bond authorizations for water pollution abatement purposes and public park and recreation purposes were directed to be submitted to state voters in November 1968.

As the bills were signed into law by Governor Evans, a luncheon was held for the full membership of the Committee of 200 in the large ballroom at the Washington Athletic Club. The room was packed with committee members, press people, and other interested residents all eagerly awaiting the detailed results of the work in Olympia.

The luncheon was a spellbinder. Dick explained each of the new Forward Thrust acts in sufficient detail to permit everyone present to be fully informed. There was a full house and the attendees hung on every word. When he concluded, without a cue, the entire audience *stood up and cheered*. It was a thrilling moment and an expression of the value of the work that had been done. It was also an exciting hint of the possibilities now within reach.

The new legislation provided authority to do many new things, including authorizing a one-time tax to create a revolving fund to buy land for low-income housing, permitting King County to issue bonds for arterial improvements located in part within cities, and permitting cities to build and operate county-financed parks located within the city limits.

In addition, new state funding was provided for King County to help finance a public stadium, and to Metro if voters approved the transit function. Substantial state capacity to make grants to cities and counties would be created if voters approved pollution abatement and parks facility bonds in the November of 1968 election.

The Committee of 200 was now empowered and energized to produce major capital facility recommendations in the form of election ordinances for adoption by the legislative bodies of King County, Metro, and the City of Seattle. An enthusiastic Phyllis Lamphere caught my eye by waving a victory "V" as the excited crowd passed out of the ballroom. The creation of a Forward Thrust capital project crusade had now become possible.

Hey, Vision! Here we come!

Better Together: Seattle Sewers

One of our hopes in creating the Committee of 200 and its Project Study Committees was to encourage joint efforts by participating governments. Solving the "Achilles heel" overflows in Seattle's combined sewer system was a great opportunity for Seattle and Metro to work together. Metro had removed all the treatment plants located around Lake Washington but had not permanently dealt with the Seattle wet-weather combined sewer overflow problem.

By 1967, Metro was intercepting and treating all dry weather sanitary sewage flows. However, during rainstorms, the old, combined storm and sanitary collection system of the City of Seattle was still plagued with backups and overflows. Metro had planned to install holding tanks along Lake Washington to prevent any direct overflows from reaching the lake, but the problem of local sewer backups was not part of Metro's responsibility. The Forward Thrust Utilities Vision Study Committee was challenged to find an acceptable solution to this critical City of Seattle crisis with its wider water quality impacts.

When combined sewers reached capacity during rainstorms, the increased flow would back up into the basements of homes and businesses and sometimes spill out onto streets, yards, and ditches. The resulting damage became a property owner's nightmare, especially when it was not the homeowner's fault. The problem was worse in some areas of the city than others and complete separation was considered too costly for the city to undertake.

No one knew Seattle's combined sewer problem better than City Engineer Roy Morse. He knew that during storms, the rainwater from roofs and streets could be as much as ten times greater than the flow of sanitary sewage. Roy understood that constructing a complete system of separate pipes for either storm or sanitary flows in a city where streets were already paved, and residential areas were fully developed, would be extremely costly. He also knew that even local overflows had potential health consequences from polluted gutters, ponds, and ground water. The health of children who played in streets, creeks, and ponds were at risk. Polluted ground water found its way into Lake Washington, the Duwamish River, and Puget Sound. The Forward Thrust Committee asked Roy whether an affordable capital project could help solve this intrinsic, combined system problem.

Roy saw Forward Thrust as a heaven-sent chance to cure a local sewage problem which had become the "Achilles heel" of his beloved Seattle's utility systems. The Forward Thrust Utilities Vision Study Committee listened carefully to his recommendation that $70 million of city general obligation bonds be issued out of the special constitutional borrowing capacity reserved for sewers. These sewer bonds would build separate pipes to remove non-polluting storm water from the City's combined system in areas subject to local back-ups and overflows. The Forward Thrust Committee agreed with Roy, that a city general obligation sewer separation bond issue would be a step forward. The Committee recommended that state help also be provided to older cities which had inherited similar overflow problems from their aging combined storm and sanitary sewer systems. Action by Seattle alone would not fully solve the pollution of Lake Washington, Puget Sound, and the Duwamish River during combined sewer overflows.

Tom Gibbs had led the development of Metro's Water Quality and Industrial Waste Control Department in 1962 and he became the technical services director of Metro following Miller's death in 1964. By 1967, he was the executive director of Metro and he was serving on the Committee of 200.

Tom was excited by the new Forward Thrust idea, knew every inch of the Metro sewer system, and was well prepared for the role of solving the difficult problems created by rainwater surges in combined sewers. He reasoned that within Seattle's combined trunk sewers and Metro's interceptors, there were capacities to temporarily store a portion of these storm water surges. He felt if these available capacities could be managed like a reservoir with central controls, the existing facilities could temporarily store rain-caused surges and release water gradually into Metro's system for treatment. This could substantially reduce the peak volumes reaching the treatment plant and greatly reduce the amount of untreated sewage overflowing to the Duwamish River and Puget Sound.

In about 1970, after the passage of the Forward Thrust measures, and with help from colleagues at Metro and EPA, Tom developed his idea into an application for an EPA demonstration grant to install central computer controls and strategic sluice gates inside existing sewer pipes. This would give engineers the ability to temporarily hold back and store the surge flows in existing pipes for short periods of time. The grant funds would be used to test this experimental system called Computer Augmented Treatment and Disposal (CATAD). If successful, the Metro Council could then give its approval to apply the concept on a larger scale. Once the CATAD system grant was approved, Metro contributed to the city the $6 million dollars previously budgeted by Metro for Lake Washington holding tanks to pay a portion of the city's cost of strategic sewer separations in those areas.

✦

CHAPTER 22

Chance of Our Lifetime

None of us can achieve our goals without the help of others.

—*Jim Ellis, "Chance of Our Lifetime" speech, January 1968*

WITH AN EMOTIONAL surge from our Forward Thrust legislative victory the Vision Study Committees went to work with renewed enthusiasm to prepare ballot measures for the voters. The Finance Committee began raising funds for the campaign to come. Simultaneous local special elections were planned for the winter of 1968. Each Vision Study Committee was challenged to move into high gear.

The idea that permeated the Committee of 200 was to create a program of capital improvements accommodating a broad spectrum of needs by creating many facilities and spaces for activities and making them widely accessible with improved transportation access. Some people want to be part of an exciting crowd at a spectator sports event. Others would rather find a natural space to find peace from the noise and hustle of urban life.

Politically, we knew that if each of us focused solely on our own special goals we would limit what could be possible if we joined forces. Indeed, all Vision Study Committees were focused on considering the complementary nature of projects. We carefully avoided forcing people to vote for two different purposes by combining them into a single ballot measure (known as log rolling). We hoped, instead, to attract the 60 percent majorities needed to pass *each* ballot measure by encouraging citizens to voluntarily consider the needs and desires of others.

Leading up to the campaign, authorizing ordinances and resolutions for each ballot measure were prepared in December of 1966 by the Forward Thrust Legal Committee and formally approved by the prosecuting attorney of King County, the corporation counsel of the City of Seattle, and with myself as the legal counsel of Metro. Each election resolution and ordinance were then adopted at public meetings by unanimous votes of the legislative bodies overseeing each jurisdiction.

It was time to tell our fellow citizens how the Committee of 200 had formed a "vision of the people" and to stress the importance of passing the entire program. After kick-off speeches in December, Paul suggested we rouse the faithful at Seattle Downtown Rotary to get a final election push from the same group which had heard the initial Forward Thrust idea two years earlier.

During December 1967 and January 1968, businesses, and groups of individuals voluntarily published testimonial ads supporting the entire program. Doorbelling was actively undertaken by hundreds of volunteers under the chairmanship of Tom Bolger. Mary Lou and I rang doorbells across a number of neighborhoods. The responses we received were overwhelmingly positive. Mary Lou loved doorbelling, saying, "It reminds me of Alaska neighboring." We both were lifted by the tidal wave of what had become a genuine public movement. Most people welcomed us when we came to their doors. Some thanked us for the work that brought the program to the voters. A few indicated they were not voting for anything, because it was too expensive. Most people said they liked the program and were willing to pay for it. Many offered to talk to friends and relatives. We found that our polls closely tracked the sentiments of the voters we saw in the districts we doorbelled.

In January 1968, I gave the final campaign speech, "Chance of Our Lifetime," which described the lasting benefits of each ballot measure, the authorized federal and state matching grants that we could capture, and the estimated annual individual taxes to be collected from each property-taxpayer over the 40-year life of the bonds to be issued. As usual, I rehearsed at home in front of Mary Lou who would interrupt to urge special emphasis, greater clarity, or to give encouraging applause. As she did for the first "Forward Thrust" speech, she suggested the title "The Chance of Our Lifetime" because, as she said, "it is!" The speech was delivered to a responsive full house in the Olympic Hotel ballroom and received favorable reporting by the press. While a voter could vote on each ballot measure as he or she chose, I emphasized the synergies that would come from approving all measures. Indeed, this was the heart of the Forward Thrust idea and of the Finance Committee's appeal for funds.

Each Forward Thrust ordinance or resolution was the product of months of work by well-prepared study committees. The February 13, 1968, election would cover eleven local bond measures. The following November 8, 1968, state election would include two state bond issues.

The parks measure became the largest per capita investment in parks ever voted on by local taxpayers. In early discussions with committee members, Parks Committee Chairs Calhoun Dickenson and Vern Williams found consensus that high priority be given to the acquisition of choice lands which were disappearing under the wave of new development. The Vision Study Committee members came from all parts of King County and understood that parks funded with King County bonds must be accessible to all residents of the county. They were eager to tackle a task that had a real chance of creating exciting, long-lasting public park benefits for the region.

Dickenson and Williams admired the Olmsted Brothers, who had created a historic, long-range vision for Seattle parks in an earlier generation and believed that the park staffs of City of Seattle and King County could come together to jointly plan and finance popular new park facilities. They brought to their work a large reservoir of knowledge, a capacity to listen, a willingness to compromise, and a large dose of contagious enthusiasm.

The final Parks Program of $118 million dollars included more than fifty miles of lake, river, and Puget Sound waterfront land, and four thousand acres of beautifully situated lands in the likely path of new development.

The park measure also provided for modest immediate improvements and preparation of a comprehensive plan for the long-term development of the Woodland Park Zoo. Construction of a new aquarium was funded, as was a new waterfront park on the downtown Seattle central waterfront. This

First Stage facility included the park site, a significant viewing aquarium, and contemplated that clean Elliott Bay water be available for long-term use as a Puget Sound teaching tool. Future expansion could create a far larger viewing, teaching, and research facility.

Facilities, like local neighborhood parks, were spread among large and small developed areas. Some swimming pools could be built on the campuses of senior high schools. The total parks system was planned to benefit every community and each of the major facilities would be made accessible to a wide range of people through the use of extended and improved public transportation.

The concept of adding reciprocal value applied to the two major transportation issues: urban arterials and public mass transportation. These two Forward Thrust committees functioned together because it was obvious to them that auto and public transit issues were closely linked, and that congestion was a common enemy. Buses needed arterials to drive on. Train stations and parking facilities needed accessibility by buses and automobiles. The committees took their lead from the new federal transit program, which had been in place for three years, and the balanced transportation objectives enacted under President Johnson. Federal guidelines were being adopted to guide federal support for construction that would encourage joint use and complimentary location of facilities whenever practical. Both the rapid transit and highway ballot proposals envisioned the use of common facilities and joint rights-of-way wherever practical.

Joint transportation planning involved a combination of funding sources: property taxes for the local bond shares of both arterials and transit, and income and gas taxes for the federal and state shares. Contracts for the joint use of space would aim for mutual economies of scale and be designed to improve service. Thus, stations for trains and park-and-ride lots for commuters would benefit expressways by reducing the uneconomic peak hour volumes that produce extraordinary traffic loads during short periods each day. We knew that space was at a premium in Seattle's constricted topography. Buses on an exclusive right-of-way lane could accommodate twice as many seated passengers in a peak hour as private cars operating in mixed traffic. A commuter train occupying one lane of space could carry as many as six to ten times more passengers than the equivalent space devoted to automobiles.

There was a need to reduce costly congestion and delay caused by traffic jams on commuting corridors at peak hours. A major purpose of the whole Forward Thrust program was to maximize the value of every project by making each a part of a whole concept.

Professional polling was done to survey voter attitudes on each of the different measures. The first poll in January 1968 showed that more than 60 percent of registered voters were likely in favor of *every* ballot measure. *The Seattle Times* and the *Post-Intelligencer* endorsed all eleven.

From the beginning, I was worried the well-known "Curmudgeon of Public Projects," Alfred J. Schweppe, might lead an attack on the whole Forward Thrust bond program. However, Schweppe had accepted an appointment to the Committee of 200, served on its legal committee, and became an active member. Still, I was pleasantly surprised when he came out enthusiastically in favor of the whole program. An article appeared on the front page of the Post-Intelligencer just one week before the vote with a picture of Schweppe and a headline "Thrust's 'Brilliant Design' Praised." In the article, Schweppe stated the 13-point program was "brilliantly and economically designed" to keep Seattle one of the most beautiful cities in the world.

Other conservative committee members could well have become opponents of the program, but most became strong supporters after participating for more than a year. This experience taught me how crucial it is to bring potential critics who are reasonable people into the early thinking and planning process. If they are ignored, their intuitive skepticism of large public programs could easily harden into active opposition.

Of course, anti-transit automobile activists were unlikely to change their minds. In fact, they led a targeted opposition to the center piece of the program—the metropolitan rapid transit system. Their opposition ads were designed to look like the testimonials which had been appearing in praise of the Forward Thrust effort but then reported that voting 'No' on the Metro Transit bill alone would cut a person's taxes in half.

The Forward Thrust mid-winter Election Day in King County was not an average special election. Voter turnout proved to be a record for a special election within King County and the subject seemed to be on everyone's lips. Most people saw it as a watershed vote. No candidates appeared on the ballot,

This experience taught me how crucial it is to bring potential critics who are reasonable people into the early thinking and planning process. If they are ignored, their intuitive skepticism of large public programs could easily harden into active opposition.

but the media portrayed the future of the area as riding on the outcome. Voter interest was intense and when the polls closed at 8 o'clock that evening, everyone was anxious to hear the results.

The election night campaign party was held at the Washington Athletic Club. As early returns came in, the headline news was the huge voter turnout, which was larger than the preceding state General Election! I remember standing at a chalkboard, updating the voting numbers as they came in. From the beginning the "Yes" votes were leading on all money related issues. In fact, they were leading with landslide numbers from 55 percent to 75 percent. From the first returns, the "Yes" votes for Metro transit were coming in with a solid majority, but this majority gradually came down as votes from outside Seattle were tallied. This was hard to watch for those of us who had worked to pass the whole program, or who saw rapid transit as the crucial centerpiece and most basic unmet need in our region.

Shortly after 8:00 o'clock p.m. Aubrey Davis, the popular mayor of Mercer Island and a leader in the Forward Thrust Committee, came into the room smiling and waving a piece of paper and saying, "Official results! Mercer Island votes 80 percent "Yes" for rapid transit!" The room erupted with cheers and when we added those votes to the running total, it brought the "Yes" votes on Metro transit to just over the needed 60 percent. Unfortunately, our euphoria was short lived. As more returns came in, the cumulative "Yes" majority for transit declined. It was never below 50 percent in favor, but it was well below the super majority needed for approval of the bonds.

The general mood of the people attending the election night party was celebratory because by varying large margins voters were saying "Yes" to all eleven money measures and ten of those were leading with more than 60 percent! The high-profile multi-purpose stadium measure was passing with more than 60 percent in favor, just one year after receiving a much lower outcome.

It was a happy evening for most county and city officials. When we left the campaign party that evening, it looked like all measures except transit would be approved. The "Yes" votes were either well over the 60 percent hurdle, or very close and leading heavily in the absentees.

However, as absentee votes were counted during the next two weeks, the important storm water issue fluctuated above and below 60 percent and finally failed to cross that barrier. Seven of the eleven money measures were finally approved by more than 60 percent of those voting. Three measures received "Yes" majorities of 58.0 to 59.5 percent and Metro Transit received a "Yes" majority of 50.9 percent.

The 1968 election results for the eleven February 13th local bond measures, as well as the two November 8th bond issues for public park and water pollution abatement projects, were a strong public endorsement of all the hours of work put in by the Forward Thrust Committee. All fourteen money measures received a majority "Yes" vote and nine of them passed the high 60 percent hurdle required for general obligation bonds and special levies.

CHAPTER 23

Triumph & Tragedy

"On February 13th the game is not for land and brick and pavement, but for us as a community of people."

—*Jim Ellis, "The Chance of Our Lifetime," speech, 1968*

THE *POST-INTELLIGENCER* called the February 13th, 1968, election "A Triumph." Indeed, the citizen action led by the Forward Thrust Committee received the Seattle area's second national All-America City Award.

However, Aubrey Davis, Carey Donworth, and I were deeply disappointed to lose our transit measure centerpiece, and Dorm Braman was crushed and outraged. Dorm's belief in the importance of rapid transit for the people of the Seattle region made him determined to see that Metro Transit not be allowed to die. In his first public comment, Dorm described the defeat of transit as a "tragic result" and urged that the issue be resubmitted. I began thinking about what we could do to create a better chance of future passage— perhaps in several stages.

The harsh fact was that a 50.9 percent "Yes" vote for Metro transit bonds was a long way from the 60 percent required by the state constitution. Professionally targeted opposition ads and high project cost had combined to knock rapid transit down from more than 64 percent "Yes" five weeks before the election, to not quite 51 percent by election night.

It was a hard loss to take. We had hoped to capitalize on the fact that two-thirds of the capital cost would be paid by federal grant under the 1964 Mass Transportation Act. Senators Magnuson and Jackson were certain that the Congress would appropriate funds for the federal share if Metro voters would approve their local share. Most supporters were convinced that an investment in rail rapid transit would be a huge long-term bargain for the Metropolitan Seattle area. It was hard to accept local failure after our hard-won federal aid had been authorized. It was even harder to accept the transit loss when the same voters approved a large local property tax bond issue to supplement federal and state aid for arterial highways.

A tragic footnote to the February 13, 1968, defeat of transit was the fact that events beyond our control began to snowball against us. As 1969 came around, it was becoming clear that the Boeing Company had grossly misjudged the timing of global demand for its jet transports. The Company had employed tens of thousands of people who turned out not to be needed.

In 1969, Boeing began lay-offs of thousands of workers and forecast steep declines in future sales in a looming national recession. It was becoming clear that these layoffs would destroy any chance of passing a major local tax measure. The transit committee of Forward Thrust and its new chairman Harry Goldie continued to work through 1968 and 1969, fine-tuning the rapid transit plan to meet critics concerns and local demands for service. However, by the winter of 1969–70, I told our Forward Thrust business backers privately that I didn't see how we could pass any rapid transit program that year. Our polls showed us below a simple majority, let alone the 60 percent required to approve the needed bond issue for a grade separated rail system. Harry, Dorm, and I had hoped that another rail rapid transit proposal might pass because it was becoming clear in Washington, D.C., that the *federal share* for transit was *going to increase to 80 percent* in a year or two. In addition, Maggie was confident he could then secure a full appropriation of the larger federal share if a local bond issue was approved by voters.

Senator Magnuson came out from Washington, D.C., to lead a Forward Thrust campaign rally at the Civic Auditorium. Maggie held up a poster-sized check for the full federal share and told the crowd he was authorized to deliver this check to our mayor if we approved the Metro Transit bond measure.

About three months before the May 1970 second-try election, polls showed us in deep trouble and Ross Cunningham of *The Seattle Times* told me, "You don't have *any* chance of winning 60 percent." Nevertheless, our business

Anti-Forward Trust bumper sticker expressed the fear of higher taxes held by many citizens if the initiative passed.

backers urged us not to give up because if we did it would further lower public confidence and increase the depth and length of our recession. We kept working, but without any real hope.

One day in April 1970, I received a telephone call from San Francisco that I could hardly believe. It was from William A. Bugge, the retired former Director of Highways for the State of Washington, who was then working as an engineer for the Bay Area Rapid Transit System (BART). He had disagreed ten years before with the idea of putting rails in the median of I-5 and had consistently opposed rail rapid transit in Seattle. He told me I had been right about rapid transit in Seattle. Since moving to the Bay Area, he had learned that rail transit is crucial for the healthy growth of cities constrained by water and land topography like San Francisco and Seattle. He said he was willing to take his three-week vacation and come to Seattle to make speeches anywhere I wanted to send him. He could help people understand the critical role rail rapid transit can perform in any tight traffic corridor.

I remember saying to him, "Bill, you have made my day. I never dreamed that I would ever get this call. I appreciate it immensely, but I have to say that our conversation is two years too late. The good Lord could come down today and speak to every neighborhood in favor of rapid transit and we wouldn't be able to pass the taxes for it. People here are deeply afraid. We are in the midst of an unexpected and serious recession, bordering on a deep depression. More than 50,000 people are *leaving* the Seattle area this year! It seems like every other block has a house for sale and it's getting worse each week. It would be a waste of your time and money to come up here. Our committee can't appear to give up, so we will continue to campaign. However, I would feel bad if you took your vacation to fight for a hopelessly lost cause."

He again offered to come but I said, "Bill, there is just no chance that we can pass rapid transit or any other tax supported program at this time. But thank you for calling. We will surely call you when our economic situation is brighter."

When election results were in on May 13, 1970, it was obvious from the first returns that the four propositions on the ballot were not going to have even a simple majority. Rapid transit did the *worst* with only 46 percent "Yes." Even storm water control, which got 59 percent in 1968, declined to 54 percent in 1970.

On election night, a small group of the faithful gathered at the Washington Athletic Club to hear the returns come in. It was a dismal evening and the mood across the room was at rock bottom. At the end of the evening, I thanked everyone for coming and for working on a lost cause, telling them there had not been anything wrong with our campaign or with their effort. It was just a time when most people could not support a tax increase for any purpose.

As we were leaving to go home, one of our loyal supporters in previous elections said, this was the last Ellis wake he'd attend, that we'd never had a chance on this vote, and to count him out on any future campaigns. Mary Lou quickly responded, "We're all tired tonight and it's late. We'll feel better in the morning." Walking to the car, I told Mary Lou how disheartening it was to have such a dedicated volunteer never want to work on campaigns again. She said, "Tomorrow will be better." Sure enough, the next morning I received a call from this same man apologizing and offering to help next time.

At home, Mary Lou gave her analysis of this, our worst defeat. "I think you and the voters need a vacation from one another. In a couple of years moods can change. You need to take a break anyway. I don't think we should try again until people can see the light at the end of this terrible depression." This view was shared by others, and the next election on transit was deferred for two-and-a-half years.

> *I think you and the voters need a vacation from one another.*
>
> —*Mary Lou*

As I reflect back on this tragic loss, I believe there was nothing we could have said or done in February 1968 or May 1970 that would have changed these two election outcomes. When confronting a 60 percent majority hurdle for a tax measure, the power of "No" is enormous. Postmortem analyses confirmed that the May 1970 ballot measures would have failed no matter what we had said or done during that campaign.

When confronting a 60 percent majority hurdle for a tax measure, the power of "No" is enormous.

A difficult challenge facing local public capital needs in Washington State is the 60 percent "Yes" vote required to approve general obligation debt. We like to think that every voter is equal in public elections. However, when voting on tax supported local debt, a "No" vote has significantly more weight than a "Yes" vote. Instead of needing 21 "Yes" votes to defeat 20 "No" votes, at least 30 "Yes" votes are required. In effect this means that each "No" voter has 50 percent more power than his neighbor who votes "Yes."

The Committee of 200 faced a double challenge. In the case of a park bond issue, for example, not only would various possible projects risk being required to be separately submitted, but the final ballot would have to pass by the overwhelming 60 percent majority of those voting.

The ultimate irony occurred when the federal funds appropriated by the Congress for Seattle Metro in 1968 and 1970 were re-directed to metropolitan Atlanta, Georgia, to fund their MARTA rapid rail transit system. This irony was compounded by the fact that Atlanta passed its rapid transit plan with 50.1 percent voting "Yes," while Seattle had voted 50.9 percent "Yes" in 1968. The future cost to Seattle area taxpayers of that result turned out to be staggering!

By the end of 1970, there was still no end in sight for the Boeing recession. King County unemployment had reached post-war record levels. There was no realistic prospect for reviving the bus rail transit plan. Still, the need to provide public transit service to the people of the metropolitan area continued. Seattle cut service and the private suburban system became insolvent. Aubrey Davis,

High Stakes Transportation
is a High Stakes Balancing Act

For years transportation issues had tended to polarize advocates into two camps: automobiles and mass transit. In the 1950s, State Highway Director Bugge had killed suggestions for designing rail rapid transit in the median of the Interstate 5 freeway project. This action effectively eliminated the lowest-cost opportunity for high-capacity rail through Seattle's narrow-waisted downtown. The consulting firm De Leuw, Cather & Company would later recommend constructing rail rapid transit on its own grade-separated right-of-way (subway). The 1964 federal Mass Transportation Act made this more expensive option financially feasible.

By 1966, all possible transportation alternatives carried high price tags. Arterial highways were sorely needed to handle growing vehicle movement and were becoming more expensive. The need for a costly new West Seattle Bridge was one of many pressing examples.

In 1996, a scaled down light rail plan was approved for a three-county area and the per capita cost to local taxpayers was more than four times greater than the 1968 plan. Delay of necessary capital investments has proved to be hard on grandchildren.

Carey Donworth, and I knew that we could not stop trying to create a public transit system to serve the Seattle metropolitan area.

During the lull between elections, we studied ways to strengthen the transit proposal and make it easier to pass. Polls taken after the 1970 rail rapid transit election showed that a change from property tax financing to sales tax financing would be more acceptable to voters. We knew that the initial cost of an all-bus system would be substantially less than the cost of a rail and bus system. There could be no regional transit system without a tax subsidy. A lower-cost bus plan paid from sales taxes would need only a simple majority vote to pass.

The Forward Thrust Committee and its City and County partners believed a new Citizens Committee should be focused solely on transit and a new all-bus and trolley plan with county-wide reach should be prepared by new consultants. We prepared a plan which would provide a sales tax of three-tenths of one percent to pay for the transit system. Republican Joel Pritchard and Democrat David Sprague were asked to lead the legislative effort.

I attended each of those meetings but was no longer acting in a high-profile position. This new effort would be managed by Metro, and the new Citizens Committee would be supported by Forward Thrust business leaders. After already failing twice, we believed this new approach would be the best chance of getting at least a modest system in place for the immediate future.

The Citizens Committee and consultants drew heavily from the Forward Thrust Transit Committee effort, but operated with a clean slate, as far as transit systems were concerned. Metro also provided the services of Larry Coffman as staff, and me as legal counsel. In addition, Metro retained Seattle public relations consultant Wally Toner and the professional engineering firm Daniel Mann, Johnson and Mendenhaul (DMJM) to design and prepare cost estimates and a long- range plan for a bus transit plan for all of King County.

The Citizens Committee painstakingly enlisted the public in preparing operating policies and standards and bus routes. Voter records were studied, and public meetings were held to determine the kind and extent of bus service the public wanted and was willing to pay for. The new system would run largely on existing streets and use renewed electric trolleys and a new fleet of gas- and diesel-powered buses. Payment would include bus fares, sales tax, and a motor vehicle excise tax credited against the existing state motor vehicle excise tax. A large number of experienced transit people participated in those meetings, along with people from the Forward Thrust Committee eager to continue working for improved transit service.

By the summer of 1972, the worst of the Boeing recession was behind us and the crisis in public transit had deepened. Service was being cut and fares rose sharply. Bus fleets were old and there were no funds for replacement.

The legislative session of 1972 turned out to be difficult. However, Dave Sprague and Larry Coffman were able to get our transit sales tax legislation through the Senate near the end of the session with leadership from Senator Greive.

The House of Representatives was a different story. Slade Gorton had left to become attorney general. Two nights before the scheduled adjournment of the House, Joel Pritchard called me to say that if we wanted to pass the Senate bill, it would be necessary for me to go with him to Olympia early the following morning to have breakfast with the Speaker and other key leaders. I drove down with Joel at 6:00 a.m. and we met in a restaurant across from the capitol. Joel had worked out a game plan in which the House leaders would take up the Senate bill and get it through Committee and Rules so it could be acted on by the House. Considering the minimal time available, I thought it was an impossible thing to do. But Joel encouraged me to work with him. He proceeded to cover all the bases using his immense credibility to go anywhere and talk with any legislator who knew him. Even though Joel was no longer a US Congressman, he was able to enter state legislative chambers and speak directly with people. Believe it or not, he actually got this thing done. The Senate bill was passed by the House and signed by Governor Evans. A surprising opportunity was created to develop a good bus system for the metropolitan area *with only a simple majority of those voting* required for local approval.

In the fall of 1972, the Metro Council put a measure on the ballot authorizing it to perform the function of metropolitan public transportation throughout King County and to levy a three-tenths of one percent sales tax to pay the cost. Many people did not think there was a chance of passage, including Mayor Ullman and me. The area was not out of the woods of the financial recession and the 1970 transit vote had been dismal. Advertising was on a slim budget with help from exhausted Forward Thrust finance committee members. But Bob Gogerty and Larry Coffman enlisted volunteers and put them to work with the simple slogan "vote for county-wide transit." This resonated with the public.

My son Bob, our family optimist, and I went to the election gathering at the Olympic Hotel and I told him before going in, "Bob, it will be a miracle if we pass this." In typical fashion, Bob said, "But Popo, there's always a chance for miracles." When returns started coming in, they showed over 50 percent voting "Yes." The numbers held and we won that election by over 56 percent, which was astonishing to me. Just as Mary Lou had hoped, voter attitudes changed and the fourth election on Metro Transit turned out to be the winner we had been trying for so long to find. It was a striking and inspiring victory. New Mayor Wes Ullman was so sure it would fail that he had prepared a statement to address the defeat and had nothing prepared for victory!

✦

It was necessary to finalize the transfer of transit properties from the City of Seattle and the Metropolitan Transit Corporation to Metro by the first of the year, less than three months away. Tom Gibbs and the Metro staff sprang into action with 6:30 a.m. meetings. They performed an incredible feat of working with, preparing for, and putting into place, a combined operating Metropolitan Transit system. This was done by using mostly Seattle transit facilities and personnel. My job was to negotiate and draft an agreement with the City of Seattle that would allow Metro to take over the operating equipment facilities and personnel of the Seattle Transit system and the Metropolitan Transit Corporation for the acquisition of its nearly defunct system. The members of the Metro Council found themselves caught up in the zeal with which Metro staff and employees worked on this difficult challenge. Metro Council Transit Committee Chairman Aubrey Davis and transit supporters on the Council, like Kent's mayor Isabel Hogan and Renton's mayor Avery Garrettor, on were on board 100 percent and helped spread the can-do spirit.

Older buses were updated with the new Metro label.

Modernized Metro bus, downtown Seattle, 1975.

New labels were pasted on old buses and title transfers were completed. Additional old buses were purchased to operate in the suburban area and the Metro Transit bus system was on the street in January 1973! It was a thrilling thing to see Metro buses on the street after so much hard work.

By the spring of 1973, the time had come to wrap up the Forward Thrust Committee. The Executive Committee met and agreed to terminate the corporation and disband the organization. We had promised in the beginning not to create another permanent civic organization to be supported by the business community. Most of the capital purposes we had sought were underway and a county-wide transit system was on the street with innovations coming.

There was still a long way to go to meet long-term rapid transit goals, but with a core bus system underway, there was a real chance of eventually realizing a larger system of public transportation for the metropolitan area. With financing and governance stepping stones in place, Metro began an innovative program destined to become a shining example of a successful bus operation. In 1983 and 1992 Metro Transit was named the best bus system in the nation by the American Public Transportation Association.

BOOK SIX

Service Beyond Self

⬥

CHAPTER 24

Spellman Builds a Kingdome

". . . good friends and integrity outlast political seasons."

—*Mary Lou*

IN THE YEARS FOLLOWING the 1962 World's Fair, two elections had been held to authorize a multi-purpose stadium for major league sports in King County. Most of those voting each time favored the measure, but the majority was less than the 60% required by our state constitution and the issue remained unsolved. With a tradition of local baseball heroes like Fred Hutchinson and popular Triple-A baseball teams, many local fans believed Seattle would be a successful major league city. When the Forward Thrust concept was being put together, Paul Siebert, Eddie Carlson and I felt that facilities for major league spectator sports should be among the iconic items included. Joseph Gandy considered a multi-purpose stadium to be a logical follow-on to the World's Fair legacy of public cultural facilities at Seattle Center. Even after the Committee of 200 was formed in 1966, the consensus process took a long time and supporters of a big-league stadium became concerned other cities would beat Seattle to the punch for major league football and baseball franchises.

When the Forward Thrust Committee program of exciting new state legislation was being prepared, Joe came to the committee and said he knew they were getting on board late, but that they'd work hard for the whole

Forward Thrust program if the committee would include the stadium in it. Most of the committee believed that the stadium should be part of any comprehensive capital program. A new stadium financing plan was developed as part of the 1967 legislative program.

Joe was as good as his word. American League president Joe Cronin, superstars Mickey Mantle, Carl Yastrzemski, and other big-league players came to Seattle to campaign for the February 1968 Forward Thrust election, saying, in effect, "If you build it, we will come." This time the multi-purpose stadium measure carried with a 62% majority.

Franklin High School graduates Dewey and Max Soriano had grown up near Sicks' Stadium in the Rainier Valley and dreamed of being the major league baseball franchise holder for Seattle. Their group secured league approval for a Seattle franchise on the premise that the recently approved multi-purpose stadium would be built.

The Sorianos called their team the Seattle Pilots. Pending completion of the new stadium, they arranged for the Pilots to play in Sicks' Seattle Stadium which was to be enlarged and refurbished for this purpose. The Pilots planned to move into the new Kingdome stadium when it was completed.

The first Seattle Pilot's season as an American League expansion team in Sicks' Stadium was disappointing. The burden of maintaining a team with relatively small attendance for several years until the Kingdome was built became too much for the Soriano family and their well-to-do partner from Cleveland, Ohio. They agreed they should sell the Pilot's franchise to an eager Milwaukee ownership group. The Forward Thrust Committee was concerned that when the new domed stadium was completed it would not have its most important tenant: Major League Baseball.

In the fall of 1969, several people got together under the leadership of Eddie Carlson, Joe Gandy, Jim Douglass, Jim Ryan, the Chamber of Commerce, and the Downtown Seattle Association to try to keep the Pilot's franchise in Seattle. They made a presentation to League owners in Oakland, California, asking what the League would require in order to hold the franchise in Seattle. At this meeting, League owners set forth what became known as the "Oakland Conditions" for retaining an American League franchise in Seattle. These conditions included specific amounts of equity and debt money that

Kingdome, 1985.

would have to be raised by a new franchise holder to buy out the Soriano group and operate the Pilot's franchise.

When no individual stepped up with enough money, Eddie Carlson held a brainstorming luncheon in his Olympic Hotel office. Attendees included Jim Douglass, Downtown Association executive director Mechlin Moore, and me. Eddie offered up a new idea that we put together a nonprofit community-owned team along the lines of the Green Bay Packers football team. He believed that enough people wanted big league baseball to buy shares of equity ownership which would be sufficient with a local bank loan to meet the "Oakland Conditions" *and* to purchase the Pilots team from its owners.

Eddie agreed to lead this group and Jim Ryan, Jim Douglass, and other businessmen agreed to support it. A private nonprofit corporation for the community-owned team was created and a fundraising campaign was launched. Subscriptions could not be more than $200,000, or less than $5,000 from any one person. The subscriptions would not be binding until enough money was pledged to meet the "Oakland Conditions" and to operate the team. Offers to pledge smaller subscriptions were received in the lobby of the Olympic Hotel. Eddie, Jim Ryan, and other business leaders each pledged $200,000 and agreed to solicit other large equity subscribers. Bill Jenkins of SeaFirst Bank headed the banking group.

The "Oakland Conditions" had set a target of $11 million to be provided by debt ($8 million) and equity ($3 million). Gordon Conger of the Preston firm and I drafted the documents to create the not-for-profit corporation and its proposals to the Pilots. This was the proposal which Eddie took to the owner's winter meeting in Chicago. When we left Seattle, $11 million dollars were deposited in an escrow account at SeaFirst Bank. This was exactly the amount that the "Oakland Conditions" required. Draft proposals to the American League for league membership of the Carlson group and purchase of the Seattle Pilots, were approved as to form by lawyers for both parties.

The owner's meeting was held in a Chicago hotel owned by Western Hotels. When we arrived, Eddie received a message from League President Joe Cronin that some of the owners would like to meet us that evening after dinner in Cronin's hotel room. We agreed to make ourselves available when they called.

While we were waiting, there was a knock at the door from one of our $200,000 subscribers. After brief pleasantries, he announced to Eddie that he expected to be named team manager after the application was approved the following day. Eddie was taken aback by this, saying he had promised subscribers that we would have professional baseball team management and he thought that none of the owners should be eligible for the job. The gentleman responded that he was fully capable of managing the team and was serious about his proposal. The details could be determined later, however, he wanted Eddie to understand up-front that he would be the team manager, or he would withdraw his subscription. Eddie stood firm on his initial statement and the disappointed subscriber left the room saying he wanted his money back immediately! Eddie told him he'd have it back tomorrow morning when the bank opens. Then Eddie closed the door behind him.

We were shaken to the core by this development, knowing we had collected only the exact amount of money required by the league. The loss of $200,000 would destroy our ability to make a responsive presentation the next morning.

We immediately began brainstorming possible people Eddie could call to fill the $200,000 hole in equity money we now needed. We were stymied.

As we frantically worried about failing to find the required money, Eddie's hotel room phone rang. It was Jim Ryan of Unico Properties calling to see how we were doing. He said he knew we were alone in Chicago and wanted to make sure that everything was going okay. He offered that if we needed another couple hundred thousand, they'd have it for us. With a big smile, Eddie said, "Ryan if you were here, we'd kiss you!"

Around midnight that evening, we finally received a call from Cronin asking us to meet with several owners in his hotel room. This late-night meeting was disturbing. We expected to be welcomed with open arms as the "Northwest Solution" for the league. Instead, we were greeted with skeptical questions and a mixed reception. Kaufman of the Kansas City Royals and Gene Autry of the Los Angeles Angels were warmly supportive. However, others wondered whether we would have the resources to sustain a competitive team, citing the financial difficulties encountered by the first Seattle franchise owners. We left the meeting concerned about the overall mixed reception. However, the next morning, the league counsel and the baseball commissioner who were also in Chicago assured us that things would work out okay.

At 10:00 a.m. we gave our presentation to the owners in a large ballroom filled with press from around the country. It was clear from newspaper articles of the previous days that the national press considered this a David and Goliath story. We were the underdog, "the little guys" who wanted to keep baseball in Seattle, and our opponents were portrayed as big business interests who were not intrigued by "non-profit experiments."

The outcome was not clear until the actual vote was taken. If there were three or less votes against us, we would be accepted under the rules of the league. If more than three votes were against us, our proposal was rejected. To our dismay, the final vote came down with four votes against us, and we had lost. This devastating blow deeply upset both Eddie and me. After the meeting, Eddie turned to me and told me he had to go to New York for a meeting, but that I was to give every subscriber their money back immediately when I returned to Seattle.

As we left the Chicago press conference Eddie turned to me and said not to feel too bad because it might have been for the best. He continued with the concern that if we'd won, this thing might have occupied us for the rest of our lives, that it was a bigger job than we figured, and that we didn't have all the power in the world behind us. When I returned to Seattle, I followed through on Eddie's request and Bill Jenkins saw that all pledged monies were returned to subscribers. I also called Attorney General Slade Gorton to tell him Eddie's group had been unable to win acceptance by the owners. Slade asked us not to let it get us down and expressed that we'd delivered a proposal that met all the "Oakland Conditions." He didn't think it would end there and that if the team left Seattle, the state and county might bring a suit for damages against the League.

In passing their resolution rejecting us, the owners assumed that they would not remove the Pilots from the city. Rather the league itself would finance the team for the next season, which would begin in a month, and observe how well it was received by local fans. This was not a comforting idea. A team playing without active local ownership and without any real promotion was not likely to sell many advance tickets and it didn't. In fact, the league moved the team to Milwaukee directly from spring training in Arizona and the team officially became the Milwaukee Brewers.

The next chapter of this odyssey began as Gorton had predicted. A lawsuit was filed by the State of Washington and King County against the American League. Leading Seattle trial lawyer William L. Dwyer was hired to represent the state and the county in an action to collect damages for the League's failure to approve the Carlson proposal. The suit was transferred to Snohomish County Superior Court for trial at the request of the league, which feared a Seattle jury would be prejudiced in our favor.

When the suit came to trial, our star witness, Eddie Carlson, was called out of town on crucial hotel business and was unable to be present. His inability to attend meant that I would have to serve as the primary witness for the county and state. I was the only one who had first-hand knowledge of the 1968 election campaign when county voters approved the taxes to pay for a publicly owned stadium. Before this election, the American League had actively sold major league baseball and a new stadium to the residents of King County. In fact, Mickey Mantle, Jimmy Piersall, and Joe Cronin were in Seattle in the run up to election night and they'd presented me a baseball signed "To Jim, with best wishes."

The purpose of their involvement and ours was not simply to build a stadium, but to build one which would be occupied by a major league baseball team when it opened. The people had voted for the excitement of big-league events and the county had proceeded diligently to issue its bonds and build the Kingdome for such events.

The trial itself lasted only three days. However, the preparation by Dwyer had been painstaking and extensive. I was on the stand for the better part of two days and answered questions about my knowledge of the league's participation in public meetings promoting the stadium. I testified that I personally watched Cronin, Mantle, and Piersall urge support of the stadium bonds at Seattle Rotary and at other key public forums in the county. I went on to describe Eddie's successful effort to create a credible ownership group and the actions of the group to meet all the league's conditions for membership. I also described the events that took place at the league meeting in Chicago where our proposal was rejected.

Dwyer had done an excellent job of discovery. When Cronin took the witness stand, he contradicted much of my testimony, but Dwyer impeached Cronin's testimony by introducing a tape that the league had made of our late-night meeting with the owners in Cronin's Chicago hotel room. The jury was familiar with both of our voices from the testimony given in court. This tape confirmed my version of history and contradicted important parts of Cronin's testimony. The tape ended dramatically with the slam of a door, followed by Cronin's voice saying, "I guess we gave them enough rope to hang themselves!"

When the jury retired to reach a verdict, they had not been out more than twenty minutes before the foreman came back to ask the court a single question: "Is the jury limited in the amount of its award to the payer of the plaintiff's complaint?" The judge responded that they were so limited, and the foreman returned to the jury room. The minute he left, the attorneys for League came across the room to our counsel table to verify with Dwyer we really wanted the team, not the money. They said they'd give us the team if he'd dismiss the lawsuit. Dwyer responded with something along the lines of, "Yes, we want a team but no more bullshit." He proposed to seal the verdict and to drop the lawsuit, *if and when* a new franchise was approved for Seattle, *and* the new team had actually played a full season in the Kingdome. In the meantime, the verdict would remain sealed. The league lawyers and owners agreed. A new Seattle franchise was granted to a group headed by Les Smith and actor Danny Kaye. All this prompted Seattle sportswriter Emmett Watson to write a column proposing that Seattle's team should be called the "Seattle Litigators" rather than Seattle Mariners.

Of course, the Kingdome had yet to be built and controversy arose at every step. In 1968, 110 potential sites were considered, including 94 recommended by individuals and 15 selected by a consulting team. The state Stadium Committee whittled this number down to 12, then down to five. After a protracted delay to consider the different sites, the County Commissioners finally selected an area of former tidelands within the railroad yard south of Seattle's King Street Station.

Building the King County Stadium—the Kingdome—south of downtown Seattle proved to be just as difficult and controversial as Mary Lou had feared before the 1968 Forward Thrust campaign. Critics protested that the sidewalks in nearby Pioneer Square would collapse from the weight of people, and that street traffic would snarl into gridlock during every event. The site selection was challenged twice. The financing plan was attacked in court. After construction finally began, the contractor walked off the job with the roof half-built! Murphy's Law was at work. (Over the years we became believers in Murphy's Law that "Whatever can go wrong WILL go wrong" and, using it as a guide to cautious planning, tried to have a fallback plan to deal with the inevitable glitches that seem to plague public programs.)

Throughout this turmoil, King County Executive John Spellman proved to be courageous and persistent. The site challenges were rebutted. Our financing plan was upheld by the Washington Supreme Court. A new contractor finished the project within available funds. The physical centerpiece of the Forward Thrust program became a reality at last—ready to house all kinds of events under its weatherproof dome, and to bring major league football and baseball to the rainy Northwest. The Kingdome was built on time and hosted Seahawks football in the fall of 1976 and Mariners baseball in the spring of 1977.

Many well-attended events took place in the Kingdome during its twenty-three years of active service. Among the most memorable were a "Final Four" NCAA basketball playoff, and the exciting early years of Seahawk football under Nordstrom Family ownership with Chuck Knox as coach and star players like Steve Largent and Jim Zorn. During the 70s and 80s, the Mariners had an impressive record of wins and losses which at times, resulted in modest attendance in the "Dome." There were some exciting games, but ownership changed hands and was on the verge of selling and moving.

During this crisis, a stable ownership group headed by a Japanese businessman was recruited by Senator Slade Gorton in 1992 to purchase the franchise and keep the team in Seattle. My brother, John Ellis, who at the time was chairman and CEO of Puget Power, was asked by Slade and business leaders to serve as the chairman of this new ownership group. John accepted the position and was instrumental in securing approval by the League for majority ownership by Nintendo Corporation's Hiroshi Yamauchi. The new group included executives from Microsoft, Boeing, and other prominent Seattle businesses. The management was well-financed, and the new owners performed their pledge to sustain the effort needed to keep the Mariners franchise *"safe at home"* in Seattle.

John hired Lou Pinella as the team's field manager and the new management built a team that included Edgar Martinez, Ken Griffey, Jr., Randy Johnson, Alex Rodriguez, and Jamie Moyer. The Mariners became a local legend while winning several division titles. By 1995, the Mariners franchise had effectively turned Seattle into a strong major-league baseball town. Under this leadership, Safeco Field, today called T-Mobile Park, was built to replace the Kingdome in 2001 and was built with spacious corridors, comfortable seating, numerous luxury suites, and an almost magical retractable roof that allowed players to play on a natural grass field in the open air more than eighty percent of the time. The Mariner's team tied the *all-time* American League, *single season* record by winning 116 games in its first year!

As Hall of Fame announcer Dave Niehaus observed, for twenty-three years the Kingdome proved to be an exciting place to play baseball, football, or any sport. With a capacity to hold 55,000 people it was a noisy place when packed with frenzied fans. The Dome's preventive maintenance by King County left

. . . the real thrill was sharing this common thread of community with total strangers.

something to be desired, and what began as a low-cost bargain gradually was rendered obsolete by high-quality competitive facilities elsewhere in the country. When interior roof tiles fell during a Kingdome game, separate new stadiums were proposed and built for baseball and football. I was chided as "the guy who built a stadium his brother wouldn't play in." Still, during its short life, the Kingdome helped bring together the people of the Seattle area in ways that only sports can do.

This special quality was brought home to me in August 1995, when the Mariners, under manager Lou Pinella, staged a late-season come-from-behind charge to force a playoff with Los Angeles for the Western Division Title. The single playoff game was held in the Kingdome. I attended the play-off with most of my family. After seesaw early innings, the game became more and more hard-fought and lasted well beyond the expected time. With the Mariners only one run behind, I had to leave early to attend an anniversary party. My daughter Lynn said, "I'll go with you Dad," and we snuck out reluctantly and started walking up Third Avenue toward my parking garage.

I remember that street traffic was minimal, and the sidewalks were almost empty. I turned to Lynn and said, "Look honey! Everyone is inside watching or listening to this game!" As we walked along Third Avenue in front of the courthouse, a small group of five or six men were huddled together outside the Morrison Hotel which then served as a low-income housing shelter. As we approached, we could see these folks were intently listening to a tiny radio. They were completely focused on the Dave Niehaus broadcast of the game. As we walked by, I said to Lynn, "*Everybody* is riveted to this darn ballgame." We went about fifty feet further when the silence on the street was broken by a roar from this small group. Turning around I shouted to the guy with the radio, "What happened?" He stood up, raised both arms and said, "We won!!" I yelled back, with two thumbs up, "Way to go!" It was a happy moment. The Mariners had made the playoffs after years of struggle. But the real thrill was sharing this common thread of community with total strangers. For that moment we were united celebrating together a win for "our" home team.

I have thought many times how difficult it is to bring the different people of a large metropolitan area together. But here was a case where a sporting event served that purpose better than we could have scripted. Over the years, major league sport franchises have produced different degrees of success. They have provided economic stimulants in good and bad times but more importantly, they have brought joy into the homes of all races and classes. I hope that the excitement of similar future events can thrill crowds for years to come. In so doing, these events continue to confirm the dreams of citizen activists, government officials, and business investors. Sporting events have the power to do far more than support a strong sports-related economy. They have the ability to unite the people of a region.

🌲

CHAPTER 25

Board of Regents:
War & Race on Campus

REGENT APPOINTMENT

In early 1965, newly elected Governor Dan Evans called to say he wanted me to serve on the Board of Regents of the University of Washington. It was an exhilarating surprise to be asked to join the loop of decision making at the hometown school where my father and mother had graduated, and where my father, my brother John, and I received law degrees. Both sets of parents were delighted with this news. I believed that my brother Bob, who had been drafted in 1943 while attending his freshman semester at UW, would have said, "Way to go, Hym!"

I knew the Evans family from my early law days when I'd met Dan's father, Les, the King County engineer at the time. Les was an easy person to talk with and enjoyed sharing views on county issues and the early history of Washington state. I often found myself extending our meetings just to listen to his stories.

The 1960s brought warning signs that the tentative US intervention in Vietnam could turn into a long and bloody war. Opposition was growing to reactivation of a military service draft. As shown in Birmingham and Los Angeles, deep racial unrest was boiling over in protests and armed police

The last official meeting of the Board of Regents with Dr. Charles E. Odegaard as president of the University of Washington in 1973. Left to right: Robert Flennaugh, R. Mort Frayn, Jack Newpert, Charles Odegaard, Robert Phillip, George Powell, Harold Shefelman, and Jim Ellis.

responses. Examples of an emerging drug and sex counterculture appeared more frequently in the mainstream press. Still, I did not really foresee the breadth or intensity of student unrest which would surface during my time as a regent.

My first meeting with the board in 1965 was calm and dignified. After new regents George Powell and I had been introduced, the board president called on University President Dr. Charles Odegaard to give his report. An hour later, without pause, he was still speaking. When I asked a question, the other regents looked shocked that anyone would be so rude as to interrupt his presentation. It was as if Charles had cast a spell and I had broken it for no good reason.

After this less-than-auspicious beginning, I soon learned why the regents regarded Charles Odegaard with near reverence. His knowledge of "the Academy" was encyclopedic. His awareness of issues and command of language was superb. As a former professor of Classical and Medieval History, he could draw scholarly analogies from his specialty with little fear of contradiction.

In 1968, Governor Evans appointed Robert F. Phillip of the Tri Cities and R. Mort Frayn of Seattle to the Board of Regents. Both of these men were outstanding regents and strong supporters of President Odegaard and his vision for a new university.

Bob Phillip was the publisher of the *Tri-City Herald* and a leader in the Republican Party in Eastern Washington where he hosted the Board of Regents as guests in his Kennewick home. He served on the Board of Regents for 19 years, the longest-serving board member.

Governor Evans' appointment of R. Mort Frayn to the Board of Regents was widely considered to be an excellent choice and strengthened the university's ability to gain funding from the state legislature. Mort had served in the State House of Representatives for many years and in his last two years served as Speaker of the House. Mort was respected and trusted by people in both parties. During his two terms on the Board of Regents, he quickly grasped Charles' goals for a "new university" and was a rock of support.

Ed Munro, one of the young Democrats whom I debated during the early 1950s, was a member of the State House of Representatives when Mort Frayn was a Republican leader. Once when Ed and I were sitting on a bench in the New York airport waiting to come home from a Metro bond delivery, Mort Frayn walked by in a crowd. Ed nudged me to say, "That's Mort Frayn. He's the only Republican I would follow anywhere." It was a real compliment coming from a leader of the opposite party.

Mort and I became political allies when he saw the positive impact that Metro was having on the Seattle area. Mort was a leading progressive Republican, serving as State Chairman of the presidential campaigns for Nelson Rockefeller and later Richard Nixon. Throughout his career, he was invariably as good as his word and universally respected. Mort's gracious wife Helen was a close partner in his political career. They warmly hosted groups in their home to help Forward Thrust or University of Washington efforts.

Charles had come to the university in August 1958, at a time when the regents were seeking strong and visionary leadership. He grasped that need and filled it to the brim. The road was neither straight, nor smooth, but his compass of ideals was steady. The institution put in place initiatives and programs that raised academic stature, built institutional capacity, and opened new doors of educational opportunity.

Odegaard's vision for a "new university" had been formed earlier in the year with the whole-hearted blessing of then Governor Rosellini and Washington state's two powerful US Senators: Henry M. Jackson and Warren G. Magnuson. The necessary capital investment for new buildings would include expensive libraries, laboratories, classrooms, and most notably, a new medical school complex. The rapid changes in analytical methods spurred by new computer technology and the creation of state-of-the-art medical research goals and methods were combined with programs of interdisciplinary study. The combination began to vault the university to new levels of educational prominence. However, it takes time for such a major vision to become a reality on the ground.

The relationship of President Odegaard with the faculty was one of mutual respect and shared dedication. Alternatively, in meetings with students, he was usually reserved and always carefully controlled. Students respected Charles but did not always feel he was connected with their concerns. Some students of the sixties looked upon the Board of Regents as coming from a different planet.

ERNIE CONRAD

Vice President Ernie Conrad was managing financial matters at the UW during Odegaard's presidency and was a key player in a group that met each morning with Charles. Conrad was an immediate convert to Odegaard's educational vision and became a creative partner in building the facilities of a "new university." Conrad began to sense a growing communication gap between the regents and university president on one hand, and the campus population of teachers, students, and employees. This information vacuum was sometimes "filled" by activists with special agendas, like Students for a Democratic Society (SDS) and other anti-Vietnam War organizations.

During this period, a national divide was opening across America caused by the increasing military intervention in Vietnam. In October 1967, more than 50,000 people marched on the Pentagon and, for the first time, national polls showed more people were opposed to the war in Vietnam than supported it.

While Charles and the regents were focusing on achieving their progressive vision for a new university, most students and their parents were thinking more about the growing US involvement in Vietnam and the activation of a military draft for men between 18 and 26 years of age. Ernie also held a bond with his many student friends that proved to be critically valuable during the coming times of campus tension. He wore the love he had for the university on his sleeve, and students and employees trusted him completely.

By the mid-1960s, the Metro cleanup of Lake Washington and the Forward Thrust public improvement effort had brought attention to Seattle's civic activists. After one meeting, Ernie said to me something close to, "Jim, you know, students would like to meet you and understand how you became involved in Metro and Forward Thrust. They won't get this from reading the *UW Daily*. If I can arrange some conversations between you and small groups of students at different locations, would you be willing to set aside some time for this?" I welcomed the opportunity and Ernie worked out available times with my secretary.

For some time, Ernie Conrad had been feeling a disconnection between the Board of Regents on one hand, and employees and students on the other. Most people on campus never showed up at regents meetings and did not know whether their views were being considered. Regents came from off-campus places and the monthly meetings were the only way members of the university community could see policy being made. Ernie saw a need to help faculty, employees, and students understand that regents were not just unknown business figures who were strangers to contemporary campus life. He knew that all the regents were residents of the state, had families, and one had draft-age children. These regents were in fact people who could understand the impact of their decisions on college students.

Ernie believed that regents had a responsibility beyond listening to staff and making decisions on their recommendations. He believed we should become aware of the range of opinions held by the large campus family and to see how policies adopted by the regents were being received. This became especially critical during the dangerous years of 1969 and 1970.

Ernie's presence as a connector of different viewpoints helped to defuse issues and prevent different views from spinning into conflicts during this volatile period of war and race-related turmoil on campus. Ernie was also a very able dollars-and-cents man, who closely followed his building projects to assure they were being proposed, contracted, and completed within budget constraints. If bonds were to be issued, he checked whether payment schedules realistically considered timely available sources. At his retirement in 1974, at the age of sixty-two, Ernie Conrad was praised by the regents for his "outstanding service in the financial and business operations of the University."

VIETNAM & ANTI-WAR PROTESTS

Vietnam was a more remote and strange place to young Americans of the 1960s than Europe had been to my generation in the 1930s. Young men of the baby boom generation faced a real prospect in the late 1960s of being drafted and sent into a difficult and deadly conflict in the distant jungles of Vietnam. When I became a regent in 1965, I was a generation removed from the students then enrolled at the university. Ernie's coffee hours showed students that Mary Lou and I were just as worried about our draft-age son Bob as their parents were worried about them.

As I became more aware of student concerns, I was also taking a harder look at my own views. In effect, Ernie and Mary Lou were changing my thinking by exposing me to the opinions of young people. They had compelling reasons for opposing participation in a deadly conflict in the former French Indochina.

By the fall of 1967, our oldest son Bob, then a student at Yale, had become convinced that the Vietnam War was "a foreign revolution with a colonial history." He took an active part in the campaign of Eugene McCarthy, the Peace Movement candidate for president. I continued to support the position of Presidents Kennedy and Johnson that American intervention was necessary to prevent an eventual communist takeover of Southeast Asia. Our opposing views were widely shared within our respective generations, and each had deep emotional conviction. I believed my brother's death in combat placed a personal duty on family members to serve their country in time of war. Bob believed that sending our armed forces into Vietnam was a mistake, did not serve the national interest of the United States, and would lead to a large and needless loss of American lives. I began to find it harder each year to defend my position.

My own opinions on the deepening Vietnam War had begun to change even before Bob went to France for his junior year abroad. By the fall of 1967, Mary Lou and I had been through several intense discussions about Vietnam and Bob's growing condemnation of the conflict. Mary Lou attended Democratic Party caucuses with Bob in spite of her previous participation with me in Republican Party activities. She said that she had come to believe the United States should get out of Vietnam because, "Our goals are just not worth the bloodshed." I believed she was reinforcing our family fabric by showing Bob her belief in him. After he returned to Yale, she persisted independently in quiet anti-war activity.

One evening when we were engaged in a serious discussion about Bob's determination not to serve in Vietnam, Mary Lou tried to soften my stance. "You know, Bob is reaching for something that will satisfy his conscience and also make you proud of him. It's up to you to support a legal alternative to military service. If you don't, his draft number will come up, he will refuse to serve, and he may end up in Canada or in jail. Remember, Judi's husband Cary was willing to enlist in the Coast Guard even though he was opposed to the war because you persuaded him that it was a life-saving form of service."

On a return business flight from New York to Seattle in early 1968, I was in my coach seat waiting for take-off. Looking out the window I watched a young man in civilian clothes run toward the plane and climb the boarding steps. He came down the aisle, sat in the empty seat next to me and said, "They're going to take me back to Nam! They're going to kill me!" I looked out the window and saw a jeep with three military policemen coming across the tarmac toward the plane. Once on board, they came straight down the aisle. When they reached my row, they asked me to step out of the way and I did. They then struggled with this young man who was belted into his seat. He continued to scream at the top of his lungs, "They're trying to kill me! They're going to take me back to Nam!" They handcuffed him and dragged him down the aisle and out of the plane into the Army jeep at the bottom of the boarding stairs.

This young man was about the same age as our son Bob. I was shaken by his screaming against the war and his being forced back to duty. I realized I had just seen a picture of what Mary Lou had feared: a young deserter being taken into custody. I began to think of what could be done to bring the war to a close and to end the military draft.

FIRST BLACK REGENT: "DR. BOB"

On March 25, 1970, five years after my appointment to the Board of Regents and during my first turn as chairman, Governor Dan Evans appointed the first African American to serve on the Board of Regents of the university. Evans made every appointment carefully with an eye to its effect on the UW. He also focused on his long-range goal of creating diversity on the Board of Regents and our common purpose of increasing the number of Black students in the state's higher education system.

Dr. Robert Flennaugh, "Dr. Bob" as he was known, was a highly regarded Seattle dentist who had graduated from the University of Washington and its School of Dentistry. At six feet and four inches tall, he had been the drum major of the UW band during his senior year. We soon became good friends and Bob's judgment and courage proved to be invaluable to the Board of Regents and administration of the University.

The issues of military research in the engineering department and military training for Reserve Officer Training Corps (ROTC) were flashpoints for anti-Vietnam War protests. The organization is a federally supported program on the UW campus and existed in many universities across the US. One spring day in 1970, the regents meeting was interrupted by a loud and angry protest in Red Square located in front of the Administration Building. This was my year chairing the board. With encouragement from the Governor and Charles, the board had invited the ASUW president and the president of the Faculty Senate to attend regents' meetings and participate in discussions, while not voting on issues.

On this day, the capable young woman who represented the ASUW on the board, informed us that an aggressive group of anti-war activists had gathered in Red Square on the campus. They had declared their intention to force their way into the Administration Building and invade the board meeting. These were tense moments. I became worried that violence could break out and asked the student representative if she would go outside to talk with her fellow students. After doing so, she returned to report that the group was determined to take part in the board meeting and could not be stopped. She suggested that a regent go outside and speak with the group. I thought this was a good idea and offered to see if the crowd could be persuaded to have a discussion outside. Bob immediately said, "I'll go with you" and Mort Frayn added a strong "Me, too." Harold Shefelman angrily grabbed the arms of his chair and said, "They will have to come and get me!"

Mort, Bob, and I started down the stairs and we found ourselves moving through a growing crowd that had begun climbing the stairs from the lobby. I was struck by the intense anger and profanity of the young women who made up a large part of the crowd. As we walked down the stairs, they pressed close on both sides forming a screaming cordon around us. The effect was chilling. By the time we got outside my throat was completely dry and I didn't know if I could actually speak. The ASUW president led us to the steps in front of the administration building and the crowd followed. It was obviously going to be difficult for *anyone* to be heard. At this point, Bob touched me on the shoulder and asked if he could speak first. I nodded approval and he proceeded to surprise everyone with the eloquence and power of his message.

Bob faced this angry White crowd and said:

I don't agree with your position on ROTC. I served in ROTC on this campus. If you ban ROTC on northern campuses, you will effectively cause the officers of the armed services to come from southern universities. I think you can understand why I believe that would be a mistake. On this campus, in this ROTC, we have a number of Black officer candidates, and have had for some time. If you shut this program down here and at other northern schools, there won't be any Black officer candidates coming out of these colleges. That would be a terrible mistake and I don't think this is what you want. I think we should find other ways of protesting government action in this war, but not stop the training of Black officers for our armed services.

Bob finished by asking the crowd a rhetorical question: *"Do you want all the officers of the United States Armed Forces to be White? Is that what you're after?"*

The crowd was silenced by his question. He had completely surprised them with the passion of his remarks and the power of his point. This was a group of liberal students who were not opposed to Blacks in the military. In fact, they were strongly in favor of it. They had not realized the consequence of eliminating ROTC from racially integrated schools. By the time Bob finished, the angry crowd was completely silent. Then one young man challenged him by saying, "You are just a lackey for these people!" Bob raised his fist and responded, "I'm not a lackey for anyone. Never have been, never will be. My father taught me to stand on my own feet and I'm doing that now!" He finished by shaking his clenched fist in anger and the young White protester backed off.

At that point, I whispered to the student body president that Dr. Flennaugh and I would agree to meet all interested students at the HUB two days later at 2:00 p.m. to discuss any issue that they were concerned about. The student body president smiled and told the crowd that this sounded like a good solution to her. She told the group they should reconvene in two days in the HUB and, for the time being, the group should go home. The group which had just minutes earlier been an angry mob was completely defused and soon everyone quietly dispersed.

Back in the regent's room, I commended our student body representative and Regent Flennaugh for their extremely effective handling of the situation and told the other members of the board I didn't think anyone else could have quieted that crowd the way Bob did. Mort reported that Bob had given one of the best short speeches he'd ever heard. The meeting continued with no further interruption.

On the appointed day, Bob and I arrived early at the HUB ballroom to find that an organized group associated with SDS had been there first and set the stage for us. SDS was an acronym for "Students for a Democratic Society," a loosely organized, left-wing, anti-war, student group with active chapters on many university campuses around the country.

They had removed all the folding chairs so that the room was empty and the floor bare. Everyone would have to sit or stand on the floor. On the empty stage were two high-back baronial chairs brought in from another building and placed in the center. The idea was for Dr. Flennaugh and I to preside like lords over students squatted below us on the floor. When we saw this scene I said to Bob, "There's no way we are going to get trapped into looking like two kings talking down to their subjects. Let's get those big chairs out of here. We can sit on the bottom steps of the stage and students can sit on the floor around us." He agreed and the two "thrones" were removed from the room.

At the scheduled time, a fairly large group of students began to assemble. Bob and I were sitting on the bottom step of the stage and the arriving students filed in and sat on the floor around us in a widening semi-circle. The ASUW president began a discussion of ROTC and the UW engineering department's government-sponsored research. The discussion was candid, and we took all questions. Bob was anti-war and straight-forward about it. I spoke in favor of the war and was forthright about my reasons. Although I had to admit that the growing war casualties and my worries about my son had weakened my conviction.

After about twenty minutes of back-and-forth discussion, an organized SDS group marched into the room in a line carrying placards. They formed a circle around the students on the floor chanting "ROTC off campus, ROTC off!" Their loud chanting drowned out the students trying to speak around us. I thought this was going to destroy the meeting. But to my surprise, a student on the floor shouted back, "Shut up, sit down, or get out!" Others chimed in agreement and the protest group was taken aback. Bob and I said nothing and within a few minutes the out-numbered group quietly left the room leaving us to a two-hour exchange with students.

The meeting created good will even though my views were shared by very few. As we left the meeting, I told Bob that his appointment to the board was the best thing that could have happened to the university at that time. There were other instances that brought this fact home in equally impressive ways, but his short speech about ROTC on the steps at Red Square, and his presence in the afternoon in the HUB, were a showcase of Bob's courage, sincerity, and leadership.

Dr. Flennaugh and I worked together on other matters over the years, and I came to believe that this man had an extraordinary ability to find common ground. The university became a leader in affirmative action programs due in large part to Bob's support for the creative leadership of President Charles Odegaard.

TENSION AROUND KENT STATE

My education about student opinions at the UW and my eventual conversion on US Vietnam War policy were led by my son Bob, my wife Mary Lou, and Ernie Conrad. Opposition to the war reached a national turning point following the Kent State University tragedy on May 4, 1970. During an anti-war protest against the previous week's US invasion of Cambodia, four Kent State students were fatally shot by National Guardsmen and two more were wounded. Immediately following the Kent State tragedy, war protests took a more aggressive turn on college campuses around the country. Three days later, on May 7, 1970, Charles Odegaard addressed an estimated crowd of 7,000 students in Red Square to declare a campus day of mourning for the Kent State victims. Kent State became a turning point for the anti-war movement in the nation. The following day, Charles joined 37 other university presidents in signing a strong letter addressed to President Nixon urging immediate withdrawal of American forces from Vietnam and Cambodia.

During this time, the University of Washington and the City of Seattle maintained the capability to quickly assemble police and the university administration was prepared to act as a last resort. On more than one occasion, riot police were hidden in the basement of the Administration Building and National Guardsmen were stationed at Pier 91 to respond to violence if a large mob was assembling. A hotline to the Governor was kept open. With a lot of luck, Conrad's student friendships, Odegaard's steady strength of purpose, and courageous action by Dean Hogness, Deputy Attorney General Jim Wilson, and faculty and student leaders, only a few incidents of school class disruption and violent injury occurred on the University of Washington campus, and these mostly during Charles' sabbatical in Europe.

When I became a member of the Board of Regents in 1965, I remember Jim Wilson, the assistant attorney general who provided legal counsel to the university, for his clear, common sense legal analyses and steady determination that lawful means be used to achieve university goals. During a time when colleges came under siege by civil rights and anti-war demonstrators, Jim Wilson was just the right lawyer to advise President Charles Odegaard and the Board of Regents. His measured and sound advice was a godsend for the university.

Protests during this time were loud and vociferous, including highly publicized marches on the I-5 freeway to downtown, but they were generally marked by a humane tone and sometimes even humor. In spite of provocative threats and intimidation, the university upheld the tenets of academic freedom, and faculty and staff kept their cool and performed their duties.

Sometimes good fortune has a lot to do with good results. In the spring of 1969, the UW chapter of the national student group, Students for a Democratic Society (SDS), planned to occupy the engineering building (Lowe Hall) as a protest against military research on the campus. A number of ROTC students and Husky athletes were determined to defend the building. A confrontation with violent possibilities seemed inevitable. The administration organized younger faculty members to be on the scene to minimize possible violence. Riot police were brought close to be available in case of an emergency and the President's office was equipped like a command post.

Charles and I had conferred with Governor Evans by phone before the Kent State events. Evans was about to leave the country on state business and knew the UW situation was a powder keg. He agreed with our plan of preparations but wanted any uniformed response to be primarily police and to be used only as a last resort. I remember his words, "I will back you, but if you have to use soldiers, you will have failed."

On one May afternoon during the Cambodia tumult, a large crowd gathered to watch an expected protest and the reaction. Hundreds of marchers approached Lane Hall, which was guarded by about a hundred student defenders clustered around the entrance. Viewing this panorama of potential trouble, it was apparent to Charles that the small number of faculty peacemakers would not be able to keep the two groups apart. It was also apparent that the hefty 2"-by-2" lumber used to carry signs could easily become clubs.

Suddenly, a flatbed truck bearing the logo of the university appeared along the campus road that passes in front of the building. Incredibly, it was loaded with small rocks for landscaping. The flatbed was followed by a small pickup truck filled with white boxes. From the second-floor office looking out the window at the scene unfolding below, Charles cursed the presence of the rock truck. The truck stopped suddenly to avoid a student and was

Jim made a point of engaging directly with students to better understand their viewpoint and concerns, as he did here at at GPSS Pack Forest retreat on November 6, 1971.

rammed from behind by the small pickup. Several white boxes spilled out on the roadway. The scene seemed about to explode into an orgy of rock throwing. As Charles waited tensely, unable to alter the course of what was happening, the students close to the truck started running away. In fact, to his utter amazement, within a matter of a few minutes the sign carriers and most of the crowd had dispersed!

The white boxes turned out to be beehives! We later learned that the bees had been sent to the university by a beekeeper in Yakima for laboratory examination of mite disease. When the boxes tipped off the truck, thousands of bees were released. After numerous bee stings, the crowd of hundreds was reduced to a few dozen and potential violence diminished to a few scuffles and thrown tomatoes.

This brewing crisis was averted by sheer luck. One reporter wrote that some protesters were convinced the bees had been a conspiracy between the university administration and a beekeeper who turned out to belong to a right-wing political organization. The truth of the matter was that no one could claim credit or blame. It was one of those miracle accidents that sometimes save us from trouble in spite of ourselves!

Mary Lou had been urging me to listen more closely to the views of our son Bob who was participating in anti-Vietnam War activity even before going east to Yale University. While Bob was in New Haven, Mary Lou arranged cookie and hot chocolate socials in our home with high school and college age neighbors and friends. Her aim was to help me understand the feelings of college age students when police came down hard on young anti-war protesters. These young neighbors were not into drugs and were willing to talk about the difficulties facing police during disruptive public protests. The result was a mutually revealing dialogue.

Mary Lou participated in my soul-searching on anti-war issues. She thought we should listen to young people in a setting where they could say what was in their hearts. She once said, "During times like these, keeping in touch with students may be just as important for regents as defending academic freedom."

I jumped at the suggestions from both Mary Lou and Ernie Conrad because I was waking up to the fact that I had much to learn about university student views. On the campus, I took part in a number of small "bull sessions" over coffee with students. These conversations arranged by Ernie were held in University Avenue restaurants, the HUB, or empty classrooms. I took all questions raised and listened carefully. Some of my long-held World War II views were beginning to change as the high cost of fighting a ground war in the jungles of Southeast Asia became apparent. I had not expected the heavy US death toll which occurred following our landing at Da Nang in 1965 and this had a profound impact on me. By 1970, it was clear that the concerns of prospective draftees were well founded. I soon learned that most of these young people were thinking for themselves and were not parroting the propaganda of an external "party-line."

I recall one meeting in an unused classroom where Ernie brought in coffee and doughnuts for everyone. The meeting lasted more than two hours and was a candid exchange of views. I voiced concerns about the effects of military conquest of South Vietnam by the Communist Viet Cong. My views were based on our World War II experience with Germany and Japan and our Korean War experience with China. Recalling the step-by-step conquest of Europe by Hitler before the US entered World War II, I thought it would be important to make an early effort to stop the Communist Chinese leadership before it had conquered and fortified Southeast Asia. I believed the hard lesson that my generation learned from watching our "catch-up" response to expansion by Germany's Hitler, Japan's Tojo, and Russia's Stalin, with their records of gross human rights abuse, should not be repeated. However, I slowly came to realize that the situation the US was confronting in Southeast Asia in the 1960s was different from the one we faced in Europe and the Pacific from 1938 to 1946 and in Korea during the 1950s.

CIVIL RIGHTS TENSIONS

One group of issues on which Mary Lou and I almost always agreed was the overdue need to address the causes and effects of racial prejudice and discrimination in America. Our views on civil rights were close to those held by many faculty and students at the University. In the 1950s, racial tensions were rising in the nation as Black citizens pushed back against "separate but equal" public schools for Black children. Actual segregation was common in southern states and de-facto segregation of housing, schools, and services occurred in many parts of the country. During the 1960s, when racial issues were added to the increasingly unpopular Vietnam War with its heavy causalities, a volatile environment spread across the nation and onto university campuses.

University of Washington students were affected by scenes of racial discrimination and conflict that appeared on television. In Seattle, public school desegregation was being carried out by controversial forced bussing of White and Black students out of their neighborhoods, with the goal of achieving more nearly representative racial levels of attendance in each school.

On the University of Washington campus, it had been apparent for years that, except for a few Black athletes, second generation Asian Americans, or visiting foreign students, the UW was almost a "lily white" undergraduate school. This was a time when courageous and patient leadership was needed and severely tested at the university. The combination of an unpopular war and rising racial tensions produced an explosive mixture when Charles and the Regents began their efforts to improve educational opportunity for Blacks at the UW.

✦

One late spring Saturday in the mid-1960s the regents were sitting in a row on the stage in Edmundson Pavilion watching graduating seniors receive their diplomas. Charles leaned down the row and whispered, "Where are the Black faces?" We had not seen any in the long line of undergraduate candidates crossing the stage. In fact, only a few graduate degree candidates (mostly foreign) were Black.

If you walked through the Quad in the 1950s and 1960s, you would seldom see a Black student carrying books. At the UW, the only visible effort to encourage minority enrollment was the recruitment of Black high school athletes by the university athletic department.

Charles led the regents' discussions on the subject of race over dinner at the mansion on several occasions. We eventually came to a consensus that some kind of affirmative action was needed to break through the effects of a long history of poor preparation of Blacks for college. A "look the other way" approach had existed from the early days of the UW. Despite this history, Charles was determined to bring a significant number of able Black high school students into the university. New efforts would include better high school preparation for college, more encouragement for qualified Black high school students to apply to the UW, and more tutoring for success after their admission. The harsh fact was that in the 1950s and 1960s, very few Black high school graduates applied to the UW and even fewer stayed through graduation. He aimed to improve this result by strengthening recruitment activity in high schools and encouraging admission of more minorities to the graduate schools of the University.

The Law School faculty developed a new admissions policy which would eventually bring a "reasonable number" of Black, Chicano, American Indian, and Filipino minorities into the state's justice system. This was done by adopting a two-tier evaluation system for minority applicants to the law school. The total capacity of the school to educate lawyers was limited to approximately 150 each year out of more than 1600 applicants. A new two-tier Law School admission policy automatically admitted applicants with very high scores on the national Law School Aptitude Test (LSAT). Most of these top-tier applicants were White. From a second tier of lower LSAT scores, a significant number of minorities were admitted and some White applicants were rejected. The purpose was to increase the minority population in each Law School class. This policy resulted in denying admission to White applicant Marco Defunis and accepting Black applicants with lower LSAT scores.

Marco Defunis sued the University of Washington in 1971 on grounds that he had been denied admission based solely on his race. In the case known as *"Defunis v. Odegaard"* the trial court ruled in favor of Defunis and he was ordered to be admitted to law school. The University appealed this decision to the Washington State Supreme Court. The State Supreme Court overruled the trial court and unanimously upheld the UW Law School special admission system as being "appropriate and necessary" to admit enough Black applicants who had the potential to successfully complete law school. Defunis appealed this decision to the United States Supreme Court which, by a 5-4 vote, vacated the State Court decision on the grounds that the issue had become "moot" because, in the years after Defunis was admitted, he continued to attend and was assured of graduating.

A majority US Supreme Court opinion on the merits of the UW admission system was not reached. One of the dissenting four judges, Justice William O. Douglas, a resident of Washington state, living near the Yakima Indian Reservation, wrote a dissenting opinion. He argued the issue was moot and demonstrated why the case should have been decided on the merits in favor of Charles Odegaard and the UW. Later decisions upheld similar admission systems designed to encourage reasonable representation of minority populations within public law schools. The lasting importance of the DeFunis case on the UW campus was to demonstrate the commitment of President Odegaard, the Board of Regents, and the university faculty to give every legal opportunity for Black applicants to be admitted to the law school.

During the 1960s, talented Black athletes were actively recruited by the UW to play a variety of sports and were given scholarship aid. Teams were highly competitive, and the university alumni and the Seattle community were emotionally involved in the success of their UW athletic teams. When the UW Huskies won Rose Bowl football championships in 1960 and 1961, Coach Jim Owens and his players became local heroes. Owens was credited with rescuing Husky football from a string of losing seasons by installing extra workout routines, strict conditioning, hard practices, and disciplined off-campus deportment. He aimed to train his players to play at a greater level of physical strength and longer sustained effort than their competitors. Rival coaches conceded that Husky teams were, by far, the toughest in the conference. One of their notorious practice sessions became known as the "Death March." A *Los Angeles Times* sportswriter famously reported, "If the Huskies were playing in the Roman Coliseum the lions wouldn't come out."

By the late 1960s, Black Husky athletes were becoming aware of their growing political power. At one point, a Black player fumbled twice in a game and was ordered to run up and down the grandstand steps twice. The player believed he had been racially singled out and quit.

Discussion evolved to the point where the players wanted to boycott. Carver Gayton, the first Black assistant coach for the Huskies who had recently been hired to reduce racial tensions, explained to them that, in his mind, the incident described didn't justify a boycott. He discussed the incident with Coach Owens that evening, hoping to reach common ground. The next afternoon, Owens confronted each player individually and demanded a pledge of 100% loyalty to him, the team, and the university.

The upshot of this was the suspension of four black athletes who would not agree to this pledge. This surprised, angered, and shocked Gayton and resulted in his decision to resign in protest. The loyalty oath at best was demeaning. After the suspensions of December 14, 1969, the team was defeated by UCLA in Los Angeles with a final score of 57-14. The trip to Los Angeles was boycotted *by all* fourteen of the Black football players. They remained in Seattle with Assistant Coach Gayton. The following week prior to the start of the UW home game vs. Stanford, Coach Owens was given a huge standing ovation by the fans.

Attorney Gary Gayton, Carver's brother, filed a suit against the university on behalf of the players. Coach Owens said he had decided to review the suspensions because there were indications of misunderstanding. Nevertheless, Carver resigned on that same day. It became an immediate crisis when the university athletic department could not end the 1969 boycott and the issue fell into the regents' laps. The value of Evans' appointment of Flennaugh as a regent was demonstrated again. With unanimous board and administration support, I appointed a committee consisting of Bob Flennaugh, Mort Frayn, and me to work on resolving the problem. We agreed between us that in meetings with the White coaches, Mort and I would do the talking and in meetings with the Black players, only Bob would speak. It took more than one meeting and community emotions were escalating. Neither players nor coaches wanted to lose the entire 1970 football season. We achieved a compromise by naming a new Black assistant coach and a Black assistant athletic director. Bob was invaluable in selling this compromise to Black players. At the same time, Mort and I were able to persuade the coaches that some settlement was better than losing recruiting competition for good Black players and watching public hostility grow as the result of a stalemate.

In April 1970, President Odegaard established a "Human Rights Commission" to investigate charges of racism within the Athletic Department. The commission issued its report in January 1971. It recommended the firing of Coach Owens and Athletic Director Joe Kearney, the hiring of a Black assistant coach, and the appointment of a Black assistant athletic director.

As the board had indicated during an earlier meeting, it was not going to fire Owens or Kearney. Our reasoning was that such action would further escalate the serious division in Seattle over the football incidents. It was a political decision on our part because we could not see a positive outcome from our firing of the coach. We saw such an action as only serving to inflame existing differences and a very tense public situation in dangerous ways. In retrospect, I believe that our decision was prudent and wise.

The politically expedient route that we took did work. There was no general public outcry against our decision to reject the Commission's recommendation to fire Owens and Kearney. Other recommendations of the Commission were adopted. Ray Jackson was hired as an assistant coach and Don Smith, a former Seattle sportswriter and AT&T executive, was appointed assistant athletic director. In the summer of 1971, Smith, Owens, and Gary Gayton, the lawyer representing the suspended athletes, made a deal with star defensive back Calvin Jones to come back to the UW with no strings attached.

The hiring of Smith and Jackson and the subsequent return of Jones went a long way toward easing the racial tensions within the football program. Many years later, reconciliation of a more complete form occurred between former players and Coach Owens before the October 25, 2003, USC game. During that game, Owens expressed regret for the pain he may have caused in the lives of Black athletes during his time as coach.

In the winter of 1969–70, a different set of racial issues threatened to disrupt the Athletic Department and the campus. Following actions at Wyoming and Texas A&M against continued athletic competition with Mormon-sponsored Brigham Young University, which discriminated against Blacks by prohibiting their ordination as priests, some Black Student Union leaders had visited Oakland and met with members of the Black Panther movement. They adopted "black power" protest methods designed to force the "white power" structure to change. This was in sharp contrast to the nonviolent methods of the national civil rights movement. A specific target of the Black Student Union (BSU) was the UW's athletic relationship with BYU. These protest leaders enlisted wider Black community support. Athletic Director Kearney could not legally break a valid contract with BYU. The campus, the press, and eventually the whole city became involved.

In early March, radical leaders of the BSU and the Seattle Liberation Front (SLF) led forcible occupations of several buildings and interrupted classes. Some property damage and a few minor injuries came of the incidents and resentment developed among students, faculty, and alumni. Chief Legal Counsel Jim Wilson urged a response through existing law enforcement means. He and his assistant attorney generals carefully interviewed dozens of witnesses, documented specific offenses, and drafted proposed court orders to be served on those who were identified as participants. King County Superior

Court reviewed this evidence, signed appropriate orders, and Seattle and King County Police made arrests. The effect was immediate and campus disruptions were stopped.

It was a clear statement that the university would not tolerate disruption of orderly conduct on the campus. Identifying individuals responsible for each injury and damage of property caused serious re-thinking by any student who wanted to get a university education. No further violent interruptions occurred on campus during the remainder of the quarter.

One of the small things done in an effort to calm community tension during the second football season of dispute was suggested by Mary Lou. She was worried that the Seattle area was becoming polarized and suggested that it might be wise for us to exchange church visits with Bob and Bernice Flennaugh. She said, "The press will notice this, and I believe our churches will be good places to show that Blacks and Whites can function in harmony with each other." It was a smart idea which the Flennaughs accepted with enthusiasm.

Mary Lou and I were first invited by Dr. Bob and Bernice to First AME Church in Seattle for their next Sunday morning service. It was an experience we would not soon forget. As we came down the street toward the church, we were met halfway up the block by a small group of women wearing Sunday-best who gave us warm hugs and effusive words of welcome before escorting us to their chapel. I remember the church was packed with Black families and I saw that the young Flennaugh boys were better dressed than ours were at their ages. As we looked around, we found ourselves surrounded by a crowded atmosphere of warmth and acceptance.

The sermon was a group activity with frequent vocal interruptions by enthusiastic congregation members. The gospel choir was incredibly good and the singing that came out of that church was genuinely moving. Mary Lou and I were jammed into a crowded pew and soon found ourselves standing on our feet and moving to the music. Afterwards, Mary Lou said to me, "That's the first call to Christ where I really felt like going, but I was sweating too much!"

The following Sunday, Bob and Bernice came as our guests to First Congregational Church in Bellevue. The contrast between the greetings was striking. Our church ushers were very polite and generous in their way, coming outside to welcome Bob and Bernice at the top of the church steps by shaking hands. The congregation politely and warmly greeted our two guests and engaged in friendly conversation, but no one was "hugging" anybody. After the service, Bob and Bernice told us that they enjoyed our minister and were moved by his sermon. As we drove home, Mary Lou and I couldn't help but remark on the dramatic contrast between our sincere but restrained Sunday worship and the effusive and heartwarming Sunday at First AME.

In the weeks and months to come, head coach Owens with the strong support of key team players and community leaders, was able to convince the public that a positive bridge was being built. This was hardly the end of racial problems on the field or in the wider community, but it was a beginning, and our friendship with the Flennaugh family continues to this day.

Looking back on his years at the university, Charles would recall that he began with awareness that his dreams would require widespread participation by university faculty and administrators. Charles was responsible for much of the conceptualizing of an enlarged community college program and of the designation of stronger four-year institutions of higher learning, as well as research universities. He understood the need to think in terms of serving the greater number of college and postgraduate student needs, beyond what the state had traditionally considered acceptable. It was not surprising to anyone watching the process that in the relatively brief period of Charles' 15-year tenure, the University of Washington rose to be recognized as one of the finest research universities in the country, and it has maintained this position ever since.

Those who realized the depth of Charles' commitment to the advancement of minority opportunities were not surprised by his programs to attract, assist, and inspire minorities to cross new thresholds. He has been honored by the Black community for assisting their achievements in graduate and professional careers. From creating the office of Vice President for Minority Affairs and appointing Sam Kelly to lead it, to adding new African American history programs, to awarding minority achievements on campus, Charles was ahead of the national university pack. He was eventually revered by most of those who once complained bitterly that he was "insensitive" to them.

I watched Charles for the last eight of his fifteen years as president of the UW and was in awe of his persistent focus on the visionary goals set forth in his inaugural address.

❦

CHAPTER 26

Freeway Park

"Systems of transportation change, but parks have a way of lasting."

—*Floyd Ellis*

ONE OF THE GOOD THINGS about having my office downtown was the chance, now and then, for working-day lunches with my father. In addition to his job as managing partner of an active commodities trading firm, Floyd served on several corporate boards, was a trustee of a mutual investment fund, and managed his own stocks and bonds with great skill. He taught me the fundamentals of personal investing and our lunch conversations were divided between grandchildren's exploits, the stock market, sports events, and current civic activity. We usually met at a quick-counter restaurant, but occasionally we would go to the Rainier Club for a game of dominoes with food served on little side tables. These times together gave me an opportunity to discuss ideas and events with a wise and loving man whose knowledge of business and finance was great, whose friends were legion, and whose support for our civic projects was unwavering. One day following lunch, we drove to Renton and watched the construction of Metro's new sewage treatment plant. On another day after his retirement, we walked across the Seneca Street Bridge to see the possibility of a park above the Interstate 5 freeway.

In the spring of 1968, I had begun taking brown-bag lunches on noontime walks as a way of relaxing. One of my destinations was the block at Sixth and Seneca Avenues. This location had been approved in the Forward Thrust election as a specific site for a downtown park. The site was then a parking lot adjoining the Interstate 5 freeway, which surged through downtown Seattle as a depressed, twelve-lane expressway under several cross-street bridges. I was struck with the possibility of building a lid over part of this large ditch as a means of extending the proposed Forward Thrust Park. Early activists led by Paul Thiry and Anne Hauberg had urged for the downtown section to be covered for its entire length before the I-5 freeway was constructed, but the highway department rejected their idea and built this portion in an open cut through the heart of the city.

The Seneca Street Bridge provided a good vantage point to view the freeway and its surrounding property. You could hear the roar of traffic below and see how this busy freeway separated the First Hill residential neighborhood from downtown. The opportunity to sew part of the city back together with a park across the freeway was an exciting prospect. However, as in so many visions, the hard part was how to build it and how to pay for it.

One morning, I drove my father downtown and he joined me for lunch, cane in hand, for the short walk over the freeway. I was lamenting the recent defeat of the Forward Thrust rapid transit ballot measure when Floyd remarked, "You never know. The park proposition might turn out to be more important than the trains. Systems of transportation change, but parks have a way of lasting."

When we reached the bridge and I explained how a park might be built across this section of freeway, Floyd's reaction was, "Are you sure it's practical? Can the engineers build it while this torrent of traffic is running?" I reminded him of developments built over active railroad tracks and he began to warm to the idea. "The concept *is* visionary, Jim. A park would certainly be a great improvement. It could even make business sense if the space you capture turns out to be worth more than the cost of building the lid."

In the weeks following the walk with my father, I took several friends across the bridge and most of them were intrigued by the possibility of a park over the freeway. Governor Dan Evans was an engineer and was fascinated by the idea. Looking at the walls of the ditch and the traffic speeding beneath us, he said, "It looks darn practical to me. We're going to appoint a new highway director soon and before we do I think he should come and talk to you about this lid." Then with a smile he added, "You can let me know if he is supportive."

A few days later George Andrews, the prospective director, took the same walk. I could see that he was genuinely excited by the park possibility. He said, "This idea is better than you think," and went on to explain how big piers had been sunk behind these walls which were deep enough to hold the hill and could make good foundations for a concrete deck. He also remarked that the median strip was wide enough for center supports and felt a lid could be done. When George was appointed Washington state highway director, he became an active promoter of the precedent-setting park over an interstate freeway.

Good friends, Mechlin Moore, who succeeded Paul Seibert as director of the Downtown Seattle Association, and Perry Johanson, a prominent local architect and partner in the Seattle firm Naramore, Bain, Brady & Johanson (NBBJ), quickly became converts. Perry contributed preliminary drawings and Mechlin hosted a brown-bag lunch for Seattle City Council members in the IBM Building conference room. The IBM Building between Third and Sixth Avenues was the new Preston law office and had a great view of the park site.

During lunch, Perry showed his drawings of a feasible lid park. After lunch, council members walked across the Seneca Street Bridge over Interstate 5, to look at the site. Among those who came with us that day were Councilman Floyd Miller who had been Seattle's lobbyist for passage of the original Metro Act; Myrtle Edwards, the chair of the City Council Parks Committee; and Phyllis Lamphere, a young, emerging council leader. Both women were members of the Committee of 200. Everyone who looked at the site that day was enthusiastic about the park idea.

By December 1968, Seattle mayor Dorm Braman was increasingly frustrated with the public criticism which goes with the job of mayor. He was deeply discouraged by the realization that he would probably not see the fulfillment of his dream of a rapid transit system. This was the year Richard Nixon was elected to his first term as president of the United States and the month his cabinet was being selected. An opportunity came open for Dorm to fill the new federal position of assistant secretary for Urban Systems and Environment. He took it.

The City Council then appointed Floyd Miller to succeed Braman as mayor. This dual change of roles turned out to be a lucky break for our park in the sky.

The greatest rewards for participating in campaigns for Metro and Forward Thrust were the many friendships that Mary Lou and I made. Ultimately, these friends proved to be decisive in the struggle to build a park over the freeway. Mary Lou once remarked that whenever the park plan ran into trouble, a friend came to the rescue. After one of these narrow escapes she said, "I think God is giving us a harvest of friendships. Look at all the people who are going to bat for this park."

As events developed, Freeway Park, as it was soon called, needed all the friends it could muster.

Shortly after Floyd Miller was appointed mayor, the designated site for the park at Sixth and Seneca appeared in a front-page news story as the location for a new office building. This was the beginning of the Boeing recession. Downtown business leaders were hungry for the economic boost which a new building would generate. They joined the developer R. C. Hedreen in urging Mayor Miller to abandon the city's plan to buy this property for a park. It soon became clear that the City of Seattle would have to condemn the property if it was to become a park, and condemnation would not be popular.

One afternoon, Myrtle Edwards and I visited Floyd Miller to urge a firm stand on condemnation of the park site. Floyd had hoped for a peaceful period as interim mayor and he grimaced when we asked him to pursue condemnation. With good reason, he was concerned that this issue would become a major fight. Myrtle encouraged him to support the idea. I remember Floyd looking hard at me and saying, "Alright, but you *better* be right."

True to his word, the new mayor held firm in the face of delegations of protesting business leaders. He and Mrs. Edwards insisted that the city keep faith with the voters who had approved a bond issue for this specific park site.

When it became clear that the mayor would not abandon the park, the property developer, R. C. Hedreen, sent his architect Tony Callison to my office to explore the possibility of a compromise. Tony was a talented architect and a friend of Mary Lou's brother-in-law, Lytle Lindeberg. The original plan showed a rectangular office building extending along Sixth Avenue from University Street to Seneca Street and occupying the entire proposed park site. Dick Hedreen was a young Seattle entrepreneur, and this proposed office building was his first major development.

In a meeting at the Preston law office, I asked Tony if he could turn the planned building around and give half the property to the city. Instead of objecting to this idea, Tony pulled out his slide rule, unrolled his drawings, and began to quietly measure dimensions. After a few moments of reflection, he smiled, "If you could get fourteen feet of unused state highway right-of-way for us, I think the building could be turned and would actually be better." In subsequent meetings with state and city representatives, the state offered the needed fourteen feet of unoccupied highway right-of-way. In exchange, the developer agreed to donate to the city a park easement covering the surface of the south half of his block. The developer proposed to build a parking garage under the city park easement and to pay for all park improvements built by the city on the surface of its park easement.

As the advantages of having both a public park and a private office building unfolded, all participants became enthusiastic about the project. The money originally allocated by the City to buy the Hedreen property suddenly became available to construct an enlarged city park across the adjoining freeway. As a result, the developer's bank increased the appraised value of the proposed office building, and the developer named the property "Park Place."

Over the next few weeks all parties worked feverishly to develop the details of an agreement between the developer, the highway department, and the city. When the agreement was finally completed and signed, the highway director successfully secured a state legislative appropriation to build an addition to the Seneca Street Bridge. It began to look like the project that Mary Lou had dubbed a "Park in the Sky" might actually happen.

The city selected the nationally recognized architectural firms Naramore, Bain, Brady & Johanson (NBBJ) of Seattle, and Lawrence Halprin & Associates of San Francisco, to design the new park lid. Halprin designated their talented designer Angela Danadjieva, a Bulgarian émigré, to lead the design effort. Our original idea had been a simple concrete slab covered with dirt, grass, and park benches. However, after modeling with clay in her studio, Angela designed a beautiful park with several waterfalls and a canyon in the highway median and, extending south of Seneca, was the Naramore Fountain entrance of Interstate 5 into the city.

The sketches that Angela drew of this expanded new concept were stunning, but her plan would cost much more than we had budgeted. We began an intensive search for additional grant money and eventually a total of thirteen different funding sources were assembled. Even with these additional revenue sources, a gap of several million dollars remained to be raised. Expanding the park south of Seneca Street and incorporating waterfalls and a canyon would make this park a spectacular addition. I remember thinking that the only way to pay such a huge cost was to increase the federal share of funds. The formula for interstate highway construction grants provided ninety percent federal funding and ten percent local participation instead of the 50/50 formula that had already been approved as a federal state highway project. George Andrews warned me that the Interstate 5 freeway had already been substantially completed and approval of our revised project and a request for interstate construction funding would be difficult and could take considerable time to secure.

CHAPTER 27

1970: Death Stalks the Family

. . . buy her a horse.

—*Jim Ellis*

IN MID-1970, Mary Lou and I found our attention turned away from public activity by a series of family tragedies.

As a young girl, our daughter, Judi, was bright and serious. She was interested in animals and collections. Her grades were good, her stamp collection was a work of art, and her closet was always neat. She loved to work in the garden with me and was an avid rockhound on family vacations.

When Judi was about 12 years old, she asked me, "Dad, what would you think if we bought a horse?"

"How could we keep a horse here?" I responded. "He'll chew up the grass and tromp over the flower beds. We just don't have enough room for him."

Judi persisted. "I could tether him so he wouldn't get into the garden, and I'll earn money to feed him. Mom thinks it would be OK."

Thus began a "buy-her-a-horse" campaign which lasted several months. As the other children joined the pro-horse forces, my resistance began to crumble; soon we purchased a large brown horse which Judi named "Flame" and the family nicknamed "Emalf" (Flame spelled backwards).

This was the beginning of a happy period in Judi's life. The horse did churn the lower lawn into a mud bowl, so we finally moved it to a pasture a few

Judi with her horse, circa 1968.

blocks away. Mary Lou became an authority on horses and their equipment so that she and Judi could enjoy the project together. Judi began studying the history of horses, their breeding, care and feeding.

When the nearby pasture was developed into home plots, we moved the horse to a farm on Raging River. In later years Judi's horses, and there were several, were kept at Ralph Dodd's farm in Redmond where Ralph, a Redmond pioneer then in his 80s, employed his handsome young nephew, Cary Cox, to help work his horse ranch.

On a warm day in early summer when Judi was about 16, she and I were talking as we weeded our vegetable garden together.

"Look at the butterflies around that patch of flowers, Dad."

I looked up and watched two butterflies circling, swooping, and almost stopping in the air. They seemed to be chasing each other. "Maybe we should plant more flowers, Judi. Butterflies are fun to have around."

She turned back toward me, "Dad, I've met a really nice boy."

I remember looking at her serious face and thinking there goes my gardening buddy, but I recovered enough to say, "If he's that nice, Judi, you'd better go to work on it."

"Don't worry, Dad, I'm working on it," Judi replied with a wide smile.

*Cary, Judi, Jim, and Mary Lou at Judi's
wedding reception in the spring of 1968.*

JUDI AND CARY

Later, Judi entered the University of Washington, but like her mother 30 years before, she was far more interested in marriage than college. Mary Lou was very close to her daughter and understood what Judi needed and wanted. I hoped that Judi would finish college, but Mary Lou disagreed. "She and Cary are just too much in love, and their life together will be raising horses. Maybe after their children are grown, she'll go back to school, but I know how she feels, and I wonder whether finishing college is really important to the business of breeding thoroughbred horses."

In the summer of 1967, when Mary Lou was planning the family trip to Europe, Judi didn't want to leave Cary for a whole summer. Mary Lou finally talked her into traveling for two weeks and coming back early with me. We both wanted Judi to have some exposure to the rest of the world before embarking on what might be an isolated farming life. The compromise worked. Judi enjoyed her experience in Europe and spoke of it afterwards,

Cary and Judi and their Mustang, 1970.

although it seemed at the time that she was thinking more about Cary than the historic sites of France.

In the spring of 1968, Judi and Cary were married in the Congregational Church in Bellevue. She and her mother worked hard together planning a wedding which was beautiful and warm. It was a joyous event and began a period of great happiness for Judi. After a honeymoon in Hawaii—a wedding gift from us—Judi's and Cary's first home was a small farmhouse a few miles from Ralph's ranch.

In the meantime, Cary had enlisted in the Coast Guard and was called to active duty in late 1968. After completing basic training, Cary was stationed in Astoria, Oregon, where he and Judi lived in a small apartment in the nearby town of Seaside. Whenever Cary could accumulate a few days off, they drove "home" to Ralph's farm in Redmond or to our house in Bellevue. The couple had announced Judi was pregnant and she looked forward to spending time with her mother to plan the numerous details surrounding

Cary and Judi with Scooter on their farmhouse property.

our grandchild's pending arrival. Judi's growing pregnancy was a source of joy for our entire family.

On a June afternoon in 1970, Mary Lou called me at the office. "Jim, something terrible has happened. Judi and Cary were just killed in an automobile accident. The State Patrol called; they want instructions on what to do."

"I'll be right home," I managed to say, feeling like a stunned ox.

The accident had occurred when an oncoming car attempted to pass a truck, killing them both.

When I came down the driveway, Mary Lou and I embraced in tears and sobs, emotionally crushed to the ground. With help from my brother John, we struggled through the burial arrangements, including a beautiful memorial service conducted by our friend, Reverend Lincoln Reed.

When we were driving back from the interment services, I remember Mary Lou saying, "Judi had a short life, but a very happy one." And I remember answering, "Thank you, honey, for telling me to buy her a horse."

Judi was just 22 years old. Once again, I found myself obsessed with the unfairness of beautiful young people with so much promise being cut down without reason. Mary Lou's pain hurt just as deeply, but she pulled herself together and concentrated on helping the rest of us through our grief. Her great strength was never more evident than during this tragic time in our lives. Their deaths clearly cast an overwhelming spell over each of us that summer.

In addition to the loss of Judi and Cary in June, Mary Lou's sister Barbara called in August sobbing, to tell us her husband, Lytle Lindeberg, had died. His death came without warning from a sudden brain hemorrhage while he was driving their boat on vacation in the San Juan Islands. Lytle had become a much-loved member of the extended Earling family and one of my closest friends. He had been an early and strong supporter of Freeway Park. An outpouring of love and tears for Lytle flowed from family and friends. A touching memorial service was held on Bainbridge Island, however Mary Lou and I found ourselves almost too worn out from grief to cry any more.

That same summer, it was becoming evident that my father's health was failing. He had suffered a mild stroke a few years earlier. Walking proved to be increasingly difficult, but Floyd continued to closely follow all family activities—including attending the events of his busy grandchildren. In September, my brother John and I hosted a 50th wedding anniversary party for Floyd and Hazel at the Rainier Club and a cadre of wonderful friends from far and wide assembled for the celebration and the anniversary couple found themselves surrounded by love.

My father died of a massive heart attack two months after the anniversary party. The loss of this unfailing family pillar left a void in our lives.

At times, it seemed like the year 1970 passed over Mary Lou and me like a grey cloud of death. We responded by pulling our remaining children close to us. After my son Bob returned from the Peace Corps to attend the funeral service for Judi and Cary, Mary Lou and I took the family on a cruise through the Inside Passage to Skagway, Alaska. At Mary Lou's urging, the family engaged in all the ship and shore activities and, when we returned home, we immersed ourselves in plans that looked forward. Family discussions of these decisions and a growing excitement about the possibilities of our "Park in the Sky" helped to turn our thoughts toward the future.

CHAPTER 28

Park in the Sky

The most important benefits are not always measurable in money.

—*Jim Ellis, "Human Environment and Public Investment," remarks,*
Seattle Junior Chamber of Commerce Luncheon, January 21, 1966

WHEN IT BECAME CLEAR that financing a full-scale park would require federal designation as an interstate highway project, Tony Callison and I went to Washington, D.C., to lobby for support. Whom should we find at the Department of Transportation but former Mayor Dorm Braman. He was sitting at his new desk in a large and almost empty office, seemingly with nothing to do. When we shared the complete set of drawings for Freeway Park, Dorm was immediately absorbed. He put all of his energy and ability into helping Washington State Highway Director George Andrews move this "first time ever" interstate project through the difficult channels of the federal Department of Transportation.

On more than one occasion, Dorm went to the Secretary of Transportation John Volpe and threatened to resign if the project was not given department support. Dorm also was the source of my appointment to the secretary's advisory council. After eighteen months in office, Dorm finally tired of the federal bureaucracy and resigned. But before leaving, he

Early development of the Freeway Park site.

had cleared a track for the approval of Freeway Park, at least so long as Secretary Volpe remained in charge.

During the two years between 1970 and 1972, the new Park Place office building was constructed. In addition, Angela's plan for Freeway Park was extended to the east by means of a proposed landscaped roof over a new multi-story city garage to be built at University Street and Hubbell Place. Angela's expanded park drawings and models were beginning to stir public excitement. Cooperation between the state highway department and the city was exemplary. Joined as allies in the effort were Seattle's newly elected Mayor Wes Uhlman, Parks Director David Towne, and later, Metro Director Dick Page, all old friends from Forward Thrust days. Additionally, Phyllis Lamphere, Paul Kraabel, and George Benson from Forward Thrust days became part of a city council that was supportive of our projects during these critical years. Of course there were local opponents, but they were few in number and had no effect on the outcome. The fate of this park would be decided in Washington, D.C.

Previously, in 1969, John Ehrlichman, who had become President Nixon's principal assistant for domestic affairs, had asked me to evaluate the administration's proposed program for water pollution abatement. This minor task eventually resulted in my appointment by the President to the National Water Commission. The activity of the commission involved monthly trips to the nation's capitol over almost four years. During this work, I became a periodic visitor to John's White House office and met his assistant, Egil "Bud" Krogh Jr.. Bud had come to the White House as a young lawyer from Seattle and impressed me with his courtesy and efficiency.

The summer of 1972 brought the completion of Angela's plans for the park and the nomination of Richard Nixon for a second term. In November, Nixon was reelected by a landslide, but his overkill campaign sowed the seeds of Watergate, and his reluctance to be forthright eventually led to the first resignation of a president of the United States. These historic national events also turned out to have a place in the history of Freeway Park.

Secretary of Transportation John A. Volpe visits
Seattle in 1972, opening a door for funding support.

Just before the 1972 election, Secretary John A. Volpe visited Seattle on a campaign swing. He had requested that his visit be publicized to assist the presidential campaign. He inspected the park site and told me he would approve interstate funding if Governor Evans requested it. The request was made, but a few weeks later Secretary Volpe learned that President Nixon did not intend to reappoint him. Our carefully planned park, having survived a tortuous path through the department's bureaucracy, found itself languishing on the secretary's desk.

Who do you think the White House sent over to watch the Department of Transportation while a new secretary went through his confirmation hearings? None other than Bud Krogh Jr.! When I checked with him on the status of the park, Bud replied that it was among a number of things stalled on the secretary's desk. He promised to inform himself by visiting the site and to prepare the matter for action by the new secretary. These steps were conscientiously taken and a couple of weeks later I received a call from Bud letting me know the project was an excellent one, everything was in order, and he was prepared to present it to the new secretary for approval in the next couple of days.

Two days later, I paused at our mailbox on my morning run and pulled out the *Seattle Post-Intelligencer*. A front-page headline screamed "Krogh resigns!" The story reported that Bud had quit and pleaded guilty to taking part in an illegal attempt to stop leaks of White House information, the so called "plumbers affair." The news hit me like a ton of bricks; I hurried home to tell Mary Lou. "Just when we were about to make it, the only person left who understands this project has resigned. Maybe the good Lord just doesn't want Freeway Park to happen."

Despite my despair, Mary Lou remained the unsinkable optimist. "You don't know that yet," she replied. "Something good could still happen."

Then, believe it or not, when I arrived at my office that very morning, a small envelope from the United States Department of Transportation was on top of the stack of mail. The letter was signed by the new secretary and in two short sentences approved Freeway Park for interstate funding. I called Mary Lou, "Beaver, we made it!"

"I knew it would happen," she laughed in reply. Minutes later my phone was ringing from an exultant George Andrews, "You pulled it off!"

Jim taking a moment along the Pigott Corridor.

Jim speaking at the dedication of Freeway Park in 1976.

The successful construction bid went to David A. Mowat Company, a well-known contractor.

During the next three years, "sidewalk supervising" became a weekly addiction for Mary Lou and me.

The city installed a project sign at the corner of Sixth and Seneca which read: "Freeway Park— through the vision of the people."

The park became the official designated American Bicentennial project for the City of Seattle and was dedicated on July 4, 1976. At the bicentennial celebration, the Seattle City Council symbolically

Freeway Park, circa 1976.

started the big waterfall by running an old fire department pumper. My grade schoolteacher Zela Vieth, who carried a banner representing nearby Plymouth Church in a long dedication procession of supporters, smiled in triumph as she walked past anti-park pickets chanting "Forward Thrust, a concrete bust!" Nothing could dampen the enthusiasm of this eighty-five-year-old teacher from John Muir School or the large crowd which had gathered to celebrate. The crowd's mood was one of surprise and delight at the beauty of their new park covering the freeway.

Mary Lou and I walked hand in hand through the completed project the day before the dedication. Angela joined us to point out each treasured detail. It was a beautiful morning. The muffled noise of the covered freeway was lost in the sound of falling water. I remember Mary Lou pulling my arm. "Look, Jim. There is a robin in that tree!" Sure enough, there he was, perched safely above the fumes and frenzy of the freeway, in a newly planted maple—chirping like he had been born there.

CHAPTER 29

The Ford Foundation Opens a Door

"Criticism is usually healthy, frequently valuable, and almost always hard to swallow. It can never be ignored."

—*Jim Ellis*

THE FROSTING ON THE CAKE of our civic work together was the twelve-year span on the board of trustees of the Ford Foundation from 1970 to 1982. On a September day in 1970, the chairman of the board of the Ford Foundation came to Seattle to tell me I was being considered for appointment to their board. I was both surprised and excited by this idea but was also sensitive to a growing concern in the law firm that I was undertaking too much time-consuming public service work without compensation. I figured I had better find out if this was a compensated position and asked early in our conversation, "What is the situation regarding expenses and compensation?" The chairman had not expected me to focus on a compensation package first. He had been attracted to my reputation for being an idealist. He looked a little puzzled but responded that the Foundation paid five thousand dollars a year and all [travel] expenses and for a spouse. I next asked if wives were allowed to be involved in board activities. He liked that question and explained spouses were briefed on Foundation work regularly by staff and were welcome to attend board meetings but could not participate in them.

We talked about the chairman's personal connection to the Northwest where he had spent part of his childhood on Bainbridge Island. He had heard of the Gazzam and Earling families. He said as he left, if we were receptive, he would get back to us with a formal invitation by November.

When I came home with this exciting news, Mary Lou and I explored the written materials the chairman had shared. We were surprised at the global reach of the Foundation's activities and fascinated by its early history. By 1970, the Ford Foundation was the largest private foundation in the world. It had begun as a family foundation for Michigan charities and grown into an international foundation concerned with global issues of human poverty, social justice, and political and economic development. Mary Lou was excited about traveling to New York four times a year as well as by the international flavor of the Foundation's work and its increasing interest in progressive women's issues. Many areas of foundation interest covered work to which Mary Lou and I had been devoting much of our life. It was almost as though our public service at the local level had been a preparatory school for decision-making at the Ford Foundation.

My name had come to the attention of Ford staff through a set of timely coincidences. A lead article in *Harper's Magazine* in the spring of 1968 was highly complementary of the citizen groups that put Metro and Forward Thrust together. In addition, a full-page article about me called "Leadership the Vital Ingredient" was published in an issue of *Time Magazine* celebrating the inauguration of Richard Nixon as President. Finally, radio and television household personality Walter Cronkite aired a ten-minute television segment on his network broadcast news program devoted to Seattle's Lake Washington clean-up. Our good luck was that this public reporting happened while Ford staff were building a list of possible names for West Coast appointments to expand its board.

Early on, our interest in Foundation work was the belief that we could actually affect problems of the urban poor in the United States. In the fall of 1971, McGeorge "Mac" Bundy, president of the foundation, called to ask me to serve as chairman of the National Affairs Committee. Two years later the name of this important committee was changed to "Urban and Rural Poverty." The committee took field trips to places which had become seed beds of racial conflict, crime, and hopelessness for millions of people. We hoped to modify Foundation resource allocations from 60 percent international and 40 percent domestic to a more equal split.

A few years after becoming committee chair, I began to raise the allocation issue during board budget discussions. At the time, Robert McNamara was serving as president of the World Bank and was a leader of the International Committee. He always had a one-line stopper along the lines of "There are more starving people in Calcutta than there are in the entire United States." Statistics and calculations tended to dominate his thinking on major decisions. But we believed his position might change if this sensitive and caring man could see the conditions of the US urban poor up close by joining our field trips to Watts in Los Angeles, Woodlawn in Chicago, or Bedford-Stuyvesant in New York. When opportunities for domestic field trips arose, however, Bob politely and firmly declined to take the extra time to inspect these sites.

MIKE SVIRIDOFF & FORD LOW-INCOME HOUSING

Mitchell "Mike" Sviridoff, the brilliant Ford vice president for domestic programs, was experimenting with a pilot program in Baltimore. A multi-block section of abandoned buildings in a crime ridden area had been acquired by the city in a tax foreclosure. Ford purchased these buildings from the city at nominal cost with the understanding that we would make the necessary investment to clean up and restore the area. By making street improvements and replacing plumbing, electrical, and structural systems serving old apartments it became possible for people with low incomes to purchase these units. They could finish individual interiors with money borrowed from a consortium of local savings and loans which the Foundation would guarantee. It was a carefully prepared program with a chance of being a model for other cities that demonstrated private capital could spark the transformation of slum areas into decent communities with housing and services affordable to low-income residents.

Mike wanted our committee to take a field trip to Baltimore where they could see how this bold concept actually working. What we really needed was for Bob and Marg McNamara to come with us. We believed it could change his approach to budget issues if he could see the impact this project was having on people's lives and the terrible conditions they were living in prior to the renovations. I urged him to come on our Baltimore field trip, which was close to his home in D.C. He answered firmly that he simply couldn't as he didn't have time for field trips, and to stop asking him to come.

I came back to the hotel room defeated and convinced I had crossed a line and would alienate him by persisting. Mary Lou responded, "Why don't you give me a crack at it? Just give me a chance to talk with him."

I said, "I've struck out swinging, he's all yours."

Mary Lou called Mac Bundy's wife, Mary, and arranged to be seated next to Bob McNamara at the next evening's dinner in the Bundy residence. She was intently listening while McNamara was talking during dinner. I thought to myself, she is really working hard but she's going to be very disappointed. After dinner Mary Lou moved over to a corner of the room with Marg McNamara engrossed in conversation.

I finally got a chance to ask Mary Lou how things went when we got back to our hotel. She was wearing a sly grin. I said, "What is that big Cheshire grin about?"

She said, "Well, would you believe the McNamaras are coming to Baltimore with us in June."

"No, I wouldn't believe it," I said.

"Trust me, they'll be there," she said quietly.

Barbara Mikulski, who would later become a senator for Maryland, was the manager of the Baltimore project and a very effective tour organizer and program promoter. To my surprised delight, Bob and Marg McNamara were present for the full day, including the afternoon tour of the site. Bob and I were accompanied by plainclothes Baltimore policemen through rough areas with broken doors and windows, interiors smelling of rotting garbage, and addicts lying on the sidewalks. We then went into areas under construction with workers busy doing structural repairs and installing utilities.

Seeing the renovations firsthand was reassuring. I remember walking through the streets and feeling hopeful. We finished by touring completed apartments and talking with residents. It was thrilling to walk in and see the pride of the new owners. The before and after contrast of these units had a powerful effect upon our entire group.

Shortly after leaving the last apartment, Bob put his hand on my shoulder and said we are doing good things here. I quickly replied, "Bob, we could do more." McNamara said if I motioned to fund the project, he'd second it.

On the train back to New York to attend our board meeting, I turned to Mike and asked, "What would you do if you had twenty million dollars to make this program national in its scope." Mike looked at me in great surprise. I said, "Trust me—I've got the votes. Put together a comprehensive program that would make sense on a national scale over a period of a few years."

The next Foundation Board meeting was in September in Delhi, India, and Mike made a full presentation of his proposed housing program modeled on the Baltimore project. The plan was to create a new organization called "Local Initiatives Support Corporation" (LISC) with help from companies who had an economic interest in the redevelopment of urban areas. It would, over a period of several years, require some twenty million dollars of Foundation funds. He had recruited insurance companies, banks, material suppliers, and construction companies to help supply capital. They committed their pledges on the assurance that LISC would come through with the grants to fund the basic property costs. It was a very impressive presentation.

When he was finished, I made brief supporting remarks and moved that staff present this proposed concept formally to the full committee and Board for action at its December meeting. Bob McNamara immediately seconded the motion and stated it would be appropriate to do it now, in Delhi, to show that we have not forgotten about the needs of people in the United States.

It carried unanimously.

I traveled frequently during my time with the Foundation and Mary Lou accompanied me on many of these trips, particularly in the early years. Her health limited her later travels. Our work took me to Senegal, Mali, Chad, Ivory Coast, Nigeria, and South Africa. We visited Thailand, Japan, India, and Nepal. The trips were wide ranging and often involved meeting and working with representatives of other charitable organizations and groups as a creator or as a financial supporter of projects. I observed

Jim with the Ford Foundation team on a trip to India.

and learned from children in the streets and from leaders across dining tables. I developed valued relationships with each trip. There were so many experiences, friendships, and stories I carried home to my civic work and family life in the years ahead. I also learned from Richard Horowitz, the young Foundation associate traveling with me in West Africa, that age is revered in Africa. My "white hair" granted me access into and out of several impactful experiences.

BISHOP TUTU

My second trip to Africa was especially memorable for the opportunity I had to meet with Bishop Desmond Tutu after our 1982 September board meeting in Nairobi, Kenya. We made our way to Johannesburg, South Africa, after the meeting. Former chairman Alex Heard had told me the Foundation was hosting a banquet at the Carlton Hotel on the evening of our arrival. I would be sitting at a table with Alex and Jean Heard, the Foundation's new director Frank Thomas, and Bishop Tutu. Bishop Tutu was the head of the Anglican Church in South Africa, the Christian religion of choice for most Whites and Blacks across South Africa.

To appease international relations and visitors, the Apartheid government of South Africa had made the Carlton Hotel open to all races. However, the rest of the city was tightly segregated with very restrictive pass laws governing any movement by Black people within Johannesburg. The large Black population living in the metropolitan area was housed in a separate community outside Johannesburg, known as Soweto. This separate community contained more than one million people and was entirely Black.

The event was a way for the Foundation to display its support for major reform of the government of South Africa and its willingness to permit Black participation. The dinner event didn't address this subject directly, but it didn't have to. The Foundation's support for opposition groups had been consistent and strong. However, it never went as far as advocating overturning the government.

There were more than one hundred people in attendance, of which the majority were Black. The dinner that evening was beautifully served, and the conversations were cordial. Our table discussion was relaxed, but there was awareness among the participants that a revolution was in progress. Everyone knew the legendary Black leader Nelson Mandela had been in jail on Robben Island off the coast of Africa for many years. The military government was strict and tough on enforcing Apartheid pass laws, and they had extremely detailed and restrictive rules in enough volume to fill a book.

That evening I found myself engaged in a conversation with Bishop Tutu. We were sitting at opposite ends of a table of ten. I had described the nonviolent leadership of American Black communities under Dr. Martin Luther King in the United States which was remarkably successful in accomplishing major changes in national laws without leading a violent revolution. I was an admirer of Dr. King and knew that the Ford Motor Company had taken strong action within South Africa to employ Blacks in its mixed-race local manufacturing plant. The Company had also built quality housing in Soweto for its Black employees.

I emphasized the religious nature of peaceful change advocated by Dr. King. It was my hope that I could inject an alternative to the violent revolution that was then brewing in South Africa. There was polite conversation for several minutes and then, when our conversation became audible to people sitting at nearby tables, I saw I had over-stepped my bounds. Bishop Tutu gave me a hard look from the end of the table and finally said in a strong voice, "Mr. Ellis, we will have our country back!" At that point, I knew I had gone too far, but I couldn't think of an immediate way out.

Bishop Tutu rose from his chair and the entire dining room fell silent as they watched him walk around the table towards me. I remember thinking Bishop Tutu was actually going to hit me! When he reached my end of the table, he stood there for a minute, then smiled. He held out his arms and gave me a huge hug saying in a loud voice, "I love an honest man!" I was very relieved and hugged him back. His gesture immediately erased the tension between us. He then invited me to come to Soweto the next day to see how they lived. He wanted me to have lunch with his family at their residence, if I could arrange a pass. He said this with a half smile, knowing that I could get a pass into any part of the city because of my affiliation with Ford. I looked over at Alex to get his approval to accept this invitation. He nodded strongly and I accepted with enthusiasm. I agreed to meet Bishop Tutu at twelve noon the following day at his home in Soweto.

I didn't continue that conversation at the table because I desperately wanted to leave well enough alone. Bishop Tutu and I resumed our seats and dinner proceeded as if nothing had happened. I did make note, however, that the incident had effectively released the tension of everyone in the room.

The following morning, I obtained my pass to enter Soweto. I would be traveling alone and arranged for an approved taxi driver to take me to Soweto. It was a revealing contrast in landscape. I was amazed by the evident military presence that the White government had installed around Soweto and Johannesburg. There was more than one military check point to get through, but finally we entered Soweto.

It was a large urban area of more than a million people and much different than I had expected. It contained mixed development with commercial areas, slum areas, and areas of nicely kept housing for the well-to-do. We drove past a new development of several square blocks of housing which had been built by the Ford Motor Company for its employees. The provincial Victorian home of Bishop Tutu was a residence fitting the Bishop of the Anglican Church of South Africa.

I was met at the door by Bishop Tutu and his wife, and was given a tour of the interior of their beautiful home. We had lunch with his wife and daughters and then the two of us adjourned to his study where we had a memorable and lengthy conversation. Interestingly, we talked almost entirely about his college experience at Cambridge and mine at Yale. We shared the fact that we each came into a new setting with different customs and strong reputations. He took delight in telling me how he had rowed with the Cambridge crew team. He greatly enjoyed his years in college and still looked forward to going back for reunions. At some point in the conversation, he asked if I'd like him to show me around Soweto so I could see what it was like. I said, "I was hoping that you would say that."

Bishop Tutu took the afternoon off and the two of us took a driving tour of the best and worst parts Soweto. It was striking to me that everywhere he went, he was considered a celebrity and I was considered a guest who was to be respected.

There were contrasts in housing. The Bishop would walk up to a home, knock on the door, and introduce me to residents of varying status. Each greeted us with open arms. It was evident that Desmond Tutu was a widely respected political and religious leader in Black South Africa.

We walked through an open market and I expressed a desire to purchase a handmade quilt from a group of women. I bought a beautiful blanket and the shop owner agreed to take care of shipping it home for me. The Bishop was pleased that I made this purchase and that it was an expensive quilt, showing my support of her quality workmanship. Overall, it was a long and wonderful day that made a lasting positive impression in my mind.

During our conversations, Bishop Tutu reminded me more than once, that he was worried about the future of his country. South Africa had become very oppressive, and he described several events of the police state that caused people to become angry, including the imprisonment and torture of prominent opposition leaders. I expressed sympathy and he understood that the Foundation could not take an active position in support of the revolution that was about to take place.

In short, it was a memorable day and I felt we became good friends.

As a footnote to this story, I did not see Desmond Tutu again until many years later when he visited Seattle in 1990. Our mayor, Norm Rice, and his wife Constance invited me to join them for a speech which Tutu was going to deliver at a large gathering at the Westin Hotel. I arrived late and didn't have a chance to shake his hand. He was sitting at the speaker's table, and I was seated at Norm's table facing Tutu not more than a few feet away. It was obvious that he did not recognize me. I decided to go up and say hello, thinking he would at least remember who I was.

I walked to the speaker's table and introduced myself, reminding him that I was the person who had spent a day with him years earlier in Soweto. He warmly acknowledged our meeting, but it was clear that he still didn't remember me. I politely excused myself and went back to my seat. Since our meeting years earlier, he had been traveling the world and meeting thousands of people. I could understand why Bishop Tutu could not remember people by name. Halfway through the luncheon, I caught him looking straight at me. He snapped his fingers and pointed towards me with a big smile. It was at that moment that I knew he had recalled our visit. I smiled back at him, remembering fondly the connection we had made so long ago in Soweto.

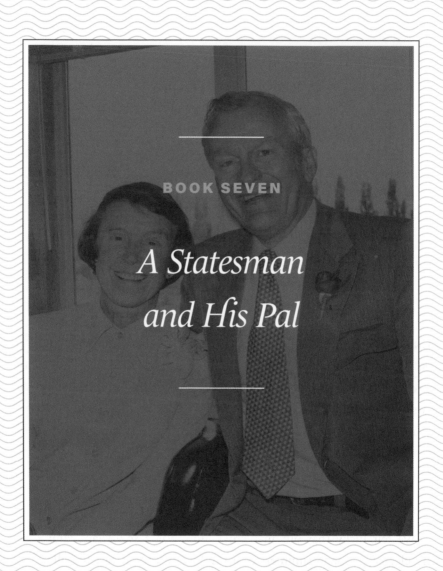

*A Statesman
and His Pal*

CHAPTER 30

Family Independence

WITH A SPEED THAT parents seldom foresee, the boys turned into men, the girls became women, and it was time for them to leave home. Mary Lou's sense of the way of life led her to encourage independence. From our early years as parents, Mary Lou worked to build a reservoir of trust and a habit of communication with all family members. This gave her many opportunities to instill feelings of responsibility and self-confidence in her young children, and to make their transition through adolescence easier and more natural.

BOB AND JUDI

We felt lucky that our first child, Bob, was a self-reliant young man who elected to spend summers as a fire lookout, to go east to college, and ultimately to join the Peace Corps after graduation. Bob always seemed to be guided by his own compass. During the years when he was breaking away, Mary Lou encouraged a career experiment in the ministry, and then helped him get a teaching job at Bush School. Bob was a natural teacher early on, and Bush proved to be the right combination of challenges and satisfactions. Later when he campaigned for the state legislature in a losing cause against a forty-year incumbent, everyone admired his initiative and determination—and he came surprisingly close to winning.

Judi was equally easy for different reasons. She was a self-disciplined girl who fell in love with Cary at an early age and set her sights on marriage, home building, and raising horses. Mary Lou and I found ourselves encouraging more schooling so the young couple would have better life chances, but we knew that marriage was right and supported the early start of their life together.

LYNN AND MARK

Lynn remembers that arriving at college was both exciting and painful. She reflected:

Mom drove me down to the University of Oregon and we spent the whole day exploring every corner of the campus, and the city of Eugene. Mom was enthusiastic about everything. The next morning as I waved goodbye, half of me wanted to call her back.

Lynn became unsure about college over the next few months as she read her brother Bob's letters describing his Peace Corps experience in Tunisia. She left school after one quarter to join him. I could see a dozen reasons not to do this, but Mary Lou saw a great chance for her daughter to mature and gain perspective.

She said, "Lynn is not ready for college now and wants her life to have a meaningful purpose. Why don't you ask Bob if he could let her live with him and if she would be safe?"

Bob responded to my letter saying, "Lynn would be safer in Tunisia than in Seattle."

We bought Lynn a plane ticket to the city of Tunis.

Lynn found work in the mountain town of Le Kef teaching English to adults, including four of the town judges! She was inspired by the country and its people, and she gained long-time friends.

When we received the tragic news that Judi and her husband Cary had died in a car accident, Lynn and Bob came home immediately to be with the family. We all stayed very close for the rest of the summer.

Lynn then studied in France for a year, worked in Ireland for a summer, and later graduated from the University of Washington.

While at the UW, she went to the wrong class and stayed to talk with the nice guy sitting next to her, Mark Erickson. In 2023, Lynn and Mark celebrate their 50th wedding anniversary.

Mark was the City Attorney in Olympia for 25 years and Lynn taught second through fifth grade there. She developed two programs for schools: The Passport Club and Sylvester's Window.

MOHAMED

Our home was always full of young guests. Different languages and voices filled the rooms of Mary Lou's household. She always found blankets, always found food, always seemed to have an available car, and always ran a relaxed, comfortable, and flexible schedule.

Some guests stayed for days. Others stayed for weeks. With this influx of visitors, it was not unusual to see sleeping bags rolled up on our deck, in the family room, and sometimes all over the house. Mary Lou made sure that a pathway was clear for me to get back and forth to my study. Distracting noises were gently moved to the other end of the house.

Our longest staying guest was Mohamed Souaiaia. Mohamed had been a student of Bob's during his Peace Corps work in Le Kef, Tunisia. When Bob returned, he sponsored Mohamed to come to this country in 1971. He and Bob first lived in a parish house in Billings, Montana, where Bob served as an interim minister in the Congregational Church, and then they moved to Seattle. Mohamed stayed in our home for several years and became a loved member of our extended family.

The contrast of our cultural backgrounds was brought into sharp focus during the first year of Mohamed's stay. One of nine children and parents who could not read or write, his view of a women's place in the home frequently clashed with our system of sharing household chores. These differences stirred arguments between Mohamed and me, which sometimes lasted for hours.

Finally, I complained to Mary Lou that Mohamed would never adapt to our way of life. She pointed out that maybe we needed to do some adapting ourselves.

Steve and Mohamed, circa 1972.

"How can we stop wars if we can't live with a culture different from ours?" she asked. Mary Lou was impressed with the integrity of Mohamed's adherence to the principles of his Muslim faith. She also thought our views of democracy and freedom would eventually be accepted by Mohamed, "if we show him that we care about him and respect his faith."

Mohamed became aware of the range of Mary Lou's humane concerns while he was still in school in Tunisia. He shared a mutual friend with Lynn from the time she'd spent teaching English in Le Kef while visiting Bob. Mohamed shared:

> *My best friend, Hamadi, once wrote to Lynn apologizing for not writing back fast enough due to a heart problem. No sooner had Lynn received the letter, than she wrote Hamadi that Mamoo (her name for Mary Lou) would fly him to Seattle for medical treatment if appropriate health care were not available in Tunisia.*

> *When my friend came to show me the letter, I was overcome. I had learned to expect generosity from Bob and Lynn. I could understand Bob and Lynn doing this—we knew each other pretty well and were very close. But Mamoo*

never met Hamadi. Later, I came to understand that this is the way Mamoo
operated. To her, Hamadi was not just a friend of a friend, but a human
being who could have died if he did not get the right care.

After graduating from Bush School in 1972, Mohamed decided to
study Arabic in Libya where he would be near the charismatic Arab leader
Muammar Qaddafi. This was during a chaotic period of Qaddafi's rule, and
we were concerned for Mohamed's safety, as well as his ability to return to
America. I was also afraid that the decision to go to Libya demonstrated our
failure to effectively share our democratic views. Mary Lou predicted that
Mohamed's idealized view of Qaddafi would change by experiencing the
regime firsthand. She was sure Mohamed's honesty and common sense would
eventually choose freedom.

His stay in Libya was a short month of hassles before leaving under threat
of expulsion and returning to Seattle.

When he lived with us for the second time, I observed a great change.
He became a contributing member of the household, was very thoughtful
toward Mary Lou, and started a serious effort to become a citizen. He put in
long hours to earn his school and college tuition and maintained good grades.

Mary Lou and I shared Mohamed's pride when he graduated Phi Beta
Kappa from the University of Washington and when he became a citizen
of the United States. Mohamed married Peggy, a girl from Boston, whose
courtship Mary Lou promoted quietly. They have four children. He was
awarded a scholarship to work on his PhD thesis.

BOB AND STEVE AND THE WORLD CYCLISTS

In 1973, Bob, then 27, began planning a bicycle trip around the world
with ten of his foreign language students at Bush School. They'd given
themselves the name World Cyclists. The mothers and fathers of these young
men and women were organized into a support group by Bob and Mary Lou.
Several of the parents were worried about the dangers of the trip and secretly
hoped their child would decide not to go. Mary Lou was equally concerned
but hid her fears under smiles of confidence and optimism during the many
preparation meetings we attended.

A few months before departure, Steve—who was then 18—decided to leave Lewis and Clark College and join the trip. He persuaded us to finance his fare by saying, "Popo, I'll be a stabilizing influence." We had been concerned that Bob would have difficulty shepherding a group of eighteen-year-olds over a span of fifteen months and 15,000 road miles. We had to agree that Steve's presence would be a big help to Bob, but our decisions to let him go put both of our sons in the same basket of dangers.

One spring afternoon when Mary Lou and I were getting our vegetable garden ready for planting, she shared her worries with me. She had confidence in Bob's leadership because of his years in the Peace Corps and his ability to speak French and Arabic. She also thought that the trip would be a good experience in independence for Steve. But she was concerned about the high visibility of the group and their route through turbulent areas of the Middle East and Central Asia.

While we were kneeling to pull grass clumps out of the freshly tilled ground, she caught my eye with a look of anxious intensity.

"You know, Jim, this trip is really going to happen. Some of the places they're going are scary! I'm worried sick that these kids won't come back in one piece."

Mary Lou felt that there must be some way that the Ford Foundation or the State Department could help reduce the risks. I knew the trip was going to be difficult and had urged the health and safety precautions that I could foresee. But the look in Mary Lou's eyes pushed me to take another step and agree to ask Dave Bell and Scoop Jackson what they thought could be done.

I knew David Bell through the Ford Foundation. He was executive vice president and in charge of its international division. The conversation with David intensified my fears about the risks of the trip. He gave helpful, practical tips about the members staying together, traveling on main roads, and spending nights in cities or towns.

US Senator Henry M. "Scoop" Jackson was a kind man and a good friend who had helped our family in the unsuccessful search for David Allen, Mary Lou's sister Nancy's son, when he was lost while climbing at the base of Mount McKinley. Senator Jackson was both helpful and reassuring. He thought steps could be taken to keep track of the young World Cyclists, through the most

The Cyclists cross Stevens Pass.

Bob and Steve talking with locals in the Atlas mountains of Morocco in 1975.

dangerous parts of the trip.

During the summer of 1975 a line of red thumbtacks began to make its way across the big map in our front hall as the bicycle caravan moved across the United States, Portugal, Spain, Morocco, Algeria, Tunisia, Sicily, Italy, Greece, and Turkey. The trip turned out to be more grueling than anyone had expected. At home, we eagerly devoured letters and extended the red tacks across the map of Syria, Jordan, Israel, Iran, and Afghanistan. When the group reached Kabul, Afghanistan, and was taken in by Mary Lou's friends from Pan American Air Lines, only four boys and one girl remained. The original group of nine had gradually narrowed to five because of illness, injuries, death in the family, and parental concerns.

The girl flew home from Kabul, but the remaining four boys pressed on to cross the Khyber Pass, between Afghanistan and Pakistan, a source of our most disturbing warnings. Steve remembers the next events:

After leaving Kabul we descended the Khyber Pass on the road to Pakistan. Suddenly a group of young children pelted us with stones. Bob jumped off his bike and started after them. Just as he grabbed one of the kids, a group of men from a cluster of tents converged on the scene. I dropped my bike and ran down, fearing the worst. The men held me back and began to give Bob a beating. It seemed our worst fears of this country were unfolding.

Then from nowhere, a car stopped on the road. Four Afghan men jumped out, ran down to us, and broke up the situation. They calmed the villagers and sent us up to the road. Then in English, the men warned us not to leave the main road again. I might add that this car was the only car we saw on the road that day. The timing was too good to have been strictly coincidental.

I now know that my parents didn't hire this carload of men to follow us through a dangerous country. However, Mamoo had pressed Popo to "do something," and Senator Jackson responded to his request with a plan that was carried out. Mamoo was often the force behind mysterious help that made our ideas work out successfully and safely.

The return of the four remaining cyclists five months later was the occasion for a major celebration. Family and friends assembled at Pleasant

Beach on Bainbridge Island to meet the bikers as they rolled into the wooded driveway and followed them on the ferry to a welcoming parade from the ferry dock to Bush School in Seattle. Bob and Steve then insisted on bicycling on to Bellevue so they could say, "we rode all the way home."

Mary Lou was popping buttons with pride and happiness that day. She had let her sons go in spite of her deepest fears. With every idea in her bag of tricks she assisted their modern odyssey. But in the end, they had made their own decisions and been taught in the real world's school. They knew more about the conditions of other nations and peoples than their parents would ever know. Above all, as Mary Lou's grin so eloquently showed, by some miracle, they had come safely home. And in the tanned faces of our sons on that morning at Pleasant Beach, we saw young men—confident, strong, and ready to build their own tomorrows.

STEVE AND KAREN

Steve had more adventure before him. The summer after the world bicycle trip, Steve met his future wife, Karen Dahl, while working in her father's bee yards in the small town of Barrett, Minnesota. The cyclists had stopped overnight at the Dahl's home, cousins of Lynn's husband Mark. When Mary Lou and I learned about their relationship, we were instantly curious to meet "Steve's girl."

Karen came to the University of Washington that fall to be near Steve, and Mary Lou found an excuse to visit her in Puyallup where she was staying with a friend. I still remember Mary Lou's excited report. "Karen is truly beautiful, and she is our kind of girl! Her feet are on the ground, and she is just what Steve needs. You'll love her!"

The accuracy of Mary Lou's prediction was attested by the prompt adoption of Karen's childhood nickname, "Tunk." Steve graduated from the University of Washington in 1978 and they were married that September in Karen's hometown.

It was Mary Lou's idea to bring a fresh whole salmon to the wedding. "Norwegians love fish," she pronounced. Mary Lou's good friend at the fish market baked the salmon, decorated it with special garnish, and packed it in dry ice for the trip. I remember holding a cold box on my lap during the flight to Minneapolis, driving through beautiful farming country, seeing green hills from the windows of a small church—and feeling the warmth of Mary Lou's hand in mine. The reception was held outdoors at Karen's family home, and we proudly set our Northwest delicacy on a checkered tablecloth. "Clag and Tunk will be a perfect match, and this salmon will be a scoop," Mary Lou said. They were, and it was!

BOB AND JEANNE

Another happy event of the late 1970s was Bob's courtship of Jeanne Sebestyen, a Reed College student who had met Bob during French classes at Bush School. Mary Lou was ingenious at finding excuses to take the young couple to dinner or visit them in Portland. Her promotion of this romance became more and more transparent as she joined Georgia Sebestyen in arranging family gatherings.

Our Mediterranean cruise in May 1980 marked the end of Mary Lou's capacity to be active. She planned and made all the arrangements for the trip. On board ship, she tired easily some days, but always managed to participate in the important events. Each evening she would insist that I take her crutches as soon as she reached the ship's dining room so that she could walk to her table unassisted. When the rest of us were on shore excursions, Mary Lou often stayed on the boat to take a nap and would be ready with a big smile to join the evening activities. I remember wondering how her smile was still able to convey its extraordinary freshness—like seeing summer for the first time.

When we returned to Seattle, Mary Lou plunged into plans for Bob's wedding. She was delighted that his bride, Jeanne, wanted to wear Mary Lou's 1944 wedding dress and to use Grandmother Tilly's home and grounds for the reception. Mary Lou insisted on standing through the long reception line at Bush School after the ceremony.

Departure from home came a little sooner in the life of each successive child. Mary Lou awoke one day to an "empty house" almost without warning and faced a gaping hole in her pattern of daily living. The independence she

Jim and Mary Lou cruising the Mediterranean in 1980.

wanted for her children had been achieved, and she was determined "not to be unhappy about something that is natural and good."

Mary Lou grabbed this chance to pursue her lifelong interest in travel. She joined Galaxy Travel, an agency created by several Bellevue women and plunged into the business with typical enthusiasm. From the start, Mary Lou did a superb job of serving her customers. She spent hours studying fare schedules to find the lowest cost flights, passed along free benefits at every chance, and personally hand-delivered most tickets. Nothing was too good for her customers. After years of watching her struggle to balance a checkbook, I was surprised to see meticulous records and reservation logs. On every business trip with me she used spare time to investigate hotels, and prepared detailed and informative reports. At home, her evenings were often spent making airline calls because reservations phone lines were less jammed at night. "This is Mary Lou at Galaxy" became a familiar sound from the family room.

Mary Lou's emphasis on service resulted in plenty of clients and a nice addition to Galaxy's revenues. However, very little money showed up on Mary Lou's bottom line; she spent most of her commissions on special benefits for her customers. We really didn't need the money and she was finally where she always wanted to be.

After several years of being a travel agent, Mary Lou's diabetes began to impact her feet and sharply limited her activity. One evening she slipped quietly next to me on the arm of our big green chair.

"Jim, I'm going to quit Galaxy. I'd rather spend my time with you than always be on the telephone when you get home. And I want to save my feet to doorbell for farmlands or take trips together."

I remember pulling her onto my lap for a long kiss and feeling a chill of fear that the time for doing things together was running out.

✦

CHAPTER 31

"Just Travelin' Along"

"If we can laugh at ourselves, we're going to be OK."

—*Mary Lou*

"**WHY DO YOU DO** so many nice things, Beaver?" I asked Mary Lou one day after we had been married for many years. "What makes you the way you are?"

"I'm really not so hard to figure out," she smiled. "Love is where I'm coming from—and where I'm going."

Mary Lou believed that love in all its forms was the end and purpose of life. She once said, "If I ever write a book of my life, it will be called, *For the Love of Jim.*"

She also believed that the roots of self-confidence began with the assurance of being loved. The more certain I became of Mary Lou's love, the stronger I grew. As Mary Lou nourished my self-worth, challenging tasks became easier to undertake.

Mary Lou believed that life and health and children are transient. She was particularly conscious of the value of play in a lifestyle that seemed so often dominated by work and pressed for time. Long before her illness, Mary Lou declared, "People don't wait in perfect preservation for the right time to do things. The best time for us to have fun together is now."

We had fun traveling.

Jim and Mary Lou, circa 1975.

Mary Lou, the kids, and I deeply valued the opportunities we had to travel far and near, from cities and backroads in distant places in the world, to the rivers and mountains of the Puget Sound, to beaches along the Washington and Oregon coasts, or simply in our own garden, the respite and chance to recharge were always treasured.

When our children were in high school, I took each of them on a trip to Washington, D.C., and for Bob and Lynn a trip to New York was added. The children gained a sense of national heritage from seeing the Statue of Liberty and visiting the White House. There were highlights and "low lights" from these trips with teenage children, including Bob's fall into the muddy Chesapeake Canal while wearing his only suit during a Washington, D.C., visit.

We had a special fondness for Hawaii. Our long love affair with Hawaii began when Mary Lou conspired with Floyd, Hazel, and Dr. Jim Haviland to heal my ulcer with a two-week rest in that "loveliest fleet of islands." After our first taste of "aloha" we couldn't get enough.

Mary Lou overlooking the harbor in Grenada while on a Caribbean cruise, circa 1960.

From the earliest opportunity, Mary Lou decided to become my indispensable companion on my long business or civic-related travels.

"Take me along. You can't remember names without me—and I'm a darn good salesman," she would say persuasively.

She conspired with several secretaries to share advance intelligence about out-of-town meetings and arranged to allow an extra day for "rest" either at the beginning or end of a trip. Mary Earling frequently offered to babysit the children, graciously opening the door for Mary Lou to travel with me.

As my law practice became more concentrated on approving the legality of municipal bonds, New York City became a frequent destination. Mary Lou loved New York and pushed hard to be a part of these trips. The result was memorable for both of us. She added dimensions of music, plays, and dancing to evenings that I probably would have spent in a hotel room watching television.

It was also obvious from our very first business trip together that Mary Lou was a major asset. She contributed to my success at bond closing dinners, meetings of the Association of Cities, the American Bar Association, the National Municipal League, the National Water Commission, and the Ford Foundation. Everyone liked Mary Lou. She always made the effort to be informed and was a superb listener. Communication came easily to her no matter what the subject or who was in attendance. Her conversations were punctuated with expressive body language and her eyes never drifted away from whomever she was speaking with.

The headquarters of the National Municipal League was located in New York, and Mary Lou and I both participated in this organization of civic dreamers and reformers from around the country. From the earliest days, the League was a source of new ideas and warm friendships. The long-time executive secretary and his wife, Bill and Peg Cassella, became close friends, as did several perennial civic activists from other parts of the country. We found that the League meetings often recharged our civic batteries.

At Mary Lou's urging we sometimes escaped from a hectic work schedule to a winter weekend on the deserted Oregon coast. For years we had combed coastal beaches looking for Japanese hand-blown glass fishing net floats without much success. The globes broke away during North Pacific storms

The family took a trip to Europe in 1968. Jim and Judi traveled with the group for two weeks of the two-and-a-half-month adventure.

and washed up on beaches from Alaska to California. Their remote origin made these floats the most exciting of beachcombing treasures.

On one trip to Beverly Beach, I secretly bought a genuine small green float with Japanese markings to "salt" in a dump of kelp for her to find. While Mary Lou was examining a piece of driftwood, I fell behind a few steps and dropped my purchased float in a drift line of kelp where she would spot it. As we turned back moments later, Mary Lou spotted the green glass ball and let out a scream of joy, retrieving it from the surf. However, the whole thing had been a little too easy and she began to quiz me.

"OK, confess. You planted this didn't you?"

After a few denials I fessed up. "I had to turn you around or the darn thing would have floated out to sea."

We spent the morning combing the beach without seeing another glass float. But the sun made the wet agates shine like jewels, and we found some beauties. Near lunchtime, Mary Lou headed back to get some food from the car for us to eat at the beach. As she was climbing over the driftwood, I suddenly heard a yell. Smiling triumphantly, she held up her trophy—a genuine green glass ball!

I scrambled over the logs to inspect her find.

"Beaver, you did it!" We hugged each other with the delight of children.

From the vantage point of passing years, I look back on that winter morning at Beverly Beach as one of the happiest days of our life together.

In November 1982, Mary Lou came up with a plan for our new daughters-in-law and son-in-law to know each other better. She made arrangements for a five-day vacation in Hawaii for the three couples. All had a ball in Waikiki and the six young people developed a closer relationship. Seeing their enthusiasm after Hawaii, Mary Lou remarked that the trip was a gift of stronger friendship. It was also the seed for a new tradition of a summer week together which has lasted for many years after. There is no better therapy for a grandfather.

✦

CHAPTER 32

Gloryoski, Zero!

Notation: "Gloryoski, Zero!" was the favorite saying of Annie Rooney, a cartoon character of the 1920s and 1930s. Her faithful dog was named "Zero." Young Annie always saw the good in events no matter what might be facing her. She seemed to say "Gloryoski, Zero!" as a statement of faith in the goodness of life.

ON AN ORDINARY WINTER morning, with rain on the roof and a working day ahead, I remember Mary Lou sitting up in bed, stretching her arms and saying, "Gloryoski, Zero! I feel great. It's a beautiful day. I love you—I'm the happiest girl in the world." In this aura of joy and confidence, Mary Lou's children and husband began each day and were inspired to believe that anything was achievable.

Mary Lou's goal was to improve the life choices of her family and friends. Her humane antennae were always out and brought us closer to people-oriented causes, to friends, and to family. She had a special way of brightening the days of the people she met. No friend or family member was ever in doubt about Mary Lou's loyalty and love. Armed with this trust, Mary Lou dared to intervene to help them reach their potential. Young people, especially, found in Mary Lou a person who understood the inner struggles and confusion they faced at turning points in their lives.

Mary Lou's common exclamation "Gloryoski Zero" drawn from a popular comic strip character, reflects Mary Lou's sunny approach to life.

Anytime was coffee time around Mary Lou's kitchen table and troubled people were attracted to this warm and friendly place. She would open the door with a welcoming smile and immediately drop whatever she was doing. She adapted her own plans with "Those things can wait," and turns her eyes on you. You would be struck by the intensity and depth of her interest in you, by the imaginative ideas that emerge, and by her eagerness to help.

Thankfully, Mary Lou and I were playmates. Mary Lou believed in her heart that she was the luckiest girl in the world. It was never hard for me to believe that I was the luckiest guy. She was a believer in the value of time, humor, and happy surprise in a loving relationship. Laughter accompanied many of our most intimate moments. The same things struck us as funny. She once said, "If we can laugh at ourselves, we're going to be OK."

The little grace-notes of living together made Mary Lou easy to love.

For instance, I remember how easy it was to make her laugh and how satisfying it was to share a casual awareness during the most ordinary moments.

Mary Lou possessed an almost mystical capacity for responding to moods. When my spirits were up, hers would lift us higher. For lonely defeats or lost elections, she prescribed long and soothing back rubs; for sleepless nights, a warm and loving hand to hold.

On evenings when I worked late at home, dish after dish of oranges would quietly appear on the table in the study. Mary Lou had learned from her mother a way of slicing oranges into sections which leaves no rind or skin. This process takes a lot of time, but the product is pure ambrosia. Whether the oranges were asked for or not, and no matter how many were devoured, the supply never stopped. Sometimes a trip to the all-night grocery was needed to keep them coming. I will swear to this day that sliced oranges restore a tiring brain. Without a doubt, they lifted my sagging spirits on those late nights. *Or was it the loving care poured into every dish?*

While Mary Lou and I were both dyed-in-the-wool optimists, I usually prepared myself to endure the possibility of failure and Mary Lou confidently expected the best right up to the end. She liked New York Yankees' baseball player and manager Yogi Berra's slogan, "It ain't over 'til it's over." This made for amusing contrasts when we watched sports on television. If the home team fell far behind, I would pronounce a fatal verdict and retreat to my study. Meanwhile, Mary Lou kept her ears faithfully tuned to the game while she continued her work. On one of those wonderful occasions when our guys made a real charge, she casually appeared in the study with a mischievous grin.

"Would you be interested in watching the Sonics if they were two points behind with three minutes to play?"

I leaped out of my chair, raced to the family room, and saw the last exciting minutes of a come-from-behind victory.

Of course, there were differences in personalities and our relationship was not always love and laughter. I was cautious, competitive, driven to achieve, trying for perfection. Mary Lou was less competitive, more willing to take chances, not afraid of failure, able to live with imperfections. We sometimes disagreed and engaged in some classic verbal battles. However, Mary Lou would never let a dispute fester. My memory of most of these "discussions" has grown a little hazy. It seemed like I usually won, but maybe that's because she never reminded me of her triumphs. Like paper lanterns floating on a pond at night,

Barbara and Lytle Lindeberg

A family story about her youngest sister, Barbara, illustrates Mary Lou's determination to intervene when she thought it would make a difference. After the breakup of an early romance while studying art in Paris, Barbara returned to Seattle and began teaching at Bush School. She lived alone and the pattern of her days provided very little social life. One Saturday afternoon the phone rang in her apartment. It was Mary Lou.

"Barb, have you ever heard of the Junior Club? I think you should join it."

Barb replied that she had heard about it but didn't want to join because she didn't drink, and it was just one of those clubs where girls go to meet boys at cocktail parties.

Mary Lou said, "Well, I think you should, Barb. How are you going to meet any men when you're stuck off teaching in a girls' school?"

Barb said she'd think about it.

"Do more than that! Now here's who you need to talk to. She's expecting you to call..."

After this insistent telephone conversation, Barbara called the name Mary Lou had given her and was invited to the next cocktail party of the Junior Club. Shortly after arriving at the party, Barbara was introduced to a shy young man from New York. They spent the evening talking about Alaska, and before too long he invited her to a dance.

I remember that Mary Lou later reported ecstatically, "My plan is working! Barb has met a man she really likes. Now, we are going to have them over for dinner. They are both shy, so help me stir up a little encouragement."

To my pleasant surprise, the man turned out to be an aspiring architect with a real interest in urban design. His understated humor reminded us of R. B., and he quickly won our affection. His name was Lytle Lindeberg and in Mary Lou's words, "Barbara and Lytle are perfect for each other."

In the best fairy tale tradition, Lytle and Barbara were married September 2, 1958, in the Episcopal Church on Bainbridge Island. They lived happily in a home that Lytle designed and raised their two wonderful daughters.

Years later Barbara said to me, "What if Mary Lou hadn't made that call?"

our separate personalities sometimes drifted apart and sometimes bumped against each other. But tenderness gentled the encounters, and when we slipped apart, Mary Lou's lantern always seemed to beckon, "come dance with me."

The onset of Mary Lou's diabetes was scary for our family, and it took some time before it was brought under control. We came to know well the symptoms of the disease. Whenever Mary Lou sensed the symptoms of insulin shock, she would swallow a little sugar and quickly bring this balance back in line. She learned to live with uncertainty, as well as with the need for discipline in measuring activities, food, insulin, and exercise. She wanted to lead as nearly as possible the kind of life that she had always led, and to continue doing things for other people. She was determined never to be a burden. I do not remember a single complaint during her long and hard battle with this terrible disease.

Once I said, "Beaver, I can't believe how you never complain at all these tough breaks. Nobody deserves them less than you. If it was me, I'd be moanin' and groanin' and gripin'."

Mary Lou smiled and winked and said, "I'm never gonna stop the rain by complainin'." As she quoted one of our favorite Burt Bacharach songs, I remember feeling her unquenchable spirit pour over me like sunlight in the morning.

Through countless setbacks, her will stayed strong. Finally, in the spring of 1982 Mary Lou's kidneys failed, her strength quickly drained away, and it was necessary to start kidney dialysis treatments.

With help from Lynn and several home nurses it was possible for me to continue working through the summer of 1982. But after returning from a Ford Foundation trip to Africa in September, I took a leave of absence from the law firm and resigned from all civic and professional activities, except the State Convention Center, so that I could care for Mary Lou full time. At Mary Lou's urging we continued to work on the Convention Center project, and the meetings of the project staff were often held in the dining room of our home. Although she was very sick and weak, Mary Lou asked for information on the progress of the design and supported the creative ideas which landscape architect Angela Danadjieva was bringing to the project. Mary Lou said, "The

JAMES R. ELLIS

903 Shoreland Drive S. E.   Bellevue, Washington 98004

Love Stays

Love stays. The only indellible relationship between lives is this specially shared awareness. The rest is dross of the smelter.

Love stays. Each human life is the sum of its moments of love. God's eternal memory is otherwise blank.

Love stays. More than suffering or happiness which slip in time from the memory of the actor, love never leaves.

Love hears its own songs. Down the valley of space and time they ring like a bell in the morning. And one for one, without fail, the hills of the heart respond — I hear, I hear.

Love Stays.

It will be beautiful, and people will love it.

—Mary Lou

concept of tying it into Freeway Park is a really good one. You need a design that will make people really want this project."

During the development of plans for the addition to Freeway Park, Mary Lou had another battle with diabetes requiring hospitalization. On the way home Mary Lou asked me to drive to Freeway Park and wheel her to the Pigott Corridor. This was some effort for her, but we managed to move the wheelchair to the bottom of the site and to 9th and University streets at the top of the hill. By now her eyesight had almost gone and there was little that she could actually see. I described the steep, brush-covered slope which then covered the site and the beautiful water cascades, ramp, and walkway that we hoped to build.

"I'm sorry, honey," I said. "I know you can't see very much."

"I REMEMBER how it looks now, and I can SEE how it's going to be. It will be beautiful, and people will love it."

One stormy evening in late October of 1983, I sat in my den putting the finishing words on a surprise anniversary poem for Mary Lou. The door of the den opens into our bedroom, which by that time had been filled with the trappings of a working hospital room. That night Mary Lou had been too weak to talk, and I thought she had slipped off to sleep. The nurses had left, and the house was quiet. I was just beginning to doze off when Mary Lou's voice came from the bedroom.

"Jim darling, I'm so glad we had four wonderful children." I moved to the edge of the bed and took her hand. "I love you, Beaver. Thank you for choosing me." We embraced and our tears mixed together. I decided not to wait until our anniversary to share the poem I had written and read it aloud to her.

"That's beautiful, Jim. I especially like the part that says, 'Our separate purposes joined complete.'"

♣

CHAPTER 33

Farmland Preservation
by Jennifer Ott

Notation: Historian Jennifer Ott reviewed Jim's papers and other historical documents related to the farmland preservation campaign. In particular, a volume of papers documenting the entire campaign made for Jim by the committee, and held in his archival collection, provided an excellent view into the workings of an Ellis-led campaign.

THE CAMPAIGNS FOR the preservation of open farmlands occurred in 1978 and 1979, after the Forward Thrust projects were well underway and while Jim served on the Ford Foundation board. While the Forward Thrust projects focused on infrastructure and facilities for a growing population, the Farmland Preservation movement grew out of a desire to manage and shape the rapidly spreading, sprawling residential and commercial development extending up the river valleys away from the towns and cities in King County. The first time Jim grew concerned about the loss of farmland publicly appears to be when he was driving back and forth across the county in the 1950s for his work on the freeholders' charter. He saw the rampant suburban growth triggered by the opening of the Lake Washington Floating Bridge (today's Interstate 90 bridge), which made it far easier to commute to the city for work.

Over time, as development increased in pace and magnitude, he also grew concerned about the impact of sprawl on the public's sense of community. If small towns in the county were allowed to merge into one unending metropolis, the character and identities of those towns like Fall City, North Bend, and Redmond, would be blurred. Jim may have been influenced by a pervasive concern in King County about repeating the mistakes of Los Angeles. Several newspaper articles in the late 1950s warned of risks associated with unchecked growth. The director of the Regional Planning Council, Robert R. McAbee, was quoted in *The Seattle Times* in 1959 as asking, "Do we want to follow the Los Angeles pattern of growth?" Another *Times* article warned, "Part of [California's] postwar boom has been decimation by the subdivider's bulldozer of orange and prune trees, peach, apricot, almond and walnut orchards and storied vineyards."

By the late 1970s, the issue was coming to a head in King County. Between 1959 and 1975, half of the county's agricultural land, 55,000 acres, had been converted to residential, commercial, and industrial use. The county's population had jumped 45% between 1940 and 1950 and another 58% by 1970. A number of people, including King County councilmembers and County Executive John Spellman, began to look for effective ways to protect farms and manage development.

In Jim's papers, the first public statements he made on the issue can be found in a speech given to the Puget Sound Association of Phi Beta Kappa on April 25, 1974. In that speech, he urged the audience to not just "decry its [growth's] possible adverse impacts," but to "act to prevent or minimize such impacts." He explained how the tools in use at that time—zoning and managing the extension of utilities to undeveloped areas—could not be relied upon, citing the loss of Green River Valley farms even though they had been zoned for agriculture as late as the 1950s, and there were no public utilities available. Instead, he argued, "The surest way to protect privately-owned open space threatened by development is to purchase the necessary property development rights out of the public purse and to pay the owner the fair value. The effect of such a purchase will be to reduce the economic pressure for the development of such property by simply taking it out of the marketplace." The next year he urged the League of Women Voters to support preservation of farmland through outright acquisition or purchase of development rights.

In January 1977, the county council took the first steps to preserve farmland, passing an ordinance setting up agricultural districts and placing a moratorium on development or extension of public utilities to about 33,000 acres within those districts. It called for an "authority" to set up the agricultural districts and to make a plan for acquiring development rights or land to prevent its development. John Spellman made a speech to the county council in June 1978 recommending the Agricultural Lands Retention Program, which would use $35 million in bonds to acquire development rights to the farms in the agricultural districts. He linked the recommendation to Jim's proposal to the county council in April 1977 to use municipal bonds to fund the initiative.

Jim campaigning for farmlands.

The following year, in September 1978, the Save Our Farmland Committee formed, with Jim, Scott Wallace, and Marilyn Ward serving as co-chairs. The committee set up an office in Pike Place Market and joined with dozens of volunteers to campaign for the bond issue measure in the November 1978 election. Jim wrote an op-ed for the *Seattle Post-Intelligencer* titled, "Color King County Green Forever." He outlined the reasons to support the measure, including the efficiency of growing food near consumers, the ineffectiveness of zoning, and the large amount of farmland lost already. He invoked the experience of

Californians, saying "In the 1920s (sic), Los Angeles and Orange counties were beautiful with orange groves and farms separating the urban development."

While there were some opponents to farmland preservation bonds, the biggest challenge to the measure was the technicalities of bond elections. Opponents argued that the initial $35 million was inadequate, that zoning was an adequate tool, and that there shouldn't be infringements on private property rights. The Save Our Farmland Committee had persuasive answers to those arguments, but they still had to compel supporters to get out and vote so they could meet the 60% approval threshold. In the first election, the measure received just short of the needed votes with 59%. In the second election, in September 1979, 77% of voters approved the measure, but not enough voters turned out to vote. Bond measures required 40% of the voters from the prior election to turn out. For the third election, in November 1979, the measure was increased to $50 million, and the committee redoubled its efforts to turn out voters.

Jim reflected on Mary Lou's role in the campaigns despite the growing toll diabetes was taking on her health. He wrote:

> She was actively involved as a campaign worker, driving her little Volkswagen all over Bellevue to install carrot-shaped campaign signs, while encouraging me and our predominantly youthful campaign workers to try again after the first election loss. In the fall of 1979, Mary Lou was confined to Swedish Hospital with a particularly severe diabetes attack, but as soon as she was able to talk, she was selling the farmlands proposition to the doctors and nurses on the staff. Some of the young campaign workers prepared a poster featuring the vegetables we had used as campaign symbols and stretched it around the inside of her hospital room.

> When she was finally released from the hospital and we were driving home, Mary Lou leaned over and said, "I know we're coming down to the wire with only a few days before the election. I'm feeling great now and want to do something to help. What do you need the most?"

> I remembered that a large 100-foot-long banner had been created to put on the fence of the Andrews farm at the intersection of I-90 and Bellevue Way.

We had been turned down flat by Mr. and Mrs. Andrews when we sent our most charming campaign workers to get permission to display the sign. These same workers had also been rebuffed in efforts to get displays mounted on reader boards at two stores in prominent locations in Bellevue. I gave Mary Lou the job of selling these promotional ideas to the Andrews family and the retail stores but didn't tell her about the previous unsuccessful efforts.

Coming home from work that night I turned off I-90 onto Bellevue Way, and there, secured to the Andrews' fence, was Mary Lou's banner. It was a quarter block long and read, "Vote Tuesday Yes for Farmlands." Then, driving farther into Bellevue, I saw the first reader board, "Vote Tuesday—Yes Farmlands," and a few blocks beyond was a second board urging a "Yes" vote.

"Honey, how did you do it?" I asked as soon as I arrived home. "Our best people were turned down trying to get those signs up. I don't know how you managed, but it's a miracle."

"It wasn't really hard to do. Mrs. Andrews is a lovely person. She just hadn't understood how the program worked," replied Mary Lou smiling. "Mrs. Andrews even helped me put the sign up. We had to struggle with that paper in the wind; that is no small sign!" In her typically enthusiastic way, Mary Lou continued, "The stores said they had just been waiting to be asked by someone they knew. None of it was really any trouble, and I didn't have to walk very much to do it."

On the following Tuesday, the Farmlands election finally carried, and a big "Yes" vote in Bellevue helped give the necessary margin.

Today, the protected farmlands support a wide network of farm-to-market relationships in King County. Farmers sell their produce at local farmers markets, the Pike Place Market, grocery stores, and through community-supported agriculture subscriptions. The farmlands also help protect rural communities from sprawl and provide open space for humans and wildlife.

CHAPTER 34

Washington State Convention Center

"The crucial ingredient that turns vision into achievement
is the will to work on your dreams for a long time."

—*Jim Ellis*

ONE EVENING DURING the winter of 1981-82, while catching up on newspapers, I came across an item about a proposal by local businessmen for a state convention and trade center to be built in downtown Seattle. The article included a diagram showing a large black square over Interstate 5 at the location of Freeway Park as the preferred site for the new trade center.

I had visions of a huge building obliterating the park and the next morning I called Governor John Spellman.

"John, I read in the paper that you are supporting a state convention center in downtown Seattle and that the favored site would be at Freeway Park over I-5."

John tried to calm my fears saying he didn't think it would be constructed *on* Freeway Park and that he thought it was just a conceptual drawing. I wasn't so sure and responded back with something along the lines of, "Please tell your group to take their darn concept out of my Park!" To which he immediately suggested I talk with the architects and assured me I'd find that the location wasn't what I was thinking. As John suggested, I called the architects who assured me that the convention center promoters were thinking of a site that would adjoin Freeway Park, but not be located on top of it.

That afternoon, John called back to see if my fire had been satisfactorily extinguished. I agreed that the plan *could* be fine, if carefully monitored. John said that if I was still worried about this, he had a solution. He could appoint me to chair the new commission that would be formed to build the convention center and I could protect my park. I told John I was fully consumed with taking care of Mary Lou and wouldn't be able to undertake such a large responsibility now. Mary Lou was sitting beside me and after hearing my conversation, I felt her tugging on my sleeve.

When I hung up, she said, "Jim you can't resign from the human race just because I'm sick. Why don't you suggest that the consultant team hold their study sessions here at the house? You could take time away from me to attend the public hearings downtown. Besides, it would give us something interesting to talk about besides worrying about me."

The next day, I called Spellman and declined to be the chair, but offered to be a member of the board and help plan the financing and construction of the new center.

That session of the Legislature successfully passed the State Convention Center Act. A new public corporation was then created and Spellman appointed me to serve as vice-chairman of its board of directors. The first task of the board was to appoint architects and engineers and determine the best site for the project. TRA Architects, Skilling Engineering, and Danadjieva-Koenig Landscape Designers, along with the renowned architect Pietro Belluschi, were employed to begin working on preliminary plans for three alternate sites: the parking lot of the Kingdome Stadium, the southeast corner of Seattle Center, and the I-5 freeway north of Freeway Park.

The private land that would be needed to develop the freeway site was owned by CHG International. Henry Griffin, the president of CHG, was extremely interested in a private co-development with the proposed Center. He offered to donate a large volume of airspace over his property to the state if the board would vote to approve the freeway site as the final Convention Center location. The City of Seattle was equally adamant in favor of the Seattle Center site. However, the Seattle Center location at Memorial Stadium would require it to be purchased for $14 million from the School District.

After much debate, the Board eventually chose the freeway site. Henry conveyed the interest in his property to the State of Washington at no cost. The architects were instructed to work toward a private/public co-development with CHG who would own and operate the retail and parking garage under the Center's exhibit and meeting floors.

The first step in evaluating the freeway site was to secure a lease of highway airspace. The State Department of Transportation joined in the planning and design of the portion of the project located over Interstate 5. Chub Foster, a retired former Deputy Director of Highways, was employed by the Convention Center to serve as the administration officer in charge of constructing the convention center.

The State Department of Transportation had become familiar with "lid projects" having worked on the Interstate 90 and Freeway Park lids. Eventually, equitable agreements were reached protecting the highway use of the corridor and conveying space above the highway for public parking and convention use. The value of the air rights conveyed was based on the appraised value of the land, less the site penalty cost of building a platform above ground and protecting the freeway beneath it. The benefits to the highway were reduction of noise impacts on adjoining properties and the restoration of pedestrian walkways which the freeway had eliminated. These benefits were calculated and offset against the price to be paid for the air rights to be purchased.

Eventually, a 65-year lease was negotiated, and the rental was determined by jointly appointed appraisers. The cost was essentially equal to the actual costs paid by the Convention Center Corporation for the work which benefited the highway.

In addition to an agreement with property owner CHG, the Convention Center needed support from business organizations, public officials, and affected property owners. During construction, it became necessary to close half of the freeway lanes at night for several weeks and traffic was detoured around the site. In a cloak of darkness, large cranes lifted steel bridge trusses into place under the illumination of bright construction lights. Each morning, the cranes were moved back to the side of the road and freeway traffic resumed. Building a lid over a major downtown artery was a dramatic process to watch.

Angela Danadjieva, along with NBBJ Architects, had just finished designing a proposed addition to Freeway Park. The addition included a landscaped pedestrian walkway and water cascade reaching from 9th and

*Karen and Steve Ellis join Jim onsite for a view
of the Convention Center project underway.*

University streets to the East Plaza of Freeway Park on First Hill. As plans
evolved for the Convention Center, opportunities arose for other connecting
pedestrian paths and plazas serving the hotels to the east and south of the site.
The design aimed to incorporate the advantages of a park along its southern
border. Walkways and a large plaza were added that connected the east plaza
of Freeway Park and the new Piggott Corridor stairway to First Hill, enhancing
the usability of the space. This dramatic section of the project was designed
by Angela, built by the City, and paid for by a gift from the Piggott family,
along with contributions from the adjoining properties which included the
Convention Center, Horizon House, and Virginia Mason Hospital.

The public/private co-development effort became a classic example of
Murphy's Law. The original owner, CHG, went bankrupt. A few months later,
the bank which had backed his promise to contribute land and costs in turn
became insolvent. Finally, the Convention Center called on an underlying
bond, which it had secured from Industrial Indemnity Corporation, to
provide the funds promised by the bank. The bond had been suggested by
Henry Griffin as a means of assuring the State that his bank would perform.

Mayor Charlie Royer and Jim cutting the ribbon for the opening of Vine Court, a 54-unit low-income apartment in the Denny Regrade neighborhood, built as part of the Convention Center project, in 1987.

Eventually, the State purchased the co-developer's property out of bankruptcy and the original center became a totally public project.

When it opened in 1988, the Convention Center was a smashing success. It won several architectural awards and has been enthusiastically received by attendees of conventions, trade shows and meetings held at this beautiful venue.

The lessons we learned from this joint development included:

- Agreements for public/private co-developments must be carefully prepared and all parties must anticipate possible worst-case scenarios.
- The use of air space over a freeway and adjacent streets for mixed use facilities can produce valuable synergies. In this particular case, the noise levels and visual impacts of the freeway upon adjoining properties were greatly reduced.

Larger downtown public park space and convention plaza space was created and greatly improved the pedestrian circulation across Interstate 5. Both residents and visitors use the pathways and the park as a shortcut to the downtown retail core and as a way to climb back up the steep grade.

This public/private development was also an overwhelming success. It included a hotel located on property owned by R.C. Hedreen and an office tower built at 7th and Pike on property acquired by the Convention Center in the CHG settlement. The City of Seattle was able to utilize space under the new Exhibit Hall, as a temporary central library until the new Seattle Public Library was completed.

While each part of this project was filled with challenges along the way, including major lawsuits to be fought and won, the results connected and reinforced the community of First Hill and the downtown commercial core. The blighted areas north of Pike Street have since been revitalized. Parks and plazas now face First Hill, while the ACT Theatre, a 24-story hotel, and retail shops face downtown. Behind these street fronts are the equivalent of four football fields of heavy-load exhibit space on one contiguous floor located four stories above Pike Street and accessible for direct floor access from the freeway by internal truck ramps.

NOTATION BY JENNIFER OTT

Not long after the center opened in 1988, Jim led the board in developing an expansion that would double its size. Another round of public debate and strong opposition ensued. The new footprint of the proposed Convention Center would displace low-income housing and groups such as The Church Council of Greater Seattle, the Tenants Union, and the Seattle Displacement Coalition campaigned for funding to build new housing. Historian Cassandra Tate interviewed Jim in 2006 and she wrote about how he "seemed genuinely hurt and puzzled to find himself being heckled by people who accused him of displacing the poor in order to cater to business interests."

The issue was resolved when the center's board agreed to build enough new housing units for everyone who would be displaced by construction. By the time it was completed in 2001, the Convention Center had also built or rehabilitated three units of low-income housing for every unit demolished to make way for the expansion.

♣

CHAPTER 35

Mountains to Sound Greenway
by Jennifer Ott

"I can grow trees, but I can't grow land."

—*Jim Ellis*

WHILE CONSTRUCTION ON the Convention Center expansion continued, the Mountains to Sound Greenway percolated up from a concept into a movement. Regional population growth threatened the things that made King County a livable place—its communities, waterways, forests, views, and open spaces. Balancing economic development and resources required a broad view, across both space and time. Jim's life work, leadership style, and dedication to place, which was imprinted upon him when he and Bob built their cabin at the Raging River, combined to make him perfectly suited to take a lead in creating a vision for a greenway and building an organization to realize that vision.

By the 1970s and 1980s, tension over development and loss of open space in King County centered on the Issaquah Alps, the three forested slopes surrounding Issaquah: Squak, Tiger, and Cougar Mountains. Squak Mountain State Park protected some lands on that hilltop, but development began to encroach on its lower elevations in the 1980s. King County Parks was acquiring parcels of land on Cougar Mountain for a regional park, but development crept up the western side. The Issaquah Alps Trails Club (IATC) had built trails across public and private lands on these slopes in the late 1970s and Harvey Manning, one of the club's co-founders, wrote books encouraging people to explore the "Alps." As thousands of people hiked these "bootleg" trails, it became necessary to formalize them and acquire access to the lands they crossed. In an early effort to reconcile the competing uses of the forested hillsides, the state Department of Natural Resources convened

This photo of Jim with the megaphone was taken in 2011 on the Seattle waterfront at the end of the 20th Anniversary Mountains to Sound Greenway Trek.

the Tiger Mountain Advisory Group in 1982 to map a path forward for managing the newly established Tiger Mountain State Forest.

That state forest was just one piece of the Alps, however. Because there were different jurisdictions and large amounts of land involved, the IATC began advocating for a regional effort to protect open space. In 1989, club member Jack Hornung wrote "'Wilderness on the Metro': A Proposed Mid-King County Natural and Recreational Corridor for Man and Beast" and club leaders Manning and Dave Kappler submitted it to the Washington Wildlife and Recreation Coalition. The title referred to the Metro 212 bus that ran between Seattle and Issaquah and emphasized the urban-rural connection.

Hornung sounded an alarm:

> So here, before the Emerald City becomes another Asphalt City, is a great opportunity to create not only a refuge for man and beast but a great green buffer which, along with other areas of open space, will help to separate and humanize the onslaught of growth. And time is of the essence—two years perhaps, certainly five years, and it will be too late.

To promote the plan, the IATC planned the Mountains to Sound March in 1990 from Snoqualmie Pass to Seattle. Jack Hornung and Ted Thomsen, an

Promotional poster for the March caught the spirit of the project's scale.

IATC member and long-time friend of Jim's, enlisted Jim as co-chair of the planning committee, along with state Commissioner of Public Lands Brian Boyle. Over a five-day hike in July, dozens of participants traversed across all or part of the route from Snoqualmie Pass to Waterfront Park in downtown Seattle. At the march's conclusion, several dignitaries spoke, including Jim, about the need to protect open space.

After the Mountains to Sound March, Jim recalled that Ted, his wife Gretchen, and Jack asked him if he would take the helm of a new organization dedicated to the Mountains to Sound Greenway. Marty Rosen at the Trust for Public Land took Jim to lunch and reiterated the offer. Jim balked at both overtures, fearing that he was fully occupied with his commitment to the Convention Center. Jim also knew he wouldn't have the office support that he had relied upon in previous campaigns now that he was retired. And, importantly, he would not have Mary Lou's guidance and support.

Despite those concerns, he considered taking on the project because it offered an opportunity to realize his commitment to Bob and continue the work he and Mary Lou had started a half-century earlier. The Greenway would protect the landscape he loved, including the Raging River watershed where his and Bob's cabin still stands, improve the quality of life for people living in King County (the Greenway would later extend east to include Kittitas County), protect and restore forests and farms, and ensure that the small towns and rural character of the Cascade foothills would be preserved. The Greenway also offered an opportunity to shape the larger region, with a far-reaching impact that zoning or other growth management tools could not achieve.

As Jim wrestled with the question, he recalled that he "talked" to Mary Lou, asking, "Honey, what the hell should I do?" He said he often consulted with her as he considered issues and felt she answered him. He intuited that she would recommend he call those people whose support he would need for the idea to succeed. So, he did.

As Jim would later recall, he called George Weyerhaeuser at his office, and miraculously, George answered his phone. Jim made his pitch, emphasizing the need to keep trees in the Greenway and that Weyerhaeuser was the largest landowner. He asked for $25,000 per year for three years and for Charlie Bingham, a Weyerhaeuser executive vice president, to support the effort as a working member of the board. After telling Jim he was naive for asking for such a small amount, George agreed.

Jim called Frank Shrontz at Boeing immediately afterward, and was shocked that he, too, answered his phone. Jim again made his pitch, emphasizing that Boeing, the largest employer in the region, would have the most people who would be using the Greenway for recreation. He again asked for $25,000 per year for three years. Frank readily agreed, after also calling Jim naive for asking for such a small amount.

The next call was to Microsoft, to his law partner's son, Bill Gates III. He didn't get him on the phone that day, but soon got a commitment for $12,500 per year.

Jim laughed when he recounted this story but also explained that he didn't "up the ante" because he felt he should stick with his original ask whenever he made a request like this. He also wanted to spread the funding to a variety of donors to build a broad, strong foundation of support for the Greenway throughout the community.

Unlike his prior projects or his legislation-specific efforts, the Greenway would need a decades-long effort and a multifaceted organization to bring it to fruition. There were similarities to the cross-jurisdictional Metro organization, but the Greenway differed in the wide variety of projects that would be undertaken, the diverse backgrounds of the board, and the need to engage with the public and enlist their widespread support over a long period. For the effort to be successful, Jim needed administrative support, partners, and a robust organization that could bring all the interested parties "under the tent."

The Trust for Public Land (TPL) provided administrative support and served as a key collaborator in realizing land and viewshed protections. Marty Rosen, TPL's president, provided office space and assigned Donna McBain as a loaned staff person. McBain, a TPL vice president, managed property acquisitions in the Pacific Northwest for TPL and her experience in finding creative ways to protect landscapes from development would be extremely valuable for the Greenway effort. TPL also assisted in facilitating public acquisition of land and conservation easements. TPL staff already had the necessary infrastructure in place to handle the funding and legal aspects. The Greenway Trust became the convenor of interested parties and facilitator of negotiations.

Jim joined with his long-time friend Ted Thomsen to incorporate the nonprofit, Mountains to Sound Greenway Trust. Ted, a lawyer, and Gretchen had lived across the hall from Jim and Mary Lou at the Shorewood Apartments when both couples were starting their families and they had remained friends over the years. Ted had a deep understanding of the legal issues that would be involved in land acquisition and conservation easements. Equal in importance to his lawyering, he and Gretchen were avid hikers and members of the IATC, so Ted, who Jim would later describe as naturally "warm and witty, without being dominating," could serve as a liaison between Jim and (the somewhat zealous) Jack Hornung and Harvey Manning.

Jim and Ted joined with Brian Boyle, who represented one of the biggest land managers in the Greenway, as commissioner of the Washington State Department of Natural Resources, to incorporate the Greenway Trust on September 10, 1991. Ted served as the secretary. Brian served on the executive committee and several of his staff members worked with the Greenway Trust in reaching its goals. Jim took on the role of president and focused on raising the funds needed to develop and implement a plan that would ensure the corridor would remain a greenway from the mountains to the sound. His extensive expertise in bringing people together from an array of backgrounds and with diverse interests was a key part of why the IATC wanted him involved and would prove to be the foundation of many of the Greenway Trust's successes.

While the incorporation process progressed, Jim turned to the next phase of organizing support for the Greenway and the organization. As Jim later explained, he knew they would need to raise tens of millions of dollars, but they didn't go straight into fundraising at meetings with potential supporters or board members. Instead, they started with the big idea for the Greenway, laying out how such a goal could be achieved and helping people understand how it could help protect the things they valued about the region. Those who worked closely with Jim at the Greenway Trust remember how inspiring and persuasive he could be in presentations and in conversations. Time and again they saw his gift for helping people see themselves in the vision he shared.

Jim started with his connections--people who had helped him in past campaigns with their time or money. He called company presidents and CEOs to recruit board members, but a number of them deferred to staff members. For example, Sally Jewell joined the board after the president of Security Pacific Bank (formerly Rainier Bank) recommended her to Jim in his place.

In October 1991, the Board of Directors met to organize the Mountains to Sound Greenway Trust. The initial board consisted of 39 members representing a wide range of interests and backgrounds. It would soon grow to more than 60 members. They needed a large number, Jim recalled, in order to pull together "all the people who needed to be involved to be successful." The area to be incorporated into the Greenway was large, with diverse interests. Jim and Ted worked carefully to find people who could bring the energy and dedication of activism, implement policies at all levels of government, influence private land management to support the Greenway vision, and raise money. Above all, they looked for people who could work with others toward the common goal.

The Executive Committee was made up of the core group of officers—Jim, Ted, Sally, Brian, and Donna—along with Kathleen Beamer, Charlie Bingham, Patsy Collins, Aubrey Davis, Gerry Johnson, Gary Locke, and Lee Springgate. This committee provided oversight to the Greenway Trust and developed proposals and projects to bring to the full board for review and discussion.

A Technical Advisory Committee (TAC) was also established at this meeting to provide expertise to the board and to create a conceptual plan in the shape of a map that described the natural, historic, and cultural assets across the Greenway. This conceptual plan would inform goals and projects in the future. Bob Rose, from the Department of Natural Resources, was named chair and he recruited a large and diverse group of people. Members included scientists, planners, foresters, land managers and park rangers, transportation and utility representatives, and many nonprofit interests including the Cattlemen's Association, bicycle advocates, and historic preservationists.

A key element of the organization's functioning was a monthly board dinner at the Preston Community Center, in the heart of the Greenway. Dinner preceded the business meeting, allowing board members time to talk. Sally Jewell remembers that Jim insisted that the dinners be provided by the Trust. He wanted all participants to share a meal together and get to know each other as individuals. This was Mary Lou's influence at work. Imbued with

Jack McCullough, Heller, Ehrman, White & McAuliffe

Dan McDonald, Washington State Senator

Larry G. McKean, The Boeing Company

J. D. MacWilliams, Mount Baker – Snoqualmie National Forest

Debbie Males, Kittitas County Planning Department

Holly Miller, Seattle Parks & Recreation Department

Dave Moffett, Ski Lifts, Inc.

Steve Morris, Seattle-King County Visitors & Convention Bureau

Sid Morison, former United States Congressman

Jon Nordby, Wright Runstad & Company

Frances North, North Bend

Mary Norton, Snoqualmie

Wilson E. O'Donnell, MOHAI

Charles Odegaard, National Park Service

Penny Peabody, King County Economic Development Council

Cleve Pinnix, Washington Parks & Recreation Commission

Irene Rinehart, former Ellensburg City Council Member

Lois Schwennesen, King County Parks, Planning & Natural Resources

Lee Springgate, City of Bellevue Parks & Recreation Department

Lucy Steers, League of Women Voters of Washington

James A. Thorpe, Washington Energy Company

David Thorud, University of Washington College of Forest Resources

Terry L. Wallgren, Key Bank of Cle Elum

Richard Zunker, Safeco Life Insurance Company

her principle of neighboring, Jim was determined to bring people together to help them discover their common interests, which would make it easier to find solutions to complex challenges in the Greenway while respecting different points of view.

Sally remembers that people sitting together over dinner were often at opposite ends of the ideological spectrum. She recalls Charlie Raines from the Sierra Club talking with Charlie Bingham from Weyerhaeuser, two organizations that were often at odds over land use in the Cascades. Terry Wallgren, a banker from Cle Elum, took board proposals to property owners in Kittitas County who often saw their interests at odds with a project originating on the west side of the Cascades. Sally shared her own appreciation of the perspectives she gained from local community activists like Mary Norton from North Bend, environmentalists like Charlie Raines, and land managers from the US Forest Service and state Department of Natural Resources that shaped her understanding of how they could work together to realize the Greenway vision.

Two additional staff members would join the Trust in the early years who were essential to its success. The first was a stroke of luck and good timing. Not long after the board was formed, Jim recalled that he was walking downtown after a Community Development Round Table lunch and saw Boeing's Frank Shrontz across the way. Frank noticed Jim looked a bit weary and asked if they needed more money. Jim responded that he really just needed more hours in the day. Two weeks later Boeing loaned a full-time executive, Ken Konigsmark, for three years (eventually extending to ten years). Boeing paid his salary, but he worked full-time for the Greenway Trust. Jim would remember, "he was incredible," and he did the "heavy lifting." Ken was the president of the IATC at that time and fully understood the vision and what was needed to get things done.

When Donna McBain left the Trust after about two years, Bob Rose recommended Nancy Keith to fill the full-time executive director position. Rose knew Keith from their conservation work in Skagit County. Nancy and Ken met with Jim each week to talk through issues and strategies and get their marching orders. They worked with the board and TAC to develop the Greenway Trust's goals, collaborative partners, and projects.

With the board, TAC, and staff in place, Jim followed a practice he had often used before in launching an idea to the public. In September 1992, he gave a speech before the Downtown Rotary titled, "Take the Greenway." In it, he laid out the problem, namely that, "Everyone engaged in the Greenway effort is spurred by a unifying fear that the power of an interstate highway to generate urban development could cause the towns along I-90 to spread into each other and create a congested highway surrounded by wall-to-wall buildings. None of us want to see this beautiful green gateway become a strip city."

Jim put his many years of public speaking experience and his deep passion for service behind promoting the Mountains to Sound Greenway project and inspiring broad public support.

He explained how the Greenway Trust would approach the project, highlighting the work the Technical Advisory Committee was doing to gather information to inform a Concept Plan and Map being developed by the landscape architects at Jones and Jones. The map would show how the Trust planned to, "preserve and enhance the scenic heart of this familiar route. . . natural beauty would be protected and in developed areas, parkway landscaping would become standard."

He then explained how the Greenway would incorporate working forests, both for practical financial reasons, but also because, "Conservation-minded people like me need to remember that if a tree farm located close to a metropolitan area becomes unprofitable it may be sold for development. Zoning has not proved to be secure long-term protection for open space." Jim would often say, "I can grow trees, but I can't grow land," which encapsulated his belief that a working forest would be better for the environment than a housing or commercial development because a logged forest can be regrown, but development meant permanent loss of green space.

He ended with a catalog of benefits that would come with the Greenway. In addition to the environmental and recreational opportunities, the Greenway would enhance tourism, preserve the region's heritage, and provide opportunities for environmental education. As with Forward Thrust, the speech generated interest and positive press that helped launch the endeavor.

The pattern of the campaign, even though it was much longer than any he had previously been involved in, shared many similarities with earlier efforts. It started with gathering people who shared an interest in an issue and strategizing with them about how to increase public awareness and how to raise financial and political support for solutions. He started with the people in his personal network who could support the effort with large donations or by providing their "gift of self," Mary Lou's description of people's sharing of their time and talents, and then extended it out from there to the broader community.

As with the other endeavors, he heeded Mary Lou's advice to find the places where people agreed or where their interests overlapped. Nancy Keith recalled that she appreciated that Jim did not see issues in terms of "white hats" and "black hats" or of good and bad. Instead, he took in a tremendous amount of information and could see both the big picture as well as the small details and find solutions that served a broad range of interests.

Nearly everyone who worked with Jim remembers his skill at bringing people together. He had a remarkable ability to inspire people with a vision for the Greenway. Members of the board, property owners, elected officials, agency staff, and community members incorporated the Greenway's goals into their work and activities, finding places where they could help the Trust achieve its vision. When assembling the pieces of a deal or a project, he would enter into a discussion with the parties involved as a negotiation, persuading people by finding common ground, or by sharing information, rather than by badgering them into agreeing with him.

Sometimes, this could be a frustrating process for those involved. Brian Boyle remembers that Jim liked to "run the railroad;" he liked to know his own preferred alternative before the discussion began and then guide others toward that choice. Nancy remembers that people would sometimes grudgingly go along with him because they could neither refute the information he provided nor the logic of his arguments, not because they wanted to embrace the solution he offered. In these discussions, Jim cultivated a shared commitment to the Greenway among the interested parties. This fostered a desire to avoid degrading or ruining the place they all valued.

The Mountains to Sound Greenway was a different effort than anything Jim had done before. There was no ballot measure at the end of the campaign. Instead of raising funds for mailers or advertising, the Greenway Trust had to find funds for making land deals, and instead of recruiting volunteers to doorbell or leaflet over a relatively short period of time, they needed people to plant trees, build trails, untangle thorny problems, and develop creative ideas over many years.

While Jim had been involved in efforts that required state, county, and local governments to carry out voter-approved plans and projects, the Greenway Trust needed those governments and public agencies to sign on to a vision and then use the tools at their disposal to help build the infrastructure, make the policies, and carry out the projects that fell within their jurisdictions. For example, Nancy Keith remembers how effective it was to have the Washington State Department of Transportation on the Greenway Trust board. At first, the board worked with transportation planners to identify ways that Interstate 90 could be modified to contribute to the Greenway experience. Before long, the agency had embraced the goals of the Greenway and independently integrated them into their own planning process. This led to things like better-designed interchanges and wildlife crossings in the mountains to ensure habitat connectivity and the ability for animals to migrate with the seasons while reducing accidents between vehicles and animals.

The scale and complexity of the Greenway project exceeded anything Jim and Mary Lou had undertaken before. It would take decades of work and collaboration with people far outside their familiar networks. That was especially true given the way the world was changing in the 1990s and 2000s. Sally Jewell worked closely with Jim, and she saw that one of his strengths was his ability to listen and a willingness to hear that he needed to do things differently. Where he had once been able to rely on calling his friends at the helms of local businesses for financial support and then move forward, he now needed to bring everyone to the table who would be affected by the proposed projects and then build support from the ground up. It was complicated and slow and required significant

Ron Sims and Jim Ellis celebrate the 7,000-acre Raging River land acquisition that completed the connection between Tiger Mountain, Rattlesnake Mountain, the Cedar River Watershed, and Taylor Mountain to form one large swath of forestland to be managed as the Raging River State Forest in 2009.

compromises. It was not an easy transition for Jim, but she saw him evolve over the years they served on the Greenway Trust board together.

The biggest difference, however, was that Jim did not have, as Sally Jewell described it, "Mary Lou there every night when he went home [as] a guiding light helping him puzzle through things." Instead, he thought about what she would have said or recommended and proceeded accordingly. He often talked about her and her ways of working with people to such a degree that Donna McBain did not realize Mary Lou had passed away years earlier until several months into working with Jim. Mary Lou was his touchstone.

In many ways the Greenway Trust was a culmination of Jim's life of service to civic projects. His dedication to the environment and the things that make the Pacific Northwest special date back to when he crisscrossed the county in support of the freeholders' charter in the 1950s. He could see then that untrammeled growth would lead to sprawl and environmental degradation.

Metro, Forward Thrust, and Farmland Preservation addressed many of the potential problems, but they were focused on the lowlands and urban areas. There were urban components to the Greenway, but it represented a new focus on maintaining the character of smaller towns and rural areas on both sides of the Cascade Crest, and on ensuring access to open space in the foothills and mountains, while supporting local economic activity.

The array of projects undertaken within the Greenway have supported and reinforced each other. Some involved acquiring large tracts of land. Rattlesnake Ridge became public land rather than homes. Snoqualmie Point Park replaced a proposed commercial development and provided a trailhead for a trail connecting with the Rattlesnake Ledge trail. Others focused on habitat continuity and development designed to be in harmony with the landscape. Jim's deep involvement with Metro and sewage management in the region led to the application of biosolids to Greenway forests. The biosolids enhanced forest growth, reduced costs to King County, and provided a funding source for additional land acquisitions and environmental education in the Greenway. Old logging roads were removed and replanted, erasing "Zorro cuts" scarring the hillsides and causing erosion. Meadowbrook and Tollgate farms were acquired as public parks with a portion of the land at each remaining as working farms, helping ensure that the towns of Snoqualmie and North Bend remain distinct and maintain their small-town character. The north entrance to the "Issaquah Gate," Grand Ridge, was left largely undeveloped, leaving the viewshed from the freeway forested and wildlife corridors connected, while still supporting housing developments in the Issaquah Highlands. The Greenway Trust played a key role in establishing the Teanaway Community Forest and developing the Yakima Basin Plan.

Jim emphasized in his speeches and writings about the Greenway, that the landscape would not ever be acquired as a whole for preservation. Instead, a significant portion of the land would remain in private ownership and part of the local economy. This meant that biosolids application on the Snoqualmie Tree Farm promoted growth of trees that would be logged; a long-term plan for the Grouse Ridge gravel mine ensured that the portion of the ridge visible from Interstate 90 would remain and the gravel pit restored and turned over to public ownership once the mining was completed. The Suncadia development

Greenway President Jim Ellis praises the partnership that brought 1,100 acres of forest land into public ownership on Rattlesnake Mountain in 1997.

near Cle Elum and the Talus development near Issaquah were both designed to minimize their environmental impact.

Jim remained involved in the Greenway Trust board for several years after he stepped down as its president in 2001. It was his longest-lasting volunteer commitment and his ethos and vision continue to shape the organization today, with one significant difference: when Jim stepped down as president of the

The Jim Ellis Birthday Tribute on August 8, 2006, at Mountain Meadows Farm launched the Mountains to Sound Greenway Legacy Fund and raised the first $1 million for this endowment in Jim's honor.

board and Sally prepared to succeed him, she talked with Jim about how she would do the job differently. She was at a different place in her life and her career, and she could not devote as many hours to the organization in the way that Jim had. Instead, she would help it transition to a stronger executive director-led model with more frequent turnover in board leadership, reducing their reliance on the early board members and on having one (remarkable) leader.

The work of the Greenway Trust has been focused on broadening the Greenway's base of support. This has been key as the "old guard" has retired. Jim's relationships were with the titans of local businesses and government leaders. To ensure the long-term stability of the organization and the Greenway, new sources of support needed to be cultivated.

To that end, the Greenway Trust has developed initiatives that will engage people who live, work, and play in the Greenway. Educational programs continue to instill appreciation of its environment and history in younger generations. Partnerships and collaborations continue to build relationships and find common ground among the many people, organizations, tribes, and governments in the Greenway. When the Mountains to Sound Greenway was designated a National Heritage Area in 2019 by the National Park Service, it provided the Greenway Trust, which was designated as the coordinating entity, with an opportunity to develop a formal cooperative management plan and a stronger foundation for collaboration with the federal government and other entities. It has also provided an opportunity to develop stronger partnerships with the Snoqualmie Tribe, the Tulalip Tribes, the Muckleshoot Indian Tribe, the Yakama Nation, and the Confederated Tribes of the Colville Reservation, all of which have connections with the lands that make up the Greenway since time immemorial.

The foundation that Jim, the staff, the board, and the TAC created in the 1990s has supported the realization of many of the Greenway Trust's goals. It also ensured that Jim and Mary Lou's commitment to Bob would outlive them. The thread running from the Raging River cabin to the brothers' deep connection with each other and on to Jim and Mary Lou's lifetime of civic work will continue into the future through the work of the Greenway Trust.

🌲

CHAPTER 36

A Future for Whom?

The future of this region will be as bright as its citizens are willing to make it.
—*Jim Ellis, Oct. 27, 2008, Forward Thrust celebration*

THERE ARE AN ALMOST infinite number of points between conception and birth when a civic project can easily die. Perhaps that's why so many promising speeches never produce anything tangible. The crucial ingredient that turns vision into achievement is the will to work on your dreams for a long time.

Looking back, every civic dream we tried to accomplish took longer than we would have guessed. Roadblocks materialized out of nowhere. Intransigent opponents never seemed to tire. In the political process whenever something could go wrong, all too frequently it would.

The Lake Washington cleanup took more than 14 years (1953 to 1967), the Metro Transit system took more than 20 years (1953 to 1973), and the rapid transit element of this concept is only recently begun to be realized. (I use the term "rapid transit" to mean a public transportation system which uses an unobstructed right of way for its main lines, regardless of the type of equipment employed.) The Kingdome stadium took more than 12 years (1963 to 1975), farmlands preservation took 11 years from concept to acquisition (1974 to 1985), Freeway Park took eight years from authorization to opening (1968 to 1976), and the Washington State Convention and Trade Center took ten years to complete.

And, of course, elections don't always come out the way you want. Over the years, about half of the ballot measures Mary Lou and I worked for were defeated. Over 30 years and 15 elections, we participated actively in the campaigns for 29 ballot measures. In these years the Washington State Constitution required that programs or projects which were paid for by property taxes above the regular local tax rate be approved by a 60 percent majority vote of the people. This was a formidable hurdle, and the most

Jim at a "Out to Lunch" event in 1981.

heartbreaking election losses were ballot measures approved by a majority of those voting but less than a 60 percent majority.

The first rapid transit proposal received a 51 percent "yes" vote and the first farmlands preservation proposal received a 59 percent "yes" vote. Neither of these passed because they failed to clear the 60 percent hurdle required by the Washington state constitution. The cleanup of Lake Washington, the metropolitan transit system, the Kingdome stadium, and the preservation of open farmlands were defeated by the voters two and even three times before they finally passed.

Huge tasks remain to keep what has been gained and to deal with even more daunting future problems. Sewage treatment technology needs to be developed which can tame and recycle a changing waste stream of chemical compounds and at the same time help conserve precious air and water resources. Problems are changing in kind and scale. The untreated run off from paved surfaces is just beginning to be effectively addressed, while the number of vehicle miles driven continues to increase. The lag between development of new products with toxic content and public awareness of their effects is challenging the development of effective source controls.

The condition of Puget Sound waters continues to suffer environmental damage from causes which are either presently unknown, widely dispersed, or extremely difficult to manage. Continuing constant testing, increased regulation, and improved technology investment will be required just to stay even. Valid lessons of hope and confidence have been taught during the years of incremental action by citizens and officials working together. This kind of human effort can clarify public thinking, focus appropriate action and, indeed, abate even the most daunting conditions of water pollution.

In the early days of our civic commitment, we discovered that if you hang on long enough, and if your cause is on the right track, the time for winning will come. Unlike a sports league, where titles are determined by comparing total wins and losses, a ballot measure can lose three times, win on the fourth, and still be enacted. Participants at any level in our system of self-government will find that success is carried on a tide of patience and persistence.

During the months and years of struggle and defeat, it was necessary, of course, to do more than just hang on. We learned the value of studying each loss and keeping our minds open to the possibilities for change. Defeat can more often become a step on the path to victory if you are willing to adapt. From each loss we learned something that would make the program better or help the public to accept it. A change in the plan or the method of financing, a different public mood, a different way of presentation, all have turned losing measures into winners. However, the first step in turning things around is to recover from the impact of losing.

Mary Lou knew how to rise from defeat. Sympathy usually lasted no longer than one night. She never talked about a lost election as a defeat, it was always, "a temporary setback." Mary Lou did not believe the saying, "Show me a good loser and I'll show you a loser." More than once she reminded me that grace in defeat can be remembered longer than the fact of defeat, and that good friends and integrity outlast political seasons. She believed that sooner or later we would rebound and try again. Her goal was to manage a quick turnaround of mood and to forestall any temptation which I might feel to make bitter public remarks. "People like someone who can take a loss in stride and look ahead," Mary Lou observed.

Criticism of all kinds is "par for the course" for civic activists, just as it is for candidates or officeholders in a free society. Criticism is usually healthy, frequently valuable, and almost always hard to swallow. It can never be ignored. It is part of the process by which voters gain awareness of the costs, risks, and alternative impacts which could flow from their decisions. If an activist can no longer accept criticism, it is time to retire from public activity.

Mary Lou understood that it took patience to follow a long path and confidence to weather criticism. Her approach to questions about the merits of our programs was to probe me quietly to see if the criticisms were being considered, to test our responses against her network of "average citizens" and to feedback constructive suggestions.

Mary Lou and I sometimes talked about the risk that our efforts would not turn out as we intended and reflected on the dreams of community activists who preceded us. Once Mary Lou asked, "Do you ever wonder what our grandchildren will think about our projects?"

We knew that the process of building cities extends from one generation to another, and that the future defies prediction. Mary Lou and I admired the efforts of the pioneers. They created parks we take for granted. They ploughed farms out of stump land and sage brush. Early Seattle residents filled the tide flats, tamed the hills, and built the Cedar River water system. They developed the schools that shaped our values, established great universities as well as a modern tradition of honest government and of caring families and neighbors. We knew that we and our contemporaries were building upon the shoulders of others. And we believed that in a later time other men and women would build upon what they found—both good and bad.

By the time many people read this book some of the projects Mary Lou and I worked on will seem like they were always part of the landscape. Others will have been changed or improved, while still others will have been torn down to make way for something different. The institutions we helped to shape may be serving well or may have grown tired and be ready for reform. No physical improvement can be truly permanent and there is no end to civic work that needs doing. A city that is alive is never finished. The ghost towns of the early West were places where no one found a way to create new jobs when the work that fed the founders played out.

By the time you try to imagine how it was to live and work in our time, the struggles, tensions, headlines, and rallies will be forgotten. Once powerful constituencies will have drifted apart. The faithful who met after lonely defeats will have gone their separate ways. It is the nature of civic and political action to be transient, the workers temporary, the causes and conflicts to find their way into newspaper morgues.

This is the natural way of healthy communities: new causes replace old causes. It is a sign of strength in democracy. The processes which nurture freedom and create places people love cannot succeed unwatched and untended. Every so often communities, like families and nations, need surges of effort to show what they can do. The real value of this effort is not so much the people helped, land preserved, water cleaned, or buildings built, but rather that citizens cared enough to do it.

From left to right, Steve and Karen Ellis, Bob and Jeanne Ellis, and Lynn and Mark Erickson at "Mary Lou's Fountain."

✦

The Ellis Children Share about Mary Lou

ON SEPTEMBER 23, 2021, we, the children of Jim and Mary Lou Ellis, were invited to a HistoryLink luncheon at the Seattle Rainier Club to speak about our father. We gathered for an early breakfast downtown and spent the beautiful morning sharing memories and walking around familiar spots. It was an emotional time as we realized again that we were surrounded by our father's prodigious contributions to the region: the cleanup of Lake Washington, wondrous parks, the Mountains to Sound Greenway, rail rapid transit, and many other vital projects that improved the quality of life in the greater Seattle area.

We strolled through Freeway Park and ended up at the Washington State Convention Center where there is a fountain in the Mezzanine honoring our mother. "Mary Lou's Fountain" has an inscription that beckons "Come sit with me." And so we did. And we reminisced. We swapped early stories of growing up with our parents and our young adult years. The thought came to all of us that any attempt to understand and characterize Jim Ellis and his lifetime of public service would have to start with Mary Lou.

Mary Lou was raised in a strong Christian Science theology. Her mother and grandmother were devout believers, and actively involved from the early days in the movement which was established in 1866. This religious foundation guided her throughout her life. Even after she left the church she often spoke of the important philosophies, which along with other religions, helped guide her.

She would often say: "Never judge someone else until you have walked in their shoes." When working on civic projects they always warmly welcomed all interested people.

As it turned out, we all described our mother in very similar ways: down-to-earth, free-spirited, unselfish almost to a fault, always positive and full of joy, caring and personally connected. She was fearless for herself, but worried for the wellbeing of others. She would never give up if she was going to bat for someone. To say that she was instinctively empathetic was an understatement. This came from Mom's ability to engage with, care for, and really listen to others. Her enthusiasm was contagious, and she liked to use the phrase *"Gloryoski Zero!"* from Little Annie Rooney. Mom would hug as long as you needed to hug.

Memories drifted back to those Christmases and special weeklong family reunion vacations with little kids in the summer. Just before she died, our mother had made Jim promise to commit to hosting an extended family vacation each year so that the cousins could stay in touch and get to know each other through shared experiences. Our father honored this promise, and his grandchildren were true beneficiaries.

There can be a tendency with time to ascribe extra human qualities to people who do great things, as if it were above our abilities to emulate. The story of Mary Lou Earling and James Reed Ellis is not the story of two saints. It is the story of two very human individuals who committed to use their special talents to help build for the better.

Our Mother Was Brave.

Brave enough to fight the terrible disease of diabetes for decades.

Brave enough to refuse to speak ill of others.

Brave enough to work for good causes, whether her own, or her family's.

Brave enough to fly a plane by herself.

Brave enough to help us all through our sorrow after Judi died.

Brave enough to live in a log cabin in the woods with small children.

Brave enough to give everything she had for love.

Through the years, when all of us were on vacation together in the family car, we would almost always sing our favorite song "Side by Side" and that song pretty much said it all:

Oh, we ain't got a barrel of money,
Maybe we're ragged and funny
But we'll travel along
Singin' a song
Side by Side

Don't know what's comin' tomorrow
Maybe its trouble and sorrow
But we'll travel the road
Sharin' our loud
Side by Side

Through all kinds of weather
What if the sky should fall?
Just as long as we're together
It really doesn't matter at all.

When they've all had their quarrels and parted
We'll be the same as we started
Just travelin' along
Singin' a song
Side by side.

Afterword *by Gary Locke*

WE SWIM IN, and boat on, the Lake Washington Jim Ellis led the charge to clean up. We ride on the county-wide Metro transit system he helped create. We picnic in and attend concerts at the many parks he established, like Luther Burbank, Marymoor, Discovery, Gas Works, and Freeway Park.

We have the Mariners and the Seahawks thanks to the Old Kingdome they played in which Jim ushered in. We feed our families fresh produce from county farmlands he preserved. We hike along the trails amidst the working forests and parks stretching along I-90, from just east of Snoqualmie Pass to Seattle, that he helped transfer from private to public ownership. And we gather in the Convention Center which helped revitalize Downtown Seattle, whose construction, financing, and expansions he oversaw.

When I was growing up, our grandparents and aunts in the mid-1950s would take us down to Leschi Beach or Mount Baker Beach to wade in the water. Mom would sometimes take us down to Seward Park if we helped her trim the edging of the backyard lawn—in those days we used hand scissors; there were no weed whackers or powered hedge trimmers! Thus, the occasional closure of Lake Washington to swimming because of pollution was profoundly felt by my sisters and me.

So in the sixth grade, when I had to choose a topic for a big research project, I chose the cleanup of Lake Washington. I was fascinated by the articles in the Seattle Public Library detailing the huge pipes—big enough to drive a truck through—being laid to carry sewage from Seattle and communities around Lake Washington to water treatment plants before being discharged into Puget Sound.

That's when I first learned of Jim Ellis. Never did I think I would ever get to meet him decades later, or I'd have the great pleasure of working with him to achieve just a few of his amazing visions of a better community for generations to come.

I finally met him in 1987 when I was in the state legislature and he was the chair of the Convention Center board. The Convention Center was in the middle of construction and was in financial trouble. The private developer in the public-private partnership that comprised the Convention Center had recently gone bankrupt and the bank that had taken over for the developer had itself gone insolvent. Costs for the project kept going up, with the state on the hook.

Jim Ellis came to the legislature in 1987 seeking additional, albeit temporary, state funding. The legislature was openly hostile. Some prominent senators accused Jim of fraud and called for a criminal grand jury investigation.

I remember one meeting in the Speaker's Office attended by leaders of the legislature and representatives of Governor Gardner. I was there as a representative of the chief budget writer of the House of Representatives. I think down deep I'd finagled my way in because I wanted to meet the man behind the project I had written about some 25 years before.

There was Jim—Father of Metro and Forward Thrust—sprawled on the floor on his hands and knees with blueprints of the Convention Center rolled out. He was excitedly pointing out the grand features of the Convention Center and how it would connect—and heal—parts of the city divided by the freeway, and how the city and state would ultimately benefit.

The Legislature grudgingly gave Jim the requested bridge loan and I gladly volunteered to form a task force to study and audit the financial premises of the Convention Center. As co-chair of the task force, I ultimately concluded the public-private partnership was detrimental to the public interest. The private-sector partners would operate the profit-generating aspects of the center while the state would operate portions that would be lucky to break even. We recommended instead, to Jim's delight, that the state take over full ownership and development of the Convention Center and that it be immediately and significantly expanded.

The terms of the expansion were actually negotiated on the back of a coaster one night in the Sheraton Hotel café between Jim and me. I am not sure who was more nervous that night!

The Legislature agreed to the extra cost of state ownership and expansion. And the rest is history—with Jim serving on the Convention Center board for the next 15 years and helping it expand two more times!

I had the great fortune of working with Jim on two other projects while I was in Olympia. The first was the renovation and sale of the Eagles Auditorium to ACT (A Contemporary Theater). Much of the opposition to the Convention Center had been focused on the displacement of housing for seniors and others on fixed income. Jim was unfairly portrayed as not caring about the Center's impact on low-income housing. But, with the Eagles Auditorium, Jim proposed that the development rights above the new ACT Theater be sold, thereby preserving the historic nature of the building, with the proceeds going to fund low-income housing. That was an easy sell to the Legislature.

The second project was the Mountains to Sound Greenway. I was a participant in the inaugural multi-day hike from Snoqualmie Pass to

Elliott Bay. I remember Jim meeting all of the hikers on the last day at the celebration on the docks at the foot of Yesler Way. He was so excited at our accomplishment and he laid out the vision of preserving from development the corridor of forests along I-90.

Whenever you encountered Jim, he had boundless energy, impatience, and humility. Whenever he pitched his projects or ideas he had this almost uncontrollable excitement that captured and drew you in, such as when I was King County Executive and he suggested using sewage sludge from the Metro sewage treatment plants to fertilize the Mountains to Sound forest lands and to have Metro *pay* the Mountains to Sound Greenways to do so. And nothing was beneath him. No task was too dirty or menial. At the age of 75, he gave me an in-depth tour of the Convention Center during construction, crawling over the steel beams and girders and going through the rat-infested Eagles Auditorium!

When you look at the many great civic achievements of our region spanning more than 50 years beginning in the 1950's, Jim is the one constant in each and every decade:

- Cleanup of Lake Washington in the late 1950's and the creation of Metro
- Forward Thrust parks and pools, the Kingdome, and the Seattle Aquarium in the 1960s
- Farmland preservation in the 1970s
- The Convention Center in the 1980s
- The Mountains to Sound Greenway Trust in the 1990s.

All these civic achievements were bold and costly initiatives that looked to the future and required the engagement of skeptical voters who ultimately had to share and embrace that vision.

While we know that it was not just all his doing, that the accomplishments we attribute to him were the collective results of the visions, leadership, and hard work of so many other people—he was nonetheless the public champion and public voice.

Jim's gift was always asking what we wanted our region to look like 20, 30, 40, years from now, then following up by bringing people together to accomplish that vision. And he never stopped. He was engaged in a never-ending process of thinking of the future.

Unfortunately, so much of politics and corporate America today is focused on the here and now. The crises of the day. The next quarterly earnings.

We need more Jim Ellises dreaming of our future and developing an action plan to make it come true; anticipating and addressing the needs of tomorrow; and tackling the pressing problems of today with long-term solutions.

The challenges confronting us today are different from those encountered by Jim and will change in the decades ahead, but they are equally important to our future way of life and our community: climate change, affordable housing, civil discourse, income inequality, and the disruptive impacts of technology.

We need more Jim Ellises—with his imagination, tenacity, selflessness, and enthusiasm—because it will take several leaders to match the impact of the one Jim Ellis whose story we chronicle in this book.

Jim is calling us not to marvel at his life but rather to come together—each participant with even a few of Jim's attributes but collectively comprising all that he was and more—to tackle the pressing issues facing our communities and to prepare for the tomorrows that seem to arrive too quickly.

Fortunately, our region is blessed with many bright, energetic, and respected civic and political leaders. With the aid of technology, they have the ability to convene residents from large swaths of our region and society to envision the future, set priorities, and develop an action plan. And the funding mechanisms to accomplish the goals are more varied and flexible than those available to Jim.

In short, there is nothing holding us back from continuing Jim's work of constantly making our region a great place to live, work, and raise a family. If we truly care about our future, we can't be dissuaded by the enormity of the challenge, the prospect of defeat, or years of hard work. If we really care, we just need to do it. We can start by coming together and creating our own vision of the future. That's how we honor the legacy of Jim Ellis.

✦

Acknowledgments

IT WAS THE LONG-HELD DREAM of HistoryLink Board President Bob Royer, Chris Bayley, and Marie McCaffrey to see that Jim Ellis' much-anticipated but unfinished manuscript was published. They saw in it a project that would fulfill a key element of HistoryLink's mission: to inform residents about our region's history so we can be better citizens and stewards of our shared future.

Completing the memoir of Jim Ellis has been a privilege and a profound responsibility. This monumental task would not have been possible without the unwavering support, dedication, and collective effort of many individuals who shared a deep admiration for the life and work of this extraordinary civic leader.

First and foremost, we extend our heartfelt gratitude to the Ellis family who graciously entrusted us with the completion of Jim's book and the preservation of his personal papers. Their trust and openness in sharing personal stories, photographs, memories, and insights about Jim have been invaluable. Additionally, the time the family spent poring over the manuscript, making revisions, and meticulously refining each chapter is a testament to their deep commitment to preserving their father's legacy. The family's dedication to this labor of love has contributed to the memoir's quality and ensured that the narrative truly reflects the essence of Jim's life and experiences.

Before Jim's book came to us, there were several professional assistants who helped Jim write the earlier manuscripts. Professional assistants included Linda Mickel, Joni Cramer, and Tamara Slater, who worked as Jim's professional assistant for many years on his book.

We owe a debt of gratitude to Jim's close colleagues and associates, especially Sally Jewell, who provided insights, anecdotes, and historical context that added depth and authenticity to the pages of this memoir. Sally's dedication to the book brought together the necessary resources and expertise to make everything happen. We couldn't have done it without her.

Our appreciation goes out to the diligent researchers and archivists who scoured countless archives, records, and interviews to unearth the historical details. We thank them for their commitment to accuracy and thoroughness throughout this process.

A special acknowledgement is extended to Documentary Media's editors Petyr Beck and Tori Smith who meticulously stitched together Jim's writings and the contributions of Jennifer Ott into a coherent and compelling narrative. Their dedication to preserving the spirit and voice of Jim's work is evident on every page.

Finally, we remember and honor Jim Ellis and Mary Lou for their will to serve and for the indelible mark they left on the Puget Sound region. Their contributions should not be forgotten and should inspire this generation and generations to come.

Special Thanks

The Ellis Family
Sally Jewell
Marie McCaffrey
Jennifer Ott
Gary Locke
Mountains to Sound Greenway Trust

This book was published thanks to the generous support of the individuals and organizations below:

The Bill and Melinda Gates Foundation

Michael and Lynn Garvey

Sally and Warren Jewell
Martha Wyckoff and Jerry Tone
Gary and Vicki Reed
Pacifica Law Group*

Brogan Thomsen, Maggie Walker, Bruce and Jeannie Nordstrom, Jerry and Lyn Grinstein, Lynn and Mark Erickson, Bob Ellis and Jeanne Sebestyen Ellis, Steve and Karen Ellis, Robert and Joan Wallace, Rob and Grayce Mitchell, Manny Rouvelas, David Tang and Daphne Tang, Donna McBain Evans and Sam Evans, K&L Gates LLP, Keehn Thomsen, Bill and Frankie Chapman, John and Laurel Nesholm, Kent and Sandra Carlson

Shannon Skinner and Tom Tanaka, Karen Daubert and Jared Smith, Stephan Coonrod and Cheryl Clark, Shannan Frisbie, Kathy Fletcher and Ken Weiner, Bart and Esme Freedman, Mike Hurley (In Memory of Ted Thomsen), Mark Wittow and Gail Gatton

*including individual contributions from Gerry Johnson, Paul Lawrence, Stacey Lewis, Faith Pettis, Deanna Gregory, Jay Reich, Taki Flevaris, Sarah Johnson, Alanna Peterson, Rich Moore, and Marni Wright

RESOURCES

HistoryLink has compiled a selection of Jim Ellis' writings as People's Histories on our website: www.historylink.org. Search keyword **Jim Ellis On.**

Jim's personal papers are archived at the Seattle Public Library. Contact the Seattle Room for more information.

CREDITS

All images courtesy of the Ellis Family Collection except where indicated:

Front Cover	Photographer: Zee Wendell
2	Mountains to Sound Greenway
136	*Seattle Daily Times*, January 30, 1960
136	*Seattle Daily Times*, December 24, 1963
147	Jim Ellis Collection, Seattle Public Library
154	Jim Ellis Collection, Seattle Public Library
158	Jim Ellis Collection, Seattle Public Library
160	Jim Ellis Collection, Seattle Public Library
163	Jim Ellis Collection, Seattle Public Library
167	Jim Ellis Collection, Seattle Public Library
169	Jim Ellis Collection, Seattle Public Library
172	Jim Ellis Collection, Seattle Public Library
173	Jim Ellis Collection, Seattle Public Library
174	Jim Ellis Collection, Seattle Public Library
199	Seattle Municipal Archives
237	Jim Ellis Collection, Seattle Public Library
246	*Seattle Daily Times*, November 3, 1965
266	*The Seattle Times*

282	Jim Ellis Collection, Seattle Public Library
288	Seattle Municipal Archives
289	Seattle Municipal Archives, 73021
293	Seattle Municipal Archives, 205761
303	Jim Ellis Collection, Seattle Public Library
315	Jim Ellis Collection, Seattle Public Library
339	Seattle Municipal Archives, 203829
340	*The Seattle Times*, 0000388AA
342a	*The Seattle Times*
342b	*The Seattle Times*
343	*The Seattle Times*
374a	Little Annie Rooney (n.d.). Newspaper Comic Strips. https://newspapercomicstripsblog.wordpress.com/2016/02/20/little-annie-rooney/
374b	Little Annie Rooney (n.d.). Newspaper Comic Strips. https://newspapercomicstripsblog.wordpress.com/2016/02/20/little-annie-rooney/
381	King County Archives
382	MOHAI, 2000.107.056.08.01
388	Jim Ellis Collection, Seattle Public Library
389	Jim Ellis Collection, Seattle Public Library
392	Mountains to Sound Greenway
393	Mountains to Sound Greenway
398	Mountains to Sound Greenway
401	Mountains to Sound Greenway
404	*The Seattle Times*
406	Jim Ellis Collection, Seattle Public Library
407	Mountains to Sound Greenway
410	Jim Ellis Collection, Seattle Public Library
Back Cover	*The Seattle Times*

INDEX